The Socialist Price Mechanism

The Socialist Price Mechanism

Edited by Alan Abouchar

Duke University Press   Durham, North Carolina   1977

© 1977, Duke University Press

L.C.C. card no. 76–4219

I.S.B.N. 0–8223–0366–3

Printed in the United States of
America by Kingsport Press

Contents

Figures

Tables

Preface

In March 1974 a symposium on the socialist price mechanism was held at the University of Toronto. The aim of the symposium was to probe in a systematic and thorough way the adequacy of socialist price concepts and price relationships to serve the diverse functions which price systems are called upon to serve—measurement, allocation, and income distribution. The papers were all contributed by specialists on the Soviet economy with formal discussions and informal participation by both Soviet specialists and non-Soviet specialists. Six papers were presented during the two-day sessions on a large variety of topics, ranging from ideological obstacles to rational price-setting to recent Hungarian price-adjustment models. A discussant was assigned to each paper and animated general discussion followed each presentation. These six papers, together with three formal discussion papers by discussants who wished to submit them for publication, and a seventh main presentation appear as chapters in this volume, which is thus a record of the proceedings. All speakers had the opportunity to revise their work, taking account of comments by their assigned discussants and others from the floor.

To the extent that the Toronto symposium was successful in developing new perspectives on socialist pricing, the credit belongs first of all to the contributors to the present volume but not to them alone. Much also is due to the other participants who were present: Richard Carson, Leonid Hurwicz, Richard Judy, Michael Manove, Paul Marer, Pavel Pelikan, Dusan Pokorny, Vladimir Treml, Martin Weitzman, and Jozef Wilzynski. Their role is gratefully acknowledged.

I would also like to thank the organizations without whose assistance the symposium would not have been possible. The generous assistance of the Canada Council provided the major financial support for the undertaking. This was supplemented by grants from two University of Toronto organizations—the Center for Russian and East European Studies* and

* Other books written by members of the Center for Russian and East European Studies are *Feeding the Russian Fur Trade* by James R. Gibson; *The Czech Renascence of the Nineteenth Century*, ed. Peter Brock and H. Gordon Skilling; *The Soviet Wood-Processing Industry: A Linear Programming Analysis of the Role of Transportation Costs in Location and Flow Patterns* by Brenton M. Barr; *Interest Groups in Soviet Politics*, ed. H. Gordon Skilling and Franklyn Griffiths; *Between Gogol' and Sevcenko* by George S. H. Luckyj; *Narrative Modes in Czech Literature* by Ludomir Dolezel; *The Collective Farm in Soviet Agriculture* by Robert C. Stuart; *Leon Trotsky and the Politics of Economic Isolation* by Richard B. Day; *Literature and Ideology in Soviet Education* by Norman Shneidman; *Guide to the Decisions of the Communist Party of the Soviet Union, 1917–1967* by

the Institute for Policy Analysis. Finally, the hospitality and cordial working environment provided by Massey College contributed in no small way to the exchange of ideas during the two days' proceedings. This is gratefully acknowledged by the editor on behalf of all participants.

Toronto   A. A.

Robert H. McNeal; and *Resolutions and Decisions of the Communist Party of the Soviet Union, 1898–1964,* ed. Robert H. McNeal.

For further information concerning price and publisher write to the Center for Russian and East European Studies, University of Toronto, 100 St. George St., Toronto, M5S 1A1, Canada.

Contributors

Alan Abouchar is Professor of Economics at the University of Toronto. His research, dealing primarily with the Soviet economy, transportation economics and planning, and urban economic analysis, has taken the form of books—*Transportation Economics and Public Policy* (Wiley-Interscience, in press); *Soviet Planning and Spatial Efficiency,* (Indiana Univ. Press, 1971)—and articles in *Journal of Political Economy, Review of Income and Wealth, Soviet Studies, Economic Development and Cultural Change, Canadian Journal of Economics, Canadian Public Policy,* and other leading professional journals and collections. He is the editor of *Matekon* (Journal of translations in Soviet mathematical economics) and the *Eastern Economic Journal.* He has served as consultant to public sector agencies in Brazil, Canada, Iraq, and Yugoslavia in the fields of transportation, urban planning, and regional economics. He holds Ph.D. (economics) and M.A. (statistics) degrees from the University of California at Berkeley, and A.M. and B.A. degrees from New York University.

Alan Brown is Professor of Economics at the University of Windsor and has earlier held positions at the University of Southern California and Indiana University. His major areas of research include Eastern European economies, international trade, and urban economics, to which fields he has contributed a number of books and articles, including *Internal Migrations: A Comparative Perspective; Urban and Social Economics in Market and Planned Economies,* Vols. I and II, ed. with Joseph Licari and Egon Neuberger (Frederick Praeger and Univ. of Windsor Press, in press); *Perspectives in Economics,* (McGraw Hill, 1968, 1971); *International Trade and Central Planning* (Univ. of California Press, 1968), ed., with Egon Neuberger; and *Economics of Higher Education* (McGraw-Hill, 1962) ed. with Seymour Harris. He received Ph.D. and A.M. Degrees from Harvard University and the B.A. from City College of New York. At present he is directing a research project on International Stagflation and Economic Reforms (sponsored by the Ford Foundation).

Janet G. Chapman is Professor of economics and Director of the Russian and East European Studies Program at the University of Pittsburgh. She received the B.A. from Swarthmore College, and M.A. and

Ph.D. (economics) from Columbia University. Her writings include *Real Wages in Soviet Russia Since 1928* (Harvard Univ. Press 1963); "Consumption" in Bergson and Kuznets, eds., *Economic Trends in the Soviet Union* (Harvard Univ. Press 1963); *Wage Variation in Soviet Industry: The Impact of the 1956–60 Wage Reform,* (The RAND Corporation, 1970); "Equal Pay for Equal Work?" in Atkinson, Dallin, and Lapidus, eds., *Russian Women* (Stanford Univ. Press, in press), and a number of other studies.

Jean-Michel Collette is an economic planning advisor with the United Nations Economic Commission for Europe, in Geneva. His research has been in the fields of Soviet investment policy, *Politique des investissements et calcul economique: l'expérience Soviétique* (Editions Cujas, 1965), and decision making and resource allocation in the social sectors, in which he has recently completed a new study. He received the Ph.D. in economics from the University of Paris.

Gregory Grossman is Professor of Economics at the University of California at Berkeley. His books on the Soviet economy and comparative economic systems include *Economic Systems,* (Prentice-Hall, 2nd ed. 1974); *Money and Plan* (Univ. of California Press, 1968), as editor; *Value and Plan* (Univ. of California Press, 1960), as editor; and *Soviet Statistics of Physical Output of Industry,* (NBER-Princeton Univ. Press, 1960). His articles have appeared in the *American Economic Review, Quarterly Journal of Economics, Soviet Studies,* and other leading journals and collections. He received the Ph.D. from Harvard and the M.A. and B.A. from the University of California.

Edward A. Hewett received the B.S. and M.S. (Economics) from Colorado State University in 1964 and 1966, and the Certificate in Soviet and East European Studies and Ph.D. (economics) in 1971 from the University of Michigan. His dissertation, entitled *Foreign Trade Prices in the Council for Mutual Economic Assistance* was published by Cambridge Univ. Press (1974). His subsequent research and writing continue to focus on the problems of intra-CMEA trade and East-West trade. Aside from frequent short trips to various CMEA countries, Professor Hewett recently spent five months in Hungary studying the problems of technology transfer in East-West trade. Since 1971 he has taught at the University of Texas at Austin, where he is now Associate Professor of Economics.

Morris Bornstein is Professor of Economics at the University of Michigan. He has also held visiting research appointments at the Russian

Research Center, Harvard University, and the Hoover Institution, Stanford University. His books include *The Soviet Economy* (with Daniel R. Fusfeld; 4th ed., Irwin, 1974); *Comparative Economic Systems* (3rd ed., Irwin, 1974, with Italian and Spanish translations); *Plan and Market: Economic Reform in Eastern Europe* (Yale Univ. Press, 1973); and *Economic Planning, East and West* (Ballinger, 1975). He has contributed chapters to a number of collective volumes, and his articles have appeared in the *American Economic Review, Quarterly Journal of Economics, Review of Economics and Statistics, Soviet Studies,* and other journals.

Aron Katsenelinboigen is Visiting Lecturer in Economics at the University of Pennsylvania and was formerly Professor of Economics at Moscow State University and Head, Department of Complex Systems, Central Mathematical-Economics Institute in Moscow. His major work on various aspects of systems theory, complex mechanization, and optimal planning theory has appeared in books and journal articles in Russian and in English translation in *Matekon.* He has recently completed two new works, *The Rebirth of Soviet Economics* (to be published by Univ. of Pennsylvania Press) and *Studies in Socialist Economic Planning* (to be published by International Arts and Sciences Press). He studied at the Moscow State Economic Institute and holds the Doctor of Economic Sciences degree as well as the Kandidatura (Ph.D.). In 1974, he was Visiting Research Economist at the University of California.

Joseph Licari, Assistant Professor of Economics, Occidental College, has published a number of papers on regional and urban economics, the theory of project evaluation, and the Hungarian economy in *Kyklos, Journal of Regional Science,* and various other collections and symposia. He is editor (with Alan Brown and Egon Neuberger) of *Urban and Social Economics in Market and Planned Economies,* Vols. I and II (Praeger Publishers and Windsor Univ. Press, 1974). He received the M.S. (engineering) from Princeton University, and the M.A. and Ph.D. (economics) from the University of Southern California. He is currently a Brookings Institution Fellow.

Francis Seton, Official Fellow of Nuffield College, Oxford, has written on Marxian economics, Soviet economic history, and problems of economic development in the *Economic Journal, Review of Economic Studies, Econometrica, Oxford Economic Papers,* and other leading journals and fora. His books include *Shadow Wages in the Chilean Economy* (Paris, 1972) and *Industrial Management, East and West,* ed.

with Anthony Silberston, (Praeger Publishers, 1973). He has served as adviser and consultant to governments of Chile, Indonesia, and Iran and various agencies of the United Nations and the United Kingdom. He received the M.A. and D.Phil. from Oxon.

Janusz Zielinski is Reader in Economics at the University of Glasgow and has held visiting appointments at Yale, Harvard, Oxford, and other major universities. His scholarly contributions on the theory and technique of economic planning have appeared in a number of books, including *Lectures on the Theory of Socialist Planning* (Oxford Univ. Press, 1968, with Spanish and Italian translations); *Planning in East Europe: Industrial Management by the State,* with M. Kaser (Bodley Head, 1970, with Arabic, Italian, and Spanish translations); and *Economic Reforms in Polish Industry* (Oxford Univ. Press, 1973), as well as several works in Polish. His major articles have appeared in the *American Economic Review, Economics of Planning, Revue de l'Est, Soviet Studies,* and other journals. He received the B.A., M.A. Ph.D. and D.Sc. degrees in economics from the Central School of Planning and Statistics in Warsaw. He is a member of the editorial board of *Soviet Studies.*

The Socialist Price Mechanism

Introduction: Efficiency and Consistency of the Price Mechanism in the Socialist Economy

Alan Abouchar

As the chapters of the present book make plain, there is some dispute concerning the operation of the price mechanism in the socialist economy. It is probably fair to say, however, that the Toronto symposium of which the present volume is the record showed that skepticism on these matters is not as thorough or deep today as it has been in the past. This proposition is advanced cautiously, and it should not be interpreted to mean that prices at present are rational, or even that price concepts are necessarily rational, but only that the eventual achievement of such rationality should not be thought to be unattainable. This is, to repeat, a cautious conclusion, and it should not be supposed that there is overall agreement regarding any of the particular aspects of the price question among the participants in the symposium. A summary statement concerning the various presentations may be useful here to explain why the editor believes that these conclusions are reasonable.

Analysis of socialist pricing might be based on the following schematic framework. We first recognize the existence of diverse objectives or functions for the price mechanism in the economy—Bornstein's well-known trinity of allocation, distribution, and measurement probably provides the best starting place—and then ask whether the Marxian theory of value is capable of providing a basis for price formation which is rational in the sense that these objectives can be harmonized. Then we must ask whether the socialist economy in general (or the Soviet economy in particular, if that is the economy whose pricing policies are being investigated) is in reality based upon these Marxian principles. If it is not, and if instead the economy has developed instruments based on alternative approaches, we would want to know whether there is anything else in the economy that renders such instruments essentially irrational. We would, of course, have to allow for an occasional irrationality or disproportion; our main concern is the more basic issue whether institutional obstacles in the economy are such as to condition a more general, economy-wide irrationality.

If, on the other hand, we did earlier conclude that the socialist economy was basing its pricing policies on Marxian *principles,* we must ask again whether the adoption of these principles in practice is necessarily fraught with irrationalities or whether any observed irrationalities creep in adventitiously over time, requiring a periodic purging. The entire analytic process could be presented by the decision tree of fig. 1.1. This simplified scheme could be made more inclusive by considering individual price instruments and functions.

The lead-off chapter (Chapter 2) by Francis Seton is concerned with the root of the decision tree, the question of ideological obstacles to rational price setting. He makes the insightful distinction between diagnostic prices and functional prices, the former being a less stringent kind of stimulus to efficiency, "optimizing prices, but only to the extent that they 'beam' the economy onto the extremal points of a production (or minimal-requirements) frontier at which the absorption of a preselected resource, i.e., labor, is minimized." A move to functional prices involves a greater reliance on price stimuli affecting resources more generally, but, he argues, if Marx's social necessity of labor is interpreted in a framework of greatest satisfaction of social needs, we find reestablished "the congruence of the cost and utility aspects of value—still the cornerstone of mainstream economics—which was seemingly discarded in favor of his 'diagnostic' value concept based on cost relationships alone." Seton argues that Russian thinkers and planners have been moving toward this view, so that the traditional stranglehold that Marxian principles were thought to have upon rational price setting and, thence, on rational planning and economic behavior is seen to be less severe.

The next contribution, Chapter 3, by Jean-Michel Collette, is a comment on Seton's chapter which also moves the question in somewhat new directions. Collette argues that Marx in fact has very little to say that might be useful to an economic planning agency about prices, viewed in a generalized way as relationships among economic categories within and between different time periods. Simply put, Marx presents too little guidance for the selection of the final bill of goods, although providing one is a prerequisite for the construction of a rational price mechanism. And even today planners have no strictly determinate way of selecting society's final output—and, moreover, it is hopeless to expect to find one. Diagnostic prices, Collette argues, are not useful for this purpose, and the amount of thought that Marx devoted to issues which are subsumed by functional prices was very slight.

Chapter 4 in the volume is my contribution, which is concerned with the traditional argument that a Marxian pricing framework neglects differential rent and interest. Implicit in such criticisms is the assumption that such mechanisms do work and work well in capitalist market econo-

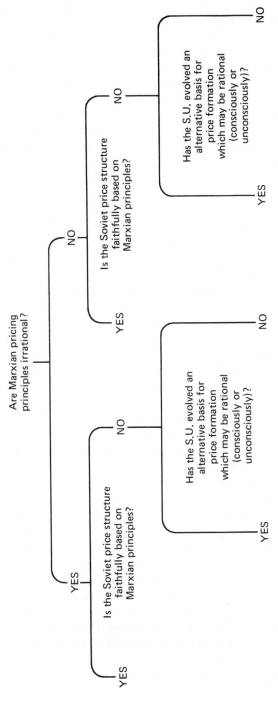

Figure 1.1

mies. Usually, these criticisms relate only to the potential for efficiency and do not consider a larger framework within which rationality is defined to reflect both efficiency and distributional considerations, as well as ability to measure welfare change over time. Accordingly, the substance of the traditional criticisms is evaluated from a comparative point of view, having in mind the different functions of prices and the different forms of economic organization. It is concluded that these instruments do not function consistently in a capitalist economy (either there is evidence of the breakdown of instruments or else there is no guarantee that the instruments will perform efficiently with respect, for instance, to long-term and short-term goals). Problems are shown to exist also in a socialist economy, but it is concluded that these are not necessarily the result of espousal of Marxian principles (indeed, there is seen to be some latitude in Marxian principles that does permit some creative improvisation by planners). The number of potential conflicts between allocative objectives, on the one hand, and distributional and measurement objectives, on the other, is seen to be no greater than that in the Western capitalist economy. Thus the conclusions of Chapter 4 relate to several branches of the tree: Marxian principles are not all that irrational within a comparative framework in which pricing in the capitalist West is imperfect; commitment to Marx does not necessarily entail a disavowal of a discount coefficient, which is one use of a capital charge; and, finally, in other cases, such as the introduction of productivity or utility considerations in the pricing of capital, surrogate instruments appear to have been fashioned to replace explicit capital charges which might be doctrinally unacceptable.

Chapter 5, by Edward Hewett, is concerned with prices and resource allocation in trade within internal CMEA trade. Hewett argues that the intra-Bloc prices are irrational from the viewpoint of the measurement of opportunity cost and so give planners incorrect price signals — raw materials are underpriced, and hence investment in their development is undervalued, while machinery is overpriced, encouraging overinvestment in manufacturing activities. These pricing policies, together with the irrationality that Hewett concludes to follow therefrom, appear to be based on general considerations and objectives for economic development rather than a reliance on Marxian value theory. In terms of the scheme that we constructed, one would conclude that inefficiency has appeared at the higher branches of the tree rather than grown from basic Marxian theory. Incidentally, Hewett provides startling evidence about the long-standing controversy concerning the Soviet Union's relationship with its CMEA trading partners, concluding on the basis of the analysis of Table 5.9 that "trade with eastern Europe is costing the Soviet Union [positively], both on average for all East European countries and also for all individual East European countries except Bulgaria and Rumania."

Gregory Grossman in Chapter 6 is concerned with the effect of price control on incentives and innovation in the Soviet economy. He argues that Soviet prices have little served the objectives of innovation since the plan era began. Many, if not most, of the problems would appear to be those implicit in any system of price control, Marxian or otherwise. He also shows that blind adherence to Marxian theory need not be invoked to explain the traditional characteristics of Soviet pricing: adherence to industry-wide average cost or labor cost of production. Rather, he argues, these are the "logical corollary" of the "ideological hostility to free markets and to free prices" which "happened to accord with the technocratic biases of the engineers and the anti-market biases of the political leaders." References to Western experience under price control in World War II, and most recently under the incipient U.S. inflation, show the general problems for efficiency that arise under price control. Thus, as in Hewett's chapter, the conclusion must be that numerous inefficiencies will result from central price planning whether oriented by Marxian principles or otherwise.

The contribution of Aron Katsenelinboigen is concerned with the interrelationship between income growth and price inflation. In Chapter 7 he argues that although inflation to date in the postwar period has been suppressed — what he calls a "disguised inflation" — there is serious danger that a much more rapid inflation could develop even in peacetime in the Soviet economy. If the pressure now being suppressed intensifies and inflation becomes a real possibility, the need for administrative methods to solve the problem will become much more urgent, since the alternative of expansion of consumer goods production will probably be unacceptable. Again we find problems relating to the price mechanism in the actual operation of the Soviet economy, but they are due not so much to the economy's adherence to Marxian principles as to the general difficulties which are involved in the control and guidance of an economy.

In Chapter 8, recent attempts to revise and analyze the price structure in a socialist economy other than the Soviet Union (Hungary) on the basis of clearly defined rationalistic models are evaluated by Alan Brown and Joseph Licari. The models, worked out in recent years by Hungarian economists, attempt to develop pricing principles within a Marxian framework. These models reflect an awareness of the need for a nonlabor cost component in prices to generate a fund for further development, which is usually accepted as a necessary lever for growth by socialist thinkers. This still leaves room for controversy, however, about the nature of this surplus component (to what should it be related?) ultimately, the two choices being labor or previously produced goods. The distribution between them is what distinguishes many of the models. One of the most interesting conclusions they draw is that even if one accepts the most orthodox viewpoint that all prices should reflect only labor, one still finds that numerous distortions creep into the price mechanism over time. This, of course, is something to which the recent Soviet reform provides ample testimony, but it is well to be reminded again so forcibly here. This means that even if labor costs (wages) truly reflect the cost of reproducing labor, prices based on wages cease to reflect these ultimate costs with the passing of time. Thus, Brown and Licari show that in 1959, prices would have had to be adjusted by considerably varying amounts in the various industries in order to have them reflect labor costs fully (they talk in terms of generating a constant overall surplus proportional to labor costs, but the conclusions are of course the same). In other words, even with the best of intentions and a commitment by planners to orthodoxy, prices deviate from labor costs with the passing of time and must be readjusted periodically in order to reflect true social costs of production, where social costs are calculated in terms of labor inputs.

In a related study in Chapter 9, Morris Bornstein argues that the various price formation models put forward during the socialist price debates in the Soviet Union and eastern Europe over the past 15 years still fail to come to grips with one of the critical determinants of rationalist pricing—utility and demand considerations. Nowhere are these considered explicitly through explicit recognition of demand curves for all final goods, or even in a semi-explicit or derivative way by including a general utility-related rent on scarce resources and inputs, including rent coefficients reflecting differential productivity of different capital goods. Therefore, he argues, the "ideal" prices generated by the price formation models cannot be said truly to represent either "welfare standard" prices or even the somewhat less demanding "efficiency prices" hypothesized by Brown and Licari in their analysis.

The price that is most important analytically from the viewpoint of a Marx-based economy is, of course, the price of labor, and it is this topic to which the final two chapters in the volume are devoted. Janet Chapman in Chapter 10 is concerned with Soviet attempts to employ this mechanism for the labor allocation function over the last forty years. Data are not available to the Russians themselves, or to the outsider, which would permit quantification of the differentials which constitute pure stimuli to worker allocation (as against skill or disutility differentials). However, one effect of such differentials would be to exacerbate the income differentials which are generated in the first place through differences in training and other costs.

The inequalities in income that do exist have traditionally been approached with some reluctance by writers on wages and incomes in the Soviet Union, reflecting presumably the discomfort felt by the leadership over the existence of such differentials. However, the picture has begun to change in the last five years, and Western analysts have been able to get an increasingly good picture of Soviet income distribution. Perhaps publication of data is itself symptomatic of a maturing attitude on the part of the Soviet leadership, a realization that wage and income differentials are essential to the allocation of labor in the Soviet economy. So, too, the attempts to explain and reconcile the empirical distribution, which is very close to lognormal, with Marxian principles. As Professor Chapman shows, utilitarian considerations must eventually be introduced, however. Thus, according to one Soviet analysis, labor is still at the root of value, but the value of this labor depends on its "complexity," which is a multiplicative rather than additive function of a number of different occupational, environmental, and other factors. This approach clearly legitimizes the further use of wage differentiation in ways unrelated to the reproduction costs of labor for the purpose of achieving the planners' given goals.

While Professor Chapman's chapter devotes primary attention to the income distribution side of wages, Janusz Zielinski in Chapter 11 is concerned with wages as prices in plan construction and implementation, and with the problems which attend these prices. Dr. Zielinski's original paper was prepared as a discussion to Professor Chapman's conference presentation, which has been revised in several important ways for Chapter 10. Prior commitments have kept Dr. Zielinski from revising his comments in the light of these revisions, but since much of his paper really represented extensions into areas not covered by Professor Chapman and offered the insight of one who has himself been close to the socialist planning process, his remarks are given here as originally presented, with minor editorial modification only of the explicit references to sections of Professor Chapman's text which were subsequently revised.

Dr. Zielinski argues that in fact in the Soviet economy, as indeed in planned sectors of Western capitalist economies, the weight of experience shows that wage differentials do not play an allocative role. In an interesting contrast between underdeveloped and centrally planned economies, he suggests that wages have actually been lower than labor productivity in the latter, a contention which he presents in support of one of the Brown-Licari theses concerning the need to introduce coefficients into prices whose effect is to deflect them from their labor cost of production where labor is measured in wage terms. Finally, he argues that real income rather than money income is the main mechanism to which workers respond, in socialist and capitalist systems, and in this case the manipulation of wages can have only a limited effect.

2

The Question of Ideological Obstacles to Rational Price Setting in Communist Countries

Francis Seton

Nuffield College, Oxford University

Antecedents

In Marxist ideology the final goal of Full Communism is a state of economic bliss where neither scarcity of means of production nor shirking of individual effort will stand in the way of human wants. The role of price relationships as scarcity signals or incentives to effort will thus have withered away and passed into oblivion along with the niggardliness of nature and man. But before these sunny uplands are reached, society must pass through Socialism, a period of struggle to overcome the scarcities and self-seeking of the past, and even under proletarian rule the ethos of accumulation must be carried over from capitalism to the new society; the worker must be deprived of some of the fruits of his effort, with the remainder accruing to him in proportion to his contribution rather than his need. In such a society the economic reckoning of cost and benefit, the bookkeeper's art, and all the paraphernalia of prices, wages, and profits must be rescued from the capitalist underworld, purged of their "exploitative" content, and universalized and perfected until they become second nature to everyone. In Lenin's vision, therefore, the role of prices will have to be greatly enhanced before there can be any justification for reducing it.

After the enforced and ill-conceived flirtation with a moneyless order under War Communism, Lenin jerked the economy back from the brink and restored price and profit incentives with a vengeance. Throughout the New Economic Policy, prices, in all their naked horror, were one of the main preoccupations of the regime. It was the low level of industrial prices resulting from the scramble for liquid resources (*razbazarovanie*) which led the government to connive at the syndication of large-scale industry, just as the opposite movement of the price scissors against agriculture gave fuel to the fateful debates of the Twelfth Party Congress and subsequent industrialization controversy. Significantly, one of the main issues around which the right and left wings of the party crystallized was the question whether the crisis should be fought by tackling the *price* scissors or the *output* scissors which threatened the worker-peasant alliance. The issue was decided in favor of pressure on prices, using a form of credit squeeze on industry and the so-called "goods intervention" through competitive imports. Prices, indeed, were the regulators invoked to save the regime, as well as the forces which were seen to pose the severest threats to it. It was no wonder that the Stalinist transformation which followed sought to emasculate prices, to render them finally harmless in a context where their defensive role was as little needed as their interference would be tolerated.

Some ideologists, to be sure, saw in this a return to the "Law of Value" from which the teleologist school were supposed to have strayed.[1] The latter had stressed a strategic, redistributive function to which the price system should be harnessed in the interests of "primitive accumulation"— the conscious and purposive spoliation of presocialist agriculture to feed the industrialization effort, untrammeled by "laws" of equivalent exchange or supply and demand, such as may be acting independently of the human will. Characteristically, the Stalinist faction posed as the saviors of the Marxian Law of Value from this particular subversion and, while professing a newfound allegiance to it in the form of cost accounting or *khozraschet,* annexed to itself the whole strategy of "primitive accumulation" through depressed agricultural prices at the point of the sword.

In principle, however, the Stalinist economy used prices as little more than accounting units through which the "control by the ruble" could be exercised. Whether we think of "current" prices, the vehicles of financial control, or of the famous 1926/27 prices which served as target- and performance-indicators, there is no evidence that physical planning or decision making on any but the lowest levels was ever swayed by price tags of any kind, except perhaps through incidental effects on aggregation—the predigestion of detail into the semblance of physical homogeneity with which the planners thought they could operate. Important breaches in this concept did of course exist: the strategy of using larger price categories as instruments of forced saving created the well-known geological rifts within the price structure, divorcing agricultural producer prices from all others and permanently separating wholesale from retail prices through the interposition of the turnover tax. In addition, the price relationships in the free labor market were, in theory at least, in-

---

1. Amongst others, this is the view of Oscar Lange (1945, p. 1277). (Full citations for authors referred to in the text and notes are listed at the end of this chapter.)

vested with a direct and genuine incentive function.[2] Equally important from an ideological point of view was the sharp dichotomy between producer-goods and consumer-goods prices, both taken at wholesale level. On a par with the rural-urban rift, this was perhaps the most significant example of what we shall later call a "functional" use of prices (in pursuit of policy) as opposed to a "diagnostic" use (aiming to reflect a given state of social relations, whether actual or idealized). The fact that producer-goods prices were held to fall short of "values" and consumer-goods prices to exceed them, and the question whether such deviations were allowable under a socialist system, posed the dilemma between the rival price concepts in the most immediate form. Under the guise of "voluntarism" versus "objectivity" in price formation, this became one of the cornerstones of the great price-value debates of 1957 and 1958.

Much could be said about the degree to which even the prices within each geological stratum broke from their moorings and took on independent roles which were not intended for them. The regime was certainly plagued by a number of dysfunctions, such as the bias toward material intensity in the pursuit of (stable-priced) output targets. It had to reckon with the disincentive effects of a form of "price and profit illusion" affecting those enterprises which wage drift or wage inflation was constantly sweeping into the "planned loss" category. The price reform of 1936 was largely designed to deal with these problems, however inadequate its timing proved to be. There were also attempts to use suitably modified prices in a genuinely allocative role, e.g., when project makers within industrial branches evaluated the competing alternatives open to them.[3] But the grand design which crystallized in the thirties confined the traditional functions of incentive creation, market clearing, and resource allocation to the broader "landscaping" of the price domain —the raising or lowering of the relative levels of various regions—and demoted individual prices within these regions to a largely administrative or accounting role.[4]

It is, however, of the nature of administrative controls that they cannot reach into the interstices of economic motivation. In a world of explicit

2. Stalin's speech (1931) spelled out the principles involved: wage policy as an instrument for differentiation of rewards and a weapon against the "fluidity" of labor ("whoever draws up wage scales on the 'principle' of wage equalization without taking into account the difference between skilled and unskilled labor breaks with Marxism, breaks with Leninism").

3. "Coefficients of scarcity" (*defitsitnost'*), special "estimate prices" (*smetnye tseny*), and various equivalence ratios were used to create strictly localized criteria of economic choice. See, e.g., Grossman 1959.

4. To say this is not to say that the authorities did not on occasion find it expedient to import traditional functions into "micro-pricing" (cf., for instance, the drastic rise in copper prices in 1937 when excessive consumption of the metal had become a serious threat). But such departures were the exception rather than the rule.

instructions, rules, and commands from the center, those at the receiving end become notoriously unresponsive to economic requirements and desiderata which the center leaves unarticulated and are apt to take excessive advantage of their residual right to interpret them in the light of their own interests. Characteristically, the Stalinist response to this took the form of proliferating the explicit signals and orders which emanated from the center, in an effort to stop each offending gap as it arose. In the field of prices, as in others, this led to a burden of detail in central decision making which greatly exceeded the planners' capacity for coordination. Official prices for the same commodity often became differentiated by brand, location of producer, type of buyer, length of haul, date of introduction, and a number of other criteria of varying economic relevance. The price setters' inability to keep all this properly attuned, and to do so in step with constantly changing costs and norms, resulted in a maze of differential profit rates, financial incentives, and well-nigh impenetrable confusion. Much of the motive force of later calls for a "rational price structure" derived from the simple need to restore some degree of uniformity, to bring order into chaos — *any* order — rather than from a desire to inject genuinely economic functions into a price system which continued to be regarded first and foremost as a tool of administration. Yet there can be no order or uniformity without some unifying principles, and if the new prices were to put an end to frustration of the social will and purpose, the least that must be asked of them was that they should "harmonize personal and collective interests." A modest and innocuous requirement, to be sure, but one that imperceptibly opened the door to the recognition of economic principles which must be studied in the abstract and to which the human will must bow. Thus the brave venture to vindicate the superiority of socialist planning over the free market by bringing prices "out of the realm of elemental forces into the domain of conscious purpose" had summoned up elemental forces of its own which demanded for their proper control a new subjection to impersonal laws, by which human affairs — after all — continued to be governed under the socialist order.

Discussion on the nature of the Law of Value had never been far below the surface during the plan era. Something like a bombshell, however, burst in 1941 in the shape of an unpublished pronouncement by Stalin to the effect that the Law of Value was, after all, in actual operation under Soviet conditions (Brus 1972, passim). It appears that higher party schools were immediately informed, essays and seminar papers were scrapped or drastically revised and others written to propagate the new line. The pronouncement was probably the imprimatur for the unsigned 1943 article in *Pod znamenem marksisma* which served as the basis for Lange's study (1945). The reference to the operation of the Law of Value in Lange's article, though scarcely more than a hint, was clearly intended to issue the much discussed law with an official certificate of naturalization. Much has also been made of the assumed espousal of the law by N. Vosnesenskii in a book in 1947 (published in English as *War Economy of the USSR* in 1948). It has been conjectured that in spite of Voznesenskii's vagueness on this issue his position was a strong one and that its implications—or at least the interpretation put upon it by Stalin—was in part responsible for Voznesenskii's fall from grace. These by no means insignificant events had pierced the surface even before the appearance of Stalin's *Economic Problems of Socialism in the USSR* in 1952, but it was only in that year that the official signal for the full resumption of discussions on the Law of Value was universally understood to have been given.

The very confusion and ambiguity of Stalin's work[5] presented a challenge to those who were drawn to the subject, at first through the need for exegesis, but later from an independent spirit which led them back to the Marxian origins of value theory. Throughout the fifties and early sixties the quest was one for a price system of the Marxian "diagnostic" type rather than for "functional" prices designed to optimize economic performance in some defined respect. We shall reserve the term "diagnostic" for price systems which are (or claim to be) descriptive of social relations. As in the case of Marxian labor values, it is their prime objective to penetrate or "see through" the veil of adventitious prices to some more illuminating reality distilling the essence of the social system to which they are thought to be appropriate. In their various forms, such as "production prices" and derivative concepts, they can have an optimizing function grafted on them, but their historical origins and raison d'être are quite distinct from those of "efficiency" or "functional" prices which will be discussed in a later section; and so—as we shall see—are their methods of construction.

"Diagnostic" Prices

Marxian labor values and "value prices"

The genealogy of diagnostic prices starts from the Marxian "labor values" defined as the socially necessary (direct and indirect) labor con-

---

5. In the most widely quoted passage Stalin chides Soviet planners for proposing nearly identical prices for grain and cotton, in spite of the higher production costs and world prices (!) of the latter. At the same time he decidedly rejects the notion that the distribution of manpower between sectors of the national economy should in any way be influenced by the Law of Value.

tent per unit of each commodity. This definition is made explicit in the formula

$$w' = w'A + l' \quad \text{or} \quad w' = l'(I - A)^{-1} \equiv l'A^0, \tag{1}$$

where w' is the row vector of n labor values (in man-hours), A the square matrix composed of the physical input coefficients of n single-commodity industries (arranged in columns), and l' the row vector of direct labor inputs needed per unit output in each industry.[6] The matrix A is sometimes known as the "technology" of the system, and its Leontief inverse $(I - A)^{-1}$ as the matrix of *full* (direct and indirect) input coefficients A^0.

The formula assumes that all material inputs are derived from industrial sectors producing single outputs[7] (for reprocessing or final use), and that "nonproduced" inputs other than direct, homogeneous labor (measured in man-hours) play no part in the determination of value. It assumes, moreover, that the production processes actually in use admit of no alternatives of equal or superior advantage from society's point of view and therefore truly reflect the "socially necessary" effort of each sector.[8]

If the last-mentioned condition is relaxed, the columns of the matrix A proliferate to equal the number of competing activities available. The unit-outputs producible with each of these may then be arranged in an expanded unit-matrix J in which the number 1 appears as many times in each row as there are activities producing the same output in the corresponding sector. The labor values of equation (1) will then emerge as the solution of a linear programing problem which seeks to maximize the aggregate labor value of a given final bill of goods y subject to the restriction that the net value produced by any activity (output value minus input value per unit) does not exceed the direct labor cost involved:

$$\max_{w' \geq 0} w'y \quad \text{subject to} \quad w'(J - A) \leq l', \tag{2}$$

where the row vector l' is now expanded to contain as many elements as there are activities.[9]

6. In what follows lowercase letters stand for row vectors when primed and for column vectors when unprimed; uppercase letters stand for matrices, and suffixed letters for scalars. The symbol I stands for the unit-matrix.

7. A slightly more general version admitting the possibility of joint production would modify this to $w'U = w'A + l$ or $w' = l'(U - A)^{-1}$, where U stands for the matrix of *output* coefficients per unit of each industrial activity (arranged in columns, like the corresponding input coefficients of A). When all n sectors are single-product industries, U turns into the unit-matrix I.

8. "Social necessity" in the sense of adequacy to the social *demand* for final output is taken for granted at this stage. We shall return to it later.

9. The problem may be interpreted as one of finding the set of compensation payments (in labor) per unit output which might be demanded by the final consumers from the producers (workers) for releasing them from the obligation of supplying the final output y. On the one hand, they would want to maximize the total payment demanded ($w'y$); on the other,

This is clearly the dual of the standard linear programing problem to find an activity program x guaranteeing the final bill of goods[10] which minimizes the total use of labor, i.e.,

$$\min_{x \geq 0} l'x \quad \text{subject to} \quad (J - A)x \geq y.$$

$$(3)$$

As is well known, the solutions of problems (2) and (3) will identify the "base activities" — in general, one column for each industrial sector in A and J — by means of which the final bill of goods may be optimally produced. All other activities are disqualified as redundant, thus making J shrink to the unit-matrix and A to a square matrix of the same dimensions (n by n). The maximization (minimization) is then trivially achieved, since the n constraints uniquely determine an equal number of surviving variables (in either of the two problems):

$$w' = l'(I-A)^{-1} \equiv l'A^0; \tag{4}$$
$$x = (I-A)^{-1}y \equiv A^0y. \tag{5}$$

Post-multiplying (4) by y and pre-multiplying (5) by l', we can see at once that the total labor resources used (n_0) may be expressed identically in terms of the direct labor coefficients (with gross outputs x) or in terms of the labor values w' (with final outputs y):

$$w'y = l'A^0y = l'x = n_0. \tag{6}$$

The last equation shows explicitly that the Marxian concept imputes to labor the whole value of the final bill of goods, i.e., the national income $w'y$, by equating it to the aggregate number of hours worked (n_0). Accordingly, the value of the national income produced *per labor-hour* ($w'y/n_0$) is by definition equal to unity.[11]

The imputation of all value to labor is not, however, the only way in which value is defined in the Marxian system. The system contains a parallel and equally important value definition — always clearly distinguished from the first — which seeks to lay bare what is conceived to be the exploitative nature of capitalism. The Marxian indictment of that social order uses labor value as a "substratum of truth" beneath the veil of those capitalist prices by means of which essentially exploitative relations are at once perpetuated and hidden from view.

Thus, if the hourly subsistence of a worker consists of a basket of n

---

they would want to set the unit payments "realistically," in the sense of not demanding greater labor compensation for any commodity than the labor effort that would be involved in producing it by the most efficient method available.

10. I.e., produces *at least* as much of each commodity for final use as specified in the desired vector y.

11. This is also the value of Marx's "net product," i.e., the sum of variable capital (v) and surplus (s) when measured per labor hour.

goods measured by the column vector h, the rations (real pay) per unit output accruing to wage earners under the capitalist system is given by the dyadic[12] matrix $B(=hl')$. By analogy with the "technology" (A), the matrix B might be described as the "biology" of the system, as it specifies the "biologically necessary" consumption inputs[13] of various goods per unit output in each industry. The sum of $A + B$, to be denoted by M, is sometimes referred to as the "augmented technology."[14] With the aid of these symbols the total cost of each output unit to the capitalist (in material and labor), when measured in terms of "value," can be defined as

$$k' = w'M = w'(A + B), \tag{7}$$

where the components $w'A$ and $w'B$ correspond respectively to the Marxian "constant" and "variable" capital (c' and v') per unit output.

The postulate of uniform exploitation of all workers specifies that the "surplus value" appropriated by capitalists, i.e., the excess of total value over the costs k', will bear the same ratio e_0 to the value of actual wage payments in each industry, i.e.,

$$s' = w' - k' = w'(I - A - B) = e_0 w'B. \tag{8}$$

This immediately leads to the second Marxian value definition:

$$w'\left(\frac{1}{1+e_0}I - BA^0\right) = 0 \quad \text{or} \quad w'(I - e_0 B^*) = 0, \tag{9}$$

where B^* stands for the matrix of full (direct and indirect) consumption input coefficients $B(I - M)^{-1}$ or BM^*.

The final version of equation (9) shows the uniform rate of exploitation e_0 as the reciprocal of an eigenvalue of the matrix B^*, say b_*, and the labor values w' as its corresponding (left-hand) eigenvector.[15] As such the w' are only determined up to a multiplicative constant which may be freely chosen, but this does not affect the essence of the matter.[16] The eigenvalue of B^*, however, is, in general, uniquely determined and may

12. The term "dyadic" denotes a matrix of rank 1 generated by multiplying a column vector by a row vector in that order, i.e., a matrix in which all columns (and rows) are proportional to each other, in our case expressing different sizes of the same "subsistence basket" of commodities.

13. The term "biology" is used here for convenience only. The interpretation of the subsistence wage minimum which sets the limit to exploitation has varied from the biological to the social and conventional in different types of Marxian exegesis.

14. The Leontief inverse of the matrix $(I - M)^{-1}$ could then be termed the "full" augmented technology M^* (by analogy with A^0 above).

15. They can in fact be identified as the *dominant* (largest) eigenvalue and corresponding eigenvector of the semipositive matrix B^*, which are known to be positive/nonnegative by the theorems of Perron and Froebenius.

16. It may be dictated by one or other of the Marxian "invariance postulates" (e.g., sum of prices = sum of values, or total surplus value = total money profits), but is formally only a matter of choosing a suitable numéraire.

be thought of as the uniform ratio of wages to the surplus value of each industry.[17]

It should be noted here that, formally speaking, a definition of this sort does not stand or fall with the assumption of fixed consumption patterns (subsistence wages) for all workers. There is nothing to prevent us from relaxing the postulate of a dyadic B-matrix ($=hl'$) and reinterpreting the surplus (s') as simply that portion of value added which is not used for workers' consumption. The values w' would then turn into a set of "value prices," determined by the requirement that the total profit arising from them be distributed among industrial sectors in strict proportion to their labor costs. The constant ratio e_0 would then appear as a universal rate of ad valorem markup on payrolls, shorn of its Marxian content and free to be vested with any ideological content whatever,[18] or with none at all.

Returning now to the Marxian interpretation of value, it is important to note that the two basic definitions — "by imputation" (1) and "by alienation" (9) — are formally equivalent: by virtue of the subsistence assumption we have

$$B = hl'. \tag{10}$$

Moreover, the value of hourly subsistence ($w'h$) must obviously equal that share of the net value created by an hour's labor (i.e., that proportion of unity)[19] which is actually paid to workers in the form of wages, i.e.,

$$w'h = \frac{1}{1 + e_0}. \tag{11}$$

Accepting the definition "by alienation" and multiplying out the bracket in the first version of equation (9), we have by virtue of (10) and (11):[20]

$$\frac{1}{1 + e_0}w' - w'hl'A^0 = \frac{1}{1 + e_0}w' - \frac{1}{1 + e_0}l'A^0 = 0. \tag{12}$$

It is immediately clear that this condition is fulfilled by the labor values as defined "by imputation" in equation (9).[21]

17. In Marxian terms: $b_* = 1/e_0 = v + s$.
18. It might for instance imply a modality of withholding wages from workers in a socialist state, in the interest of a faster advance toward communism.
19. See equation (6) and the subsequent paragraph.
20. By using (10) and (11) we are implicitly choosing the multiplicative constant (numéraire) which was lacking in the original definition "by alienation" (9).
21. Professor Morishima (1973b) has noted this and other instances of the multifaceted nature of the Marxian value concept. His proofs of equivalence are in some respects very close to those given here. They are, however, complicated by insistence on the traditional subdivision of the economy into the two Marxian "departments" (producer goods and consumer goods).

Production prices (classical version)

The second diagnostic price concept introduced by Marx is the "production price" intended to reflect the central tendency of fluctuating market prices under capitalism. In their original form, production prices u' allow a uniform markup or profit rate g_0 on the production cost (material plus wage costs) of all industries, i.e.,

$$u' = (1 + g_0)(u'A + u_0l') \quad \text{or} \quad u' = u_0l'\left(\frac{1}{1 + g_0}I - A\right)^{-1}, \quad (13)$$

where u_0 stands for the hourly wage.[22]

The cost of material inputs $u'A$ is here conceived to include outlays on the purchase of fixed capital, as the period of production is taken by Marx to be long enough to "turn over" the whole of the capital stock in use. Given this assumption, an equilibrium price system of the "production" type would arise from the tendency of capitalists to shift their capital (= cost inputs) from one industry to another until all interbranch differentials in the rate of profit earned on this have been eliminated.

Maintaining the Marxian subsistence assumption implies the equality of the wage with the cost of hourly subsistence in current prices, i.e.,

$$u'h = u_0, \quad (14)$$

and therefore

$$u_0l' = u'hl' = u'B. \quad (15)$$

Accordingly we can rewrite equation (13) in the homogeneous form

$$u' = (u' + g_0u')M \quad \text{or} \quad u'(I - g_0M^*) = 0, \quad (16)$$

where M stands for the "augmented technology" $A + B$ as before, and M^* for the corresponding "full" (direct and indirect) coefficients $M(I - M)^{-1}$.

In the final version of (16) the uniform rate of profit emerges as the reciprocal of the dominant[23] eigenvalue of M^*, and the production prices as the corresponding eigenvector.[24] The latter are again determined up to a multiplicative constant only, but assume a fixed absolute size by virtue of (14).

A massive literature on the problem of converting classical production

---

22. The definition in this form is incomplete, as the value of g_0 remains to be determined. This can only be done with the aid of a homogeneous equation of the form (16) below.

23. See n. 15 above, by analogy.

24. A number of important theorems relating the rate of profit g_0 to the rate of exploitation e_0 (essentially through the mathematical links between the dominants of B^* and M^*) have been established by Morishima, Okishio, and me. The most interesting of these is the necessary dominance (superior size) of e_0 over g_0, implying that positive profits in terms of production prices must entail a positive "rate of exploitation" as defined by Marx.

prices into labor values, and vice versa, was called into being by the imperfection of Marx's own attempt to solve the "Transformation Problem."[25] The earlier solutions which imparted full consistency into the treatment were wholly dependent on a particular partitioning of the economy (e.g., producer goods, wage goods, and luxury goods), thereby precluding normal feedback effects and to that extent lacking full generality. Later solutions, however, established the viability and consistency of both price systems and value systems without these restrictions and confirmed most of Marx's conjectures on their comparative characteristics.

Production prices (modern version)

As the third diagnostic price concept we must consider production prices in the guise in which they are used or advocated in a contemporary context in communist countries. These differ from the classical production prices of the preceding section only in rejecting the "capital-swallowing" production period which Marx assumed and postulating uniformity for the rate of profit on *capital stock*. Such a concept is much more in accord with practical needs and allows value appraisals within meaningfully limited time horizons. It requires for its definition an implied knowledge of the capital-output ratios k_{ij} which relate the physical capital stock originating in the production of sector i to the output unit of the sector in which it is utilized (j). If the n-by-n matrix of these ratios[26] is denoted by K, the definition of production prices v becomes

$$v' = v'A + v_0 l' + f_0 v'K = v_0 l'(I - A - f_0 K)^{-1}, \qquad (17)$$

where v_0 stands for the hourly wage and f_0 for the uniform rate of profit on capital stock.[27]

Given the subsistence assumption, we have again

$$v'h = v_0 \quad \text{and} \qquad (18)$$

$$v_0 l' = v'hl' = v'B, \qquad (19)$$

from which we derive the alternative, homogeneous definition

$$v' = v'M + f_0 v'K \quad \text{or} \quad v'(I - f_0 K^*) = 0, \qquad (20)$$

where K^* stands for the matrix of "full" capital coefficients $K(I - M)^{-1}$.

25. Marx, *Capital* (Kerr ed.), vol. 3; Bortkiewicz 1907; Sweezy 1946; Winternitz 1948, p. 276; Meek 1956, p. 94; Seton 1956/57, p. 149; Morishima and Seton 1961; Okishio 1963; Samuelson 1971, p. 399; Morishima 1973b.

26. The ratios are variously defined to include or to exclude stocks of *working* capital (inventories) by different advocates of this system and may therefore encompass contributions from producing sectors other than those supplying fixed capital (inventory ratios). Any sector i which does not provide capital stock of any kind (e.g., a service sector) will contribute a zero row to the matrix.

27. This rate remains to be determined; see equation (20) below.

Again the uniform profit rate on capital emerges as the reciprocal of a dominant eigenvalue, this time that of the augmented technology K^*. The production-price structure itself is identified with that of the corresponding left-hand eigenvector, with absolute size determined by equation (18).

Multichannel prices. A synthesis of value prices and production prices came into vogue in some people's democracies (notably Czechoslovakia and Hungary) and in the Soviet Union during the second half of the sixties. These are the so-called "multichannel prices" (mostly two- or three-channel) which allow simultaneously for several types of uniform markups—a constant rate on payroll (r_1), another on the capital stock (r_2), and a third on total prime cost (r_3)—thus implying a threefold division of the surplus. With the hourly wage unit equal to p_0, these prices (p') may be defined as

$$p' = (p'A + p_0l') + r_1p_0l' + r_2p'K + r_3(p'A + p_0l'), \tag{21}$$

where the first bracket measures prime costs, and the remainder the surplus value or profit.

In explicit form the same equation can be written as

$$p' = r_0p_0l'(I - r_2K - r_3A)^{-1} = p'(r_1, r_2, r_3), \tag{22}$$

where r_0 stands for $1 + r_1 + r_3$.

By virtue of the subsistence assumptions in terms of the new prices we have

$$p'h = p_0 \quad \text{and} \tag{23}$$

$$p_0l' = p'hl' = p'B, \tag{24}$$

which yields the definition of p' in homogeneous form:

$$p'(I - r_1B^* - r_2K^* - r_3M^*) = p'(I - R^*) = 0. \tag{25}$$

It is easily seen from (25) that all previously considered diagnostic prices are special cases of the three-channel prices $p'(r_1, r_2, r_3)$, obtained by setting two of the three uniform ratios equal to zero, i.e.:

$p'(e_0, 0, 0) = w'$ value prices; see (9);
$p'(0, f_0, 0) = v'$ production prices (modern version); see (20);
$p'(0, 0, g_0) = u'$ classical production prices,[28] see (16).

28. This identity is of course formal only, since the original definition of these prices assumes a lengthening of the production period to accommodate the whole lifespan of fixed capital; in these conditions the coefficients of A and B which are involved in the definition would take on a different meaning from that implicit in v', or in w' with a more limited time horizon.

As in the case of the derivative "one-channel" prices, however, the uniform rates r cannot be freely chosen, but are restricted in their degree of freedom by the requirement that the n homogeneous equations of (25) be nontrivially solvable for the n dependent variables p'. In other words, the r's must be so adjusted to each other that the matrix $R^* \equiv r_1 B^* + r_2 K^* + r_3 M^*$ comes to have unity for its (dominant) eigenvalue.[29]

This means that only two of the r's can be chosen freely, within such limits as will allow the consequential value of the third to remain positive. The restriction becomes clearer if instead of attempting to choose the markups directly, we start out with the freely chosen ratios in which they are to stand to each other, say $s_1 : s_2 : s_3$. In that case each r_i will be some constant fraction of the corresponding s, say s_i/s_*, and equation (25) can be written

$$p'(s_* I - s_1 B^* - s_2 K^* - s_3 M^*) = p'(s_* I - S^*) = 0, \qquad (26)$$

where S^* stands for the matrix $s_1 B^* + s_2 K^* + s_3 M^*$.

The matrix S^* may then be constructed with three arbitrarily chosen s-ratios and the constant divisor s_* determined as its dominant eigenvalue. A consistent set of markup ratios r_i can then be computed from

$$r_i = s_i/s_* \cdots \text{ for } i = 1, 2, 3. \qquad (27)$$

It goes without saying that this procedure could be used for the definition and computation of diagnostic prices with any number of "channels" (profit segments geared to different cost or input elements). The genus "multichannel" price is thereby characterized with complete generality, provided only that the markups are "channeled" through surplus value (profit).

Two-channel prices. A special case of considerable practical interest arises when the third markup ratio in equations (21), (22), and (26) is equated to zero (i.e., r_3 or $s_3 = 0$). We are then left with "two-channel" prices $q' = p'(r_1, r_2, 0)$ of a kind which have served – in intention at least – as a basis for a number of official price reforms in eastern Europe and the Soviet Union (Sekerka et al. 1967). With hourly wages at q_0 and markups on payroll and capital respectively equal to r_1 and r_2, these prices are defined by

$$q' = (q'A + q_0 l') + r_1 q_0 l' + r_2 q' K = (l + r_1) q_0 l' (I - r_2 K)^{-1}. \qquad (28)$$

Given, further, the usual subsistence or workers' consumption matrix B, the two r's can be determined from their arbitrarily chosen ratio $s_1 : s_2$

---

29. Equation (25) will have no solution for p' other than zeros unless the determinant $|I - R^*|$ vanishes. This is by definition equivalent to the requirement of a unit eigenvalue for R^*.

by finding the dominant eigenvalue s_* of the appropriate matrix from the determinantal equation

$$|s_*I - (s_1B^* + s_2K^*)| = 0, \tag{29}$$

and equating each r_i to the corresponding ratio s_i/s_*. We have then incorporated a markup on payroll and a "capital charge," either of which — but not both — may in effect be chosen freely.

In a number of countries, particularly Hungary (Brody 1965), attempts were made on a conceptual plane to eliminate this remaining element of arbitrariness and restore two-channel prices to the wholly "objective" status which many advocates of such systems regard as desirable. These took the form of identifying the payroll charge as a payment for the use of human capital "stored up" in education, health, professional training, etc., and originally contributed by various industrial sectors (including services), in much the same way as the physical capital stock. A matrix of human capital requirements per unit output (H) is then construed to exist (by analogy with the physical capital coefficients K), and the derived value of this "stock" as used by each industry ($q'H$) is charged against the surplus at the same rate as any other capital stock, i.e., at the rate r_2. This postulates the notional equality

$$r_1q_0l' = r_1q'B = r_2q'H. \tag{30}$$

Equation (28) is thereby transformed into

$$q' = (q'A + q'B) + r_2q'(K + H) \equiv q'M + r_2q'C, \tag{31}$$

where C stands for the total capital matrix $K + H$.

The defining equation then takes on the familiar form

$$q'(I - r_2C^*) = 0, \tag{32}$$

where C^* stands for the "full" total capital coefficients $C(I - M)^{-1}$, and r_2 for the reciprocal of its dominant eigenvalue. The procedure can thus be seen to reduce this version of prices into a "one-channel" system based on a wider concept of the capital stock.

The free choice of the two markups is of course restored if the price system is to be confined to the producer or wholesale level and insulated from consumer prices by a turnover tax or similar device. In this case equation (28) may be used without the eigenvalue requirements of the subsequent discussion, as the resulting price structure no longer has to ensure overall consistency throughout the economy.[30]

30. Hungarian two-channel price computations in the middle sixties were based on a markup of 25 to 30 percent on payroll, assuming some $2\frac{1}{2}$ to $3\frac{1}{2}$ man-years' "investment" in each worker; this was taken to imply a capital charge of 10 percent; see Brody 1965, p. 65.

Elements of optimality in diagnostic prices. Although the price concepts discussed so far originated in attempts at "social diagnosis" or economic systemization rather than quests for optimal guidelines, some claims could be—and occasionally *have* been—advanced on their behalf in this respect also. These claims are highly theoretical and rest on assumptions of doubtful relevance to economic reality; they should nonetheless be mentioned here, even if cursorily.

Taking the "total production prices" of equation (32) as our example, it can be shown that the consistent use of all nonconsumed output for investment in capital (physical or human) would result in a growth of the capital stock eventually converging to a steady rate, and that this rate would equal the reciprocal of the dominant eigenvalue of the matrix of full capital coefficients C^*, say c_*. Accordingly, any change in production methods which serves to reduce this value will raise the eventual growth rate of the capital stock once "golden age" conditions are reached. But the simplest way of ascertaining whether the introduction of a new technique will have the effect of reducing c_* is precisely to value all the inputs involved in total production prices q' and to test whether the cost-to-price ratio of the relevant commodity would be lowered in these terms. This may be shown by recalling that the dominant of the matrix A, say a_0, can always be expressed by "valuing" any of its columns in terms of the corresponding (left-hand) eigenvector, say a'; for by definition we have

$$a'(a_0 I - A) = 0. \tag{33}$$

Post-multiplying by the r-th-column vector of the unit matrix i_r,[31] and multiplying out, we can write

$$a_0 a' i_r = a' A i_r = a' r, \tag{34}$$

where r stands for the r-th column of A. Since $a' i_r$ is simply the r-th element of the eigenvector a_r, we have finally

$$a_0 = a' r / a_r. \tag{35}$$

The last ratio is evidently the cost-to-price ratio referred to above, with A being interpreted as the full capital matrix C^*, and a' as the total production prices q', which we know to be proportionate to the (dominant) left-hand eigenvector of C^* (see 32).

Additional proofs are needed to show that the test remains valid when the new techniques are appraised in production prices *prior* to their introduction. If this is so, however, it is legitimate to claim that these prices furnish valid guidelines for the choice of techniques, given that it is desired to achieve the highest possible growth rate in "golden age" conditions. Parallel claims, *mutatis mutandis,* can be made for the other types

31. The vector has a unit in the r-th position, and zeros everywhere else.

of "one-channel" prices discussed,[32] while it may be conjectured that multichannel prices will be of similar help in maximizing eventual growth rates with a policy of profit disposal exemplified by formula (25) or (29).

It should be noted, however, that the claims rest on the highly unrealistic assumption that all input coefficients and capital-output ratios remain fixed from the moment the new techniques are introduced until "golden age" conditions are reached. In particular, no provision is made for the possibility of price changes inducing further shifts in technology.

Revised Marxian prices. A different kind of optimality, this time of a static sort, can be claimed for a special variety of prices analyzed by von Weizsäcker and Samuelson (1971) as "synchronized labor requirement costs" and by others as "Austrian synchronized labor costs."[33]

Perhaps the simplest way of interpreting these is to postulate "golden age" conditions from the start, and to identify them as the direct and indirect requirements of labor per unit output, *given that simultaneous provision is to be made for the ploughing back necessary to sustain the steady growth rate r_0.* They are, in fact, the "labor costs of production and growth" defined by

$$z' = z'A + l' + r_0(z'A + l').$$ (36)

The formula is easily recognized as the definition of Marxian labor values w' (equation 1) augmented by the last term on the left-hand side to allow for the cost of additional inputs needed to secure growth at the rate r_0. It can be made explicit in the form

$$z' = l'\left(\frac{1}{1 + r_0}I - A\right)^{-1} \equiv \pi'(r_0).$$ (37)

This, however, is clearly identical with the classical ("bourgeois") production price,[34] with the steady growth-rate[35] substituted for the uniform rate of profit g_0.

In von Weizsäcker and Samuelson's paper the "rationality" of these prices is predicated on an implicit valuation of man-hours in accordance with the time period of their absorption, given the labor supply then pre-

32. Value prices for instance could be used to scan available techniques for choices which would maximize "golden age" growth on the assumption that nonconsumed output would be consistently used to add to workers' consumption in the next period. The maximized growth rate would of course be different if this strategy were adopted.

33. Wolfstetter 1973, p. 787. The two concepts are identical up to a multiplicative constant only; see below.

34. Equation (13) with money wages u_0 equated to unity (without loss of generality). In the interest of consistency with other parts of this chapter, my notation departs from that of the authors quoted.

35. If growth is coupled with steady labor-augmenting technical progress at the rate s_0, the formula would need to be modified by putting $(1 + r_0)(1 + s_0)$ in the place of $(1 + r_0)$; see von Weizsäcker and Samuelson.

vailing: if wine requires the same input as grapejuice, but does so one period earlier—when labor resources were scarcer by the factor $(1 + r_0)$, then it ought "rationally" to be dearer than grapejuice by the same factor. Formula (36) is therefore seen by these authors as a "rational" modification (correction) of the Marxian value definition[36]—in conditions where a steady growth rate is to be maintained. The relationship between classical production prices u', synchronized labor costs z', and Marxian labor values could be expressed in concise terms as

$$u' = l'\left(\frac{1}{1+g_0}I - A\right)^{-1} \equiv \pi'(g_0); \tag{38}$$

$$z' = l'\left(\frac{1}{1+r_0}I - A\right)^{-1} \equiv \pi'(r_0);$$

$$w' = l'(I - A)^{-1} \equiv \pi'(0).$$

A more explicit form of static optimality is claimed by Wolfstetter (1973) for his closely related "Austrian labor costs," defined as

$$t' = t'A(1 + r_0) + l' \equiv (1 + r_0)\pi'(r_0). \tag{39}$$

These differ from the previously discussed z' only by the constant factor $1 + r_0$, and are capable of identifying the most efficient (i.e., labor-saving) subset among the available production techniques, given a required growth rate r_0 and any desired bill of goods y for final consumption. The subset will be the one to yield the cheapest t-values (commodity for commodity) of all the possible sets and will form the optimal base associated with the solution of the linear programing problem

$$\min_{\hat{x} \geq 0} \hat{l}'\hat{x} \quad \text{subject to} \quad \hat{x} - (1 + r_0)\hat{A}\hat{x} \geq y. \tag{40}$$

Here x stands for the vector of outputs, and the sign $\hat{}$ indicates the proliferation of vector and matrix elements in line with the number of alternative techniques available for the production of each.[37]

Functional Prices

Demand factors in price

Diagnostic prices, which have been the subject of discussion so far, are constructed without explicit regard to the pattern of demand and utility

36. The von Weizsäcker and Samuelson 1971 version of that definition is not quite coincident with mine. They regard Marxian values m' as the solutions of $m' = m'A + (1 + e_0)l' = (1 + e_0)l'(I - A)^{-1}$, which differs from my definition by the factor $(1 + e_0)$. It would seem to imply that "unpaid" labor (e_0l') was an addition to direct labor (l') rather than a constituent part of it, and leaves the rate of exploitation e_0 to be determined exogenously.
37. I.e., the matrix A is rectangular, with as many rows as there are commodities and as many columns as there are activities (techniques) for their production.

which it is the aim of all productive activity to serve. They *may* be described as optimizing prices, but only to the extent that they "beam" the economy on to the extremal points of a production (or minimal-requirements) frontier at which the absorption of a preselected resource, i.e., labor, is minimized.

The transition to functional prices in the traditional sense requires a clear conceptual separation between the objectives (objective function) of the system and the resource constraints which define the *masse de manœuvre* (production possibilities) for their attainment. In communist countries this transition was made without an open breach with ideology through the subtle reinterpretation of the epithet "socially necessary" by which Marx qualifies the labor time measuring the value of commodities: labor time spent on the production of goods which do not correspond in quantity or assortment to the "maximal possible satisfaction of needs" cannot be regarded as "socially necessary" and is therefore (partially) disqualified as a true measure of value. This notion at once reestablishes the congruence of the cost and utility aspects of value — still the cornerstone of mainstream economics — which was seemingly discarded by Marx in favor of his "diagnostic" value concept based on cost relationships alone.

The argument is well illustrated in a recent work of exposition by a Soviet author, N. I. Shekhet (1972), exemplifying a whole typology of similar approaches. Assume a two-commodity economy with labor as the only scarce factor capable of producing on or below the line A_1A_2 whose slope[38] measures the labor requirement of good 1 in terms of good 2 ($l \equiv l_1/l_2$). Given indifference curves of the family I_1 and I_2, the traditional optimum occurs at point L, where the slope of the highest attainable curve (the ratio of marginal utilities u_1/u_2) coincides with the slope of the production frontier l_1/l_2. If faulty planning or implementation results in output assortment M (instead of L) the cost ratio would still be l, but the market prices needed to optimize consumption would now have to stand in the ratio $m(\equiv m_1/m_2)$. Presumably — though Shekhet does not say so — this "deviation of prices from values" would betoken a waste of labor proportional to A_1B_1 (or A_2B_2), the distance measuring the portion of *actual* labor time embodied in M which was not "socially necessary" for the attainment of the level of satisfaction achieved.[39]

This simple piece of apparatus may be used to establish a fairly illuminating relationship between market prices and labor values, not recognized by Shekhet. Assume that the elasticity of the indifference curve at M is ϵ times that at the equilibrium point L, i.e., that the faulty

38. For ease of reference, the angles in Fig. 2.1 are identified by their tangent (i.e., the slopes of the relevant lines).

39. The same level could have been reached at N with labor time proportional to OB_1. The value ratio at point N, however, is indeterminate, since the point is not on the production frontier.

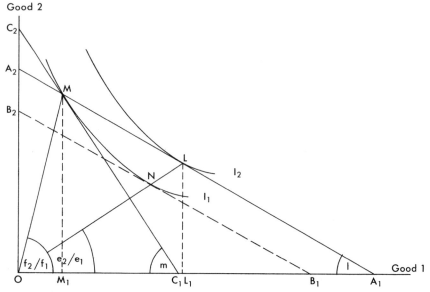

Figure 2.1

plan has forced on consumers an "elasticity bias" equivalent to ϵ. We then have

$$E_M = \epsilon E_L \quad \text{(or } M_1O/M_1C_1 = \epsilon L_1O/L_1A_1\text{)}. \tag{41}$$

Given that the output proportions are e_2/e_1 and f_2/f_1 at points L and M respectively, the equation could be written

$$\frac{M_1M/M_1C_1}{M_1M/M_1O} = \epsilon \frac{L_1L/L_1A_1}{L_1L/L_1O} \quad \text{or} \quad \frac{m}{f_2/f_1} = \epsilon \frac{l}{e_2/e_1}.$$

If we now define the "supply bias" (in favor of good 1) as the cross ratio

$$\sigma = \frac{f_1/e_1}{f_2/e_2}, \tag{42}$$

we can finally express the ratio of price to value (good 1 in terms of good 2) as

$$m/l = \epsilon/\sigma \tag{43}$$

The equation says that the deviation of market price from labor value is greater, the smaller the planners' "supply bias" and the larger the enforced "elasticity bias" of consumers in favor of the commodity in question.[40] The absence of both kinds of bias ($\epsilon = \sigma = 1$) would of course signify the coincidence of value and price.

40. A "bias" below unity is of course a bias *against* the commodity.

Shekhet recognizes this theorem only in the very special case where the utility function is of the generalized Cobb-Douglas type and implies constant elasticities at all points of the indifference map. This eliminates the possibility of elasticity bias ($\epsilon = 1$) and makes the deviation of market price from value uniquely dependent on the "objective" distortions in the output pattern.

In the general case, however, it is clear that even with labor as the single "limitational" factor of production and without variations in returns, the deviation of prices from values will crucially depend on demand and utility patterns.

The optimal equilibrium condition at point L of Fig. 2.1 can be identified as the solution of a nonlinear programing problem of the form

$$\max_{x \geq 0} \phi(x), \quad \text{subject to} \quad l'x = l_0, \tag{44}$$

where the x's are the coordinates of production points (outputs), the objective function $\phi(x)$ defines the utility index of indifference curves, and the limit on the input constraint is given by the total available labor time l_0. If optimal prices (π_1, π_2) are identified as marginal utilities ($\partial\phi/\partial x$), the familiar solution involving the Lagrangian multiplier ν_1 emerges as

$$\pi' = \phi'_x = \nu_1 l', \tag{45}$$

i.e., the optimal situation requires that prices be proportional to (direct) labor content.

This solution remains valid when the number of commodities expands indefinitely and when feedback effects (input-output) are allowed for. Assume, in fact, that *final* outputs y are related to total outputs x by

$$x = Ax + y, \text{ i.e., } x = (I - A)^{-1}y, \tag{46}$$

where A is the matrix of input coefficients. Then problem (44) is transformed into

$$\max_{y \geq 0} f(y), \quad \text{subject to} \quad w'y = l_0, \tag{47}$$

where w' stands for the Marxian (direct and indirect) labor values $l'(I - A)^{-1}$, as given in equation (1) above.

The corresponding solution for the marginal utilities of *final* output p_1, p_2 will then be

$$p' = \nu_1 w', \tag{48}$$

which establishes the proportionality of optimal prices and labor values in this more general case.

Nonlabor factors of production

It remains to be seen whether variation in returns, as associated with the existence of more than one limitational factor, imposes necessary departures from ideological purity which have so far been avoided. One would normally expect this to be so, but Marxist authors have shown great ingenuity in circumventing this by the use of conceptual devices of various sorts.

One such procedure has been explored most recently also by N. I. Shekhet (1972), but is contained in more or less explicit form in many of the price paradigms which are now common coinage in communist countries. It starts by slightly transforming the labor constraint and using available labor *power* (rather than available labor *time*) as the crucial limitation under this head.[41] The difference arises from the Marxian distinction between the labor time actually absorbed in production (l_0) and that portion of it (λ_0) which generates the wage goods "necessary" to maintain the existing labor force constant in quantity and quality (health, etc.). The excess of l_0 over λ_0 is of course the Marxian "surplus" without which neither capitalist exploitation nor socialist accumulation would be possible. Corresponding to this reduced form of labor time there is a reduced form of commodity values, say ω', which measures only labor content *exclusive of the surplus per unit output* ($l' - \lambda'$), such that

$$\omega' = \omega'A + \lambda' \quad \text{or} \quad \omega' = \lambda'(I - A)^{-1}, \tag{49}$$

where λ' stands for labor power per unit output. The similarity with equation (1) for surplus-inclusive values (w' and l') will be evident.

Put in terms of this labor power, the problem of equation (47) becomes

$$\max_{y \geq 0} f(y), \quad \text{subject to} \quad \omega'y = \lambda_0, \tag{50}$$

and has solutions strictly proportional to (48), i.e.,

$$p' = \nu_1\omega'. \tag{51}$$

In this form, however, it is easier to generalize the problem by the addition of, say, two more constraints—one limiting the use of capital resources to a total of κ_0 and the other the use of some natural resource or nonproducible material to a total of μ_0 tons.[42] The problem then presents itself as

$$\max_{y \geq 0} f(y) \quad \text{subject to} \quad \begin{cases} v'y = \kappa_0 \\ \omega'y = \lambda_0 \\ \eta'y = \mu_0 \end{cases} \tag{52}$$

41. This is my own interpretation of the formal procedure used and does not necessarily command the assent of the Soviet author quoted.

42. We may be forgiven here for skirting round the problems of measurement—especially in the case of capital—since these are not peculiar to the present issue. Suffice it to say that some physical form of measurement must be intended. Indeed, the Russian term used for capital by Shekhet is *edinovremennye zatraty truda* which seems to me to defy translation ("synchronized labor" or "once-for-all labor"?).

Solving by the method of Lagrangian multipliers ν_1, ν_2, and ν_3, we obtain equations for the marginal utilities

$$f_y' = \nu_1 v' + \nu_2 \omega' + \nu_3 \eta'. \tag{53}$$

Optimal prices are thus linear combinations of the reduced labor values ω' and the (direct and indirect) requirements of the two other limitational factors per unit output (v' and η'). The Lagrangian multipliers figuring in these combinations have their familiar meaning of "marginal factor productivities," i.e., they measure the improvement in the optimal value of the objective function $f(y)$ obtainable by increasing the availability of each limitational factor by one unit.

So far the solution in no way departs from the Western (mainstream) mold and does not single out the factor labor for any special value-determining function. In the interpretation of communist authors, however, such a role is easily restored to it. All that needs to be done is to postulate optimal prices ζ' proportional to those of (52) while equating the proportionality factor to the inverse of the marginal productivity of labor (ν_2), i.e.,

$$\zeta' = \omega' + \frac{\nu_1}{\nu_2} v' + \frac{\nu_3}{\nu_2} \eta' \equiv \omega' + \phi_0 v' + \psi_0 \eta'. \tag{54}$$

When the coefficients ϕ_0 and ψ_0 are recognized as the "marginal productivities" of the nonlabor factors *in terms of labor,* these prices can with some justification be described as "modified socially necessary labor inputs" and presented as a more sophisticated, but no less orthodox, version of Marxian values.[43] The coefficients are usually described as the "normative coefficients of economic effectiveness" of producible and nonreproducible means of production,[44] and for their calculation are similar to those used to determine interest rates and differential rents in mainstream economics.

Other ways of justifying capital and rental charges in terms of the labor theory of value have been proposed at various times, but the method described here distills what seems to me the essence of the matter: nonlabor factors of production are evaluated according to the amount of labor which would be needed to replace them with equivalent effect on the objective function (at the margin). They are allowed to play a part in the determination of value because they "save" (or "add to") labor resources in this sense. To many this may appear as little more than a semantic trick, but in the circumstances described its legitimacy is hardly

43. The expression quoted is the Russian "modifitsirovannye obshchestvennye neobkhodimye zatraty truda" taken from Shekhet 1972, pp. 71 and 72. The same construct is, however, used by many other authors with similar ideological commitments.

44. "Normativnye koefitsienty ekonomicheskoi effektivnosti edinovremennykh zatrat truda i novosproizvodimykh sredstv proizvodstva." Shekhet, p. 72.

a matter worth discussing. Whether capital and land are "separate" factors of production or merely "aids to labor" is of little consequence — except to fetishists of various kinds — so long as pricing and distribution rules are independent of the chosen interpretation, as in this instance they appear to be.

Marginalism and "objectivity"

Up to the mid-fifties and beyond, the use of a general utility function of the form $f(y)$ and its maximization subject to resource constraints would have been ruled out of court by Marxist ideologists as a lapse into the twin heresies of "subjectivism" and marginalist economics.[45] It needed the rising prestige of the Soviet mathematical school, associated with the names of Kantorovich, Novozhilov, Lurye, Konüs, Nemchinov, et alii, to legitimize such procedures within defined limits and under stringent safeguards in ideological interpretation. Even now, however, in spite of powerful institutional backing, they have not secured the solid spiritual citizenship which would put them beyond the reach of sporadic, and occasionally concerted, political attack from the die-hard Marxist establishment.[46]

It is not surprising therefore that the original conception of these ideas, in which, notwithstanding all obstacles, Soviet economists played an outstanding and even pioneering role, should have occurred in the safety of an ideological straitjacket in which the general utility function was pressed into a very special linear form involving technologically rather than "subjectively" determined coefficients. In Kantorovich's formulation of 1939[47] the "utility" to be maximized is measured by the physical output of a composite good (or subassembly), each unit of which requires fixed quantities $(h_1, h_2, \ldots, h_n)$ of n different components. The "resources" for the production of these are m machines, each capable of being used up to 24 hours a day and of producing any of the required components at certain rates per hour which are technologically given (e.g., $q_{1j}, q_{2j}, \ldots, q_{nj}$ for the j-th machine). There are accordingly $mn + 1$ different activities, i.e., producing q_{ij} units of component i by using machine j for one hour plus engaging in the costless assembly of the composite good by "producing" ($=$ using) $-h_i$ of each component. If the activity k ($= ij$) is used at intensity x_k, i.e., for x_k hours per day, and if x_0 units of

45. For the relationship between marginalist methods and the new type of linear economics, see Hicks's article "Linear Theory," pp. 75–113.

46. For recent instances involving also econometrics and automated planning systems, see early 1973 issues of *Planovoe khozoaistvo* and a defensive article by I. Solovev in *Pravda* of 4 June 1973. Further exchanges and reports of special meetings appeared in the September and October (1973) issues of *Planovoe khozoaistvo* and in *Pravda* of 2 December 1973.

47. Kantorovich 1939. For a lucid review, see Johansen 1966.

the composite good are produced, the constraints are evidently of the form (for all i and j):

$$\sum_{i=1}^{n} x_{ij} \leq 24; \quad \sum_{j=1}^{m} q_{ij}x_{ij} \geq h_i x_0 \quad \text{or} \quad x_0 \leq \min_i \left(\sum_{j=1}^{m} q_{ij}x_{ij}/h_i \right). \quad (55)$$

Since the components have no intrinsic utility outside the composite good of which they form a part, the objective function reduces to the physical output volume of the latter, i.e., all price coefficients p_k other than p_0 disappear, and when the latter is taken as unity[48] we have:

$$\max f(x_1, \ldots, x_{mn}, x_0) \equiv x_0, \quad \text{subject to} \quad (55). \quad (56)$$

The marginalist or "subjectivist" element therefore disappears with this ingenious "technocratization" of what is essentially a programing problem in the universally accepted sense. We need only restore the generality of the function (56) and of the constraints (55) to see what must have been obvious to Kantorovich himself—that he was solving the classical Lagrangian problem of maximizing $f(x_1, x_2, \ldots)$ subject to a number of linear constraints.

The solution of the dual problem establishes shadow prices for an hour's use of each machine (r_j) in such a way that the value of total machine time is minimized; it also determines a derivative value for each component (s_i) which can at most equal the shadow price of the machine time necessary to produce it on the best-adapted ("cheapest-producing") machine, and which together must exhaust the price of the composite good $(= 1)$; i.e., for all i and j:

$$\min_{r,s} 24 \sum_{j=1}^{m} r_j, \text{ subject to } s_i \leq \min_j (r_j/q_{ij}) \text{ and } \sum_{i=1}^{n} s_i h_i = 1. \quad (57)$$

Again, this is nothing but a special "objectivist" formulation of the normal linear programing dual which justifies Kantorovich's own characterization of shadow prices as "objectively determined valuations" (*ob'ektivno obuslovlennye otsenki*).

Similar variants of problems formally indistinguishable from the search for constrained maxima (or minima) of general functions by Lagrangian methods abound in Soviet and other communist literature (Nemchinov 1963; Novozhilov 1964). In almost every case the objective function is linearized and interpreted in a technological or biological way ("scientific consumption norms"), while in others it is confined to a special subclass of functions which allow "marginal" derivatives to reach equality with "average" values at the required optima (Konüs 1967, pp. 72–83).

None of the paradigms which have come to my knowledge either fall

---

48. Without loss of generality.

short of or go beyond the understanding of optimal pricing as dual production problems, as it has now been generally accepted in the West; nor do they fail to appreciate the related theorems of "complementary slackness," etc. Moreover, in none of them have I found the special Marxian interpretation of procedures or results standing materially in the way of the essential insights or practical applications that may be achieved.

Functional prices as planning aids

In a world where the sheer number of variables and constraints jostling for inclusion in programing exercises vastly exceeds the capacity of computers, and where the fixed coefficients, technological or otherwise, may be counted in tens of thousands, it would be the height of quixotism to dish out the mathematical blueprints to any one group of central planners and expect them to supply the concrete structures to which the formal solution algorithms could be applied. Special methods for the gradual exploration of unknown coefficients or constraints and for the devolution of excessive detail to specialist subgroups have therefore been developed in both East and West. To the extent that these take the form of iterative procedures or "dialogues" between a central planning organ conversant only with aggregative macrostructures and a number of subordinate groups (whether sectors or regions),[49] they are generally known as "decomposition algorithms" or "multilevel planning" and are intended to converge to a final solution approaching the optimum of the fully disaggregated, but not directly manageable, problem. Both prices and quantitative targets may be integral parts of the dialogue, subject to progressive revision as the process develops toward the desired optimum.

Apart from the pioneering work of Dantzig and Wolfe (1961) it is not surprising that eastern European countries and the Soviet Union should have devoted the most sustained efforts to experiments of this kind. The Hungarians have been prominent in this field (Kornai and Liptak 1965; Porwit 1968; Simon 1968; Ujlaki 1969; references in Hare 1973), but some of their conceptually valuable work has been dogged by difficulties about the convergence of the iteration procedure. The Soviet Central Institute of Mathematical Economics (TsEMI) has been feeling its way toward a particularly ambitious conceptual apparatus which allows the objective function itself to be gradually revised in the process of iteration.[50]

49. Some variants of the procedure iterate information flows among subgroups without the need for an overall center. A full discussion of these and related methods is contained in the as yet unpublished doctoral dissertation by P. G. Hare (1973), to whom I am indebted for a number of insights in this field.

50. Information has been supplied to various international conferences by Academician N. P. Fedorenko and others.

None of these procedures, however, appears to alter the concept of price or its relation to the Marxian ideology, once the "functional" principle is accepted. They merely facilitate or render possible a cooperative effort to solve a problem "by parts" when it cannot be fully comprehended or digested by any single authority. Their great merit, however, is to bring the mathematical schemata within the bounds of practical possibility and thereby to intensify the interest and commitment, as well as the suspicion, with which their development is generally followed.

It is most doubtful whether any of the communist countries has fully integrated such procedures into the actual planning process. Where they do play a part, they appear to be used as ex post checks on operational plans which have been devised by traditional methods, and may at best serve as marginal correctives. Indeed, there is evidence that Hungarian mathematical planners expressly formulate or alter their objective function in such a way as to keep the deviation of their optima from the officially sponsored plan within preassigned bounds (Hare 1973). This is a form of political realism which recognizes the arbitrariness and uncertainty that must attach to any preformulated objective and exposes the rigid separation of ends and means implicit in functional prices for what it really is — a mathematical fiction which may evaporate in the polluted air of practical reality. How, indeed, can we be sure of our aims before the optimal means for their attainment are known and are themselves evaluated on a scale of preferences of which we may only then become aware? It is this interdependence and uncertainty which may yet restore the "diagnostic" or similarly systematized prices to the status of "rational" planning parameters which the present functional prices appear to deny them. After all, "rational" may be interpreted as the best attainable with *desired,* rather than *available,* means, and this may not be open to discovery by price parameters alone.[51] Moreover, what would be "rational," given complete knowledge, may be irrational in the face of uncertainty, and some forms of consistency without conscious optimization may become rational where the hidden costs of information are prohibitive. We are not as yet advanced enough to assess the costs and benefits of "diagnostic" versus "functional" prices with any degree of confidence.

It will be evident from the foregoing pages that the prevalent ideology of communist countries allows scope for a large variety of price-setting methods, fully as sophisticated in theoretical insight and policy orientation as any that have been devised in the West. The ideology does impose certain constraints on the interpretation of these methods and gives special sanction to a battery of expository devices and a hallowed vocabulary.

51. Evidence of some "price pessimism" is already appearing in the country most advanced in programing and decomposition methods. See Kornai and Martos 1973.

This can be cumbrous and time-wasting on occasion, but does not to my mind constitute an "obstacle to rational price setting" in any reasonable sense in which this term may be taken.

Where such obstacles do arise, they must be laid at the door of vested interests rather than ideology. There is the planners' commitment to "set" prices instead of allowing them to be "formed" on free or controlled markets, and once they are set, administrative necessity or convenience may result in their introduction or persistence during periods when any contingent claims to rationality may have ceased to exist. Even here, however, certain well-known breaches have occurred in the shape of "limit" and "free" prices, and some of the sophisticated models which are being hatched in the "think tanks" of Novosibirsk are said to make special provision for such price domains within an iterative procedure of the "multilevel" type.[52] Advanced methods allowing for uncertainty and incorporating the "cost of information" in the optimization process are surely as familiar to mathematical economists in communist countries as they are in the West.

Whether these developments will be allowed their proper scope in the future is a matter of power politics, and whether they will find practical application, a matter of experience and savoir faire. It is not to my mind a matter of ideology, though ideology, with all its totems and taboos will no doubt continue to be invoked on both sides of the fence.

52. Personal reports from foreign visitors to Akademgorod.

References

The list is not intended to be exhaustive.

Bachurin, A. 1957. O deistvii zakona stoimosti i tsenoobrazovanii v SSSR. *Voprosy ekonomiki,* no. 2.

Belkin, V. D., ed. 1963. *Tseny edinogo urovnia i ekonomicheskie izmereniia na ikh osnove.* Moscow: Mysl'.

Bortkiewicz, L. von. 1907. Wertrechnung und Preisrechnung im Marxschen System. *Archiv für Sozialwissenschaft und Sozialpolitik,* vol. 25. English translation, Value and price in the Marxian system, *International Economic Papers,* no. 2, 1952.

Boyarskii, A. 1973. Matematicheskie metody i optimal'noe planirovanie. *Voprosy ekonomiki,* Nov.

Brody, A. 1965. Three types of price system. *Economics of Planning,* no. 3.

———. 1970. *Proportions, prices and planning.* Amsterdam.

Brus, W. 1972. *The market in a socialist economy.* London.

———. 1955. Zu einigen Problemen der Einwirkung des Wertgesetzes auf die sozialistische Produktion. *Wirtschaftswissenschaft,* no. 3. Berlin. English translation, Socialist production and the law of value, *International Economic Papers*, no. 7, 1957.

Campbell, R. W. 1961. Marx, Kantorovich, and Novozhilov. *Slavic Review*, no. 3.

Czikoś-Nagy, B. 1968. *Pricing in Hungary*. London.

Dantzig, G. B., and P. Wolfe. 1961. The decomposition algorithm for linear programs. *Econometrica*, Oct.

Diachenko, V. 1968. Osnova tseny v sotsialisticheskom khoziaistve. *Voprosy ekonomiki*, no. 10.

Federenko, N. P. 1966. Optimal'noe planirovanie i tsenoobrazovanie. *Vestnik Akademii Nauk*, no. 2.

———. 1966. Tsena i optimal'noe planirovanie. *Kommunist*, no. 8.

———. 1968. *O razrabotke sistemy optimal'nogo planirovaniia i upravleniia narodonym khoziaistvom*. Moscow.

Grossman, G. 1959. Industrial prices in the USSR. *American Economic Review*, May.

Haffner, F. 1968. *Das sowjetische Preissystem*. Berlin.

Hare, P. G. 1973. Hungarian planning models based on input-output. D.phil. diss., Oxford Univ.

Hicks, J. R. 1966. Linear theory. In *Surveys of economic theory*, vol. 3. London.

Hirsch, H. 1957. *Mengenplanung und Preisplanung in der Sowjetunion*. Tübingen.

Ippolitov, S., and E. Figurnov. 1973. Sootnoshenie tsen i polnykh zatrat truda. *Voprosy ekonomiki*, no. 5.

Johansen, L. 1966. Soviet mathematical economics. *Economic Journal*, Sept.

Kantor, L. M. 1964. *Tsenoobrazovanie v SSSR*. Moscow: Ekonomike.

Kantorovich. L. V. 1939. *Matematicheskie metody organizatsii planirovaniia i proizvodstva*. Leningrad Univ. Reprinted in English, *Management Science*, July 1960.

———. 1940. Ob odnom effektivnom metode resheniia nekotorykh klassov ekstremal'nykh problem. *Doklady Akademii Nauk SSSR*, vol. 28.

———. 1959. *Ekonomicheskii raschet nailuchego ispol'zovaniia resursov*. Moscow: Akademiia Nauk. English translation, *The best use of economic resources*, Oxford, 1965.

Kats, A. 1960. Ekonomikicheskaia teoriia i primenenie matematiki v ekonomike. *Voprosy ekonomiki*, no. 11.

Kondrashev, D. D. 1963. *Tsena i stoimost' v sotsialisticheskom khoziaistve*. Moscow: Izd. sotsial'no-ekonomicheskoi literatury.

Konüs, A. A. 1967. On the tendency for the rate of profit to fall. In *Socialism, capitalism, and economic growth*, ed. C. H. Feinstein. Cambridge.

Kornai, J. 1967. *Mathematical planning of structural decisions*. Amsterdam.

———, and Th. Liptak. 1965. Two-level planning. *Econometrica*, Jan.

———, and B. Martos. 1973. Autonomous control of the economic system. *Econometrica*, May.

Kronrod, Ia. 1970. *Zakon stoimosti i sotsialisticheskaia ekonomiia*. Moscow: Nauka.

Kulikov, A. G. 1957. Zakon stoimosti v SSSR. *Voprosy ekonomiki*, no. 9.

Lange, O. 1945. Marxian economics in the Soviet Union. *American Economic Review*, March.

———. 1953. Prawa economiczne socjalizmu w swïetle ostatniej pracy Jozefa Stalina. *Nauska Polska*, no. 1. Warsaw. English translation, The economic laws of socialist society in the light of Joseph Stalin's last work, *International Economic Papers*, no. 4, 1954.

Lenin, V. I. 1954. *Concerning the so-called question of markets*. Written in 1893. Moscow: Foreign Language Publishing House.

Malyshev, I. S. 1960. *Obshchestvennyi uchet truda i tsena pri sotsializme*. Moscow: Izd. sotsial'no-ekonomicheskoi literatury.

Malyshev, Y. 1957. Nekotorye voprosy tsenoobrazovaniia v sotsialisticheskom khoziaistve. *Voprosy ekonomiki*, no. 3. English translation, Some problems of price formation in a socialist economy, *International Economic Papers*, no. 10, 1960.

Mayzenberg, A. 1956. *Tsenoobrazovanie v narodnom khoziaistve SSSR*. Moscow: Gos. izd. politicheskoi literatury.

Meek, R. 1956. Some notes on the transformation problem. *Economic Journal*, March.

Mendel'son, A. 1963. *Stoimost' i tsena*. Moscow: Ekonomizdat.

Morishima, M. 1973a. Marx in the light of modern economic theory: an inaugural lecture. London School of Economics, Nov. Typescript.

———. 1973b. *Marx's Economics*. Cambridge.

———, and F. Seton. 1961. Aggregation in Leontief matrices and the labour theory of value. *Econometrica*, April.

Nemchinov, V. S. 1960. Stoimost' i tsena pri sotsializme. *Voprosy ekonomiki*, no. 12.

———. 1963. Osnovnye kontury modeli planavogo tsenoobrazovaniia. *Voprosy ekonomiki*, Dec. English translation, Basic elements of a model of planned price formation, in *Socialist Economics*, ed. A. Nove and D. M. Nuti. Harmondsworth, 1972.

———, ed. 1964. *The use of mathematics in economics*. Cambridge, Mass.

Novozhilov, V. V. 1939. Metody soizmereniia narodnokhozaistvennoi effektivnosti planovykh i proektnykh variantov. *Transactions, Leningrad Industrial Institute*, no. 4.

———. 1946. Metody nakhozhdeniia minimuma zatrat v sotsialisticheskom khoziaistve. *Transactions, Leningrad Polytechnic Institute*, no. 1. Partial English translation, On choosing between investment projects, *International Economic Papers*, no. 6, 1956.

———. 1964. Teoriia trudovoi stoimosti i matematika. *Voprosy ekonomiki*, Dec.

———. 1965. *Zakon stoimosti i planovoe tsenoobrazovanie: problemy primeneniia matematiki v sotsialisticheskoi ekonomike*, sbornik 2. Leningrad Univ.

———. 1970. O probleme razvitiia teorii optimal'nogo planirovaniia na sovremennom etape. *Voprosy ekonomiki*, no. 10.

Okishio, N. 1963. A mathematical note on Marxian theorems. *Weltwirtschaftliches Archiv*.

Ostrovitianov, K. V. 1959. *Zakon stoimosti i ego ispol'zovanie v narodnom khoziaistve SSSR*. Moscow.

Plenum Nauchnogo Soveta AN. 1969. Optimal'noe planirovanie i upravlenie narodnym khoziaistvom. *Ekonomika i matematicheskie metody*, no. 3.

Porwit, K. 1968. The central plan in a system of multilevel planning. *Közgazdasági Szemle*, Nov. In Hungarian.

Samuelson, P. 1971. Understanding the Marxian notion of exploitation. *Journal of Economic Literature*, June.

Sekerka, B., O. Kyn, and L. Hejl. 1967. Price systems computable from input-output coefficients. Paper delivered to International Conference at Geneva. Prague.

Seton, F. 1956/57. The transformation problem. *Review of Economic Studies*, vol. 24, no. 3.

Shekhet, N. I. 1972. *Planovaia tsena v sisteme ekonomicheskikh kategorii sotsializma*. Moscow: Moscow Univ.

Simon, Gy. 1968. A dynamic model of national economic price programming. *Szigma*, no. 1.

Stalin, J. 1952a. *The tasks of business executives: new conditions, new tasks in economic construction*. Moscow: Foreign Language Publishing House. Originally published in 1931.

————. 1952b. *Economic problems of socialism in the USSR*. Moscow: Foreign Language Publishing House.

Stoliarov, S. G. 1969. *O tsenakh i tsenoobrazovanii v SSSR*. Moscow: Statistika.

Strumilin, S. G. 1946. Faktor vremeni v proektirovkakh kapital'nykh vlozhenii. *Izvestiya Akademii Nauk, Otdel economiki i prava*, no. 3. English translation, The time factor in capital investment projects, *International Economic Papers*, no. 1, 1951.

————. 1957. Zakon stoimosti i izmerenie obshchestvennykh izderzhek proizvodstva v sotsialisticheskom khoziaistve. *Planovoe khoziaistvo*, no. 2.

Sweezy, P. 1946. *Theory of capitalist development*. London.

Turetskii, Sh. A. 1957. K voprosu o sootnoshenii tsen i stoimosti. *Voprosy ekonomiki*, no. 5.

————. 1959. *Ocherki planovogo tsenoobrazovaniia v SSSR*. Moscow: Gospolitizdat.

Ujlaki, Zs. 1969. A long-term multi-time-period, aggregated programming model. *Szigma*, no. 1.

Voznesenskii, N. 1948. *War economy of the USSR in the period of the patriotic war*. Moscow: Foreign Languages Publishing House. (Original Russian edition in 1947.)

Weizsäcker, C. C. von. 1971. A new labor theory of value for rational planning through use of the bourgeois profit rate. *Proceedings of the National Academy of Sciences, U.S.A.*, vol. 68, June.

————. 1973. Morishima and Marx. *Economic Journal*, Dec.

Winternitz, T. 1948. A solution to the so-called transformation problem. *Economic Journal*, June.

Wolfstetter, E. 1973. Surplus labour, synchronized labour costs, and Marx's labour theory of value. *Economic Journal*, Sept.

3

Marxian Constraints on Price Rationality

Jean-Michel Collette

United Nations Economic Commission for Europe

An analysis of Marxian constraints on price rationality in a Soviet-type economy raises three broad questions which will serve as a background for commenting upon Professor Seton's very clear and comprehensive contribution to the Symposium, Chapter 2 in this book. The first question relates to the position of Marx and Engels, the founding fathers of the doctrine examined here, with regard to the problem of price setting in a socialist economy. The second concerns the position of the two authors mentioned with regard to pricing theories developed by other economists during their lifetimes. The third question, which has been extensively treated in Professor Seton's chapter, is the use by Soviet theoreticians of the analytical tools developed by Marx in his descriptions of "value and price phenomena" in a capitalist system.

Following a classical framework, I shall refer to prices as any relationship falling under the following categories: (a) relationships between goods and services consumed during a given period; (b) relationships between goods and services consumed during this period and those consumed during later periods; (c) relationships between goods and services consumed during any given period and the quantity of labor required for this production; and (d) relationships between the quantity of labor required for a given production and other factors of production. Relationships defined under (a) and (b) can be regarded as "final" (output) categories; they correspond, respectively, to the price of consumers' goods and the interest rate. Relationships (c) and (d), which are "instrumental" (input) categories, are reflected in wages and the price of capital goods, including land.

The author is a staff member of the United Nations Economic Commission for Europe. The opinions put forward are presented in a personal capacity and should not be regarded as representing the opinion of the organization to which the author belongs.

Prices are set when the following elements are determined:

1. Categories (inputs or outputs, as the case may be) between which price relationships are established;
2. Agents establishing these relationships;
3. Objectives optimized by these agents;
4. Operations through which objectives are optimized;
5. Information required for carrying out these operations;
6. Agents providing this information;
7. Operations carried out by these agents;
8. Incentives for performing these operations.

The categories listed should be viewed as the constituent elements of a system by reference to which progress achieved in the direction of a greater rationality—i.e., efficiency in resource allocation—can be assessed.

Marx-Engels and the problem of rationality in price setting under socialism

Marx's and Engels' chief interest did not lie primarily in the construction of a normative theory of socialism. Their main concern was the functioning—development and breakdown—of capitalist systems. Only broad and fragmented indications can accordingly be derived from the few works—essentially, the *Critique of the Gotha Programme, Anti-Dühring,* and to a lesser extent *Capital* (volumes 2 and 3)—where Marx and Engels expounded their views on the socialist and communist societies they envisaged. Table 3.1 is a brief—and tentative—listing of the kind of indications which can be derived from a careful reading of the works mentioned.

No indication can be found in Marx's or Engels' works of the type of information and incentives required for performing efficiently the calculations referred to above.

The problems likely to be encountered in the process of price setting and for which some clues, however broad and vague, can be found in Marx' or Engels' works are marked with a cross in Table 3.2. There is scarcely any doubt that, even when considered jointly, the elements listed provide little guidance as to the type of mechanisms by which social welfare under socialism might be optimized in some way, and price relationships set accordingly. The attitude of Marx toward early pioneers of modern pricing theory tends to confirm the fact that the "founding fathers" of scientific socialism attached little importance indeed to the problems tackled here.

Table 3.1 Elements of a price-setting system for which information has been provided by Marx and/or Engels.

Element	Nature of information provided
1. Input or output categories between which price relationships are established	A few indications in the *Gotha Programme*[a] on (i) the growing importance of community services under socialism, and (ii) wage differentials.
2. Agents establishing relationships between the above categories	Broad references in *Anti-Dühring*, part III, to the existence under socialism of a plan drawn up by society at large which is intended, to a large but undefined extent, to replace decisions made by individuals.[b]
3–4. Objectives optimized by agents responsible for price setting, and operations through which objectives are optimized.	Indications in *Anti-Dühring* and volume 2 of *Capital* that under socialism economic calculation will be performed directly in labor time.[c]

a. In the first section of the *Gotha Programme* (par. 3), Marx points out that the part of the social product which is intended for the "common satisfaction of needs, such as schools, health services, etc.," should "grow considerably, from the outset" (i.e., from the first phase of the process of socialist construction) "in comparison with present-day society" and should keep on "growing in proportion as the new society develops."

b. According to Engels, "anarchy in the process of social production will be replaced" under socialism by "conscious organization on a planned basis (ersetzt durch planmässige bewusste Organisation)." Less explicit references to the existence of a central plan (as opposed to the spontaneous decisions of producers and consumers) can be found also in *Capital*.

c. According to Engels, once society owns the means of production, it can calculate directly how many hours of labor are contained in a steam engine, in a bushel of wheat, etc. It could never occur to society that the quantity of labor put into product, which is thus known in an absolute and direct way, should be expressed in a third product. This assertion, which is developed in the above-mentioned work, is fully consistent with the following thesis expounded by Marx in the last paragraph of vol. 2 of *Capital:* "In the case of socialized production, the money-capital is eliminated. Society distributes labour-power and means of production to the different lines of occupation. The producers may eventually receive paper checks, by means of which they withdraw from the social supply of means of consumption a share corresponding to their labour time."

Marx's attitude toward the works of early exponents of modern pricing theories

Although efforts aimed at developing modern pricing theories were still in their infancy during Marx's life (the date of his death, 1883, coincides with the publication of Edgeworth's well-known article on optimization theory!), pioneering works had been or were in the process of being published — Cournot's, Gossen's, and Walras's, to name a few in chronological order — when Marx put forward his main theories. But in spite of Marx's tremendous capacity for absorbing new knowledge — a capacity

Table 3.2 Elements taken into account by Marx and Engels in their analysis of socialist systems.

Element	A Final goods and services	B Time	C Labor	D Land and capital
1. Categories (A, B, C, D) between which price relationships are established	X		X	
2. Agents establishing these relationships	X			X
3. Objectives optimized by these agents	X			
4. Operations through which objectives are optimized	X		X	X
5. Information required for carrying out these operations				
6. Agents providing this information				
7. Operations through which agents obtain the information required				
8. Incentives for carrying out these operations				

attested to by the numerous notebooks he kept of all his reading[1] — and a real (but little-used) interest in mathematics applied to the study of economic phenomena,[2] no reference whatsoever can be found in Marx's

1. Marx made extensive notes of his readings, which, fortunately, have not been destroyed. More than two hundred notebooks, most of them unpublished, are stored in the Amsterdam Institute of Social History. For more details on the notebooks and their utilization, see Maximilien Rubel, "Les cahiers de lecture de Karl Marx," *International Review of Social History* 2 (1957), part 1, pp. 392–420. This article contains, inter alia, a brief review of the contents of the notebooks completed in 1851 by Marx on the problem of ground rent. An interesting fact in this connection is the absence of any reference to the pioneering work of H. von Thünen, *Der isolierte Staat,* published in 1826. One may, in the same vein, contrast the extensive references devoted by Marx in the *Capital* to such minor economists as H. F. Storch (*Considérations sur la nature du revenu national,* Paris, 1824) or G. Ramsay (*An Essay on the Development of Wealth,* Edinburgh, 1836) with his utter silence concerning Cournot's *Recherches sur les principes mathématiques de la théorie de la richesse* (Paris, 1838); translated as *Researches into the Mathematical Principles of the Theory of Wealth* (New York, 1960). It may be noted incidentally that while J. Schumpeter paid tribute in his *History of Economic Analysis* to the work of G. Ramsay, he had apparently little regard for H. F. Storch's contribution to the development of economic knowledge, to which he devotes only a few lines!

2. Marx's interest in mathematics applied to economics, in particular differential calculus, which dates back to the years 1858–1863 had been prompted by difficulties encountered in the development of the "reproduction" schemes presented in vol. 2 of *Capital.* For more details on Marx's position in this respect, see M. Rubel's introduction to *Oeuvres de Karl Marx,* Bibliothèque de la Pléiade (Paris, 1963); and *K. Marks i socialisticheskaia ekonomika* (Moscow, Ekonomika, 1968), pp. 352–57. Marx's mathematical "notebooks" have recently been published in a bilingual edition, under the title K. Marks, *Matematicheskie rukopisi* (Moscow: Nauka, 1968), 639 pp.

published works or in his correspondence to the authors listed. This ignorance of works which are nowadays regarded as major contributions to the development of modern allocation theory can easily be ascribed to the fact that Marx's approach to economic phenomena was essentially sociological and bore little if any relationship to contemporary planning theory.[3] Any evaluation of the role played by Marxian doctrine in the development of Soviet pricing theory should take this factor into account.

Two alternatives were available for Soviet planners and theoreticians when they started their work on the development of a price system adapted to the needs of their society. The first was to devise entirely new concepts and methodological tools—a perfectly legitimate course of action in view of the limitations of Marxian theory in the fields analyzed above. The second was to adapt the tools devised by Marx for other types of problems and other "social formations" to the needs of planning in a socialist economy—a no less legitimate (and probably *safer*) course of action in view of the role played by Marxian "categories" in the development of Soviet thought.

Scope of recent Soviet pricing theories reviewed by Professor Seton

Professor Seton has demonstrated in a convincing way that the Marxian concepts used by Soviet economists in their attempts to devise a rational pricing theory allow scope for a large variety of methods, "fully as sophisticated in theoretical insight and policy orientation as any that have been devised in the West." In spite of undeniable, and in some cases exceptional, theoretical achievements, the methods which have been developed suffer from a number of limitations which can be briefly recorded by using Professor Seton's distinction between "diagnostic" and "functional" prices.

Diagnostic prices. The various pricing methods which have been related to the diagnostic type theories can be regarded as valid contributions to the problems which are identified in Table 3.3 with an X. They all assume, at least implicitly, that the decisions regarding (a) the choice of final output, (b) its allocation over time, and (c) its distribution to and among wage earners have been made when input prices are set. The prices (or scarcity relationships) which are derived from the various maximizing schemes put forward are those which, to quote Seton, "beam the economy on to the extremal points of a production frontier at which the absorption of preselected resources is minimized." They perform a useful function, but assume that the basic problems identified in

3. This point has been stressed by several authors, and especially by T. B. Bottomore and M. Rubel in *Karl Marx, Selected Writings in Sociology and Social Philosophy* (London: Penguin Books, 1963), Introd., pp. 27–28.

Table 3.3. Elements taken into account by Soviet theoreticians

Element	A Final goods and services	B Time	C Labor	D Land and capital
1. Categories (A, B, C, D) between which price relationships are established				X
2. Agents establishing these relationships				X
3. Objectives optimized by these agents	?	?	?	X
4. Operations through which objectives are optimized	?	?	?	X
5. Information required for carrying out these operations				X
6. Agents providing this information				X
7. Operations through which agents obtain the information required				X
8. Incentives for carrying out these operations				X

columns A, B, and C of Table 3.3 have been solved satisfactorily, a condition which imposes severe limitations on the practical applications of this method, except for dealing with problems of a narrow "operations research" type.

Functional prices. Although the development of "functional prices" may be considered a considerable broadening of existing theories, I would personally be inclined to regard these theories as partial attempts to solve the problems identified in Table 3.3 by a question mark.

As was pointed out by Academician N. P. Fedorenko in a book published in 1968, basic questions relating to the choice of the final output are still dealt with in a highly intuitive way:

> Man's various needs can be met by a large number of combinations of consumers' goods. The relative utility [svranitel'naia tsennost'] of each good from the point of view of its contribution to meeting the needs of society is determined in the process of drawing up the plan. . . . This means in practice that each consumers' good receives an evaluation which determines by what amount the welfare of society increases when one additional unit of good is produced. In present conditions the decisions of planning organs are based more on the intuition and practical experience of planner-economists than on a precise assessment of the utility of consumers' goods.[4]

4. N. P. Fedorenko, *O razrabotke sistemy optimalñogo funktsionirovaniia ekonomiki* (Moscow: Nauka, 1968), pp. 33–34. To give a complete picture, one should add that the

And I, for one, fail to see how the various "functional" pricing theories which have been reviewed come to grips with these and related problems. Much therefore remains to be done in order to "fill" the blank spaces of Table 3.3, and therefore to overcome the methodological—and political—obstacles to a greater rationality in price setting.

---

same type of problem is encountered in the setting of "norms" or standards (physical and/or financial) used in the planning of nonmarket sectors. In spite of efforts aimed at developing more "scientific" approaches, frequent references can be found in Soviet specialized literature to the empirical and intuitive nature of instruments utilized in practice.

The Consistency and Efficiency
of Interest and Economic Rent

Alan Abouchar

University of Toronto

I. Purpose and Plan of Study

I.1. *Introduction*

Scholars have often noted that by denying to interest and economic rent any right to be considered as proper cost categories, the Marxian theory of value deprives planners who would build a price system upon it of two very important price instruments which could play an important role in a price system which is used as a basis for decentralized decision making in the economy.[1] Critics of the neglect of these instruments have

I would like to thank the Center for Russian and East European Studies and the Ford Foundation for a part-time leave grant during which this study was written.

1. In fact, as it happens, Soviet economics today is somewhat schizophrenic about the use of these categories, sometimes recognizing their rightful and essential purpose and sometimes not, but being at best seriously divided about their use. For example, the latest *Great Soviet Encyclopedia* (*BSE*), expanding on the article of the previous edition, acknowledges for differential rent a rightful place in the Soviet economy, but justifies it, not as a means to promote rational decentralized decision making, but as an instrument to transfer surplus product to the state budget. *BSE*, 1970, vol. 8, pp. 332–33. The latest edition has not yet reached the P's (at the Toronto library at any rate). The previous edition quite forcefully relegated *protsent* to the category of an irrational capitalist price instrument—irrational since it represented a price based on the use value of the capital rather than its cost of production, a notion that is very hard to reconcile with the legitimacy of differential rent—which, of course, originates for the same reason. In any event, the recent fairly complete acceptance of the new Standard Methodology (Abouchar 1973) and its proposal of, inter alia, a specific discount rate, which is certainly one purpose of the rate of interest under equilibrium planning, suggests that the article on *protsent* in the *BSE* may be in process of revision. (For full citation of works referred to in this chapter, see the references listed at the end of the chapter).

Since this chapter was written, there has been more movement to reinterpret Marx as a precursor of the modern theory of optimization and price rationality. In a recent article in *Ekonomika i matemachiskie metody*, N. Ia. Petrakov goes further than anyone has done to date in asserting the preeminence of Marx in this field, relegating those of his disciples who insisted on a strict labor cost of production approach to the intellectual scrap heap of history along with Ricardo and Smith, on the one hand, and those who overstressed utility, on the other. The paper is remarkable for its absolute conviction. Two citations may convey its flavor: "Optimal valuations are not the antithesis of a plan (similar to the spontaneous explicitly or implicitly referred to resource allocation. However, it is possible that these instruments, when instituted for purposes of resource allocation, may influence in an undesirable way the ability of the price system to serve other functions. It is even possible that when an instrument is applied to one kind of resource allocation (e.g., short-term allocation), long-term allocative inefficiencies may arise.

The objective of the present chapter is to analyze the foregoing possibility for the most important functions of a price system. Four functions are distinguished. These are

(1) Short-term efficiency in resource allocation;
(2) Long-term allocative efficiency;
(3) Income distribution; and
(4) Measurement of performance over time.

By "efficiency of the price system" we will mean the ability of the price system to service the two allocation functions. "Consistency" will refer to the ability of the price system to service simultaneously all four functions in a manner which is consistent with the basic goals of the society.

I.2. *The four functions of the price system*

Before we can proceed we must explain the four functions of the price mechanism and establish criteria to determine whether to expect offsetting or consistent movements. We will first make the simplifying assumption that prices can be broken down into components:

(1) Labor costs based on the reproduction cost of labor which can be accurately and unambiguously measured;
(2) Rents; and
(3) Interest.

Apart from the assumption of unambiguous measurability of labor costs, this assumption is unexceptionable.

---

market regulator) and are not a temporary 'prop' in the planning control system, the necessity of which is elicited by the remnants of the 'birthmarks' in the system of production relations of socialism, but are an organic component of the mechanism for planned centralized control" (p. 665). And (p. 671): "These words are heard today with great urgency. They might have been especially intended by Engels for economists who in recent years have set enthusiastically to the task of calculating labor time and who attempt by these means to adjust the price system. Direct and full labor costs are calculated, and comparisons between levels of labor content and prices in different sectors of the national economy are compared. From these comparisons numerous conclusions are derived about deviations between prices and labor norms. But what does it mean, for example, to show that the price for chemical products, calculated according to labor norms, is twice as high, or, conversely, half as high as the currently existing price? What practical actions should be undertaken on the basis of such information?"

In all cases to be considered we will be interested in the degree to which an instrument designed for one function can serve the other function (or even the own function itself) as compared with adding nothing to the labor cost of production.

I.2.1. *Short-term and long-term allocative efficiency.* Essentially, by "short-term decisions" we mean decisions in an environment which is not undergoing major changes, while the framework for long-term decisions permits such changes. The distinction cannot be defined unambiguously and uniquely for all the aspects of our analysis. For our analysis of interest, short-term decisions may be thought of as decisions which leave the capital stock intact — net investment is zero. In principle, there could be technological change, but for simplicity in exposition we will neglect such change. Even in such a setting, obviously, decisions must be made concerning the use of capital, and the prices for all goods should be designed to encourage users under decentralized decision making to choose the right combinations of labor and capital for their operations.[2] For example:

(1) Should conveyor belts or men and shovels move coal in a lime kiln?
(2) Should hewn timber or concrete be used for pilings in a river dock?
(3) To update one of Böhm-Bawerk's examples, should huge stripping machines and explosives be used for mining, or hand tools and dynamite, or unadorned raw human muscle?

Even if the economy is not growing, decisions like the foregoing must be made about the use of goods which have varying degrees of capital intensity. If the economy is growing, a growing capital stock and, hence, net investment is implied. Decisions relating to the use of capital when there is net investment will be termed long-term decisions.

For the analysis of economic rent, short-term decisions are those which are made with respect to optimization of this year's production and with a fixed available supply of the resource, while long-term decisions consider the production pattern over time. Decisions will generally be different if the resource is exhaustible, since potential exhaustion would alter the relative rents of different resources over time, and, hence, the optimal use patterns.

It will be recognized, of course, that in practice the two frameworks

2. Strictly speaking, the capital charge for short-term decisions defined in this way is an economic rent, a price component showing the advantage of using a unit of capital or the intermediate or final good produced by the capital good rather than a good produced entirely by labor. We consider it in Section II below, on interest, together with long-term capital charges, since both relate to the factor capital.

cannot be so easily distinguished. The economy does not concern itself with short-term decisions this year, long-term next, and so on. Moreover, even a sectoral compartmentalization cannot be given, long-term decisions being made in one part of the economy, short-term in another (although some agents will certainly be more concerned — perhaps exclusively concerned — with one term rather than the other). But the fact that they cannot be separated should not be considered a limitation on the conclusions of the study. Rather, this is the main source of difficulty in the harmonization of allocation goals, one of the most important of the conflicts that we will study. A similar problem arises in Western microtheory when the short runs and long runs are treated in isolation, and optimization within one framework may be consistent with or imply a state short of optimal in the other run.

I.2.2. *Income distribution.* Income distribution objectives can be influenced through the price system. For example, public transit reductions to the elderly, subsidized pricing of school lunches, and food price discounts to welfare recipients, all represent attempts to influence income distribution through the price mechanism.

To determine whether a given price instrument is consistent with the economy's income-distribution objectives, we must have a way to determine what the income-distribution objectives of the economy are. In our analysis we will be concerned with three economic systems — the neoclassical system, the capitalist market economy, and the Soviet-type economy. Although there is some room for controversy on this issue, it seems reasonable to argue that the neoclassical economy has no explicit distributional goals: that distribution is right which emerges from the solution of the resource-optimization problem. For the other two economies, we will take greater income equality as the goal, i.e., income distribution is better if it is more equal, all or most other things being equal. That is, we recognize the possibility that some inequality may be required to create incentives to promote economic growth, but subject to this qualification, the more nearly equal, the better.

I.2.3. *Performance measurement.* The usual measure of performance of an economy over time is the increase in its output as measured by some national income indicator. For a number of reasons, such measures are well known to be inadequate indicators of the change in the economy's welfare. Among other things, some goods go into the estimate of the aggregate measure with prices that do not measure welfare correctly. Any unit of a class of good enters the total at the price of the observed market transaction, although the value of the good to many users will be greater. Accordingly, the recorded measure in any year falls short of the dollar value of the true welfare. But if the relative shortfall were constant over time, there would be no problem. If the shortfall varies between the two years being compared, the change in welfare will be different from the measured income change.

The problem just mentioned cannot be avoided simply by making comparisons according to the price weights of one of the two years in an attempt, in effect, to introduce the same relative distortion into both years and neutralize the difference distortion between years. Any attempt to do so would introduce a new "index number" bias, as is well known. However, the true relative welfare change is known to lie between the relative changes in the national income aggregates measured in the beginning year and end year prices, respectively. That is, denoting these ratios, as is customary, by

$$\frac{P_1 Q_2}{P_1 Q_1} \quad \text{and} \quad \frac{P_2 Q_2}{P_2 Q_1},$$

where the subscripts refer to use of beginning and end year prices and quantities, and for expositional simplicity omitting the commodity subscripts and summation notation, we know that under all but extremely abnormal conditions the ratio of the first to the second will exceed unity. We also know that the first ratio overstates and the second ratio understates the true change in welfare.[3] This range, of course, can be very wide.

We will assume that the prices P_1 and P_2 are measured entirely in labor costs. Then the objective of the analysis of the effect of the rent and interest price instruments is to determine whether inclusion of these instruments in the prices of the two years used to measure national income will define a narrower range for the true welfare change than the prices which omit these categories. If we denote by a prime mark (') the prices which include the instrument in question, will the ratio

$$\frac{P'_1 Q_2}{P'_1 Q_1} \Big/ \frac{P'_2 Q_2}{P'_2 Q_1}$$

be greater or less than the ratio of the measured income ratios weighted in rent-exclusive (or interest-exclusive) prices, viz.,

$$\frac{P_1 Q_2}{P_1 Q_1} \Big/ \frac{P_2 Q_2}{P_2 Q_1} ?$$

3. There are really two "true" welfare changes, one viewed from each of the two temporal vantage points. If we denote the true change from the standpoint of the beginning year by dW_1 and that from the standpoint of the end year by dW_2, it will normally be the situation that

$$\frac{P_2 Q_2}{P_2 Q_1} < dW_2 < dW_1 < \frac{P_1 Q_2}{P_1 Q_1}.$$

For a good treatment of this problem see Usher 1968, part 1.

We will for convenience refer to these ratios as Gerschenkron ratios, named for the man who first made us aware of their deep economic significance, and denote them by G' and G, respectively. Then the aim of our analysis of the effect of the price components on welfare measurement can be stated as determining whether the ratio G/G' is greater or less than unity. If it is greater than unity, we will say that performance measurement (i.e., the welfare interpretation of growth measurement) is enhanced, since the difference in national-income growth calculated by price weights of either of the two years will be narrower than when the price weights do not include the component under investigation.

I.3. *Plan of the chapter*

The chapter proceeds through a comparative logical analysis of efficiency and consistency of economic rent and interest as price components under three different economic frameworks:

(1) The pure neoclassical system;
(2) The capitalist market economy (essentially the neoclassical model shorn of its purity and better reflecting market frictions); and
(3) The socialist economy, as represented by the Soviet Union.

This comparative approach enables us to specify the concepts and relationships in a clearer way than would be possible if we went directly to the Soviet economy, the setting of primary interest to us in this volume. In addition, as noted, the analysis is logical rather than empirical in the sense that we draw conclusions concerning consistency and efficiency on the basis of observations concerning the behavior of models which abstract from some of the specific institutional features of the economies which they represent, even while, in the case of (2) and (3), they come closer to real life than their corresponding ideal forms: the laissez-faire neoclassical model and the pure socialist model of some of the nineteenth-century utopians or of the period of full communism. By proceeding in this way it is hoped, first of all, to distinguish, when necessary, between those characteristics which rent and interest display in the pure theory of economic optimization, which usually is based on analysis with a neoclassical model, and the guise which they assume in the more realistic representation of capitalism. Using the standard of this more realistic capitalist model rather than the pure model will enable us to form better judgments concerning the adequacy or inadequacy of these concepts and practices in the basic socialist economy. In the same way, by abstracting from some peculiar institutional features of the Soviet Union today, we can determine whether there is anything inherently irrational about the treatment of these price components in a socialist economy, or whether problems which do arise in fact are simply the consequences of transitory features of the economy which could be corrected without serious doctrinal or organizational adjustments.

Whether a characteristic is inherent in the model of an economy or is adventitious depends, of course, on how the economy is defined. A characteristic which is not inherent when the economy is defined in one way may be inherent when the economy is defined to include some special function or characteristic. Since the question of what does constitute the essential socialist economy is itself a matter of some dispute, it is first necessary to sketch the organizational and operational framework presupposed in the analysis. I have in mind an economy with state ownership of the means of production, central planning of certain basic proportions and large investment decisions, and at least a mild preference for distributional equality. Current operations *may* be centrally planned or they may be oriented by market relations; the traditional criticism of the socialist price system applies under both variants; i.e., the price system is said to be incapable of furnishing rational guidelines to decision makers under central planning, or of eliciting (planners' or consumers') welfare-maximizing behavior by firms through the market, since, according to Marx, value is created wholly by labor power and if value is to equal price, there can be no room for differential rents, which, however, do indicate the opportunity cost of using one resource rather than another.

Certain present or past institutional features of the actual Soviet economy may not be inherent in an economy as just specified. For example, it would be difficult to argue that the recent imposition of a 6 percent capital charge in the Soviet Union was inherent in the economy—difficult, if only because the charge was just recently adopted after forty years of operating without such a charge. Thus, to evaluate the efficiency of interest in the basic Soviet-type economy we would not consider either the concept of this charge or the specific value adopted for it. On the other hand, once we have formulated certain criteria for rational capital charges, we can evaluate the adequacy of some specific instruments actually existing in the economy being evaluated. I will attempt a few such evaluations during the course of the study. Similar problems of distinguishing between phenomena which are an inherent part of the economy and those which are merely transitory arise, of course, in the analysis of the capitalist market economy.

The analysis is summarized in Tables 4.1 and 4.3, which show the relationships that exist for the three economies between each of these price components and the four major functions which are of concern to us. Interest is considered in Section II and economic rent in Section III below.

II. Interest

II.1. *Introduction*

The concept of interest most relevant to this discussion is the traditional view of interest as the variable through which the demand for investment as a function of productivity is equilibrated with the willingness of people to abstain from consumption. That is, we think in terms of something like a natural rate of interest. We will not have to concern ourselves with the rate of interest in the Keynesian sense of the variable simultaneously determined by the interplay of the real investment sector equilibrating productivity and thrift, on the one hand, and the monetary sector, on the other. The reason for this unconcern is not that the Soviet economy does not need to worry about monetary policy and inflation — it does — or that the bond market in the Soviet Union is limited — it is. Rather, we can neglect this part of the interest-determination relationship as simply a temporary disturbance of the economy from its long-term equilibrium path; for example, if the money supply is increased and the LM curve shifts to cut the IS curve at a lower interest rate at higher money income, this new rate will become the new equilibrium, with all prices undergoing a one-time change. If the original money supply is restored, we will be back to the former equilibrium.

For similar reasons, we can abstract from inflationary monetary effects at full employment, or in an economy with structural unemployment, under which the interest rate comes to include an inflation-hedge component to induce those on the money side of the equation to purchase financial instruments with income expressed in money rather than real terms and the IS curve moving to the right.

Table 4.1 shows the interfunctional relationships for interest in the three economies. Each row in the table designates a function which may be performed by the instrument, and each column denotes a different function. The square defined by the intersection of a row and a column shows the influence exerted by the instrument, when applied for the row function, on the function shown in the column head. A positive effect is indicated by a plus sign, a negative effect by a minus sign, neutrality by a zero, and indeterminacy by a question mark. NC, KM, and SS denote the neoclassical, capitalist market, and Soviet socialist economies respectively.

II.2. *The neoclassical economy*

Table 4.1 shows the relationships for interest. For the neoclassical economy there are no inconsistencies. Examination of the reasons for this will lay the groundwork for analysis of the capitalist market economy and the Soviet-type economy.

Table 4.1. Interfunctional relations for interest in three economies.

Instrument applied for function shown in row	Effect on function shown in column			
	Resource allocation		Income distribution	Performance measurement
	Short term	Long term		
Resource allocation: short-term	NC + KM + SS +	NC $\begin{cases} 1.^a + \\ 2.\ probably + \end{cases}$ KM SS +	NC + KM − SS −	NC − KM − SS −
Resource allocation: long-term	NC Probably + KM − SS +	NC + KM ? SS +	NC + KM − SS 0	NC 0 KM − SS 0

^{a} Position 1 refers to effect of incorporation of short-term capital charge in prices of capital goods. Position 2 refers to further use of short-term charge in place of long-term charge for investment decisions (π in place of $\bar{p}$).

II.2.1. *The short-term instrument and efficiency.* Fig. 4.1 provides the necessary information to analyze the efficient relative prices for short-term decisions. The economy starts with a capital stock of K_1 and a labor availability of L_1. The cost of reproducing a unit of labor is taken as unity. Hence, the total value of the labor resources available to the economy is L_1. This labor can all be spent in the production of consumption goods, without using any capital, or it can be combined with varying amounts of capital to produce different quantities of consumption goods. For example, we may draw a line between K_1 and L_1. The point of tangency at A between this line and an isoquant I' represents one output of final consumption, although the economy can do better. To produce this output would require the use of K_A units of capital and L_A units of labor. Some of this labor will be used directly for the production of goods and some will tend machines. In addition it will be necessary to replace the capital that is used up.

Capital is also measured in terms of the labor used to produce it. A unit of capital is defined as that amount which can be produced by one unit of labor, so that the cost of a unit of capital, on this scale, is equal to the reproduction cost of labor. Since capital is measured in units of labor cost of reproduction, the necessary labor required to produce any given amount of capital is found along the straight-line segment perpendicular to the 45° ray from the origin. In this case it is the line segment K_1L_2. Production at point A requires K_A units of capital and L_A units of labor. But the labor necessary to reproduce the K_A units of capital is L_3. Therefore $L_A + L_3 (= L^*)$ units of labor would be necessary to maintain production of the output of isoquant I' at point A. This is less than L_1 and would leave $L_1 - L^*$, which can then be spent entirely on consump-

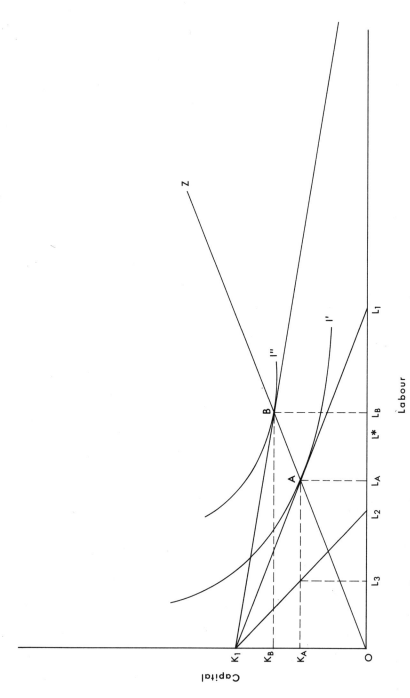

Figure 4.1. Determination of short-term equilibrium capital/labor price ratio.

tion-goods production. Alternatively, part of it could produce more capital. If it is used to produce consumption goods entirely, the annual output of the economy will be equal to that represented by the isoquant I′ plus an amount $L_1 - L^*$.

Assuming that the production function is homothetic, as is usual in neoclassical theory, the expansion path for the economy would be along the ray through A, denoted OZ. Along this ray capital and labor are combined in the proportion K_A/L_A. The labor L^* is allotted in proportions L_3/L^* to the production of capital to replace capital being used up, and L_A/L^* to combine with the capital in the production of final goods. The remaining labor $(L_1 - L^*)$ will also be divided in this ratio. This will lead to production on isoquant I″ going through the expansion path at B.

We can draw an isocost through point B. This has the equation $P_L L + P_K K = P_L L_1$. Since the price of labor is taken as unity, this reduces to $L + P_K K = L_1$, giving a price for a unit of capital of $P_K = (L_1 - L)/K$. This implies a premium for capital over its cost of production of $[(L_1 - L)/K] - 1$, which we will denote $\bar{\pi}$. If the market price of capital is set at this level, there will be an efficient use of capital and labor under a profit-maximization constraint. Only those processes would substitute capital for labor which could by doing so replace at least $1 + \bar{\pi}$ unit of labor with each unit of capital.

It may be helpful to illustrate the foregoing description with a small numerical example. Assume that to produce 100 meters of cloth requires 100 man-hours, priced at $1 per hour. The value of the output is $100. Alternatively, suppose that a machine can be produced using 40 man-hours and can subsequently be combined with 50 man-hours to produce the same 100 meters. By relieving 50 man-hours of labor for application elsewhere, the machine (costing 40 man-hours to produce) generates a contribution of 25 percent to the economy beyond its labor cost of production. If an economic rent or interest of 25 percent is then included in the price of the machine, we can be sure that nobody will buy it and use it except by putting it to use to produce at least $50 worth of some other product (valued in terms of labor). For efficiency, the machine price reflects the opportunity cost, π, of using the machine in one activity rather than another and ensures short-term efficiency.

The charge for capital derived in the foregoing way will promote short-term allocative efficiency, which is denoted by a plus sign in the short-term row-column intersection. To examine the effect of this capital charge on long-term allocation we must first analyze the relationship between long-term efficiency and capital charges.

II.2.2. *The long-term instrument and efficiency.* Long-term allocative efficiency involves choices in the distribution of consumption over time.

The time path of consumption is determined by the amount of investment in the economy, and the productivity of capital in the last project undertaken in any year must just exceed the rate at which society is willing to exchange consumption today for consumption in the future. This rate is usually termed the "marginal rate of time preference," but we prefer to call it the equilibrium marginal rate of substitution, $\overline{MRS}$; the bar indicates that it is the equilibrium value that is intended.[4]

In order to make rational decisions concerning investment, society through individual firms, must balance the future payoff against present sacrifice. This may be done through a calculation such as the internal rate of return. The internal rate of return of a project is the value of ρ that equates to zero the expression $\sum_{T=1}^{T} V_t (1+\rho)^{-t} - I$, where V_t is the gross output (net of current operating costs, but gross of depreciation of the initial investment) in year t, and I is the investment cost of the project. That is, the flow of output, discounted by the internal rate of return emerging as the solution, will be just equal to the investment cost undertaken for the project. All projects with a value of ρ greater than $\overline{MRS}$ should be undertaken, with the final project to be chosen having a value $\bar{\rho} = \overline{MRS}$.

The internal rate of return calculation is made on the side, so to speak, and does not introduce any adjustment to the price structure. However, the investment cost I will be based on prices of two kinds of inputs, labor and capital. The capital inputs to the investment project already reflect a premium, the capital charge that emerges from the solution diagramed in Fig. 4.1. There is no logical reason for this to be the same as $\bar{\rho}$, the investment criterion cutoff. In other words there are two rates of interest or capital charge, and they control different kinds of decision. Note that in the long-term decision, a project can be undertaken provided that it passes both tests, i.e., that (1) it has a return at least as great as the calculated

---

4. The term "marginal rate of time preference" suggests that there is some systematic bias in favor of consumption today, although in fact there need be none. This is easy to show through indifference-curve analysis of consumption of present and future goods. The consumer can be seen to have a positive rate of substitution $(MRS - 1) > 0$ for either good in relation to the other depending on which side of the 45° line through the origin he finds himself on. The usual justification for the assumed bias in favor of present consumption is impatience or hedonism, for which there is a long tradition in the literature. Böhm-Bawerk recognized this tradition (and others as well) and added his "third reason" for the existence of a positive rate of interest, namely, the productivity of capital which is what we stress here (see Böhm-Bawerk 1959, book IV, ch. 1). Had indifference analysis been developed during his time, Böhm-Bawerk would undoubtedly have reached this conclusion himself and recognized the sufficiency of his "third reason." That no systematic preference is necessary was expressed succinctly by Patinkin 1972, p. 30. "More generally," he argued, "the fact that an individual will, at the margin, insist on receiving more than one unit of future goods to compensate him for foregoing one unit of present goods is not necessarily the *cause* of the existence of interest but its *effect:* he insists on receiving more because he has the alternative of obtaining more by lending out at interest the money that would be released from current consumption by saving."

long-term rate of substitution of future for present consumption, the marginal project having an internal rate of return just equal to $\bar{\rho} = \overline{MRS}$, and (2) even the capital inputs in the marginal project will cover their opportunity cost in terms of the burden that is imposed elsewhere on the economy by using them for this investment project rather than for some other purpose as measured by the capital premium $\bar{\pi}$.

Thus, it is proper to speak of two efficient capital charges, one for short-term allocative decisions and one for long-term. But long-term decisions are made on the basis of relative labor and capital prices which reflect, first of all, the short-term opportunity cost of capital. In the first place we can say, therefore, that use of the short-term instrument is consistent with long-term allocative efficiency, and a plus sign is entered in position 1 in the short-term/long-term intersection. Efficient long-term allocation would still require something beyond that, however—i.e., that any project i must meet the criterion $\rho_i > \rho = \overline{MRS}$. We turn now to the question of what happens if $\bar{\pi}$ is assumed to be equal to $\bar{\rho}$ and is used as the cutoff for project selection.

Although it would take further investigation to establish the fact, it seems a reasonable speculation to suppose that if the choice is between using $\bar{\pi}$ or zero in place of $\bar{\rho}$ in the absence of knowledge of what $\bar{\rho}$ really is, it would be better to use the value of $\bar{\pi}$ for $\bar{\rho}$ if the difference between them is less than the size of $\bar{\rho}$ itself (i.e., is closer to $\bar{\rho}$ than $\bar{\rho}$ is to zero), and to use zero if the difference is greater. Moreover, it seems reasonable to suspect that this would be the case, and this would be the more true the higher $\bar{\rho}$ is. Accordingly, the short-term/long-term intersection square in Table 4.1 shows that there is probably a positive correlation between the use of $\bar{\pi}$ in place of the $\bar{\rho}$, although this is not absolutely certain.

For similar reasons, the effect of using $\bar{\rho}$ in the absence of knowledge of $\bar{\pi}$ is also probably positive, as is shown in the first square of the second row. The effect on efficiency of using $\bar{\rho}$ for long-term allocation is, of course, positive.

II.2.3. *Distribution and measurement.* We turn now to income distribution. In the neoclassical framework, there is no normative judgment concerning income distribution. That income distribution is correct which emerges from the optimal behavior of the economy. That behavior is optimal which results when the correct price signals are given in the first place. Hence, if capital is correctly priced relatively to labor—and if final-product prices are based on the cost of inputs based on such prices which are necessary to produce them—behavior is presumed optimal and the resulting income distribution would be correct. Hence, the correlation between the short-term capital charge and income-distribution objectives is positive.

Analysis of the influence of the interest charge used for long-term decisions on the productivity and, hence, the price of capital and the income of capitalists would require that additional information be given concerning the effect that would result from directing capital goods into the production of capital goods rather than into consumption goods directly. If the effect is one of raising productivity, the price of capital will rise (since its opportunity cost will rise), and income will be more concentrated in the hands of capitalists. If the effect is one of reducing the average productivity differential of capital over labor, it will reduce the price of capital, and hence the income share to capital owners. In either case, the resulting distribution would be "correct," since there are no other normative guidelines.

The effect of the inclusion of a short-term interest charge on performance measurement is negative. Since this charge really partakes of the nature of a rent (a rent on capital), the reasons for this conclusion will be better understood following the discussion in Section III below of the effect of rents on the performance measurement criterion (the ratio of the Gerschenkron ratios which exclude and include economic rents).

The long-term capital criterion, which in this neoclassical framework is used as a decision rule without being actually translated into the output prices, will not affect measurement at all. While its use would be expected to increase welfare by rationalizing the time path of investment, what is at issue in the performance measurement column is the question whether the use of certain prices leads to a reading on national output change which sets narrower bounds on the change in welfare than the use of some other sets of prices.

II.3. *The capitalist market economy*

The main systemic differences when we move from the pure neoclassical model to the capitalist market economy are the existence of frictions of various kinds (externalities and indivisibilities, primarily), uncertainty, and a wide variety of products and production processes in place of the one-product, two-factor model. Some of these differences are essential and some — the presence of numerous industries and products and a wide spectrum of production techniques for any product, for example — merely complicate the empirical verification of the relationships which we are attempting to analyze.

II.3.1. *The short-term instrument and efficiency*. Assuming a reasonable degree of competition in the capitalist market economy, we would expect the short-term capital charge to equal the productivity differential of capital. Thus, the short-term row-column intersection will show a positive relationship. It will also promote rational long-term decisions for reasons similar to those put forward in the earlier exposition.

II.3.2. *The long-term instrument and efficiency.* The long-term relationships are more complicated. The positive relationships of the neo-classical model cannot, without further specification, be presumed to hold here, either in the long-term/short-term square or even in the long-term row-column intersection if, as is usually the case, the interest on funds borrowed for physical investment activities comes to be included in the price of the outputs rather than treated as a factor share to be paid out of the stream of quasi-rents which the physical capital asset earns.

The problems may be easily shown. Suppose some product presently costs $3.66 per unit and is produced in an annual output of 755 units. The average cost consists of labor, materials, and entrepreneurship. The process could be speeded up through the introduction of a new machine costing $10,000 and depreciating at $1 per unit of output. Materials and labor costs under this new process amount to $2.50, including the $1 depreciation. Equilibrium output under the new price would be 1,000 units a year. The $\overline{MRS}$ is known to be 8 percent. In this case, substitution of the new process would reduce the annual unit cost by $1.16, or $875.85 in all. This exceeds the 8 percent rate which reflects the tangency between annual capital productivity growth and the marginal rate of intertemporal substitution. Demand is assumed to be linear. In this situation, two possibilities must be distinguished:

(1) The annual interest cost of $800 will be incorporated into the price base. If the producer maximizes profit, he will continue to produce at the present level of 755 units annually. If consumers continue to have to pay the former prices, they will be unable to purchase additional goods that could be produced by the liberated resources which amount to $875.85. Unemployment would result or, if conditions were competitive, prices for the resources of the kind being liberated would fall and these released resources would find reemployment. In practice, this could not be assured.

(2) Product prices are lowered to their new level of $2.50. The released resources are reabsorbed directly, as consumers now only have to spend $1,887.50 to purchase their prior quantities of the good. Part of their new purchasing power is spent directly on this product, and output rises to 1,000 units. The rest is spent on other goods. All released resources are reabsorbed.

The second alternative, which would be the ideal, is obviously incompatible with market relations, since it would make no provision for repayment of the loan instrument. Therefore, final evaluation must depend on one's views about the nature of competition and how it relates to the ability of the economy to reabsorb the released resources under the first alternative, in which the producer incorporates the interest charge into the selling price. Thus, the result might be no better than under the second alternative, but it is difficult to say how much worse one should expect it to be. Accordingly, we indicate this uncertainty with an indeterminacy for the capitalist market economy.

The foregoing comments on the treatment of long-term interest suggest, then, that there will be allocative inefficiencies on decisions in the short-term allocative framework. Short-term decisions will be based on prices that include these additional interest charges, which are not related to the productivity of capital as a substitute for labor. (They presumably already include such productivity differentials. If they do not, then a negative rather than a positive sign should be entered in the short-term row-column intersection.) In this way the consumer's trade-off between capital-intensive and labor-intensive consumption will be distorted. Short-term decisions will be inefficient.

II.3.3. *Distribution and measurement.* Income distribution objectives in the capitalist market economy cannot be stated categorically. But it is generally believed that while income differentials should provide incentives, inequality should not be "too great." At any given moment of time there will be some income inequality, a large amount, indeed. It seems safe to say that most people would feel that changes would be desirable which were in the direction of *less* rather than *more* inequality as compared with the situation which obtains at any given moment of time.

If we accept the foregoing as the income distribution goal for the capitalist market economy, we see that both short-term and long-term interest instruments are inconsistent with distributional objectives. For the short-term instrument, this inconsistency may be easily seen by the way the interest is added to the cost of reproduction of the capital good, increasing the revenues to its owner and, hence, raising his command over consumption goods.

The long-term instrument also makes income distribution more unequal. (The investment act itself would exacerbate income inequalities, although undoubtedly it would increase income levels.) Since the long-term interest frequently does come to be included in the price of the capital good and to be passed along to the user at the next stage, as we have seen, it does actually contribute to distributional inequality.

Finally, the measurement of performance. The effects here are negative, for reasons whose explanation is better postponed until Section III.2.3, where the relationships between rent and measurement are discussed.

II.4. *The socialist economy*

The relations for the socialist economy are somewhat better than those for the capitalist market economy, with only two negative relations, neutrality in two squares, and four positive relations. This is probably at variance with most people's expectations on this score. Part of the paradox lies in the way one distinguishes between what is inherent and what is transitory in the socialist economy.

II.4.1. Definition of interest concepts: The short-term instrument. In accordance with the preceding discussion, interest, for short-term decisions, is the productivity differential of capital over labor, and any output will be priced according to the labor intensity and capital intensity of the inputs into its production. Capital intensity is defined by prices which include this productivity differential. Such a definition, of course, opens up the possibility that there may exist a productivity differential which is not explicitly added to the output price or called a capital charge or interest. But such differentials may actually exist in the Soviet economy. Indeed, there *have* always existed differentials since the start of industrialization, i.e., since the Soviet Union started on the planned route to industrialization which has always been taken as the essence of Soviet growth. These have taken the form of the differentiated wages which were instituted in the 1930s, although the precise amounts of the differentials may not have corresponded exactly to the productivity differentials that we would like them to equal.

In the Soviet mode of reckoning, the costs of capital goods and consumer goods may be resolved entirely into labor cost.[5] How is labor cost itself to be measured? The common practice is to treat the wages bill as the labor cost for any industry. But the wage in a capital-goods industry already has a premium over the wage in consumption-goods industries, and this premium appears not to be related to the cost of reproducing the labor itself. For example, Bergson gives an example of a cashier's wage differential of 89 percent between the meat processing and nonferrous metals industries (1964, p. 117). More generally (Aganbegian and Maier 1959), industrial variation in average wages has been very wide, and this appears to be due to causes other than labor reproduction cost. Thus the average wage in the coal industry is over twice as high as that in the food industry (Aganbegian and Maier 1959, p. 187). That the capital-goods industries and those producing primarily for their support have been favored with high wage incentives is generally agreed. This conscious wage policy is evidenced in the tremendous transformation in the industry

5. This discussion is taken from Abouchar 1973b.

ranking which accompanied the five-year plans. For example, only three of the nine industries ranking highest in average wage in 1956 were among the nine highest in 1924! The four highest in 1956 — coal, iron mining, steel, and petroleum — ranked 10, 15, 13, and 11 in 1924 and 14, 12, 9, and 8 in 1928 (p. 190)!

The force behind the radical change in interindustry wage structure was undoubtedly the competition for workers in the 1930s, with wages in Soviet industry rising by nearly 400 percent during the 1930s. Officials were unable to stem the tide. As Holzman has put it: "True, wages were set by the state; but these scales presented no obstacle to wage inflation because of the widespread upgrading, illegitimate use of bonus money, and other such devices. The labour market was in such a turmoil that in 1930, for example, workers in large scale industry changed jobs, on the average, more than one and one-half times a year" (Holzman 1960, p. 176). With firms in such a situation it was natural that the firms with a greener go-ahead signal from the top, i.e., heavy industry, would outbid the traditional industries, leading to the change in rankings observed by Aganbegian and Maier.[6]

What is the significance of these wage comparisons?[7] They are very persuasive evidence that the values of capital goods, if based simply on the labor costs of the input components, as measured by wages, already contain a premium over their labor cost of production. For the sake of illustration consider the following example shown in Table 4.2. The

6. That the practice has been institutionalized and obtains today is shown most clearly by Kapustin 1964, p. 286: "Under socialism where wages are administered in a planned manner, socialist society, with an eye to the development of the national economy, and, hence, the standard of living of all the people, consciously introduces adjustments into the wage level for different industries, to provide a higher wage level for workers with identical skills in the leading industries." In a recent analysis, Kirsch (1972, p. 174) concludes that "Soviet economists simply hold that the initial basic rate [of an industry] should be further adjusted for a branch's importance or its expected growth so that certain industries are 'first in line' in hiring additional workers." He cites here various Soviet works up to 1964.

7. The extent to which wage premia reflect productivity differentials in terms of planners' priorities is discussed in the chapters by Chapman and Zielinski, 10 and 11 in this volume. Chapman argues that wage premia reflect priorities, although she finds little evidence for this position in a rank correlation between changes in average wages and employment in Soviet industries, while Zielinski argues that such negative evidence, together with historical experience in English planning, implies that premia are not used to guide labor. On the other hand, the shifts in average wages shown by Aganbegian and Maier are striking evidence that wage premia do reflect priorities, since the key industries, such as steel and coal, are the ones that rose fastest. We hasten to observe that this need not be a conscious policy. It may well simply "have happened" under the pressure of events. As Holzman has shown, in the prewar Soviet economy the banking sector was imposing severe constraints, most notably its "real bills" policy, which in principle required that loans be made only against commercial documents such as invoices. It seems reasonable to suppose that the enforcement of this policy by the bank was weakest where the high-priority sectors were concerned, and this in turn implies that these industries would have had the greatest latitude for raising wages in their bid to attract labor, thus providing logical corroboration to the data of Aganbegian and Maier.

Table 4.2. Hypothetical analysis of price-labor cost relationship.

		Food industry	
	Nonferrous metals industry	Production by N.F. worker if he transferred to food industry	Production by food industry worker
1. Value of output	150	114	60
2. Cost of materials (including capital consumption)	74	38	20
3. Wage	76	58	40
4. Reproduction cost of labor	58	58	40
5. Value added $(1 - 2)$	76	76	40
6. Net value added $(5 - 4)$	18	18	0

nonferrous metals industry has an average wage 90 percent higher than the average food industry wage (Aganbegian and Maier 1959, p. 187). Suppose that half of this difference is due to greater training requirements and other factors influencing the reproduction cost of labor, and that half constitutes an incentive to attract labor to this industry, which the planners wish to favor. Suppose that in one week the food worker produces food valued at 60 rubles (60 kilograms of canned fish, say) while the nonferrous worker produces a capital good valued at 150 rubles, all output valued in terms of wages actually paid. This is shown in Table 4.2. The direct (own industry) labor inputs into food and nonferrous metals are, let us say, 40 and 76 rubles' worth of each man's labor respectively. Now, since the nonferrous worker is a superior worker, one week's work by him, if it were applied in the food industry, would produce, say, 114 rubles of product (114 kilos of canned fish). The opportunity cost of employing this man in nonferrous metals production is, then, 18 rubles, which is the differential net-value-added that he would have created in the food industry (Table 4.2, line 6). We should certainly wish to impute such a charge to the nonferrous metals industry.

In the ideal hypothetical example of Table 4.2 the opportunity cost is precisely the amount of the wage incentive in the nonferrous metals industry. Therefore, the price of the capital good, based on the wage cost of production, already is ample to cover this opportunity cost, and therefore it would be wrong to add another interest imputation. Unfortunately, however, there is no way to tell how closely this wage premium does in fact correspond to the opportunity cost and, hence, whether an additional interest imputation is required. One argument for an increase in interest would be that since so many capital investment projects were being undertaken simultaneously – a frequent complaint in the Soviet press –

the interest rate should have been raised to help stem the flow to consumption and increase the resources available for investment. This argument assumes that the projects being undertaken *were* all justified and that the prices should have been restructured to allow that to be apparent by comparing cost and benefit.

To summarize, the industry wage premia existing in heavy industry since the mid-'30s have played the role of an interest surrogate to raise prices of capital relatively to labor. They have worked in the direction of more rational short-term resource allocation in the economy. We have also argued that differentiation of wages was a necessary adjunct to the rapid industrialization which the economy sought, the rapid industrialization itself being an inherent part of the Soviet model, being, indeed, the quintessence of the Soviet approach to development. Accordingly, we would argue, the Soviet-type economy *does* generate wage premia which can serve the role which the short-term interest instrument is called upon to play in the West.[8] To say this is definitely not to say, however, that the industry premia which evolved were necessarily the correct ones. Or to put it another way, in actual circumstances there is no mechanism to ensure that the wage premia which subsequently determine the prices of the industry's output will coincide with output productivity differentials. But in principle there is no reason why they could not. In any event, the premia which are imposed help to promote the correct allocation. Accordingly, we observe positive relations in the short-term row-column intersection.

II.4.2. *Definition of interest concepts: the long-term instrument.* The long-term instrument should be used in a way which is neutral with respect to relative input prices; i.e., it should not impose upon price a further capital charge beyond the short-term productivity differential which, we have argued, is reflected, although probably not with complete accuracy, by the industry wage differentials. The proper use of the long-term instrument is to provide a cutoff for selecting projects on the basis of their internal rates of return, i.e., a value for $\bar{\rho}$. This is at the same time the rate of discount which should be used to commensurate future output with present output.

8. Recently, after many years of debate, Soviet capital goods were marked up by 6 percent to include an interest component. As Campbell has argued (1968), this could lead to inefficiencies, since the markup was applied on the original capital, and, serving as it would as a basis for enterprise performance evaluation, might lead managers to scrap machinery prematurely. However, the imposition of the markup is an administrative regulation, and is of recent vintage. It is not clear whether managers will have discretion about imposing the charge. If they have, the implied inefficiency need not result. The 6 percent charge, then, does not seem to be inherent in the Soviet-type economy, either the stipulated quantity (which, for all one can tell, may be the right amount to add to the capital charge already existing by way of the wage differential) or the particular method of imposing it on the undepreciated cost.

For many years before the decree on the use of the Standard Methodology in 1960 ("Tipovaia metodika," 1960)[9] and also subsequently, although to a lesser extent, there had been general opposition to the use of such an instrument in the Soviet economy on the ground that it resembled an interest rate and was inconsistent with Marxian principles. However, the long-term instrument proposed here does not enter the prices of commodities and so does not lead them away from values based on their labor cost of reproduction. Thus, strictly speaking, it would be difficult to object to it on the basis of Marxian value theory. Rather, it simply provides a decision rule to guide investments. Its consistency with Marxian theory would have to be evaluated on the basis of whether or not it leads to production patterns which would be at variance with Marx's views. It seems safe to say that the production patterns would be difficult to infer from any of Marx's writings; surely his theory of value does not imply any unambiguous rule for determining what sectors, industries, or projects to invest in. However, since any economy must devise some criterion for determining what investments to make, and since it can go only so far on the basis of political criteria, it is almost certainly the case that a criterion such as $\bar{p}$ would emerge eventually — indeed, the fact that it *did* emerge in the face of the rigid opposition of those camps which believed themselves orthodox in their commitment to Marxism is perhaps the surest testimonial to this conjecture. At the same time, the fact that the Soviet economy has no mechanism whereby the instrument can be incorporated into the price of goods — unlike the capitalist market economy, which, as we have seen, has mechanisms that frequently do effect such an incorporation — causes the Soviet instrument to have a positive relationship with both short-term and long-term resource-allocation functions.

II.4.3. *Some problems in practice.* The short-term instrument almost certainly represents a force for rational short-term and long-term decision making, since it permits all commodities to reflect their capital intensity, and thus the opportunity cost of producing any particular good. The empirical problem would be, as noted, to determine how closely the wage differentials approximate the productivity differentials of the outputs. Present-day data are wholly inadequate to support any conjectures.

On the other hand, there are some problems in the actual application of the long-term interest instrument. But since the obvious examples do not seem to arise for reasons inherent in the organization of the economy, they do not contradict the essential conclusion reached above. We will consider two problems which may be observed in practice.

9. The Standard Methodology was revised and a new version presented in 1969 ("Tipovaia metodika" 1969). A comparison of the two and an assessment of the workability of the new one are contained in Abouchar 1973a.

The first problem is that the new standard methodology, in effect, decrees two different rates for $\bar{p}$, .12 and .08. The first rate (.12) is the normative coefficient of effectiveness, which is to be used as the cutoff point for choosing between alternative technologies for accomplishing a given task — an increment in production by a steel mill (TM, 1969, p. 12), for example. The second rate (.08) is the rate of discount which is to be used to commensurate future income and cost streams.

The second problem concerns the actual use — or misuse — of the long-term instrument. As just implied, the cutoff for investment selection should be the same as the coefficient used to discount future cost or production streams. However, there has long been a tendency to use nothing at all. (Perhaps this will change with the new provision, just cited, that future magnitudes must be discounted — discounted not only in project appraisal as a basis for investment decisions but also in the elaboration of broad policies for which the optimal variant necessarily involves considerations of the cost of long-lived capital.) Thus, one finds discussions of alternative cost behavior in which future costs are not discounted by any rate of discount at all. For example, in (Ialovenko 1966) an analysis of optimal tractor life, there was no recognition that a tractor performing 25,000 hectares of standardized ploughing in three years cost the economy less than one tractor doing the same acreage in ten years, since in the first case the stock of tractors to do the same work in any year would be smaller, thus freeing some resources for use in other productive activity in the economy. (A prior decision between using any tractor at all and using only hand labor is not affected in principle; such decisions should be based on a comparison of the price of hand labor and the tractor cost, which is based on the short-term interest, which is supposed to be equal to the wage premium for the production of tractors.)

Recognition of the lower opportunity costs implied by a smaller stock might have an important bearing on major policy decisions. For example, recognition of the advantages of more intensive utilization of capital might lead agriculture to seek various forms of rationalization, such as custom combining (Abouchar and Needles 1975). It is true, of course, that the machine tractor stations were an attempt to utilize agricultural capital more intensively, an attempt which ultimately proved to have tremendous organizational shortcomings, but this does not rule out the possibility of other kinds of equipment sharing in agriculture. Custom combining, where the equipment can move over wide geophysical-meteorological belts to follow the harvest, might well present an efficient approach without the problems arising in conflicting schedules that the local orientation of machine tractor stations encountered. But as long as the implied savings of the reduced agricultural capital stock are ignored, such a policy is not likely to be investigated. However, this neglect does not reflect inherent systemic shortcomings in the Soviet-type economy, but rather some misinformed practices.[10]

II.4.4. *Evaluation of capital charge instruments for distribution and measurement.* The effects of the short-term capital charge or interest surrogate on income distribution are negative, naturally, since the industry coefficients represent large sources of wage discrepancy. The magnitude cannot be conjectured, of course. Empirical data are inconclusive, since industry differentials also reflect a number of factors other than incentive premia, especially skill differentials, part of which could be justified by higher skill-reproduction costs. Another part reflects labor disutility, which may bulk larger in some industries than in others. The industry incentives, however, do exacerbate income inequalities.

The effect of the long-term capital charge on income distribution is neutral, since there is no way for the long-term interest instrument to be reflected in profits, bonuses, or wages, as in the neoclassical system.

The effects of the interest or capital charge instruments on performance measurement are similar to those in the neoclassical system as we will see below.

II.5. *Summary of the interest instrument*

The interest mechanism in the capitalist market economy shows a greater number of conflicts than in the Soviet-type economy, where we found the relationships between short-term and long-term allocative instruments to be consistent, and where the distribution and measurement conflicts were fewer. Even in the absence of an explicit short-term capital charge, we argued, the wage differentials could serve the purpose. This conclusion, one must add, relates to the number of conflicts rather than their seriousness. Conceivably, the inconsistencies in the Soviet-type economy (the relationships between short-term interest and distribution and performance) could be much greater than those in the capitalist market economy. Or vice versa. There is simply no way to aggregate the effects on the different functions into a single measure, or to combine the overall effects into a summary indicator.

It should be added that even when the interfunctional relationships are positive, it does not follow that one economy may not be superior to the other. For example, while the wage differentials play the role of a short-term instrument in the Soviet economy, there is no guarantee that their levels are the correct, socially efficient ones. Thus, while in principle we

10. Perhaps with the new provision for discounting in the 1969 Standard Methodology there will be an increasing awareness of the return through rapid recoupment of capital costs. But this neglect in the first place, I believe, does not reflect inherent systemic shortcomings in the Soviet-type economy, but rather some misinformed practices.

can say that these serve the cause of efficiency (a plus sign in the short-term row-column square), in fact they may not be doing so. If they do not, and if the short-term instrument in the capitalist market economy does, the latter will in fact be superior in practice. But unless one could find an inherent incapacity in the Soviet-type economy to achieve the correct wage premia levels, one could not say that the capitalist market economy was inherently superior on this score.

III. Economic Rent

III.1. *Introduction*

We will define economic rent as the difference between the market price or earnings of a factor and the minimum price that the factor owner would accept for a unit use of that factor. This definition appears to cover three definitions that are put forward in the literature and which are sometimes believed to be alternative rather than consistent concepts:

1. The surplus earnings or price of a factor over the minimum necessary to retain it in its present use;
2. The surplus earnings or price of a factor over its highest earnings or price in an alternative use;
3. The surplus earnings or price of a factor over the earnings or price of the next best factor in the use to which the first factor is applied.

Some writers have stressed the differences in these definitions, but if we define the frame of analysis appropriately, the three concepts really reduce to the same idea. For example, Mishan (1959) has contrasted the use of the first definition by Boulding and Benham to the use by Samuelson and Stigler of the second. But, obviously, the minimum earnings necessary to retain a factor in its present use will depend on its earnings potential in another use.

That the third definition is also equivalent to the first two is easy to see. We think in terms of characteristics of factors (this factor and all others which provide the same characteristics) and construct a supply curve with the rent-exclusive cost of a unit of the characteristic on the vertical axis. Then we arrange all the factors on the horizontal axis, with those having the lowest rent-exclusive cost first, and those providing a unit of the characteristic at successively higher costs following. The economic rent is then the difference between rent-exclusive costs of inframarginal units of factors and the price at the demand-supply intersection. This would also be the surplus earnings in definition 1.

As noted in Section I, for purposes of rent analysis, short-term decisions are those which are made with respect to optimization of production this year (or in some other short period) with a fixed supply of a scarce resource. Long-term decisions cover production over long time periods. The main differences in the price instruments will arise because of resource exhaustibility; exhaustion will alter the relative rents over time, and, hence, optimal use patterns. Our analysis of efficiency, then, aims to study whether rents designed for short-term optimization also lead to long-term optimization.

Finally, we must introduce a new price instrument into the discussion. This is economic rent designed for purposes of income distribution. It is shown in the third row of Table 4.3. Real-life examples of this rent include differentiated agricultural procurement or industrial wholesale prices. We consider the three economies in turn.

III.2. *The neoclassical economy*

III.2.1. *Allocative efficiency: allocation-related rents.* In the neoclassical economy, rents will arise naturally in the course of daily activities, reflecting the cost advantages of certain factors or inputs. Table 4.3 shows the interfunctional relations for rent in all three economies. Rents which arise because of short-term scarcities promote short-term interfirm efficiency by rationing the existing fixed quantity of the factor among the uses which make the greatest contribution to the economy and ensuring that the cost imposed on society by forcing a second user to a less efficient resource is offset by the social gain accruing from the use of the first resource by those whose demand price exceeds the rent-inclusive price.

Table 4.3. Interfunctional relations for economic rent in neoclassical, capitalist, and socialist economies. (Relations are the same for all three economies.)

Instrument applied for function shown in row	Effect on function shown in column			
	Resource allocation		Income distribution	Performance measurement
	Short-term	Long-term		
Resource allocation: short-term	+	?	−	−
Resource allocation: long-term	?	+	−	−
Income distribution	?	?	+	0

An example which recurs frequently in the Soviet context is the relationship between oil and coal. Oil has a much lower labor cost of production than coal. If oil is priced on the basis of its kilocalorie content relatively to coal, so that its price includes a rent, we would know that any oil user who forces a user elsewhere to use coal is contributing to society through his output a value at least equal to the cost imposed on society by forcing the second user to resort to coal.[11] This result would hold both under more market-oriented operating conditions, with profit serving as the critical success indicator, and under central planning of current operations.

What of the short-term/long-term square? If short-term rents are included in prices under profit maximization, resource locations with positive rents will be developed through new investment, those with the highest rents being developed first. This ensures intertemporal efficiency. On the other hand, inclusion of short-term rents in the price of resources may have inefficient results. This can be seen in the following way.

If the resource is priced at rent-exclusive cost of production, many firms will be encouraged to expand into activities which use this resource as an intermediate good. The resource will now be used up more rapidly. This will hasten the day when the economy will have to resort to higher-cost alternatives, either the sources which are now highest-cost and are temporarily abandoned, or to further high-cost resources not now envisaged. If the gain to the economy from using the low-cost (i.e., low in terms of rent-exclusive production costs) resource today exceeds the higher cost of the alternative resource in the future (discounted, of course by the equilibrium interest rate of Section II), its use today should be encouraged rather than discouraged. But if the short-term rents are added to the cost of production of the resource to determine its market price, its use will be discouraged. On the other hand, if the gain today falls short of the present value of the higher cost which accelerated use of the resource today would impose on the economy at a future date, use today should be discouraged. Determination of all these relationships is an empirical matter, but it would be supposed that for some resources the higher future costs would be greater and for others less than the benefit to the economy from using the resource more rapidly today.

Now, in the neoclassical economy, determination of the rents at any given time would take account of all the conflicting demands for the resource (i.e., the demands for use today and the future effect of earlier exhaustion), would balance all competing uses, and would result in a number yielding a price which, when related to any other price, would

11. We are abstracting from quality variations in coal or oil, as well as transport costs, all of which of course are other sources of rent generation whose consideration would present no new problems of principle but would complicate the presentation unnecessarily.

reflect the two-way (interfirm, intertemporal) marginal productivity of the resource. This adaptability is the potential for efficiency of the rent instrument. In practice, however, when it is argued that rents should be included in prices and the Soviet system is criticized for its inability to generate rents, the criticism implicitly assumes that a neoclassical solution equating relative rent-inclusive prices on the two-way margin is a reasonably realizable goal. But, in fact, such a goal is very hard to attain. In fact, if the system of rent-inclusive prices is concerned solely with short-term efficiency, there will necessarily be many cases of inefficiency in long-term decisions, as described in the preceding paragraph. To emphasize this fact, we will indicate in the short-term/long-term square that the overall efficiency of long-term decisions based on the short-term rents is indeterminate, there being some cases of negative and some cases of positive influence.

We now consider long-term rent. This is designed to enable firms to equate intertemporal productivity-price ratios. Its analysis is symmetrical with that of short-term rent. I.e., it may have both positive and negative consequences on short-term allocation, while it has a positive influence on long-term allocative efficiency. The qualifications made above concerning the logical emergence of a single rent to equate interfirm, intertemporal marginal productivity-price ratios continue to apply, of course. But again, unless both sets of allocative decisions are considered simultaneously, a rent designed for long-term allocative efficiency can have inefficient short-term consequences.

III.2.2. *Allocative efficiency: distribution-related rents.* We turn next to the analysis of the effect of distribution-related rents on the several functions of interest. An income distribution rent may be thought of as a tax on a factor equal to the rent that is generated by the market, or some proportion thereof. An example in recent Western experience is the Canadian imposition of a federal unit export tax on crude oil for U.S. markets, designed to transfer the windfall gains arising from the increase in Arab oil prices and the Arab oil embargo.

The resource-allocation column intersections with the distribution row are indeterminate. The reason is that the person on whom the rent is imposed will fall to a lower welfare level. But he will produce more, and the ultimate issue whether his extra output will increase society's welfare more than his own welfare reduction cannot be answered in general. Sometimes it may; at other times it may not.

Mishan's analysis of 1959 is a good starting point. He showed that any attempt to transfer the rent as a lump sum is not neutral with respect to welfare levels. According to his analysis, there may be an increase in the amount supplied to achieve the same income, i.e., a welfare reduction.

The same is true if prices are adjusted by the distributional rents. They may lead to a higher output, but they will also result in a welfare loss. A welfare reduction for the same input is one form of inefficiency—indeed, perhaps the single best way to define economic inefficiency.

The foregoing results are shown in fig. 4.2. Income is shown on the

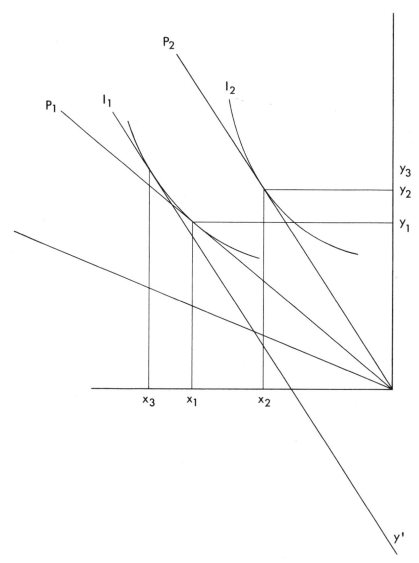

Figure 4.2. Determination of income distribution rent and final market price and output.

Y-axis and labor input, in days worked, on the X-axis. I_1 and I_2 represent the indifference curves of two different workers, in two different regions, say. Movements to the left indicate greater labor inputs. (The indifference curve families are the same, however.) The nature of their locations leads to different productivity for the two workers. Any two points on an indifference curve indicate combinations of work and income between which the worker is indifferent. The second worker is on a higher indifference curve (I_2) since he is more productive and has become accustomed to higher earnings. He is willing to work the same amount as the first worker only if he receives a higher income.

The daily income of the first worker is p_1. The relation between total income and total work input is given by the ray P_1. The tangency of P_1 and I_1 shows his equilibrium income and labor input, y_1 and x_1, respectively. The wage for the second worker is p_2, and his equilibrium income and labor input are y_2 and x_2, respectively. To equalize welfare for the two workers requires a reduction in the second worker's income. If an annual lump-sum tax of Oy' is imposed on the second worker, leaving his unit wage untouched (p_2), he will increase his labor input to x_3 and his net income to y_3. Thus, he will have the same welfare as the first worker (they are now on the same indifference curve), but he will work more hours and earn more money. This presentation follows Mishan's diagram, although Mishan's presentation related to shifts in wages and indifference curves for the same worker.

If the daily wage rather than the gross annual income is adjusted through taxation, we must distribute the annual tax Oy' over the total days worked and subtract it from the daily earning p_2. This gives a daily net income $p_2 - (Oy'/x)$, which is nonlinear. However, total income will equal $x[p_2 - (Oy'/x)]$, or $xp_2 - Oy'$, and we will have the same income line and solution as in the case of the lump-sum rent. The wage earner's welfare is again less than it was previously (when he was on I_2), although his income is higher. He is also producing more (the increase is $x_3 - x_2$). The critical question for estimation of final welfare change is whether this increased output will generate an increase in social welfare in excess of the welfare reduction of the individual concerned.

The same analysis as for labor would hold for any given commodity. For example, if income is related to profits, and profits are higher for firms supplying a better-quality resource (since these firms earn rents), they could be forced to pay a lump-sum tax or a tax per unit, which is the essence of the differentiated settlement price. Again, the critical issue is whether the increased output of the producer generates a welfare improvement greater than the producer's welfare reduction; whether, that is, there is an advance toward Pareto optimality.

It warrants stressing that this analysis has run in terms of maximization of welfare, which Pareto analysis really requires, rather than national income. Frequently—perhaps usually—Western economists really think in terms of national income when they analyze welfare, noting tangentially that the two are not the same thing and that they would really prefer to measure welfare if they could. Indeed, it is almost the tradition to think in this way, and, moreover, it is national income which is undeniably the preoccupation of economic policy makers and analysts in government and academic circles. The same tradition is surely also relevant to the Soviet scene, and even more apparent, for there personal-utility maximization is not even rendered lip service. If this Soviet tradition were followed here, we would have to conclude that the distribution-related rent was efficient, since it did increase national income. All this is worth noting here since there is probably a tendency in some circles to insist on a Pareto-type, utility-maximizing criterion to measure the efficiency and desirability of the Soviet economy, while applying a national-output maximization criterion in their own countries.

III.2.3. *Income distribution and performance measurement.* As noted, a single rent instrument should logically emerge in the neoclassical model, and its effect would be to distribute income more nearly in proportion to (intertemporal and interfirm) marginal value productivity of factors. Such a distribution of income, because of its efficiency implication, would constitute the normative neoclassical distribution criterion. The existence of a single rent criterion, optimizing both at a given moment in time *and over* time, is consistent with the distribution goal.

Regarding the twin one-way criteria—short-term and long-term rent considered separately—we cannot be so sure. If resource A has a high short-term rent, but because of its huge supply may be considered virtually inexhaustible, the single two-way rent should be low. The resource owner's income would be lower under the long-term instrument and higher under the short-term instrument as compared with the single two-way norm of the preceding paragraph. Accordingly, a negative relationship is shown in both allocation squares in the distribution column.

The effect of the income-distribution-related rent on income distribution is positive. The income-distribution objective of the neoclassical system is simply the one which accords with intertemporal and intersectoral allocative efficiency. The rents which would be generated thereby would accrue to factor owners, and it would not be necessary to impose such devices administratively. Hence, no rents would have to be designed for income-distribution objectives.

We turn finally to performance measurement. The effectiveness of a price instrument with regard to performance measurement is determined by the value of the ratio G/G' where G and G' are respectively the Gerschenkron ratios

$$\frac{\Sigma P_1 Q_2}{\Sigma P_1 Q_1} \Big/ \frac{\Sigma P_2 Q_2}{\Sigma P_2 Q_1} \quad \text{and} \quad \frac{\Sigma P'_1 Q_2}{\Sigma P'_1 Q_1} \Big/ \frac{\Sigma P'_2 Q_2}{\Sigma P'_2 Q_1}, \tag{1}$$

where the primed P's indicate prices which include the price instrument being investigated, and the unprimed P's are the prices which reflect the labor cost of production.

We start by disaggregating each summand into two summands, one summing over all goods on which economic rents might arise and one summing over all other goods. We will denote goods in the first set by a tilde and in the second by a bar. Then each ratio in the Gerschenkron ratio may be written as the ratio of two summands, e.g.,

$$\frac{\Sigma P_1 Q_2}{\Sigma P_1 Q_1} = \frac{\Sigma P_1 \tilde{Q}_2 + \Sigma P_1 \bar{Q}_2}{\Sigma P_1 \tilde{Q}_1 + \Sigma P_1 \bar{Q}_1}. \tag{2}$$

Goods marked by a tilde we will term class 1 and those by a bar, class 2.

For simplicity, we will assume that all the commodities denoted by a tilde are used for the same purpose, so that they can be considered as inputs to a cost curve showing the relationship between price on the vertical axis and activity level or consumption on the horizontal. The rent-exclusive cost curve is given by the curve BCD in fig. 4.3. As successively inferior (harder to find, deeper to drill, more difficult conditions to work, etc.) resources are brought into play, rent-exclusive costs of production rise. Fig. 4.3 also shows the demand curves for class 1 products for the beginning and end years of the period being studied. The production (equal to consumption) of the class 1 commodities for the two years is shown by $\tilde{Q}_1$ and $\tilde{Q}_2$.

The class 1 output in the second year exceeds that of the first year by $\tilde{Q}_2 - \tilde{Q}_1$. We do not know what the cost of producing this output would have been in year 1, since we have observations on input costs only as far as $\tilde{Q}_1$. But since this additional output uses as input the resource which is used in the last unit of output in year 1, in the normal course of things we would assume that the year 1 cost of each unit of input to produce the additional output would have been equal to the cost of the last unit of year 1 input, which is P_e. The early-year weighted output for class 1 goods in year 2 (weighted by the rent-exclusive prices) is given by the area $ABCE\tilde{Q}_2$, and the early-year output in year 1 rent-exclusive prices, by $ABC\tilde{Q}_1$. Meanwhile, since the rent-exclusive costs for the inputs used to produce up to $\tilde{Q}_1$ do not change between the two years, the late-year weighted year 1 output continues to be what it is in the first year, namely

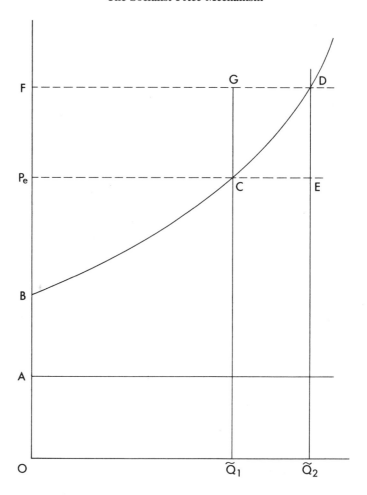

Volume of resource use

Figure 4.3. Determination of national income accounting prices for two periods (two activity levels).

$ABC\tilde{Q}_1$, while the late-year weighted year 2 output is given by $ABCD\tilde{Q}_2$. These relationships are shown in fig. 4.4.

We turn now to the rent-inclusive prices. If the price of each of the inframarginal inputs is made to include the rent as defined in Section III.2.1, the total resource input in any year will be a rectangle, whether measured by year 1 or year 2 prices. For example, the rent-inclusive value PQ for the year 1 output in year 1 rent-inclusive prices would be $AP_eC\tilde{Q}_1$, and that for year 2 output in year 1 rent-inclusive prices would be $AP_eE\tilde{Q}_2$.

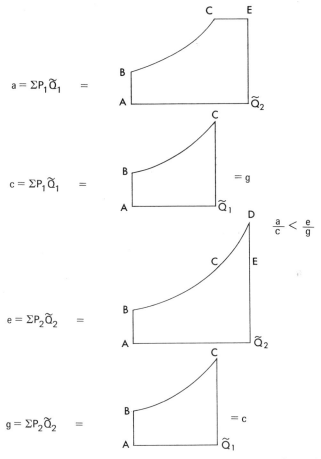

Figure 4.4. Correspondence between areas of fig. 4.3 and components of Gerschenkron ratio expressed in rent-exclusive prices.

Similarly, rent-inclusive outputs for the year 1, and year 2 outputs in year 2 prices, would be given by the rectangles $AFGC\tilde{Q}_1$ and $AFDE\tilde{Q}_2$. The four rent-inclusive relationships are shown in fig. 4.5.

To see what will happen, we write out the Gerschenkron ratios in full, showing the division of goods in outputs between the two classes. We have

$$G = \frac{\dfrac{\Sigma P_1 \tilde{Q}_2 + \Sigma P_1 \overline{Q}_2}{\Sigma P_1 \tilde{Q}_1 + \Sigma P_1 \overline{Q}_1}}{\dfrac{\Sigma P_2 \tilde{Q}_2 + \Sigma P_2 \overline{Q}_2}{\Sigma P_2 \tilde{Q}_1 + \Sigma P_2 \overline{Q}_1}}$$

$$G' = \frac{\dfrac{\Sigma P'_1 \tilde{Q}_2 + \Sigma P'_1 \overline{\overline{Q}}_2}{\Sigma P'_1 \tilde{Q}_1 + \Sigma P'_1 \overline{Q}_1}}{\dfrac{\Sigma P'_2 \tilde{Q}_2 + \Sigma P'_2 \overline{\overline{Q}}_2}{\Sigma P'_2 \tilde{Q}_1 + \Sigma P'_2 \overline{Q}_1}}. \tag{4}$$

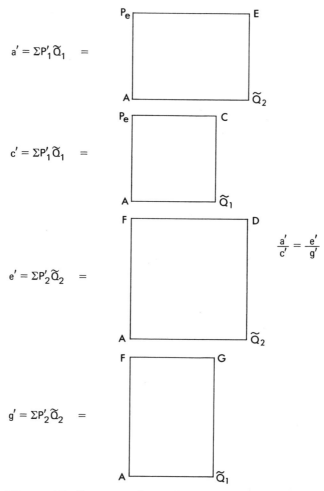

Figure 4.5. Correspondence between areas of fig. 4.3 and components of Gerschenkron ratio expressed in rent-inclusive prices.

We will rewrite these, substituting a single letter for each summand. Using the notation of Fig. 4.4 for the class 1 summands, and b, d, f, and h for the class 2 summands, we write:

$$\theta = \frac{G}{G'} = \frac{\dfrac{\dfrac{\dfrac{\dfrac{a+b}{c+d}}{e+f}}{g+h}}{\dfrac{\dfrac{\dfrac{a'+b'}{c'+d'}}{e'+f'}}{g'+h'}}}{} . \tag{5}$$

Since the class 2 components do not have rents, we know that $b = b'$, $d = d'$, etc. Also, it will in normal situations be the case that $b/d > f/h$ (i.e., one output will normally appear greater relatively to a second output when both are valued by prices of the second situation).

We rewrite the performance measurement ratio as follows:

$$\theta = \frac{G}{G'} = \frac{\dfrac{a+b}{c+d}}{\dfrac{a'+b'}{c'+d'}} \cdot \frac{\dfrac{e'+f'}{g'+h'}}{\dfrac{e+f}{g+h}} . \tag{6}$$

To evaluate θ we note that if at least one of the ratios

$$\frac{\dfrac{a}{c}}{\dfrac{a'}{c'}} \cdot \frac{\dfrac{e'}{g'}}{\dfrac{e}{g}} \tag{7}$$

and

$$\frac{\dfrac{b}{d}}{\dfrac{b'}{d'}} \cdot \frac{\dfrac{f'}{h'}}{\dfrac{f}{h}} \tag{8}$$

exceeds unity while the other is equal to unity, θ in (6) is certainly greater than unity. Likewise, if at least one is less than unity while the other is no greater than unity, θ is less than unity. (The converse of both of these statements is not true.) Expression (8) is equal to unity since it involves ratios of class 2 outputs for which the question of rent-exclusive prices does not arise (i.e., $b = b'$, etc.). To evaluate expression (7) we note that

$$\frac{a'}{c'} = \frac{e'}{g'} = k \text{ (see Fig. 4.5)};$$

therefore (7) may be written

$$\frac{a/c}{k} \cdot \frac{k}{e/g}.\tag{9}$$

But since $(a/c) < (e/g)$, expression (9) < 1, and θ is less than unity. Therefore, the Gerschenkron ratio expressed in rent-exclusive prices (G) gives a smaller range than the ratio expressed in rent-inclusive prices (G'). Hence, if we include rents in prices, we will tend to give a less precise reading on welfare change over time. The conclusion just derived applies to a situation in which the same cost curve relates to year 1 and year 2, the costs in year 2 being found simply by moving along the curve. It might happen, however, that there is a shift of this curve, rather than a movement along the curve. In this case evaluation of the ratio G/G' is less certain. We would have to make assumptions concerning the details of the form of the curves.

III.3. *Capitalist market economy*

The interfunctional relations for the capitalist market economy are just the same as in the neoclassical model. The negative entries in the first two income distribution squares are prompted by the same considerations as the negative entries in the analysis of short-term interest — they tend to make distribution more unequal, since they will accrue to factor owners, while the income distribution objective of the economy, insofar as it can be said to be explicitly formulated at all, tends to be in the direction of greater equality. (In the neoclassical economy the effects of the short-term and long-term instruments are negative because they differ from the income distribution that would be observed if rents simultaneously took account of both long-term and short-term horizons, which is the desideratum for income distribution in that economy.) The entry in the third row is positive because the income-distribution rent would tend to make income distribution more equal, and this is adjudged the goal.

The short-term/long-term relations are especially interesting in today's fuel crisis, and it may be that the difficulties in harmonizing the rents for the two horizons are so serious as to outweigh the considerations for all other resources and make the balance definitely negative. Any brief exposure to the wide range of pricing arguments put forward by oil-producing interests — firms, countries, and provinces and states — and the arguments of users looking for "equity" — provinces, whole countries, regions — shows, first of all, the conflicts between income-distribution-related rents and allocation rents. But even the question of long-term vs. short-term is hopelessly muddled. Does anyone have any idea what the long-term rent should be (i.e., the rent which should optimize the decisions of users to adopt petroleum-based technologies and the pace of adoption)? Does anyone know what the short-term rent should be (including a negative component to pay society for whatever environmental effects are now imposed by exploration and production)?

But it is not simply a problem of lack of information. Suppose that an oil producer knew how high the long-term rent should be to reflect the opportunity cost imposed on the economy fifty years from now when the economy would have to resort to a different fuel or different technology, discounted to the present. Users would willingly pay this rent to the supplier to use his oil rather than be driven to the next resource. By discounting to today, the supplier could compare the profit to be made in the future with the profit to be made today and would adjust today's supply to maximize his discounted profit stream. Decreasing today's supply would raise today's price while it would raise future supply and lower future price; increasing today's supply would have reverse effects. Guided by the discount rate, the supplier would adjust his supply patterns to maximize the present value of the profit stream (including rents). But for this to be socially optimal, the discount rate must be the value $\bar{\rho}$ which we calculated in Section II. In fact, the supplier will probably be guided by the bank rate of interest, which may differ sharply from $\bar{\rho}$. In this case, we will not get the optimal output pattern over time, and the short-term rents implied by the actual distribution pattern will differ from the correct intertemporal, intersectoral rents which efficiency calls for. In addition, of course, in the absence of knowledge of future demand curves, the manager of the firm could not even determine the correct parameters to solve the intertemporal use pattern were he merely to be given the value $\bar{\rho}$.

Income-distribution-related rents would have the same indeterminate effect as in the neoclassical system. This point is of special importance today, when policy is being formulated regarding oil producers' windfall profits and oil pricing, and suggests that the two main "equitable" approaches may be unjustified from a welfare viewpoint. Administrative price control would allow all Canadians to buy petroleum products at a "fair price." Alternatively, a unit royalty would be transferred to the federal budget (or even, for that matter, to the province) the difference between mid-1973 production costs and the new price dictated largely by OPEC prices. The first example would be implicit income distribution; the second, provided the federal royalty revenue were distributed in certain ways, would be explicit income distribution. Similar considerations are being bruited in the United States, and, of course, similar conclusions apply.

Evidently, any of these oil-pricing policies could lead to inefficiency, i.e., to a reduction in welfare below the level of Pareto optimality, although the chances would be slight. The analysis is the same as in the discussion and diagram illustrating the neoclassical situation. The producer increases both his output and his income. He is on a lower indifference curve, however, and so suffers a welfare loss. The amount is probably slight in the case of the oil producer, however, and the welfare gain to others associated with the higher output will probably exceed it. In the case of other commodities or forms of labor, the situation would not be so predictable. Therefore, the income distribution/allocation squares are shown as indeterminate, as in the neoclassical case.

III.4. *The socialist economy*

The interfunctional rent relations for the neoclassical and capitalist market economies are the same as those of the socialist economy. They have the same basic weaknesses, although these may arise for different reasons, especially in the income-distribution rents. We will first examine the influences of allocation instruments and then turn to the distribution-related rents.

III.4.1. *Allocative instruments: effect of allocation instruments on allocative efficiency.* The short-term row-column square and the long-term row-column square present no problem—relations are positive for reasons described in Section III.2 on the neoclassical economy.

The short-term/long-term square and the long-term/short-term square present the same kind of problems for the socialist economy as we observed in the other two systems. Consider the example of the short-term instrument. This will have a positive effect on short-term allocative efficiency, but a positive or negative effect on long-term efficiency. It will have a positive effect insofar as the rent discourages the rapid exhaustion of the resource which would result if firms were encouraged by lower prices to employ technologies or produce output using the resource in question and were driven, following its exhaustion, to high-cost substitutes. On the other hand, the short-term rent may lead to long-term inefficiency, since planners may not receive correct price signals. For example, suppose there are two ore bodies in two different regions, the one in the more populated and developed region, possibly having lower extraction costs per ton, but with higher costs per ton in terms of standardized output (i.e., considering its mineral content). In this case, the output of the deposit in the new region will earn a rent as the difference between its costs of extraction and transport to the old region, and the production cost in the old region. If this rent is included in the pit-head price, planners trying to decide on the location of production facilities using this ore as an input—a long-term decision—will not see the cost advantage of this aspect of their operations, since the price they will be faced with will be higher than the rent-exclusive cost. As a matter of fact,

Soviet pricemakers have almost always had regionally differentiated prices based on cost of production, which do provide a better clue to regional development decisions (which are, of course, a form of long-term decision) than do short-term rent-inclusive prices.

III.4.2. *Allocative instruments: effect of allocation instruments upon distribution and measurement.* Both the short-term and long-term rents would aggravate income inequalities as compared with a rent-exclusive price structure. This aggravation would occur in both agriculture and industry as the firms benefiting by the rents would have higher profits, and managerial bonuses would rise. Differentials would also develop in profit-related housing and other noncash income. Measurement of macroeconomic performance would meet the same problems as were encountered in the analysis of the neoclassical system.

III.4.3. *Income-distribution instruments: allocative efficiency.* The most obvious examples of prices based on distribution-related rents are the regionally differentiated agricultural procurement prices and industry settlement prices, which provide for differentiated payments to suppliers and a single price to users. Since they tend to relate each supplier's income to his costs, in principle they equalize profits of suppliers; and since they result in the same cost to users, it is easier to evaluate users according to their profit performance. A policy of "equal income for equal value added" can be pursued by tying managerial bonuses and worker incentives to the firm's profits.

That such distribution-related rents may lead to allocative inefficiency follows from the theoretical analysis of Section III.2.2. Whether or not they are allocatively inefficient, according to that analysis, will depend on the incremental social welfare generated by the increased output of the producer (or from the resource input on which the income-distribution rent is levied, i.e., whose unit price is reduced to compensate for some differential natural advantage). It is also easy to show that in the actual circumstances of the Soviet economy, such rents would indeed lead to allocative inefficiency, although the reasoning is not as tidy as in the theoretical exposition. The same conclusion almost certainly applies to any other real economy. Hence, if the income-distribution rents are applied, an inefficiency will result.

Before we begin our analysis, a few words concerning the Soviet treatment of economic rent will be in order. Differential rent has long been recognized as a proper category in a price system. It exists in two forms, I and II. Differential rent I is traditionally associated with differential land productivity and in recent years has been specifically linked to more workable mineral deposits. (The final paragraph of the 1970 *Encyclo-*

pedia article on differential rent makes this adjustment [*BSE*, 8:984.]). Differential rent II is said to result from "the differential productivity of marginal investment: its size and rate increase in a planned manner in conditions of intensification and scientific and technological progress in agriculture; it remains almost wholly within agriculture" (*ibid.*).

Writers seem generally to agree that differential rent is consistent with Marxism, since it enables the socialist economy to transfer the surplus value of agriculture to the service of the state. Thus, it is viewed primarily as a distribution instrument, if only in a negative way; i.e., it keeps the better-placed farmers from getting rich. To the extent, of course, that as a result of industrial growth, everybody will be better off in the future, differential rent provides a larger pot to share in the future, one in which the farmers will presumably share, so that it can be said to promote egalitarian income distribution in the long run. This path to the justification of differential rent—together with the statement that differential rent II is to be left to the farmers—suggests an income-distribution bias in the Soviet view of differential rent. It is not seen principally as a mechanism for promoting economic efficiency. There is no hint of such notions in the *Encyclopedia* article. An article by L. Zaitsev (1969), Deputy Director of the Kolkhoz Affairs Administration of the USSR Ministry of Agriculture, discusses differential rent exclusively from this viewpoint. Finally, writers who frequently champion the cause of allocative efficiency stress the absence of a rent mechanism from cost manipulations today (see Kantorovich et al. 1970), which again shows that in practice today differential rent is viewed almost exclusively as an income-distribution instrument.

One indication of concern with the allocative aspects of rent is contained in a recent study by Brusilovskaia et al. (1967) of the Institute of Economics of the Academy of Sciences.[12] The authors observe a decline of nearly 50 percent in the share of coal and increases of 67 percent in the shares of oil and gas in the national fuel balance between 1958 and 1966. Meanwhile, coal production costs (sebestoimost') rose by 13 percent while oil and gas costs decreased by 16 percent and 30 percent respectively between 1950 and 1966. Today these differences are compensated for by including rents on the lower cost fuels in the form of turnover taxes and fixed rental payments to the budget. The authors sense that if these use and prime cost trends continue there will be problems. Although they do not quite express the problem of short-term vs. long-term rents, this is what seems to be behind their statement that: "With a further increase in the oil and gas shares in the fuel balance, the average

---

12. While not explicitly recognizing the efficiency aspects, this seems to be what they have in mind in part of their discussion of rent and fixed charges (p. 44ff) which also reveals some understanding of the short-term vs. long-term conflicts.

level of objectively necessary labour costs and the prices for fuel will, obviously, be determined not by the costs in the coal industry, but by the average industry wide costs in the fuel industry as a whole. This, naturally, limits the possibility for collecting differential rents through the oil and gas prices, and leads to a relatively low rate of profit planned in coal prices.

Because of this, the need for using a system of settlement prices in the coal industry will increase in the future rather than diminish." (pp. 46–47). The authors seem to mean that as oil and gas become still more important, and their prime costs less, the spread between coal and other fuel prime costs, and hence the implied rent, would become so great as to give false signals about the use of oil and gas. Accordingly, at some future point, they should be divorced, with oil and gas prices geared primarily to their own prime cost, which would give good long-term signals, since they would encourage the development of the activities that use these low cost inputs.

Given this bent, it is not surprising that most Soviet discussion of differential rent has revolved around the question of what mechanism should be used to transfer the differential rent. Differentiated zonal agricultural procurement prices, differentiated income taxes, and differentiated land rents, in isolation or in combination, are the most frequently espoused mechanisms. None of the discussion has concerned itself with the effect on efficiency and, with the exception of one Estonian writer, Bronshtein, most discussants have concerned themselves with the doctrinal compatibility of the alternatives rather than their economic advantages or disadvantages. It is rarely recognized that procurement-price differentiation is a very difficult matter and would open tremendous potentials for abuse of the kind that results in inefficiency. To be sure, if the country could be divided into a number of clearly defined zones of varying agricultural potential, agricultural procurement prices could be differentiated by zone, location in a zone being a proxy for the differential productivity of land. Farmers in relatively productive zones would receive less per ton, the differentials being calculated to allow each farmer the same annual income. Articles giving the average land values in different regions contribute to the impression that is created that this zoning is easy to carry out. For example, Cheremushkin (1967, p. 87) gives values for 90 organizational subordinations—Yakut ASSR, Altai Krai, Estonia, etc.—but even these political divisions are extremely coarse.[13]

The fact is that the country does not divide up into distinct, homogeneous zones. There are large productivity differences even in small areas.

13. Incidentally, there are also serious differences between Cheremushkin's study and one by Romanchenko which shows Estonia with an arable land value of 99 rubles vs. a USSR average of 197 (1969, p. 15), i.e., twice as high. This compares with a USSR/Estonian arable land ratio of .77 in Cheremushkin's study (p. 87).

For example, a recent study by El'met showed that farms in Estonia were distributed over a wide range of grain productivities; according to his study, the shortfall in income per hectare under grain (from the theoretical maximum) ranges between zero and 125 rubles (1973, pp. 720–21). Since he nowhere states what the theoretical maximum is, it is difficult to assess the significance of these shortfalls, but since he considers as significant an average reduction in the shortfall of 45 rubles which would result from a more rational cropping pattern, this shortfall under grain monoculture appears significant.

Given the existence of such wide differences even within such a small republic, how does an administrator determine where they are and rate the various farms? He cannot do it simply on the basis of large zones. There may be too many variables to permit the handicapper to isolate the effect of the land. For example, if he looks simply at last year's experience, he has to find a way to commensurate output of flax on one farm, say, with fruits on another, not to speak of livestock, dairying, and so on. If he restricts himself to flax alone, say, how can he be sure that the differential productivity between two farms is due to the land rather than the ability and sweat of the farmers? He cannot. Therefore, if he makes a practice of simply giving a higher procurement price to those with lower output per hectare to equalize annual earnings, he will, to be sure, be giving something to those whose land is inherently less productive, but he will also be encouraging incompetent or otherwise unproductive labor, since farmers will have no incentive to improve their performance. How widespread this phenomenon would be is, of course, an unanswered question. But some writers do not seem to consider it a problem. For example, E. Brianskikh, writing in 1964, confidently describes grain production costs, determines the "optimal net income," and calculates the resulting rents per centner and per hectare on eight collective farms in the Zav'ialovskii raion of Udmurt ASSR without asking whether, possibly, capital differences or differences in worker competence might account for the different costs. If it is the capital differences, the effect of his proposal would be to deny a rent to capital, since the farms being worked more capital-intensively would receive lower prices, and as a result the incentive to invest in equipment would be reduced. The prime costs on what one would have thought would be a relatively homogeneous area (a single raion) vary from 3.0 to 7.3 rubles per centner—a spread of nearly 1.8 times the lowest cost (Brianskikh, p. 108).[14] However, we

14. The prime cost appears to exclude any physical measure of labor input. (It also excludes "optimal net income," which was assumed to be equal to 40 percent of prime cost.) Prime cost would then reflect mechanization, irrigation, technique, and labor utilization (e.g., the private plot/common land labor mix), as well as natural fertility. For this reason, the more mechanized the activity, the higher would prime cost appear, although, of course, total "real" cost of production (with labor assigned some value) would presumably be lower.

should be careful with such comparisons. As noted, the land itself may be homogeneous and may in fact lend itself to incorporation in a system of zonal rents. It may be that the writer's calculations are simply ill-founded.

Before concluding this section we should briefly consider the possibilities for imposing income-distribution rents on the output of industry. The purpose of such a rent would be similar to its purpose in agriculture. In industry it would work somewhat differently, however. In agriculture the state procurement agency is the middleman and deducts the rent at the procurement stage by paying a differentiated procurement price; but an industry income-distribution rent would involve a per-unit tax imposed by the state. Such a policy would depend for its success on the ability to know what the rent should be, which would require reliable knowledge on the operating conditions of plants in each industry. But the prospects for ever acquiring such knowledge are extremely bleak. While the Soviet-type economy would have some advantages over the capitalist market economy in the acquisition of such information—a view reinforced by the present dilemma facing U.S. energy policy officials trying to gain access to petroleum refinery data—even in a relatively homogeneous industry like petroleum refining, it is very difficult to transform raw data into a basis for determining relative interplant production advantages, which is a necessary prelude to the setting of rents. This is not a peculiar feature of the Soviet economy, but rather inheres in the nature of the industry. And if it is so difficult in the relatively simple petroleum industry, as the details of a recent study show (Arushanian et al. 1973), it is bound to be much more difficult in industries with more diverse products and more varied technologies. In this study, forty-five refineries were ranked according to expert valuation and according to eleven "objective factors." The two sets of rankings were far from coincident, and only three plants were graded consistently by all four experts.

III.4.4. *Income-distribution instruments: distribution and measurement.* In the light of the comments at the opening of the last section, III.4.3, the effect of income-distribution rents on income distribution is positive—incomes are made more nearly equal.

Finally, we consider the effect of income-distribution rents on the measurement of performance. To do this we must keep clear the distinction between these rents and short-term or long-term rents in order to isolate the effect of the former (the latter, we saw above, would have a negative effect in the case that seemed the more reasonable representation of reality). Regarding the income-distribution rents, we note that there would be no effects of the type introduced by short-term and long-term rents, since final prices would not be affected. For example, the ore industry wholesale price might include a rent component, say to forestall exhaustion, but the effect of this rent is already considered in the allocation/distribution square. Income-distribution rents would show up in differentiated enterprise prices for the two ore bodies. But these would not affect the estimates of GNP, merely the division of profits.

III.5. *Summary of rent instruments*

The interfunctional rent relations for the socialist economy are the same as those for the capitalist market and neoclassical economies, although sometimes for different reasons. Again, we cannot divine an overall measure since (1) any weighting of the different interfunctional relations would be arbitrary and (2) the seriousness of any particular inconsistency or the attractiveness of any particular positive relationship cannot be known.

It may be useful to summarize some of the main points of the discussion, however. First, we observe that it is very hard to guess the right rents for any function, the short-term rent being somewhat easier in this regard in either real world economy. But generally speaking, even the short-term rent may be suboptimal for short-term allocation; the right long-term rent is likely to be much more difficult for long-term objectives in both real world economies. Reference to the current fuel-pricing problems should suffice to convince those who are more sanguine about the prospects for the capitalist market economy.

It is interesting to note in this regard that primary emphasis in Soviet theory and practice seems to be given to rent as an income-distribution instrument. We have argued that this will lead to allocative inefficiency by encouraging prodigal management, since if income-distribution rents are imposed – in the form of differential procurement prices, fixed rental payments by mineral sites, or differentiated budget contributions by industrial enterprises – there is no incentive to cut production costs: if the difference between selling price and production cost goes to the state in the form of a rent, thrift has nothing going for it.

Finally, we note the negative effect of allocation-related rents on performance measurement. Since this aspect of the price system is of less importance than the others, this is not a telling indictment.

IV. Conclusion

The arguments presented here question some of the traditional criticisms concerning the inherent weakness of the price mechanism under socialism. The price mechanism here appears to have a smaller number of consistency conflicts than in the capitalist market economy, although, as we have said several times through the chapter, the number of occurrences is only one dimension of the problem: the seriousness of each occurrence would have to be assessed and some way would have to be found to commensurate them before any overall statement could be made concerning the relative merits of the two price systems. Nevertheless, the study shows clearly that the socialist price mechanism, in principle, is not as feeble as has frequently been supposed.

It may be helpful to set down the main points that emerge from the presentation:

1. Although Marx does not legitimize the incorporation of economic rent and capital charges into the price system, since they do not reflect labor costs, which constitute the true source of value, the socialist economy does not necessarily forswear their use, either explicitly or implicitly.

2. The short-term interest (capital charge or capital rent) function under socialism can be performed by a surrogate measure, the interindustry wage differentials. It has been in the USSR since the early plan era, but we can only speculate how efficient it has been.

3. The long-term interest instrument should find its use as a criterion for selecting investment streams rather than as a component of prices. Such a use would include commensuration of quantities over time (i.e., discounting future outputs or imputing costs to immobilized capital) for analysis of investment opportunities and for broad evaluation of operating or organizational policies. We cited the example of custom combining which cannot be dealt with unless the advantage of more intensive use of equipment under such a policy is explicitly considered by imputing a capital cost to the more distant use of the equipment. But while the interest should be used at the stage of deciding whether to undertake an investment, it should not be reflected in a proportional increase of all prices of the output stream flowing from the investment. Some outputs will have higher prices, some lower, the overall profit being enough to cover total interest costs which, ideally, reflect the opportunity cost of capital. We note that in many sectors in the capitalist economy, such as real estate, there is a tendency to think in terms of a 6–10 percent rate of return to capital *after* interest charges are made. To the extent that this is the case, this instrument did not serve long-term allocation objectives efficiently under capitalism, while the practice in socialist economy does, since the charges do not get incorporated into market prices.

We should also observe that to say that the matter is well handled potentially is not to say that there are no inconsistencies or inefficiencies at all. Undoubtedly, as just noted, there are many errors made in actual project evaluation. In addition, there is continuing ambiguity and conceptual misunderstanding in the design of the rules. This is evidenced most clearly by the coexistence of an 8 percent rate of discount and a 12 percent net benefit as the cutoff for calculations by a Fisherian-type rate of return over cost, not to speak of some of the other inconsistencies in investment allocation which have been discussed elsewhere (Abouchar 1973a). On the other hand, the many ambiguities and conflicts in investment criteria put forth by Westerners suggest that, even apart from the inefficiency problem of incorporation of interest in market prices, which is unavoidable in the capitalist market economy, efficient use of long-term capital charge instruments is not to be attained in the immediate future.

4. Ideally, a two-way allocation-related rent should optimize the intertemporal and intersectoral trade-offs in the use of a resource within a framework of total optimization. It would be extremely difficult to consider correctly all the factors that must be considered in designing such rents. Accordingly, people tend to think in terms of short-term and long-term rents.

5. Rent instruments in all economies involve several potential inefficiencies and inconsistencies. The short-term/long-term and long-term/short-term relationships are all sources of potential inefficiency, i.e., we may get optimal results in one time frame and wrong ones in the other. In all economies allocation-related rents would lead to greater income inequalities. They might worsen performance measurement (according to the criterion we have employed) under certain conditions.

6. Moreover, it is extremely difficult in practice to determine the correct level of rent even for short-term or long-term efficiency in the market economy or the socialist economy. Short-term rents are probably less difficult to deal with, however.

7. On the whole, Soviet rent instruments in practice are oriented primarily to distributional considerations. This being so, they take the form primarily of fixed rental payments and turnover taxes in some extractive industries, such as fossil fuels, and differential procurement prices. Their effect on allocative efficiency is indeterminate. Their use must worsen performance measurement in the sense discussed in this chapter (i.e., introduce greater ambiguity in the welfare interpretation of measured national income in prices of various periods). On the other hand, they enhance income equality objectives, which is undoubtedly more important from the viewpoint of national welfare.

8. While most discussion of rent in the Soviet Union seems to be concerned implicitly or explicitly with distributional considerations, there do exist rents designed for objectives of short-term allocational efficiency, primarily in the fuel sector.

References

Abouchar, Alan. 1973a. The new Soviet standard methodology for investment allocation. *Soviet Studies*, Jan.
_____. 1973b. Les primes de salaire comme succédané d'interêt en Union Soviétique. *Revue de l'Est*, April.
_____, and Daniel Needles. 1975. Custom combining: a neglected opportunity for Soviet agriculture. *Canadian Slavonic Papers*, 1975, no. 1.
Aganbegian, A. G., and V. F. Maier. 1959. *Zarabotnaia plata v SSSR* (*Wages in the USSR*). Moscow: Gosplanizdat.
Arushanian, I. I., V. Z. Belenkii, A. I. Levin, and V. B. Tkach. 1973. Klassifikatsiia predpriiatii neftepererabatyvaiushchei promyshlennosti po usloviiam ikh khoziaistvennoi deiatel'nosti (Classification of oil refineries according to their operating conditions). *Ekon. i mat. met.* (*Economics and Mathematical Methods*), vol. 9, no. 3. English translation in *Matekon* 11 (1974), no. 1.
Bergson, Abram. 1964. *The economics of Soviet planning.* New Haven and London: Yale Univ. Press.
Böhm-Bawerk, Eugen. 1959. *Capital and interest:* vol. 2. *The positive theory of capital.* Translated by George D. Huncke. South Holland, Ill.: Libertarian Press.
Bol'shaia sovetskaia entsiklopediia (*The great Soviet encyclopedia*). 1970, vol. 8. Referred to as *BSE*.
Bornstein, Morris. 1966. Soviet price theory and policy. In *New directions in the Soviet economy*, part 1. U.S. Congress, Joint Economic Committee. Washington: US GPO. Reprinted in *The Soviet economy*, by Bornstein and Fusfeld, 3d edition. Homewood, Ill.: Irwin, 1970.
Brianskikh, E. 1964. Ob ischislenii differentsial'noi renty v kolkhozakh Udmurtskoi ASSR (Calculation of differential rent on the collective farms of Udmurt ASSR). *Ekonomika sel'skogo khoziaistva* (*Economics of Agriculture*), no. 7.
Bronshtein, M. 1964. O vyravnivanii uslovii vosproizvodstva v kolkhozakh (On the equalization of production conditions on collective farms). *Ekon sel's. khoz.*, no. 8.
_____. 1972. Vnutrizonal'noe vyravnivanie uslovii proizvodstva v sel'skom khoziaistve (Interzonal equalization of production conditions in agriculture). *Voprosy ekonomiki* (*Problems of Economics*), no. 4.
Brusilovskaia, N. A., A. G. Gogoberidze, L. D. Oblomskaia, and N. N. Kosinova. 1969. *Teoreticheskie osnovy i metodika postroeniia raschetnykh tsen* (*Theoretical principles and methods for constructing settlement prices.*) Moscow.
BSE, see Bol'shaia sovetskaia entsiklopediia.
Campbell, Robert. 1968. Economic reform in the USSR. *American Economic Review*, May. Reprinted in *The Soviet economy*, by Bornstein and Fusfeld, 3d edition. Homewood, Ill.: Irwin, 1970.
Cheremushkin, S. 1967. O stoimostnoi otsenke zemli (On the valuation of land). *Ekon. sel's. khoz.*, no. 12.
El'met, Kh. A. 1973. K voprosu o razmeshchenii sel'skokhoziaistvennykh kultur (On the location of agricultural crops). *Ekon. i mat. met.*, vol. 9, no. 4. English translation in *Matekon* 11 (1974), no. 1.
Holzman, Franklyn. 1960. Soviet inflationary pressures, 1928–1957: causes and cures. *Quarterly Journal of Economics*, May.
Ialovenko, F. 1966. Metodika opredeleniia srokov sluzhby traktorov (Methodology for determining tractor service life). *Ekon. sel's. khoz.*, no. 4.

Kantorovich, L. V., V. N. Bogachev, and V. L. Makarov. 1970. Ob otsenke effektivnosti kapital'nykh zatrat' (On the measurement of the effectiveness of capital expenditures). *Ekon. i mat. met.,* vol. 6, no. 6. English translation in *Matekon* 8 (1970), no. 1.

Kapustin, E. I. 1964. *Kachestvo truda i zarabotnaia plata (Labor quality and wages).* Moscow: Mysl'.

Kirsch, Leonard J. 1972. *Soviet wages: changes in structure and administration since 1956.* Cambridge: MIT Press.

Mishan, E. J. 1959. Rent as a measure of welfare change. *American Economic Review,* June.

Patinkin, Don. 1972. Interest. In *Studies in monetary economics.* New York: Harper and Row.

Petrakov, N. Ia. 1974. K probleme soizmereniia zatrat i rezul'tatov (On the problem of comparing costs and results), *Ekon. i mat. met.,* vol. 10, no. 4.

Romanchenko, G. 1969. Otsenka zemli i differentsial'naia renta (The valuation of land and differential rent). *Ekon. sel's. khoz.,* no. 9.

Shackle, G. L. S. 1967. Recent theories concerning the nature and role of interest. In *Surveys of economic theory:* vol. 1. *Money, interest, and welfare* London and Toronto: Macmillan; New York: St. Martin's Press.

Tipovaia metodika opredeleniia ekonomicheskoi effektivnosti kapital'nykh vlozhenii i novoi tekhniki v narodnom khoziaistve SSSR. (TM-60). 1960. (Standard methodology for determining the economic effectiveness of capital investments in new equipment in the national economy of the USSR). *Planovoe khoziaistvo (The planned economy),* no. 3. Referred to as TM-1960.

Tipovaia metodika opredeleniia ekonomicheskoi ·effektivnosti kapital'nykh vlozhenii. 1969. *Ekonomicheskaia gazeta (The Economic Gazette),* no. 39. Translated as TM-69: Standard methodology for determining the economic effectiveness of capital investments. *Matekon* 8 (1970), no. 1. Referred to as TM-1969.

Usher, Dan. 1968. *The price mechanism and the meaning of national income statistics.* Oxford: Clarendon Press.

5

Prices and Resource Allocation in Intra-CMEA Trade

Edward A. Hewett

University of Texas, Austin

I. Introduction

This chapter seeks to analyze the role of the foreign trade price (ftp) system in resource allocation among members of the Council for Mutual Economic Assistance (CMEA).[1] This will of necessity be a very tentative assessment, since many of the data needed for a full analysis are not available. The writings of CMEA economists concerning the price system are frequently contradictory, misleading (frequently inadvertently), and typically of low quality. Finally, interviews in eastern Europe on foreign trade, and particularly on ftp's, are difficult to arrange and generally uninformative. Most of this subject matter remains under the rubric of "state secret," not, I am convinced, because there is much to hide, but more probably because there was something to hide in the late 1940s and early 1950s.

Since I am discussing the price *system* in the economic system controlling intra-CMEA trade, the data problems are not fatal; there are enough data to allow the use of simple analytical tools in understanding how the price system operates, what role it now plays in allocating resources, and what its future role might be. It is typical in actual systems that the de facto institutions which serve to allocate resources will differ significantly from de jure institutions. While this paper concerns only de facto institutions, the de jure institutions are an important part of the story, and they are discussed in Section II. In Section III I discuss the structure of CMEA ftp's; in Section IV, the economics of intra-CMEA trade;

1. CMEA, which is also referred to as CEMA and COMECON, is a political-economic association of socialist countries. The present membership is Bulgaria, Cuba, Czechoslovakia, East Germany, Hungary, Mongolia, Poland, Rumania, and the Soviet Union. For purposes of this paper "CMEA" will designate only the European members of CMEA; i.e., Cuba and Mongolia are not discussed.

and in Section V I speculate on the future of the CMEA resource allocation mechanism.

II. Trade and Price Agreements in Intra-CMEA Trade

Trade agreements

Intra-CMEA trade is formally controlled through a web of bilaterally negotiated five-year *trade agreements* and annual *trade protocols*. The distinction between these is similar to that in the typical CMEA centrally planned economy: the main proportions and important quantities are set in the five-year agreements, while annual protocols are primarily intended to implement the long-term agreements.

Formal responsibility for negotiating the long-term trade agreements rests with the ministries of foreign trade (MFT). However, the lengthy preparatory work is supposed to involve the entire planning apparatus of each country in a process of plan coordination. For example, one Czech economist reports that his country initiated bilateral negotiations on the 1971–75 trade agreements in 1968. The negotiations, which coincided with calculations for the 1971–75 five-year plan, primarily involved planning agencies "which predetermined in considerable detail, the structure of future deliveries" (Kostak, p. 1). Ultimately most CMEA countries hope for detailed multilateral plan-coordination for trade flows and investments; at present, "coordination" seems primarily to consist of bilateral alignment of material balances for a few key materials (Csikós-Nagy, p. 218).

The long-term trade agreements set at a central level either value or quantitative quotas for most intra-CMEA trade. For example, the 1971–75 agreements had quotas covering about 85–90 percent of projected trade (Kiss, p. 179). The value quotas evidently cover somewhat aggregated product groups, primarily in relatively sophisticated commodity classes; the quantitative quotas for these products are set at a decentralized level, i.e., by foreign trade enterprises, during negotiations for the annual trade protocols (Csikós-Nagy, p. 219). In 1966 and 1967 about 40 percent of Hungarian exports and 30 percent of imports were governed by value quotas in the long-term agreements with CMEA trade partners (Kiss, p. 174). Centrally determined quantitative quotas generally cover primary products, typical intermediate products, and some mass-produced commodities (Csikós-Nagy, p. 219). These quotas account for about 50–60 percent of the intra-CMEA trade projected in the long-term trade agreements (Ausch, p. 171).

Table 5.1 presents data showing the number of quotas (both value and

Table 5.1. Number of items specified in Hungarian trade agreements.

Year:	Long-term agreement			Short-term agreement				
	58–60	61–65	66–70	59	60	62	65	66
Partner:								
Bulgaria	46	83	134	175	151	167	166	151
Czechoslovakia	106	185	303	384	401	400	424	380
East Germany	150	251	372	584	638	725	552	546
Poland	53	101	202	192	191	191	252	237
Rumania	37	112	96	134	151	174	180	158
Soviet Union	118	207	553	307	295	348	455	768

Source: Ausch, p. 172.

quantitative) in Hungarian-CMEA trade during 1958–70. These include quotas at various levels of aggregation. The number of quotas in Hungary's long-term agreements has approximately tripled with all CMEA countries; it has almost quintupled with the Soviet Union. For all of the years reported here, there have been more quotas in the annual protocols than the long-term agreements. However, the number of quotas in the protocols did not change significantly during 1959–66, except with the Soviet Union, so that, by 1966, for all Hungarian trade with CMEA, the number of quotas in the protocols exceeded that in the long-term agreements by only about a third.

In principle, long-term agreements stipulate a zero trade balance (excluding long-term credits). For example, in the USSR-Rumanian agreements covering 1961–65, there was a clause which specified that if an imbalance remained at the end of a year, the parties would negotiate compensating deliveries to be completed by April 1 of the following year (Usenko, p. 11). The annual trade protocols implement the long-term agreements, precisely for the quantitative quotas, and after lower-level negotiations (mostly among foreign trade organizations) for the value quotas. Also, during the annual negotiations, quotas are set for that proportion of trade not specified in value or quantity quotas in the long-term agreements. Additional deliveries are also set at that time.

These long-term trade agreements, particularly the Soviet agreements with other CMEA members, play a fundamental role in determining the level of output throughout CMEA. In order to give some notion of the magnitudes involved, I discuss below a succession of data to document the share of exports and imports in CMEA countries' foreign trade; the share of other CMEA countries in CMEA trade with the world; and the share of raw materials and semifabricates in total trade, intra-CMEA trade, and Soviet-CMEA trade.

It is difficult to derive comparable estimates of export (import)/national income ratios for CMEA and capitalist countries. One major difficulty is that CMEA national income concepts differ from Western concepts. Also CMEA foreign trade data are typically reported in foreign trade prices, which creates additional problems because foreign trade prices are unrelated to domestic prices; hence, de facto exchange rates differ by sector and in effect by product. The official exchange rates do not reflect this dispersion, and, in addition, official rates are usually overvalued. Therefore, even if the national income problem can be solved, it is still necessary to estimate sector-specific exchange rates. In addition, as I will show later, CMEA prices are above world prices; therefore, a complete procedure would estimate exchange rates by sector and region. The six estimates of export/national income ratios in Table 5.2 represent several different efforts to deal with these problems. All four estimating techniques used a single price set to adjust for the differences in foreign trade and domestic prices. The data in columns (1) and (2) include an additional adjustment to compensate for an overvaluation of the CMEA foreign trade ruble in most product groups.[2] Since the estimates use three different price sets and three concepts of national income, the numbers should not be the same. Columns (1) and (2) differ solely because of the exclusion of services and inclusion of depreciation in column (2). Columns (2) and (3) should not necessarily be the same, since they were done on the basis of two different price systems (and probably two different input-output tables); still, they should be close, and with the exception of Czechoslovakia, they are. Columns (3) and (5) would be expected to differ somewhat because GDP includes all services, which GMP does not account for. The ECE estimates that GDP is about 125 percent of GMP (UN ECE 70, p. 48). Dividing column (3) by 125 still leaves a substantial gap; either the GMP estimates in column (3) are too low, or the GDP estimates in column (5) are too high. The ECE notes that the column (5) and (6) estimates are experimental; thus, we should probably consider these estimates as the low end of a confidence interval for export/GDP ratios in eastern Europe. The high end is probably columns (2)–(3) adjusted downward by 25 percent.

Columns (4) and (6) reflect an upward trend in export/GDP (GMP) ratios in eastern Europe, similar to trends in western Europe. In the regression analysis which I discuss below, the ECE estimated that, after allowance for changes in independent variables, export/GDP ratios increased five percentage points between 1953–57 and 1963–67 for a sample of 23 western and eastern European countries (ibid., p. 49). Data for the Soviet Union have not been included here. Holzman estimates their export/GNP ratio as 2.3–2.6 percent in 1959 (Holzman 1963, p.

2. For example, Bulgarian exports of the same fuel to socialist markets will carry about a 14% higher price (in Bulgarian levs) than exports of the same product to capitalist markets. For estimates of the overvaluation by sector, see Ausch, pp. 230–32.

Table 5.2. Ratio of exports to various measures of national income in eastern Europe: 1958–67.

Income measure: Prices: Year: Column no.: Country	Nat. inc.[a] 60 cwm[d] 1960 (1)	GMP[b] 60 cwm[d] 1960 (2)	GMP[b] dp[e] 1958–62 (3)	GMP[b] dp[e] 1963–67 (4)	GDP[c] 65 cwm[f] 1958–62 (5)	GDP[c] 65 cwm[f] 1963–67 (6)
Bulgaria	24.6	29.1	28.7	40.3	11.3	15.7
Czechoslovakia	24.5	28.7	15.6	19.2	10.4	12.8
East Germany	20.4	23.9	n.d.	n.d.	n.d.	n.d.
Hungary	23.1	27.3	23.3	29.4	10.9	13.7
Poland	13.7	17.1	16.4	19.8	5.7	6.9
Rumania	16.3	19.0	n.d.	n.d.	n.d.	n.d.

Sources: Cols. (1)–(2): Ausch, pp. 56–57; cols. (3)–(6): UN ECE 70, pp. 48–49.
a. National income. Defined as value added, excluding depreciation and including an estimate of services.
b. Gross material product. Defined as value added, excluding services and transport, but including depreciation.
c. Gross domestic product. The UN definition: value added, depreciation, and services all included.
d. 1960 capitalist world market prices were used in the valuation. Exports and national income (or GMP) computed using an input-output table of unspecified dimensions.
e. Domestic prices, via an input-output table, were used to value exports and GMP.
f. Exports are valued in 1965 dollars at official exchange rates. GDP (also in 1965 dollars) was approximated by first estimating correlations between 36 physical indicators and GDP for 29 West European and "overseas" countries, then applying those coefficients to the same physical indicators for the four East European countries, and finally averaging the 36 estimates of GDP for each East European country to obtain a single estimate.

290); it probably has increased about one half of a percentage point since then.[3]

CMEA export/GDP ratios are probably lower than those typical of West European countries, even after allowance for the level of development and size of the country. For example, the ECE regressed the estimates in column (5) of Table 5.2, along with export/GDP estimates for Rumania, East Germany, and seventeen West European countries on a set of two independent variables: per capita GDP (as a proxy for the level of development) and the square root of population (as a proxy for country size). According to those estimates, Rumania and Bulgaria had export/GDP ratios far above those predicted, Hungary is about at the level predicted, and the remainder of the CMEA countries were below the predicted ratios.[4]

The underlying GDP estimates are crude, and possibly too high. Nevertheless, it seems that, given the level of development and size of the CMEA countries, most of them are probably less dependent on trade than comparable Western countries, and certainly not more dependent. The two interesting exceptions are the two least developed CMEA members, Bulgaria and Rumania.

These issues aside, the data in Table 5.2 indicate that foreign trade is a significant proportion of national income in the East European economies. The share of intra-CMEA trade in East European foreign trade is quite substantial. Table 5.3 shows official estimates of the proportion of each member's foreign trade turnover which is with other CMEA members. These data have an upward bias in them since, as mentioned earlier, intra-CMEA ftp's (converted by official exchange rates) lie above world market prices. The exact amount of bias is difficult to estimate precisely,

3. Current price exports rose 130% between 1960 and 1970 (CMEA 71, p. 35). I estimate that Soviet export prices fell about 10% during that period (Hewett 1974a). Therefore real exports rose about 140%. National income rose about 100% over the same period (CMEA 71. p. 35). Thus if the national income growth rate approximates that for GNP, the export/GNP ratio may have risen to about 3.0% (240%/200% times 2.5%).

4. The regression equation for the 1958–62 average is

$$x/y = 11.780 + .009994y/p - .072104p^{1/2}, \ R^2 = .89,$$

where x is exports, y is GDP, and p is population. No test statistics are reported.

The difference between actual and calculated export/GDP ratios, divided by the actual ratios (all for 1958–62), are these:

Bulgaria	1.29
Czechoslovakia	.67
East Germany	.81
Hungary	1.05
Poland	.87
Rumania	1.75

The ECE also ran regressions for 1953–57 and 1963–67, and in some cases the results do vary by period.

Table 5.3. Ratio of trade turnover with CMEA countries to total trade turnover, 1970.

Bulgaria	74.4
Czechoslovakia	64.2
East Germany	67.3
Hungary	62.1
Poland	63.1
Rumania	49.3
Soviet Union	55.6

Source: CMEA 71, p. 342.

but a rough adjustment is all that is needed here. I would estimate that most of these shares are no more than five percentage points too high.[5]

Table 5.4 shows the 1969 commodity structure of all CMEA countries' trade with CMEA and with the world; and of each CMEA country's trade with the world, with CMEA, and with the USSR.

Somewhere around 40 percent of East European imports are primary products, presumably almost all inputs for industry; in imports from the Soviet Union the ratios are much higher, in the range of 60–70 percent. In exchange for those primary products, the East European countries are shipping the Soviet Union machinery, equipment, and consumer goods combined, far in excess of the proportions they export of those commodities to all markets. These goods essentially have no other outlets on world markets (except possibly LDC's), and they are in excess supply in CMEA; the primary products do have outlets on world markets, and are in deficit on CMEA markets. Apparently some East European industries have idle capacity solely because of a shortage of primary products and semifabricate inputs (Zhukov and Ol'sevich, p. 20). Consequently the Soviet Union is presently in the position of exporting high-value (at world market prices) primary products in exchange for low-value (at wmp's) products. And if the Soviet Union did not sell the raw materials, eastern Europe would probably not have the material means of payment to obtain the products on alternate markets.

With these data in mind, the significance of the long-term trade agreements, particularly with the Soviet Union, is more apparent. The im-

5. That is a ceiling. Ausch estimates that 1963 CMEA ftp's were about 17% above wmp's, but CMEA ftp's dropped between 5% and 10% during the 1964–66 price review; wmp's did not change significantly. Therefore the 1970 overvaluation was probably in the neighborhood of 15%. For a country such as Bulgaria, with a 74% share of CMEA trade at official prices, the adjusted share would be about three points lower.

Table 5.4. Commodity structure of CMEA countries' trade with other CMEA countries, and with the world, 1969.

	Commodity groups							
	Exports[a]				Imports[a]			
Direction of trade	I	II	III	IV	I	II	III	IV
1. CMEA–CMEA	39.4	34.7	9.5	12.6	41.2	35.0	9.5	12.8
2. CMEA–world	32.5	39.1	11.2	11.6	35.1	40.0	13.0	11.0
3. Bulgaria–world	28.1	20.7	36.1	15.1	40.1	48.9	5.6	5.0
4. –CMEA	31.8	14.9	35.2	18.1	46.4	42.7	4.5	6.4
5.[b] –USSR	29.2	11.1	36.5	23.2	36.5	56.3	2.7	4.5
6. Czech.–world	50.2	29.4	3.9	16.5	33.4	47.9	15.0	8.5
7. –CMEA	60.6	22.8	1.6	15.0	34.3	44.0	13.4	8.3
8.[b] –USSR	55.8	20.2	1.4	22.6	14.8	68.9	14.5	1.7
9. East Ger.–world	50.5	24.7	4.8	20.0	34.1	44.3	17.1	4.5
10. –CMEA	59.3	21.2	.4	19.1	37.8	40.0	13.5	4.7
11.[b] –USSR	57.3	11.7	0	31.0	18.1	68.0	13.2	.8
12. Hungary–world	32.4	24.7	21.8	21.1	31.0	53.7	7.7	7.6
13. –CMEA	43.2	15.8	17.3	23.7	34.6	53.2	5.4	6.8
14.[b] –USSR	45.0	5.4	19.9	29.7	18.3	72.4	6.8	2.5
15. Poland–world	38.5	32.8	13.1	15.6	36.4	43.1	9.6	6.1
16. –CMEA	52.7	25.9	2.8	18.6	42.8	42.4	8.4	6.4
17. –USSR	37.4	28.8	.7	33.2	19.0	66.1	12.0	2.8
18. Rumania–world	22.6	43.2	16.1	18.1	39.6	49.5	5.4	5.5
19. –CMEA	26.5	38.1	14.0	21.4	48.2	43.1	2.7	6.0
20.[b] –USSR	20.8	40.2	8.7	30.3	31.1	66.2	.9	1.7
21. USSR–world[c]	21.5	53.6	8.4	2.7	35.1	29.9	15.1	18.3
22. –CMEA[c]	22.7	54.5	10.1	2.5	44.2	19.2	9.1	23.6

Source: All rows except 5, 8, 11, 14, 17, 20: Bożyk, p. 16. The remaining rows are estimated by the author from Soviet foreign trade statistics. For details of the estimation technique, see Hewett, p. 64.

a. I — Industrial machinery and equipment (including spare parts); II — fuels, raw materials (other than food), other materials; III — foodstuffs and raw materials for foodstuffs; IV — manufactured consumer goods.

b. These data were constrained to sum to unity; however, they actually represent a distribution of somewhere between 80% and 100% of reported trade. The actual number is usually around 90%, but depends on the trade flow.

c. These do not add to 100. Apparently they are reported trade divided by all trade, and reported trade falls about 10% below total trade in exports, and about 3% below in imports for Soviet-CMEA trade (see Marer 1972a).

portance of the Soviet Union as a supplier of raw materials, and its willingness to act as a "sink" for some finished products, combined with its sheer size relative to other trade partners, dictate that East European countries conclude their trade agreements first with the Soviet Union, and then with other East European countries. As Kiss puts it,

In general each CMEA country strives to ensure most of its raw material needs by contractual purchases from the Soviet Union, and to take thereby an advantage over other CMEA partners. At the same time, they usually envisage to purchase certain kinds of raw materials from other partner countries, and this practice leads sometimes to oversecuring of purchases. At such occurrence, again, the most convenient solution is to request the Soviet Union to cancel the preliminary order [Kiss, p. 180].

This is only one of several manifestations of a passivity on the part of the Soviet Union which has hitherto received little attention in the literature.

As corroboration of Kiss's assertion, Table 5.5 presents information on the dates the 1966–70 long-term trade agreements were signed. While the dates of signing cannot be regarded as a certain indicator of the order of negotiations, they are probably a good approximation. Of the six East European countries, all but Bulgaria and Rumania signed first with the Soviet Union and then with the remaining five partners; Bulgaria and Rumania concluded their mutual agreement before either signed with the Soviet Union.

Price agreements

The CMEA ftp system has existed in some form since the late 1940s when the CMEA countries negotiated their first trade agreements. It has become infinitely more complex than it was then; but in fundamentals it has changed very little. For present purposes there is no need to go into the history of the system, or the details of its operation, since discussions are available elsewhere.[6] Instead, I will simply outline the fundamental principles on which the system operates.

Prices in intra-CMEA trade are one of the major items in the bilateral

6. See, e.g., Marer 1972b or Hewett 1974b, especially ch. 2.

Table 5.5. Signing dates for the 1966–70 intra-CMEA long-term trade agreements (month/date/year).

	Cz.	E. Ger.	Hun.	Po.	Ru.	USSR
Bulgaria	1/9/66	12/20/65	10/25/65	2/1/66	9/17/65	10/13/65
Czechoslovakia		12/21/65	11/21/65	1/8/66	6/17/66	9/5/65
East Germany			12/15/65	12/30/65	1/22/66	12/3/65
Hungary				11/23/65	1/25/66	10/20/65
Poland					1/4/66	11/18/65
Rumania						12/24/65

Source: Biulletin' ekonomicheskoi informatsii 5, no. 32 (Oct. 1966):61–62.

negotiations of the five-year trade agreements between ministries of foreign trade. These negotiations are referred to as "price revisions," which indeed they are, since typically they concern, for the most part, price *indices* for very detailed product groups (i.e., an agreement might stipulate that prices for ETN group 269 in 1971–75 trade will be 115 percent of those prices during 1966–70 trade). It is now apparently the general practice that prices in intra-CMEA trade change only at five-year intervals as a result of negotiations for the five-year trade agreements; price negotiations in the intervening years primarily concern new products. For all but a few very important products, actual prices are negotiated by foreign trade enterprises under the constraint that, for detailed product groups, the weighted price changes remain within bounds agreed upon by the ministries (Ausch, p. 97).

In theory, one would expect to find, not one price system in CMEA, but rather twenty-one price systems: one for each bilateral trade agreement. In the absence of a market, there is no strong pressure for unified prices. Also, the centralized determination of quantities "liberates" prices from their function as signals in a resource allocation mechanism. All that remains for them to do is to set the aggregate terms of trade, and any of an infinite set of relative prices could do that.

In fact, the CMEA countries have sought to collectively agree on "rules of the game" for bilateral negotiations which endeavor to create a single set of CMEA ftp's similar in structure to wmp's. The formal justification for using wmp's rather than actual domestic prices in individual CMEA countries is couched in Marxian concepts of values and prices of production. However, the essence of the actual motivation is that wmp's are estimates of true opportunity costs to CMEA countries.[7] Economic considerations aside, relative domestic prices in individual CMEA countries are fixed and different, and wmp's would seem to be the sole candidate for a single price base acceptable to all member countries.[8]

In practice it is wmp's for some past period which are designated to serve as the base for CMEA ftp's in subsequent periods; this "base period" is determined in multilateral negotiations among all CMEA members. Thus, it was decided that wmp's in 1957 would serve as a base for CMEA ftp's during 1958–64. Then in 1964–66 there was a transition to a new set of ftp's for the 1966–70 trade agreements, which were negotiated on the basis of an average of 1960–64 wmp's. According to my

7. For a typical treatment in the Marxian terms, see Tarnovskii and Mitrovanova, chs. 1 and 2.

8. These differences, which have always existed, are attributable not only to different real costs among the CMEA economies but also to differences in the rules for setting domestic prices among the CMEA countries. See, e.g., Kobzar and Stromtsov.

estimates, the 1964–66 price changes caused about a 20 percent drop in Soviet terms of trade with the CMEA countries as a whole (Hewett 1974a, ch. 3).

It is not clear whether or not there was another price revision during negotiations for the 1971–75 trade agreements. There has been no broad discussion of such changes, comparable to the discussion which accompanied the 1964–66 price changes. On the other hand, there has been mention of a 1966–70 price base (RFE 1972). In addition, the Soviet foreign trade yearbook publishes quantity indices for Soviet-CMEA trade which make it possible to estimate price indices and thus changes in Soviet-CMEA terms of trade. Those data indicate substantial price changes in 1971 and 1972 (the latest year for which I have data) which brought about a further decrease in Soviet-CMEA terms of trade.[9] My independent estimates corroborate the general accuracy of the price indices derived from Soviet sources (Hewett 1974b, p. 90). Thus it would seem that substantial price changes have occurred during the early years of the 1971–75 trade agreements. We cannot ascertain from these data how the price changes are distributed among commodity groups, or what the new official price base is.

There is no guarantee that CMEA ftp's will reflect wmp's. The Price Clause written into all intra-CMEA trade agreements does stipulate that negotiators must base their initial price bids on documentation of wmp's existing in the designated base period. However, it permits numerous "adjustments" to the wmp, in order to transform it into a true measure of value; and it allows deviations from value in certain cases. Thus CMEA

9. The price indices derived from official Soviet sources are computed by dividing Laspeyres quantity indices of Soviet-CMEA exports (imports) into indices of changes in the total value of exports (imports); thus the price indices are estimates of the true Paasche index. Based on 1960 weights, official Soviet data show that in 1970 Soviet terms of trade with eastern Europe were .81 of their 1960 value (Hewett 1974b, p. 90). Since 1970 the quantity indices have been shifted to a 1965 base. I have adjusted that back to 1960 by using the estimate of 1965 terms of trade relative to 1960 and have obtained the following results for 1970–72:

Soviet-CMEA terms of trade (1960 = 100)

	Export prices	Import prices	Terms of trade
1970	.88	1.11	.79
1971	.90	1.17	.77
1972	.85	1.19	.71

Source: MFT 70 and 72.

The 1970 figure from the 1965-weighted index (.79) differs slightly from that based on the 1960-weighted index (.81), but not substantially. As the data show, since 1970 Soviet-CMEA terms of trade have continued to decline, because of changes in both export prices and import prices.

ftp's could vary substantially from wmp's and still be consistent with the Price Clause.[10]

Also, as CMEA negotiators have discovered, it is no simple affair to locate "the" wmp for CMEA products. First, most products have a broad distribution of wmp's, depending on the details of the price quotations and sometimes subtle differences in the characteristics of the products themselves. Thus, documented wmp's can vary greatly for individual products.[11] Second, many CMEA products have no similar counterparts on world markets, and naturally negotiators on each side differ substantially (each in his own favor) on the appropriate adjustment to the wmp (Zhukov and Ol'sevich, p. 33).

Trade in parts of products, which is quite important in intracapitalist trade, and is supposed to grow in significance in intra-CMEA trade, presents yet a third set of problems. Much of the intracapitalist trade in these products is subject to secret interfirm agreements or else it is intrafirm, and thus in effect subject to a secret agreement. In either case a wmp cannot be found, and CMEA countries have only highly inflated spare-parts prices on which to rely (Karmnov and Cheburakov, p. 109).

In summary, the CMEA ftp system in a de jure sense is a Price Clause included in foreign trade agreements which constrains negotiators to justify their price bids by documenting prices existing in some past period on world markets. For various reasons this Price Clause sanctions widely divergent "legal" price bids, and there is no mechanism specified for resolving the resulting conflicts. Certainly one cannot be certain, solely on the basis of the Price Clause, that the structure of CMEA ftp's approximates wmp's. On the contrary, these rules would "support" a multitude of quite diverse price systems.

III. The Structure of CMEA ftp's

Thus, knowing about how prices are negotiated in CMEA trade contributes very little to knowing what the actual structure of intra-CMEA prices is; the set of possible negotiated price systems literally coincides with the set of all possible price systems. Therefore only the study of actual CMEA ftp's will actually make it possible to ascertain the structure of those prices.

10. For details on the adjustments and deviations, see Hewett 1974b, ch. 2.

11. For example, Bartha states that in CMEA price negotiations, supporting wmp's for machinery and equipment can differ by as much as 60%, while for primary products the variation is no more than 10%. See Bartha, p. 9.

If sufficient data were available, it would be possible to test several hypotheses:

(1) CMEA ftp's are unified, i.e., prices for the same commodity in different transactions are equal;
(2) CMEA ftp's equal wmp's for comparable products in the official base period; or
(3) CMEA ftp's are not unified, but they equal the exporters' wholesale prices in various CMEA countries.

These are only three of the many possibilities which have been suggested or implied in the literature, and which are all possible outcomes of the negotiating process.

Unfortunately adequate data do not exist: no CMEA ftp's are published; unit values (average prices) can be estimated only for a portion of total trade flows, and there are well-known drawbacks to using unit values as estimates of prices; wmp's are hard to estimate, and so on. Therefore it is necessary to rely on scraps and pieces to guess at the structure of CMEA ftp's.

Hypothesis (1) is fairly easily disposed of. There are many allusions in the literature, especially in discussions on convertibility, to the effect that CMEA ftp's are not unified. This has been confirmed in the work of both CMEA and non-CMEA economists.[12] The most telling data are from the Hungarian Ministry of Foreign Trade, as they were reported by Ausch (p. 80). These data indicate that of 1,020 commodities which Hungary exported to more than one socialist country in 1964–65, 169 differed in price by more than 50 percent; and 293 differed by more than 25 percent. Ausch compares these data to information for 1935 on Hungarian exports, and 1947 on French exports; in both cases the deviations in prices of homogeneous commodities are substantially smaller. The Ministry's data from the 1964–65 price review indicate that other CMEA countries have the same dispersion in their export prices to CMEA.

It seems likely, therefore, that there are indeed many CMEA ftp systems, possibly as many as the twenty-one mentioned earlier. I will abstract from that in discussing the remaining hypotheses, but it should be understood that when "the" structure of CMEA ftp's is being discussed, the term refers in actuality to an average structure.

It is now generally conceded that, using wmp's as a standard, machinery and equipment have *relatively* higher prices in CMEA, while primary products have somewhat lower prices, and agricultural products much lower prices. In addition, the official exchange rates are overvalued.

12. See Hewett 1974b, pp. 49–52, for a discussion of the literature.

Probably the best information, again from Ausch, is given in column (1) of Table 5.6. Ausch estimated that prices on all East European exports in 1960 were 24 percent above world market prices converted at official exchange rates; for machinery the overvaluation was 39 percent; for fuels, mineral raw materials, and metals it was only 17 percent.

The remaining columns of Table 5.6 are, it must be emphasized, a very crude attempt to estimate the impact that price trends in world markets and on CMEA markets have had in the 1960s. For purposes of comparison to Ausch's overall ratio of 1.24 for ftp's in 1960 relative to wmp's in 1957–61, I have used the same weighting scheme for the subsequent four columns: East European exports, excluding the USSR. Column (2) is an estimate of the relationship between 1960 ftp's and the official price base for those ftp's, 1957 wmp's. The correspondence is not terribly

Table 5.6. An approximation of the relationship of CMEA ftp's to wmp's, 1960–68.

Commodity group	60 ftp's / 57–61 wmp's (1)	60 ftp's / 57 wmp's (2)	68 ftp's / 60 ftp's (3)	68 ftp's / 60–64 wmp's (4)	68 ftp's / 68 wmp's (5)
Total	1.24	1.21	.99	1.27	1.21
Machinery and equip.	1.39	1.46	1.02	1.34	1.22
Fuels, min. raw mats., and metals	1.17	1.10	.84	1.02	1.00
Agric. prods.	1.06	1.01	.97	1.02	1.12
Food	1.00	.93	1.06	1.07	1.03
Mfd. cons. goods	1.25	1.23	1.14	1.43	1.37

Sources: Col. (1): Ausch pp. 230–32 (I have averaged his fuel and power and metallurgy ratios into fuels, min. raw mats., and metals). *Col. (2):* Using UN data on world export unit values, I have estimated the difference between 1957 wmp's and an average of 1957–61 wmp's. I used the resulting ratios to deflate column (1). The ratios and the sources are given in Table 5.7. *Col. (3):* These are based on indices of Soviet and Polish export unit values to CMEA which I computed and reported (Hewett 1974b, pp. 78–79). The indices for machinery and equipment and for fuels, mineral raw materials, and metals are weighted averages of the Soviet and Polish indices for those categories (the weights are .2, Poland, and .8, Soviet Union, which approximate the ratio of their total exports to CMEA in 1960). The agricultural products and food indices are Soviet indices; Polish exports in those product groups were too small to obtain reliable estimates. The manufactured consumer goods index is the Polish export index; Soviet exports were not large enough to calculate a reliable index. *Col. (4):* Column (3) divided by column (b) of Table 5.7 below, then multiplied by column (1). *Col. (5):* Column (3) divided by column (c) of Table 5.7, then multiplied by column (1). *Cols. 2–5:* The totals have been derived by taking a weighted average of the rows, where the weights are, for columns (2) and (3), the distribution of total East European exports in 1960 excluding the Soviet Union; for columns (4) and (5) the weights are from the same trade flows in 1968. The choice of weights is motivated to derive numbers comparable to Ausch's; and he used 1960 East European exports. When I aggregate column (1) using the 1960 weights, I get 1.22 instead of 1.24; but the difference may be because my data source (Marer 1972a, pp. 53, 61) does not have distribution data for East Germany; Ausch did have those data.

good; machinery is priced more than 45 percent higher than the world market level; fuels, mineral raw materials, and metals, 10 percent higher; food is below the world market level. Since the overvaluation is about 20 percent, the relative prices of all products except machinery and manufactured consumer goods lie fairly significantly below wmp levels.

Column (3) shows that, using East European exports to all countries as weights, the 1964–65 price review left the level of CMEA ftp's practically unchanged. However, relative prices changed considerably: fuels, mineral raw materials, and metals prices fell relative to all other prices. Column (4) shows that overall, 1968 CMEA ftp's were about the same amount above their official (1960–64) price base, as 1960 prices had been above their official (1957) price base. Machinery has fallen slightly to about 135 percent of its official base; fuels, mineral raw materials, and metals are almost equal to the base, and manufactured consumer goods are way above the base.[13] Finally, as column (5) shows, since 1960–64, wmp's have approached CMEA ftp's in machinery and equipment, di-

13. The price index for manufactured consumer goods was an extremely difficult one to estimate and the resulting estimates may be off by a considerable amount.

Table 5.7. Wmp's in several periods relative to 1957–61 wmp's.

Commodity group	57 wmp's / 57–61 wmp's (a)	60–64 wmp's / 57–61 wmp's (b)	68 wmp's / 57–61 wmp's (c)
1. Machinery and equip.	.95	1.05	1.16
2. Fuels, min. raw mats., and metals	1.07	.96	.98
3. Agric. prods.	1.07	1.01	.92
4. Food	1.08	.99	1.03
5. Mfd. cons. goods	1.02	1.00	1.04

Source and computational technique: These data are all based on UN unit value indices covering total world exports, where the base year is 1963. The procedure in each case was to average the price indices (relative to 1963) for the 1957–61 period, then divide those into, respectively, the index values for 1957, into an average of the 1960–64 values, and into the 1968 values. The UN commodity groups of Tables 5.6 and 5.7 are based on the Standard International Trade Classification (SITC), while the data from Hewett 1974b and presumably Ausch's data (although he does not say so) are based on the *Edinaia tovarnaia nomenklatura* (ETN), which is used by most CMEA countries in reporting their foreign trade data. These are basically different classification schemes. However, at an aggregated product group level, such as is used in the two tables above, fairly close correspondence can be achieved between the two systems. (For a detailed discussion and comparison of the two classification schemes, see Marer 1972a.) The sources for Table 5.7, plus the SITC-ETN correspondence for the five product groups, are: For row (1) (machinery and equipment; ETN 1, SITC 1) and (5) (manufactured consumer goods; ETN 4, 9, SITC 6, 8): UN MBS 65, xxv, and UN MBS 70, xvii. For remaining rows: UN 71, pp. 8 (food; ETN 6–8, SITC 0 + 1), 35 (agricultural products; ETN 5, SITC 2, 4), and 65 (fuels, mineral raw materials, and metals; ETN 2, SITC 3).

verged for agricultural products, and changed only a small amount for the other product groups.

These adjustments to Ausch's data are crude; and, in addition, Ausch's methodology is not completely explicated, so there are some questions about his data. Even so, it seems safe to conclude that CMEA ftp's are higher than wmp's, and that prices of machinery and equipment relative to fuels, mineral raw materials, and metals are much higher in CMEA than on world markets.

These data do confirm some predictions one might make, based solely on the descriptions of price negotiations in CMEA. The wmp's which are probably easiest to document and identify are those for fuels, mineral raw materials, metals, agricultural products, and goods; machinery and manufactured consumer goods are probably the most difficult to find wmp's for. Thus negotiators mutually agree on relatively high prices where there is great leeway (in the latter two product groups); where there is little leeway, they are forced to stay close to actual wmp's in the base period.

These data provide some notion of the real power of the Price Clause. Machinery, which was in excess supply in CMEA throughout the 1960s, rose in price relative to fuels, mineral raw materials, and metals, which were in excess demand. I will discuss below the impact of those "counter-economic" price changes.

It would be interesting, if the data were available, to try to ascertain the relationship between wmp's and ftp's on a product-by-product basis. If these relations reflect those at the aggregate product-group level, then one would expect fairly close approximation of relative prices in primary products, and little correspondence in machinery and manufactured consumer goods. The only information available for primary products is from Ausch, who presents data for a few primary products to show that in fact wmp's and CMEA ftp's even for these products are not very closely related (Ausch, pp. 89–90). Until more information becomes available, the relationship between world market prices and CMEA foreign trade prices remains unknown.

The data are not much better for machinery and manufactured consumer goods. There are a number of statements in the literature to the effect that it is the wholesale price of the exporter, and not the wmp, which determines the ftp. Of course, using domestic prices to justify a CMEA ftp is technically forbidden by the Price Clause. Still, this poses no serious impediment to the clever negotiator, who apparently can, and usually does, find a wmp which supports the ftp derived from the domestic price (Ausch, pp. 95–96; Zhukov and Ol'sevich, p. 59).

Of course, the asking price of an exporter need not be accepted by the importer; thus it would be quite conceivable that domestic prices are the

Table 5.8. Soviet wholesale prices and CMEA contractual prices, 1966.

	USSR wholesale price	CMEA ftp
Cutting lathes (1500 mm)	100	100
25-Horsepower tractor	73	45
Caterpillar tractor DT-54-A	87	129
4-Ton truck	88	91
Passenger car ("Moskvich-407")	65	25
General purpose freight car (58-ton)	204	204
5-Ton portal crane	3329	2071
Grinding machine	318	231
Home refrigerator	6	2
Wristwatch ("Pobeda")	.2	.1

starting point for exporters, yet the actual set of CMEA ftp's would diverge from domestic prices. The small amount of data available suggests that something of the sort might be operating. Table 5.8 presents data on relative Soviet wholesale prices and CMEA ftp's in 1966 for ten Soviet exports. Zhukov and Ol'sevich present similar data for 1960 for thirteen commodities, which in a few cases are identical to the sample in Table 5.6 and in the remaining cases are of similar types.

In both samples the data indicate that regardless of exporters', intentions, CMEA ftp's differ substantially from domestic wholesale prices. Until more substantial data sets are available, the relationship of ftp's to domestic prices on a product-by-product basis is a matter of conjecture. I suspect that these results will stand, i.e., that CMEA ftp's are not closely related to the domestic costs of exporters for machinery and manufactured consumer goods.

IV. The Economics of Resource Allocation in CMEA

Moving from the price system to resource allocation is practically a non sequitur in the world of de jure intra-CMEA trade. It is planners who allocate resources, and prices merely assist planners. To quote Tarnovskii and Mitrofanova (pp. 22–23)

The exchange of commodities is accomplished through money, which emerges as a universal equivalent, expressing commodities. . . . However, commodity production in the countries of the world socialist system differs fundamentally from capitalist commodity production. . . . Commodity production is subservient to the requirements of the construction of socialism and communism. . . .

The law of value is used by socialist states for the strengthening of the planned socialist economy.

Thus, in terms of the aspirations of planners, all they ask is that *prices reinforce plans*. The central planning bureaus and the ministries of the various countries will, individually and in bilateral negotiations, decide on new additions to capacity, shifts in the use of current capacity, and trade flows.

The intention to maintain passive prices appears, for the most part, to have been successful in CMEA. Until the reforms in the late 1960s, all CMEA countries had completely isolated the domestic price system from ftp's by a system of subsidies and taxes: typically, producers would sell goods at the producers' wholesale prices and buy either at the industrial wholesale price or the retail price. In this system it was only planners, and not producers or foreign trade enterprises, who could "read" the domestic cost/ftp signals and possibly respond to changes in the gains from trade. The structure of CMEA ftp's is so out of line with the structure of demand and of wmp's that it obviously could not withstand the operation of a genuine intra-CMEA market. Therefore, I suspect that even with the economic reforms, the insulation between CMEA ftp's and domestic costs probably remains intact.[14]

Even if CMEA ftp's do not influence producers, do they influence planners? Typically the answer is that they do not. Obviously, at the level of individual commodities or even of commodity groups, there is no way planners could really build ftp's into their physical allocation schemes. If planners wish to plan quantities, without markets or multi-level planning schemes, then we can say a priori that prices could not influence them in any systematic fashion.[15]

But then, asking if *individual* prices affect *central* planners is really the wrong question. A more appropriate question is this: Do CMEA ftp's in some aggregate sense influence planners in CMEA? And here the answer may well be in the affirmative. It seems that many of the real allocative decisions in CMEA, which ostensibly are independent of prices, in fact are a faithful reflection of those strange relative CMEA ftp's.

I will state the argument in brief, then fill in the details. The CMEA price system, albeit irrational to its core, still sends out signals as if it measured opportunity costs in intra-CMEA trade. For planners these prices measure opportunity costs in the sense that, after the fact, they

14. The reforms in Bulgaria, Rumania, and the Soviet Union have left the subsidy system intact. The remaining East European countries are using some form of shadow rates to induce producers and foreign trade enterprises to compete on foreign markets and economize on imported inputs. Hungary is probably the furthest along in this area of reforms. My impression is that even here, the only truly active ftp's are capitalist prices which do reflect true opportunity costs.

15. For an elaboration of this point, see Hewett 1974b, ch. 4.

register the cost of machinery in terms of iron ore, etc. And because of the price-determination mechanism, these opportunity costs have been fairly stable over time, as Table 5.6 has shown: average prices of machinery have been high; average prices of raw materials have been low. Consequently the gains from trade at a fairly aggregated level have strongly signaled increased investment in and exports of machinery; conversely they have signaled no further investment in and curtailed exports of raw materials. And these signals, although "false" in a true opportunity cost sense, are quite real as a historical record. Thus it is hardly surprising that planners have tended to overinvest in machinery and underinvest in primary products.[16]

To fill in this argument, I begin with estimates of the gains from trade implied by the CMEA ftp system. Ferenc Kozma has published estimates for seven CMEA countries, and eleven sectors in each country, of the direct and indirect factor costs of producing a million 1959–60 foreign trade rubles. Those estimates are summarized in Table 5.9.

The data which support these numbers are a result of research by a CMEA research group in the Hungarian Academy of Sciences. They revalued in the late 1950s the input-output tables for each CMEA

16. I do not wish to imply that relative CMEA ftp's are the sole reason for overinvestment in machinery and equipment, but only that they are one reason. For example, Stalinist industrialization policies, and the fact that the mechanism in intra-CMEA trade makes specialization difficult, also must be mentioned as sources of the pressures to overinvest in this area.

Table 5.9. Total direct and indirect factor requirements (in man-hours) required for producing 1,000,000 1959–60 foreign trade rubles for the CMEA countries in 1960.

	ETN no.[a]	Bulg.	Czech.	E. Ger.	Hung.	Pol.	Rum.	SU
Machinery and equipment	1	453	190	184	325	342	351	151
Fuels, min. raw mats., and metals[b]	2	902	253	233	506	409	508	181
Chemicals	3	515	218	185	501	494	467	227
Building mats.	4	490	275	230	432	549	531	86
Agric. prods. (exc. food)	5–7	902	508	409	670	863	1472	670
Food	8	723	394	368	611	784	984	468
Mfd. cons. goods[c]	9	555	285	908	456	485	472	402

Source: Kozma, p. 38.

a. These are the commodity category numbers according to the CMEA trade nomenclature, *Edinaia Tovarnaia Nomenklatura* (ETN). For a detailed discussion of that classification scheme, see Marer 1972a, pp. 309–22.

b. This is a simple average of Kozma's coefficients for four industries: electrical energy, fuel, ferrous metal products, and nonferrous metal products.

c. This is a simple average of Kozma's coefficients for two industries, textiles and other light industrial products.

country at 1959–60 ftp's (each table apparently an eleven-sector table), and they revalued all outputs at the same prices. The tables include two primary factors, labor and capital, and those coefficients were used to estimate the direct and indirect factor requirements of producing one million 1959–60 foreign trade rubles. However they have combined direct and indirect factor requirements for each sector into one measure by restating depreciation in terms of its equivalent in man-hours, then adding the resulting quantity to the actual direct and indirect man-hour requirements.[17]

The coefficients in Table 5.9 are given by the following formula:

$$f_j^{k,1}(I - A_j)^{-1} = \mathrm{TFR}_j \, (j = 1, \ldots, 7) \tag{1}$$

where

> $f_j^{k,1}$ is an eleven-element vector stating direct labor and capital (in man-hours) requirements for producing 1,000,000 1959–60 foreign trade rubles in country j;
>
> A_j is the technology matrix for country j (11×11), where the prices used in its construction are 1959–60 CMEA ftp's;
>
> TFR_j is the vector of direct plus indirect (i.e., total) factor requirements in country j for producing 1,000,000 1959–60 foreign trade rubles.

Table 5.9 contains the seven TFR_j vectors, aggregated into seven sectors in order to correspond to the one-digit CMEA trade nomenclature (ETN).

The economic interpretation of the A_j's is that they permit the estimation of value-added in CMEA ftp's for each CMEA country. That serves our purposes perfectly, since we seek to estimate the gains from trade implied by the structure of CMEA ftp's. The use of ftp's means that one of the determinants of the level and structure of the direct and indirect factor requirements in Table 5.9 is the level and structure of CMEA ftp's. If intra-CMEA machinery prices increase 10 percent, and raw materials prices fall 10 percent, then, ceteris paribus, the factor requirements for producing 1,000,000 foreign trade rubles' worth of machinery fall 10 percent and those for raw materials rise 10 percent. Eleven sectors is an abysmally low level of disaggregation with which to work, and the results below are to be understood as only very general indications of the actual orders of magnitude.

The gains from trade will be defined as the ratio of the estimated resource cost of exports to the potential resource cost of full import substitution. The input-output approximation of that is,

---

17. The coefficients for converting capital depreciation into man-hours are not specified, nor is the methodology. The most complete discussion of the methodology of which I am aware is in Kovásznai, Kozma, et al., passim, esp. p. 81.

$$\frac{TFR_jEX_j}{TFR_jIM_j} = GFT_j \qquad (2)$$

where $EX_j(IM_j)$ is a vector of exports (imports) valued in 1959–60 ftp's, and GFT_j is the gains from trade in country j. Even if all of the data are correct for the input-output table, this estimate is probably biased upward. It assumes that export production and import substitution production have the same factor requirements as average production in the economy. In fact, exports may be of higher quality (and cost) than average for their industry. What is probably more important, though, is that the same is almost sure to be true for imports. In fact, in the short run a production function will probably not even exist for most noncompetitive imports. Thus it seems likely that even if export requirements are underestimated somewhat, import requirements will be even more so, and the GFT_j estimates will be biased upward.

The data in Table 5.10 use equation (2) to estimate GFT_j in Soviet–East European trade from the Soviet point of view and from the East European point of view. For example, the number 1.41 in column (1) is an estimate of Soviet gains from trade with eastern Europe; it indicates that it actually cost the Soviet Union 41 percent more resources (direct and indirect) to export to Hungary than it would have cost it to substitute domestic production for the imports from Hungary. As I mentioned earlier, there is probably some upward bias in the number. The number .69 in column (4) estimates that foreign trade allowed Czechoslovakia to save about 30 percent of the resources it would have expended had it produced all of its 1960 Soviet imports domestically without importing them; again, this number could be biased upward (i.e., the savings could be more than 30 percent).

Columns (2) and (5) show how the gains from trade would have changed if only ftp's (and therefore factor requirements) had changed between 1960 and 1970, but not the distribution of trade. Columns (3) and (6) show the full impact of changes in prices and the distribution of trade between 1960 and 1970 on the gains from trade. The estimates in columns (2) to (6) are particularly crude, since they do not take account of changes in production functions which occurred during the 1960s; they assume that the total factor requirements changed solely because ftp's changed.

Even with the wide confidence intervals implied by all the reservations with the data mentioned above, the results are startling. One would expect that all of the numbers in columns (1), (3), (4), and (6) were less than 1, which would reflect mutual gains from trade. In fact, however, it appears that trade with eastern Europe is costing the Soviet Union, both, on average, for all East European countries and also for all individual East European countries except Bulgaria and Rumania. While there is the

Table 5.10. Soviet and East European perceptions of gains from their mutual trade, 1960 and 1970.

	Soviet gains from trade with CMEA countries			East European gains from trade with the Soviet Union		
	1960 (1)	1970 (2)	1970 (3)	1960 (4)	1970 (5)	1970 (6)
Bulgaria	.72	.63	.64	.97	.71	.73
Czechoslovakia	1.68	1.95	1.66	.69	.58	.61
East Germany	1.68	2.20	1.65	.72	.58	.66
Hungary	1.41	1.60	1.08	.78	.63	.74
Poland	1.26	1.29	1.25	.74	.72	.78
Rumania	.89	.81	.78	1.19	1.12	.89
Weighted average	1.38	1.67	1.28	—	—	—

Columns (1) and (4) are computed using a variant of equation (2), the TFR_j estimates in Table 5.9, and estimates of the distribution of Soviet trade with individual East European countries (the latter from computer runs relating to Hewett 1974b, ch. 3; weights for the most important commodity groups are reported in that source). The actual formula is:

$$GFT_j = \frac{TFR_j EX_j^{*.60}}{TFR_j IM_j^{*.60}}$$

where $EX_j^{*.60}$ ($IM_j^{*.60}$) is a vector representing the 1960 percentage distribution of exports (imports) for the seven commodity groups identified in Table 5.9. This formula is equivalent to equation (2) in the text if there is a zero balance of trade, which is a reasonable assumption, since we are only interested in estimating typical gains from trade. Columns (2) and (5) were computed by deflating the TFR_j for changes during 1960–70 in an average of Soviet export and import prices to and from all CMEA countries (Hewett 1974b, pp. 78–79). In cases such as machinery and equipment where there were price indices for both exports and imports, I used a simple average to deflate the total factor requirements in that sector for the seven countries. Then the GFT_j were computed, using the same formula as above, and the 1960 trade weights. This is an approximation of what the gains from trade would have been in 1970 if the distribution of trade had not changed. Columns (3) and (6) are calculated as for (2) and (5) except that 1970 trade weights are used.

possibility that upward bias has pushed some of the numbers above unity, that does not seem as likely as for the East European estimates, since most Soviet imports from East Europe are in machinery or manufactured consumer goods, products which the Soviet Union is probably capable of producing at only somewhat higher than (domestic) average costs.

The changes in ftp's in the 1960s would have made the losses even larger had the Soviet Union not managed adjustments in the trade structure, primarily by shifting exports away from food and nonagricultural raw materials, and toward machinery. The "gains" from trade could have been as high as 1.67 for Soviet trade with the six European members; because of shifts in the composition of trade, the actual figure comes out 1.28. Table 5.11 contains estimates of the composition of Soviet-CMEA trade in 1960 and 1970.

Column (4) of Table 5.10 suggests that all East European countries save Rumania perceived gains from trading with the Soviet Union in

Table 5.11. Composition of Soviet trade with eastern Europe, 1955–70.

	ETN no.	1960	1970
Soviet exports			
Total		1.00	1.00
Machinery and equipment	1	.12	.20
Fuels, mineral raw mats., and metals	2	.47	.50
Agric. prods. (exc. food)	5	.17	.13
Raw mats. for production of food	7	.13	.06
Soviet imports			
Total		1.00	1.00
Machinery and equipment	1	.46	.44
Fuels, mineral raw mats., and metals	2	.16	.08
Agric. prods. (exc. food)	5	.03	.02
Food	8	.04	.08
Mfd. cons. goods	9	.20	.29

Source: Hewett 1974b, p. 79.

1960; by 1970, Rumania too perceived gains from trade. For all East European countries except Rumania the price changes alone improved their gains from trade substantially, but the changes in composition of trade diminished the realized gains from trade. The East European estimates are probably biased upward substantially, since some of the raw materials and fuels those countries import from the Soviet Union either could not be produced in requisite quantity at all in eastern Europe or could only be produced at enormous expense.

Fig. 5.1 combines in a simplified two-sector format some of the main conclusions suggested by these data, and data discussed earlier, on the economics of intra-CMEA trade. The curve EE is a representative East European country's transformation curve between machinery and raw materials; SS is a similar curve for the Soviet Union. They are drawn to suggest the Soviet comparative advantage in raw materials production, and the East European comparative advantage in machinery production. CMEA ftp's are designated by the dashed lines; wmp's by the solid lines.

Without trade barriers, CMEA ftp's would equal wmp's, and eastern Europe would specialize in machinery *relative to the Soviet Union;* however, eastern Europe would be producing more raw materials than it presently does. At CMEA ftp's eastern Europe is encouraged to specialize almost totally in machinery, and the Soviet Union is encouraged to produce much more machinery than it would at wmp's.

In fact relative costs and production lie in both countries at points intermediate to A and B, or A′ and B′, e.g., at the points C and C′. It is from these latter points that trade occurs. East Europe exports machinery

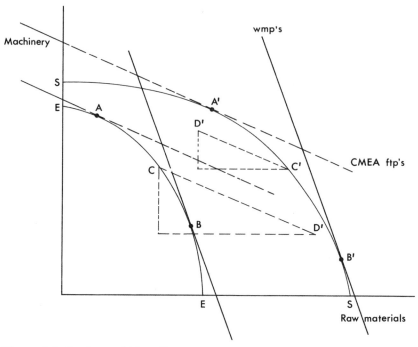

Figure 5.1. Soviet and East European gains from trade.

to the Soviet Union in exchange for primary products at terms of trade far above wmp's and (as Table 5.10 shows) far above internal rates of transformation. Thus eastern Europe trades to point D, outside its production possibilities curve. The reverse side of that bargain for the Soviet Union has it trading raw materials for machinery at terms of trade below domestic rates of transformation. It ends up at point D', inside its transformation curve.

The CMEA countries are aware of the terms of trade generated by CMEA ftp's; the USSR and Bulgaria have complained of poor terms of trade with CMEA since the late 1950s. From the point of view of those raw materials producers "it is not infrequently more profitable to satisfy demand with domestic production (even though it will be less efficient than that of the main exporter) than to pay for imports of finished products with exports or raw materials and agricultural products at relatively unfavorable foreign trade prices" (Os'mova, p. 130). Prices on machinery and equipment are so high that even very inefficient producers can sell at a profit. From the point of view of the machinery exporter then, "it is more profitable to export machinery in exchange for raw materials, fuel, and food, than to develop international specialization within machine-building, chemical industries, etc." (Zhukov and Ol'sevich, p. 19). Simultaneously, there has been a pronounced tendency to constantly expand the mix of exports, instead of specializing in a limited number of lines (ibid., p. 43).

The consequences of this situation are readily apparent. Intra-CMEA trade in 1963 prices has grown during the 1955–69 period at almost 8.4 percent, while CMEA trade with the world has grown at 8.5 percent.[18] Yet, intra-CMEA trade in primary products over that same period grew at a slower rate than CMEA exports to the world of primary products (respectively, 4.7 percent p.a. and 6.8 percent p.a.). Intra-CMEA trade in all manufactures has grown faster than CMEA exports to the world of all manufactures (respectively, 10.6 and 9.5 percent). These divergences in growth rates — both the higher rate of growth in machinery vs. primary product exports, and the relatively high rate of growth in CMEA-CMEA machinery trade — are cited endlessly in the CMEA economic press as signs of "improvement" in the structure of CMEA exports. For individual countries that may be true, but the collective result is an oversupply of machinery and a dearth of primary products on CMEA markets, with no signs that either will change.

Imagine what would happen if the CMEA countries decided to maintain quantitative controls on CMEA trade with the other world areas, but to (1) allow CMEA ftp's to fluctuate, and (2) also allow individual enterprises to respond to those prices. The result would probably be an enormous relative increase in primary-product prices, relative to machinery prices. Simultaneously one would expect a relative decrease in the demand for primary products relative to machinery.

Interestingly enough, it seems that to some extent the effects listed above have begun to occur without the imagined change. Without proclamations and conferences, a second informal price system has arisen in CMEA trade which partially compensates for the distortions of the formal system. It is typically called the "one-to-one rule," but has been referred to as "direct barter" (Csikós-Nagy, p. 220), "structural exchange" (Kiss, p. 174), and "barter in kind" (Ausch, p. 112).

One-to-one applies for the most part to trade among the small CMEA countries; as I show below, Soviet-CMEA trade is subject to different rules. The principles of one-to-one are simple. The formal prices of CMEA products, denominated in foreign trade rubles, have been progressively replaced by informal prices, denominated in terms of the relative "hardness" of commodities. The extremely "hard" commodities are in effect those which are in demand on CMEA markets, and which can be sold at their full formal prices on world (hard currency) markets.

18. These data, and those immediately following, are from UN ECE 72, p. 27.

Extremely "soft" commodities are those in excess supply in CMEA which would sell on world markets, if at all, only at relatively low prices.[19]

The one-to-one rule is that negotiators will exchange hard goods only for hard goods, and can sell soft goods only if they will buy soft goods from the other side. As an approximation, this means machine for machine, primary product for primary product. This intra-CMEA trade is a variation of pure barter, where any of a number of individual commodities of a similar type (degree of hardness) will serve as "currency" for buying similar types of commodities, and where the formal prices play a role as "exchange rates" among the "currencies."

The one-to-one rule operates only in trade among the small CMEA countries; Soviet-CMEA trade is primarily hard Soviet commodities for soft East European commodities. And even in intra–East European trade excluding the Soviet Union the one-to-one rule is not strictly applied, i.e., the structures of individual bilateral trade flows differ in the two directions. It seems likely that the one-to-one rule is applied strenuously only on the margin, i.e., to increases in trade. Therefore one would expect the structure of exports and imports in intra–East European trade should be converging. The effects of the one-to-one rule are apparent in the data presented in Table 5.12 on changes in the composition of East European–Soviet and East European–CMEA (excluding the Soviet Union) trade flows.

Looking first at Czech and Polish trade with CMEA excluding the USSR, we note that the ratio of Czech exports to imports for four commodity groups did not change substantially between 1958 and 1968. Simultaneously, however, there was a shift in exports and imports toward machinery and equipment, and from fuels, raw materials, and other materials. In Polish trade with CMEA excluding the USSR, the ratio of exports to imports by commodity group converged substantially toward unity during 1958–68. In addition, exports and imports shifted toward machinery and away from other product groups. The one-to-one rule seems most apparent in Polish CMEA trade; but of course in Czech trade it would be hard to tell if one-to-one was operating, since by 1958 the structure of Czech-CMEA (excluding the USSR) trade was already quite similar in exports and imports.

In both countries' trade with the USSR the data show an increasing divergence in net imports by commodity group. To an increasing extent over the period, the Soviet Union is selling primary products (mostly

19. See Ausch, pp. 111–13. Ausch attributes hardness to high capital requirements, high content of imports from capitalist countries, and high marginal import/GNP ratios (presumably as a proxy for demand). But actually the first two simply restate the problem: at fixed, relatively low CMEA ftp's the supply of many products falls below demand because those prices will not allow many producers to recoup basic factor costs.

Table 5.12. Composition of trade[a] of two CMEA countries with other CMEA countries (excluding the USSR) and with the USSR: 1958 and 1968.

| | | Czech trade with CMEA (exc. USSR) | | | | Czech trade with the USSR | | | | Ratio of exports to imports by commodity group | | | |
| | | Exports | | Imports | | Exports | | Imports | | Trade with CMEA (exc. USSR) | | Trade with the USSR | |
	ETN no.	1958 (1)	1968 (2)	1958 (3)	1968 (4)	1958 (5)	1968 (6)	1958 (7)	1968 (8)	1958[b] (9)	1968[c] (10)	1958[d] (11)	1968[e] (12)
Industrial mach. and equip.	1	.37	.51	.31	.41	.42	.54	.11	.13	1.19	1.24	3.82	4.15
Fuels, raw mats. (nonfood), and other mats.	2–5	.44	.36	.45	.34	.30	.20	.58	.62	.98	1.06	.52	.32
Foodstuffs and raw mats. for foodstuffs	6–8	.03	.02	.19	.12	.05	.01	.28	.23	.16	.17	.18	.04
Mfd. cons. goods	9	.16	.11	.05	.13	.23	.25	.03	.02	3.20	.85	7.67	12.50
		Polish trade with CMEA (exc. USSR)				Polish trade with the USSR							
Industrial mach. and equip.	1	.13	.40	.37	.48	.39	.44	.14	.20	.35	.83	2.79	2.20
Fuels, raw mats. (nonfood), and other mats.	2–5	.79	.42	.38	.34	.48	.23	.71	.65	2.08	1.24	.68	.32
Foodstuffs and raw mats. for foodstuffs	6–8	.06	.08	.05	.05	.06	.02	.09	.12	1.20	1.60	.66	.17
Mfd. cons. goods	9	.02	.10	.19	.14	.06	.30	.06	.03	.20	.71	1.00	10.00

Source: Marer 1972a, pp. 88, 95, 96, 103, 112, 119, 120, 127.

a. Soviet and east European sources do not report the composition of all trade. These figures represent the commodity distribution of reported trade; reported trade is typically between 80% and 100% of actual trade, with a median value of about 90%.

b. Col. (3)/col. (1).

c. Col. (4)/col. (2).

d. Col. (7)/col. (5).

e. Col. (8)/col. (6).

hard goods) for machinery, equipment, and manufactured consumer goods (mostly soft goods).

It should now be apparent why one-to-one resembles the hypothetical results allowing the free fluctuation of prices in intra-CMEA trade. In the area where one-to-one operates – intra-CMEA trade excluding the USSR – the products which would have relatively low prices in a market (machinery and equipment) are indeed ranked as "soft," hence low-priced, in the informal price system. Consequently, exchange in these products is at a high and growing level. The opposite is true for a high price, and the volume of this exchange is (relatively) falling.

For this informal system to work as well in all ways as the hypothetical liberation of prices, several additional preconditions would have to be satisfied. First, producers would have to be receiving the message that relative informal prices valued certain products much more or much less than formal prices. Also, informal prices within product groups (i.e., rankings of "hardness" within the group of "hard" goods) would be necessary to stimulate economizing behavior. Finally, it would have to operate for all of intra-CMEA trade.

In fact the informal price system seems to fulfill none of these conditions. It appears that planners and producers are still more impressed by formal prices; informal prices are very difficult to work into investment efficiency formulae, foreign trade efficiency formulae, etc. "Hardness" is a poor informational vehicle to communicate the subtle innuendoes of scarcity. Still, *something* does get through and, possibly with a long lag, informal prices may have some impact. It is also clear from this that the second condition is not fulfilled. Relative informal prices probably do not exist for most specific commodities in CMEA. Thus the informal price system has only partially compensated for the distortion of its formal counterpart. Likewise the third condition is not fulfilled since Soviet–East European trade does not operate according to the one-to-one rule.

V. The Future of the CMEA Resource Allocation Mechanism

I think most students of the CMEA economies would agree that the eventual culmination of the reform movements of the 1960s will be genuine decentralization concerning decisions on production, productive technologies, sales, and to some extent investment, and an increasing reliance on profits as incentives and prices as signals. Decentralization will most probably be only to the level of industrial associations, an outcome not so much different from the highly concentrated industries in Western countries. The Hungarian model, in its fundamentals, seems a likely prototype for the future economic system, at least for small CMEA countries. Without any attempt at predicting a timetable, it seems fruitful to ask what the CMEA ftp system will be like in the context of trade among "reformed" CMEA economies.

The system as it stands now is totally at variance with the spirit and substance of those reforms, and it can only act as an impediment to their full realization. The reforms are giving more autonomy to industrial associations and individual enterprises. In addition, they are seeking to introduce price systems which carry useful information on opportunity costs, and incentive schemes which emphasize the marketability of production, in lieu of the volume of production. For small CMEA countries dependent on foreign trade, the reformed domestic price systems must include, in the enterprise's calculus, foreign trade prices to induce those enterprises to economize on imports and maximize profits on sales in exports. That means bringing ftp's through equilibrium exchange rates directly into the firm's receipts and costs.

The combination of decentralization, profit maximization, and CMEA ftp's as they are currently determined would obviously be short-lived and disastrous. Relatively low prices on many primary products would discourage investment in and the production and export of goods needed in CMEA; simultaneously they would induce artificially high import demand for CMEA-produced primary products. The opposite would be the case for machinery and equipment. Prices would dutifully remain frozen even in the face of the serious disequilibria, and enterprises would soon learn that the posted prices were not prices at all. Assuming that planners would wish to avoid either anarchy or a CMEA-wide black market, one of three results would follow: (1) either the price system would have to be reformed; (2) planners would have to negotiate centrally and require enterprises to produce, export, and import certain goods; or (3) each CMEA country would need to construct a tariff system to reflect the informal, more realistic prices already implied in negotiations.

Taking these alternatives in reverse order, the last seems least likely as the sole solution. True, capitalist countries use tariffs, but for different reasons. They seek to shield domestic producers from actual supply-and-demand conditions on world markets. On the other hand, this hypothetical tariff system in the CMEA countries would seek to *apprise* domestic producers of supply and demand trends on CMEA markets. Even aside from the absurdity of this solution the information requirements would seem to preclude its feasibility.

The second alternative—the administrative solution—is the old system again, at least for foreign trade. That seems a likely outcome in the short run, but could hardly be a long-run solution if planners genuinely seek increased factor efficiency. Specialization, particularly intra-industry specialization, is a crucial instrument for those goals in the case of foreign-trade-dependent economies. And I think most CMEA economists would agree that specialization and decentralization are inextricably linked; centralized intra-industry specialization is what CMEA has been attempting for over fifteen years, and it is obviously cumbersome, costly, and of minimal effectiveness.

The long-term prospect would seem to be for a CMEA ftp system providing a flexible, accurate vehicle for injecting into domestic price systems information on real opportunity costs. This is the only type of price system consistent with the reformed economic systems discussed in CMEA, and implemented most completely in Hungary. That also means a price system where ftp's, domestic prices, and wmp's have similar structures, not because of decrees, but as a natural outcome of the operation of a market.

The transition to such a system will probably involve a process similar to the formation of a customs union. As a first step, CMEA ftp's will gradually be linked to domestic prices converted by some estimate of an equilibrium exchange rate (such as the conversion rates now in use in Hungary); presumably, high tariffs will initially protect domestic producers. Of course these domestic prices will have to be flexible if they are to serve their information function to the fullest. There will also have to be some move toward intra-CMEA convertibility, if only within the context of bilateral payments agreements.

This first step should make an important difference in intra-CMEA trade in that an exporter's wholesale prices plus a tariff will communicate to importers the full costs of their contemplated purchases; and changes in relative domestic costs will be transmitted among the CMEA countries. After this first step, the remaining steps will be those involved in the typical case of forming a customs union.

That is, the second step will be to unify domestic prices in CMEA through some program of mutual tariff reductions. This will cause substantial reallocation of resources, presumably mostly to the good, as relatively efficient producers of individual products in CMEA become the relatively most important producers of those products. There would be some trade diversion, but presumably the resulting costs would be swamped by the benefits of trade creation. It is during this second step that convertibility within CMEA should be achieved.

During all of this period there is presumably a common external tariff to protect developing CMEA industry from the full effect of world competition. There will also probably be at least payments agreements, if not commodity convertibility with non-CMEA countries. At the end of this stage the CMEA economy will, in many important respects, institutionally resemble the EEC.

The final step will be the integration of CMEA into the world economy, a process identical in its form to the integration of individual CMEA economies into a customs union. Thus there will be achievement of convertibility with other economies and a mutual reduction of tariff barriers.

While such a scenario will not be fully played out in the near future, the first stage may not be that far away. The transformation of CMEA ftp's into export prices of domestic producers has been discussed since the late 1950s under the heading of an "Independent Price Basis" (IPB: *sobstvennaia baza tsen*) in CMEA. This proposal arose out of dissatisfaction on the part of CMEA primary-product exporters (Bulgaria and the USSR for the most part) with their terms of trade. The argument was that exporters would be able to recoup their production costs, hence that CMEA ftp's should reflect some weighted average of domestic prices in CMEA.[20]

IPB was regarded by its most zealous supporters as an end in itself, not a first step along the road outlined above. Furthermore, it was simply a recommendation for a change in ftp's, not a change in the ftp system. There was no hint that export and import plans might need to be changed; rather, the idea was that whatever the export and import plans were, exporters should make a profit on the goods they agreed to export. The proposal in this early form was inconsistent with the reform movements in CMEA and therefore it was ultimately doomed.

The study and debate about IPB reached a crescendo in the mid-1960s.[21] The outcome was a defeat of IPB as a final system because it implied regional autarky for CMEA. More importantly, the debates seem to have produced a more sophisticated understanding of the interconnections of the CMEA ftp system with the domestic economic systems. Also, the research, which actually involved attempts to quantify an IPB, produced a formidable body of data documenting the incredible diversity among CMEA countries in domestic prices and domestic price determination techniques.[22]

The price system was again considered in the context of reforming the entire intra-CMEA foreign trade mechanism during discussions concerning the Comprehensive Program which was passed by CMEA in 1971 (CMEA 71b). This is an ambitious, but contradictory, blueprint of a reform of CMEA which would not be completed until the late 1980s. It encompasses all aspects of intra-CMEA economic relations: joint planning, direct links among various hierarchical levels, specialization,

20. For more details on IPB, see Hewett 1974b, ch. 5.
21. Földi and Kiss contains an excellent collection of papers stating the major positions in the debate.
22. The Csikós-Nagy article in Földi and Kiss represents probably the most coherent view of the infeasibility and undesirability of IPB. Zhukov and Ol'sevich summarizes the empirical research.

scientific-technical cooperation, joint forecasting, and so on. This program contains no specific recommendation on prices. But other aspects of stage 1 are listed as goals: convertibility, realistic conversion ratios to replace official exchange rates, and an increasing role for the market in intra-CMEA resource allocation. If these other conditions are implemented, then there is little question what form the price system must take. In fact there are signs that unification of CMEA price-determination *techniques* is under active consideration, which is a necessary prelude to unification of prices themselves.[23]

It may be that some time in the late 1970s there will be a transition to an IPB, but only as a first stage, and accompanied by the other measures discussed above. Such a change would make economic sense, although it could create serious political pressures. Zhukov and Ol'sevich estimate that the following price changes shown in Table 5.13 would have resulted from introducing IPB in 1964 (pp. 140–59). We can also infer (Table 5.14) from the data in Zhukov and Ol'sevich[24] what changes would have occurred in the terms of trade if IPB had been introduced (*ibid.*, p. 159).

These data imply a substantial redistribution of national income from machinery producers to primary-products producers. And since the 1964–65 price changes, which increased the terms of trade of machinery exporters, the shift to IPB would involve even more of a redistribution of national income.

Even the stage-1 change, then, will be a painful one for the CMEA countries. Nevertheless, it seems an unavoidable "down payment" for the ultimate success of economic reforms in the individual CMEA countries.

23. Kobzar and Stromtsov discusses the different price determination systems in CMEA and some possibilities for unification. Also, evidently the heads of all price offices in CMEA are now meeting in a new committee formed under CMEA auspices, probably to study price unification problems. The first meeting was held 15–17 January 1974 in Moscow (*Pravda*, 19 Jan. 1974).

24. Zhukov and Ol'sevich, p. 159, contains estimates of 1964 exports and imports of each CMEA country to all others denominated in existing contract prices and the estimated IPB prices. I take the percentage change in the value of exports divided by the percentage change in the value of imports as an estimate of the terms of trade changes.

Table 5.13.

	ETN no.	IPB price 1964 CMEA ftp
Machinery and equip.	1	.90
Fuels, mineral raw mats., and metals	2	1.7
Chemicals and const. materials	3–4	1.6
Agric. raw mats. (nonfood)	5–6	1.8
Food	7–8	2.0
Mfd. cons. goods	9	1.5

Table 5.14.

	Terms of trade with CMEA in 1964 ftp = 100
Bulgaria	1.11
Czechoslovakia	.85
East Germany	.74
Hungary	.96
Poland	.97
Soviet Union	1.09

References

Ausch, Sándor. 1972. *Theory and practice of CMEA cooperations.* Budapest: Akadémiai Kiadó.

Bartha, F. 1967. Trends in the development of socialist foreign trade prices. *Külkereskedelem (Foreign Trade)* 9 (Sept.):271–72. Translated in *JPRS, TEEFT* no. 363 (10 Oct.): 6–12 [MCUSGP 17859-31/1967].

Biulletin' ekonomicheskoi informatsii (Bulletin of Economic Information) 5, no. 32 (Oct. 1966).

Bożyk, Paweł. 1973. Economic integration of Poland with the C.M.E.A. countries and economic relations with the West. (In English.) *Handel Zagraniczny,* special edition for the 43d Poznan Trade Fair. Pp. 15–18.

CMEA 71a: Sovet Ekonomicheskoi Vzaimopomoshchi (Council for Mutual Economic Assistance), Sekretariat, *Statisticheskii ezhegodnik stran-chlenov Soveta ekonomicheskoi vzaimopomoshchi,* 1971.

CMEA 71b: *Kompleksnaia programma dal'neishego uglubleniia i sovershenstvovaniia sotrudnichestva i razvitiia sotsialisticheskoi ekonomicheskoi integratsii stran-chlenov SEV (Comprehensive program for the further deepening and improvement of cooperation and the development of socialist economic integration of the member countries of CMEA).* Bucharest: Sovet ekonomicheskoi vzaimopomoshchi (Council for Mutual Economic Assistance), 1971.

Csikós-Nagy, Béla. 1973. *Socialist economic policy.* Budapest: Akadémiai Kiadó.

Földi, T., and T. Kiss, editors. 1969. *Socialist world market prices.* Budapest: Akadémiai Kiadó.

Hewett, Edward A. 1974a. Estimating price indices from unit values: a new technique with application to Soviet terms of trade, 1955–70. In *Studies in Soviet terms of trade, 1913–70,* edited by E. Hewett and M. Dohan. Bloomington, Ind.: International Development Research Center Report.

————. 1974b. *Foreign trade prices in the Council for Mutual Economic Assistance.* London: Cambridge Univ. Press.

Holzman, Franklyn. 1963. Foreign trade. In *Economic trends in the Soviet Union,* edited by A. Bergson and S. Kuznets. Cambridge: Harvard Univ. Press. Pp. 282–332.

————. 1968. The ruble exchange rate and Soviet foreign trade pricing policies, 1921–1961. *American Economic Review* 58, no. 4 (Sept.): 803–25.

Karmnov, Iu., and M. Cheburakov. 1973. Sovershenstvovanie upravleniia otraslevoi integratsii stran-chlenov SEV (Improvement in the management of the sectoral integration of the CMEA countries). *Voprosy ekonomiki (Problems of Economics)*, no. 7, pp. 103–12.

Kiss, Tibor. 1971. *International division of labor in open economies with special regard to the CMEA*. Budapest: Akadémiai Kiadó.

Kobzar', E., and A. Stromtsov. 1974. Sblizheniie metodov vnutrennego tseno-obrazovaniia (The convergence of internal price-determination techniques). *Ekonomicheskaia gazeta*, no. 3 (Jan.): 20.

Kostak, Vitezslav. 1971. 1971–75 Czechoslovak trade with other socialist countries discussed. *Zahranicni Obchod (Foreign Trade)* 6 (June): 1–18. Translated in *JPRS* TEEEIA no. 574 (3 Dec.): 1–18 [MCUSGP 844-10/1972].

Kovásznai, Gy., F. Kozma, et al. 1967. On the interrelations between the socialist international division of labor and the efficiency of production. In *For the progress of Marxist economics*, edited by T. Földi. Budapest: Akadémiai Kiadó. Pp. 78–100.

Kozma, F. 1971. Some theoretical problems regarding socialist integration and the levelling of economic development. Hungarian Scientific Council for World Economy, *Trends in World Economy*, no. 6.

Marer, Paul. 1972a. *Soviet and East European foreign trade, 1946–69: statistical compendium and guide*. Bloomington: Indiana Univ. Press.

————. 1972b. *Postwar pricing and price patterns in socialist foreign trade*. IDRC Report no. 1. Bloomington, Ind.: International Development Research Center.

MFT: Ministry of Foreign Trade (USSR). 1970, 1972. *Vneshniaia torgovlia SSSR za 19—, statisticheskii obzor (Foreign trade of the USSR in 19—, statistical compendium)*. Moscow: Vneshtorgizdat. Published in 1971 and 1973.

Os'mova, N. M. 1969. *Khoziaistvennye reformy i mezhdunarodnoe sotsialisti-cheskoe razdelenie truda (Economic reforms and the international socialist division of labor)*. Moscow: Moscow Univ.

RFE: Radio Free Europe. 1972. Hungarian situation report 28 (25 July).

Tarnovskii, I., and N. M. Mitrofanova. 1968. *Stoimost' i tsena na mirovom sotsialisticheskom rynke (Value and price on the world socialist market)*. Moscow: Nauka.

UN 71: United Nations, Statistical Office. 1971. *Price movements of basic commodities in international trade: 1950–1970*. Series M, no. 29, Rev. 1/ Add. 1. New York: United Nations.

UN ECE 70: United Nations. 1970. Economic Commission for Europe. *Economic Bulletin for Europe* 21, no. 1.

UN ECE 72: United Nations, 1972. Economic Commission for Europe. *Economic survey of Europe in 1971*, part 1: *The European economy from the 1950's to the 1970's*. New York.

UN MBS 65: United Nations. 1965. *Monthly Bulletin of Statistics*, Nov.

UN MBS 70: United Nations. 1970b. *Monthly Bulletin of Statistics*, Nov.

Usenko, E. 1962. Soglasheniia sotsialisticheskikh stran o vzaimnykh postavkakh tovarov (Agreements of the socialist countries on their mutual deliveries of commodities). *Vneshniaia torgovlia (Foreign Trade)* 7: 5–13.

Zhukov, V. N., and Iu. Ia. Ol'sevich. 1969. *Teoreticheskie i metodologicheskie problemy sovershenstvovaniia tsenoobrazovaniia na rynke SEV (Theoretical and methodological problems of the improvement of price formation on the CMEA market)*. Moscow: Nauka.

6

Price Control, Incentives, and
Innovation in the Soviet Economy

Gregory Grossman

University of California, Berkeley

For nearly two decades now, since the great debate on the law of value and price formation surfaced after the Twentieth Party Congress, prices of producer goods and of certain factors of production have been at the center of attention of those who would improve the operation of the Soviet economy. The sharp contrast with the situation of the previous quarter-century, when—despite Stalin's belated and confused lip service to the law of value—prices within the state sectors were regarded in both official theory and actual practice as all but irrelevant to the functioning of the economy, need hardly be stressed for the benefit of students of Soviet economic thought. When in 1956 the pendulum swung in the opposite direction, it swung with considerable force and emphasis, as though all concerned were eager to make up for lost time.

The first phase of the post-1956 literature on prices—the so-called debate on the law of value[1] —was concerned primarily with what Francis Seton in Chapter 2 of this volume felicitously calls "diagnostic prices," i.e., prices as they *ought* to be according to some first principles of Marxist doctrine. Such principles, however, proved to be varied and ambiguous enough to spawn a considerable variety of diagnoses and prescriptions. In any case, in an atmosphere of diminishing scholasticism, diagnostic prices could not for very long hold the limelight of discussion, for they served neither the needs of efficient planning and management

It is a pleasure to gratefully acknowledge the research assistance of Ewa Krzyśćiak and Pauline Andrews, and the financial support of the Institutes of International Studies and of Business and Economic Research, both of the University of California, Berkeley.

1. There are now many Western works describing and appraising this debate. Among them one should mention Alfred Zauberman, "The Soviet Debate on the Law of Value and Price Formation," in *Value and Plan,* ed. Gregory Grossman (Berkeley: Univ. of California Press, 1960), pp. 17–35, and Morris Bornstein, "The Soviet Price Reform Discussion," *Quarterly Journal of Economics,* 68, no. 1: 25–48.

nor those of the Party and bureaucracy to run things in the wonted manner without hindrance from abstract tenets. And so already in the early sixties the limelight on the intellectual stage shifted to price proposals resting on rigorous theoretical formulations of a praxeological nature, such as Kantorovich's "objectively determined valuations" and the "prices of the optimal plan" put forth and championed by the Central Economic-Mathematical Institute.[2] In price-setting practice, however, control remained firmly with the bureaucracy, and although the Price Reform of 1966–67 did incorporate some conceptual and calculational innovations, it did not in any fundamental manner subvert the traditional Soviet approach to the nature and role of prices in the centrally planned and administered economy.

It is not our intention here to dwell on the debates. Suffice it to note that there was broad agreement (among otherwise very diverse bodies of opinion) on two basic propositions. First, there was a general rejection – though for very different reasons – of the traditional (Stalinist) formula: wholesale price equals average industrywide cost of production plus a small margin of profit. Second, there was agreement (embracing a wide gamut of theoreticians, but also apparently some practitioners) that in the future wholesale prices ought to play a more active role in the economy than they had theretofore, although just what role or roles, in what ways, and on what theoretical grounds were objects of the intense controversy. We might note in passing – anticipating our later discussion – that more active prices necessarily imply also more flexible prices.

The intense and profound disagreements in regard to the nature and functions of prices of course tended to reflect even more basic differences among the disputants – i.e., differences in conceptions of the economic process in a socialist economy, of relations between economic institutions and the ends of social activity, and perhaps in conceptions of the ends themselves. The debate on prices was an integral part of the debate on a forthcoming economic reform, and both debates of course had their parallels in nearly every other communist country of eastern Europe.

In the Soviet Union, a major turning point occurred in 1965, a year that saw two landmark events in this regard. The first of these (and the better known one) was the announcement at the end of September of the "new system of planning and economic stimulation," more commonly known as the Economic Reform of 1965. The governing materials of the economic reform had only little to say about prices, and their chief importance for our purpose lies in that they failed to provide for a sig-

2. An extensive account and a sympathetic critique of the prices proposed by mathematical optimizers will be found in Michael Ellman, *Planning Problems in the USSR: The Contribution of Mathematical Economics to Their Solution, 1960–1971* (Cambridge: Cambridge Univ. Press, 1973).

nificant systemic rearrangement of the whole economy. This being the case, whatever they might have provided in regard to prices proper could be at best by way of a rather limited reform of their role in the economy. Such indeed was the case.

The other landmark event of 1965 actually anticipated the announcement of the economic reform by some months; it was the establishment in April 1965 of the State Price Board (*Gosudarstvennyi komitet tsen*).[3] Whereas the economic reform determined the limits of the function of prices in the economy, and therefore also largely their nature and the general ways of their formation, the establishment of the State Price Board (hereinafter, SPB) was the first step toward creating a corresponding administrative framework for the setting and supervising of prices. One offspring of these two events was the reform of wholesale prices of 1966–67.[4]

While the price reform will be taken up in a later section of this chapter, its logical connection with the Economic Reform of 1965 might be pointed out at this juncture. The essence of the economic reform was the stimulation of more effective operation within each enterprise, rather than the creation of a more efficient system of interrelations between enterprises, or between enterprises and their superiors among managerial and planning bodies. In this regard, stress was laid on enhancing incentives for the firm as a whole (say, by giving it greater investment opportunities) and for its personnel, especially its managerial personnel. The source of these incentives is the firm's profit. Hence, a major objective of the price reform has been to widen profit margins in general and to make them more uniform among industries, for the so-called normally operating firms.

The prices introduced in 1966–67 were of course controlled prices, like those that they supplanted. The economic reform did not look forward to attaining equilibria in individual producer-good markets; consequently, it presupposed the continuation of price control. And since it did not introduce measures that would significantly weaken the pressure of aggregate demand on aggregate supply, it also virtually ensured that price control would continue to be maintained for anti-inflationary reasons. Moreover, the "conservative" way in which the economic reform actually was carried out only tended to reinforce the role of price control. Thus, the tendencies on the side of prices and on

3. The history of the establishment of SPB and related institutions is conveniently summarized in Friedrich Haffner, *Das sowjetische Preissystem* (Berlin: Duncker & Humbolt, 1968), pp. 162ff.

4. Hereinafter, unless qualified, "price" will stand for wholesale price of an industrial product. I know of no systematic Western study of Soviet prices in construction. A recent work on railroad rates, with special reference to revisions of 1965 and 1967, is Chantal Beaucourt, "Système tarifaire et réforme des prix en U.R.S.S.," *Cahiers de l'I.S.E.A.: Economies et Sociétés*, 5, no. 1 (Jan. 1971): 171–226.

the side of the decision-making arrangements seem to have been mutually reinforcing.

On the other hand, the somewhat increased importance of value magnitudes (profit, total sales) among the success indicators of the enterprise under the 1965 system, the heightened emphasis on personal and enterprise material incentives, and the consequently greater distributive and allocative implications of the actual prices, perforce increased the potential significance of prices as parameters of short-term decision making. By the same token, the possibility of using prices instrumentally to bring about desired allocative results was also enhanced. And indeed, a concerted attempt has been made to activize prices somewhat in two specific and closely delimited areas, to help solve two of the more intractable and venerable problems in the Soviet economy: namely, stimulating technical progress, and improving the quality of industrial products, in both cases at the enterprise level. In both respects, administrative methods have proved to be quite ineffectual. While such methods have not been abandoned, they are being increasingly supplemented by "economic methods," i.e., by manipulating the material incentives to the firm and to its relevant personnel through more flexible and more purposive prices for finished products. This approach will be examined in some detail below.

In sum, thanks to increased size and importance of material incentives and their closer link with the actual prices received by the industrial producers, "economic methods" of guiding the performance of enterprises have become more feasible since 1965. Yet there is always the danger that the activization of certain prices, given the continued presence of a strong seller's market, will invite inflation, and in its wake various unintended distributive and allocative effects. In other words, in this regard the authorities face a trade-off between the pace of innovation, on the one hand, and price stability and certain distributive and other desiderata, on the other. Alternatively, one may speak of a trade-off between inflation and technological sluggishness. We will return to this issue after discussion of price control in general, of the 1966–67 Price Reform, and of the changing conceptions regarding the role of wholesale prices in certain areas of the economy.

Price control

Whatever else it may have been since the start of the Plan Era, Soviet policy in regard to wholesale prices of industrial commodities has been eminently one of strict and comprehensive *price control*. This comprehensive price control has been in effect much longer than in any other country in modern times. And yet, some basic questions can be asked about its rationale. If prices in the state sector perform almost entirely "passive" functions, as is often stated, why should the avoidance of open inflation in this sector be of such importance to the authorities? What would it matter from a resource-allocative standpoint if prices were not under strict control, and presumably subject to a continuous inflationary trend, so long as the economy is planned and administered primarily in physical terms or in the famous "constant prices" (which are little more than aggregates of physical units with a common monetary denominator)? What would it matter also from the distributive standpoint, so long as property and entrepreneurial income flows to the state and not to individuals, so long as the treasury can easily enough siphon funds from here to there, and so long as retail prices are in any case divorced from wholesale prices by large and elastic turnover taxes and subsidies? The informed reader can without doubt anticipate the answers; namely, that wholesale prices are passive but not altogether so, that they do have some allocative consequences,[5] and that something of what might justifiably be called entrepreneurial and property income has a tendency to settle — nay, is often intended to settle — in the pockets of individuals. Hence, price changes have both allocative and distributive effects. In sum — to paraphrase the old saw about hypocrisy, vice, and virtue — Soviet price control is the unwitting tribute that authority pays to spontaneity, that the planning principle pays to *khozraschet* and to personal acquisitiveness.

In any economic system, the Soviet not excluded, price control carries with it a certain logic. It must deny, or at least curtail, the force of demand, for otherwise there is no rationale for the intervention of political authority (except for primarily bureaucratic or demagogic reasons). Consequently it must invoke administrative and extra-economic principles for the determination of the fixed or ceiling prices, principles that can be cast in the form of a relatively easily understandable criterion, and which invoke certain notions of equity or doctrinal venerability for the sake of general acceptance. The criterion should be an *objective* one, in the sense that its use ought not depend unduly on an informational base that is much more accessible to the controlled than to his customers or to the controller, such as the producer's own cost of production. Lastly,

---

5. A good summary of the allocative role of Soviet prices is by Morris Bornstein in "The Soviet Price System," *AER* 52, no. 1 (March 1962): 66–68. Comprehensive surveys of the Soviet price system, theory and practice, by Western authors are: Henri Denis and Marie Lavigne, *Le problème des prix en Union Soviétique* (Paris: Cujas, 1965), Morris Bornstein, "Soviet Price Theory and Policy," U.S. Congress, Joint Economic Committee, *New Directions in the Soviet Economy,* Part I, (Washington: U.S. G.P.O., 1966), pp. 65–98, and Haffner, *Das sowjetische Preissystem.* A well-known analysis of Soviet "industrial materials prices" from the standpoint of Western theory is Abram Bergson, *The Economics of Soviet Planning* (New Haven: Yale Univ. Press, 1964), ch. 8. I have earlier addressed myself to the subject in "Industrial Prices in the USSR," *AER,* 49, no. 2 (May 1959): 50–64.

since any price control program is essentially unmanageable under any conditions, administrative convenience is a major desideratum for the controller.

The objective criteria fall into two broad groups: (1) historical (base period) prices, and (2) current or expected costs. In the latter case there are again two possibilities: (a) a price authority that is independent of both the producer and the consumer sets the actual prices on the basis of costs computed by or submitted to it; and (b) the price authority does not set the actual prices but rather lays down the rules by which cost-determined prices are calculated by the interested party or parties (although the authority retains the right to audit and, if necessary, adjust such prices).[6]

In the first case, that of the historical standard, prices are frozen (or price ceilings are imposed) as of a certain date prior to the imposition of control, as in the United States in 1942, 1950, 1971, and 1973. It has nearly all the advantages listed above, not the least that prices of the recent past are much more accessible to the buyers (and, hence, also to the controllers) than, say, the producer's costs. Perhaps it also has an intuitive appeal to the public on grounds of equity. It has, however, the great disadvantage of ephemerality, for exceptions have to be allowed almost from the start and mount very quickly. The exceptions have to invoke a different criterion—and if demand is to be thwarted there is really only one criterion left, that of cost. Since the initial reason for the price control is probably some major structural change—on either the demand side, or the supply side, or both—and possibly certain concomitant changes in social values, the life of historical prices is likely to be quite brief.

The Soviets used the historical criterion during the early years of the Plan Era, but since then they have had little choice but to set calculated prices, which means employing some cost criterion.[7] Moreover, almost necessarily the relevant cost has had to be average cost for the industry, rather than marginal cost or average cost of the marginal firm. After all,

6. This classification is similar to that of Donald H. Wallace in his very useful survey of price and other wartime controls, *Economic Controls and Defense* (New York: Twentieth Century Fund, 1953), esp. ch. 9. Our three criteria correspond to Wallace's "freeze ceilings," "dollar-and-cents ceilings," and "formula ceilings." He points out that formula ceilings—our case 2(b)—permit decentralized price setting, which largely resolves into margin control, and are particularly appropriate for new products—all of which is apposite to understanding Soviet attempts at imparting flexibility to price controls in order to spur innovation.

7. To be sure, the notorious 1926/27 "constant" prices, a species of historical prices, remained in effect for planning and statistical purposes until 1949/50. Their perdurance was possible because, on one hand, they quickly drifted away from their historical base, and on the other hand, they were of little importance for the actual planning of either financial flows or of production in industry (even though firms' global production targets continued to be expressed in these prices until 1949), and not at all for the planning of investment.

with the establishment of the command economy the chief function of wholesale prices became the "accounting" (*uchetnaia*) function, i.e., planning and controlling the financial flows of the enterprise and the branch. For this purpose, industry average cost is clearly suited better than the other two kinds of cost. Even more is this true of the comparative function of price—comparing the cost in an individual firm with costs in the industry as a whole—for purposes of revealing what the Soviets call "production reserves," i.e., waste and inefficiency. Lastly, the fear of inflation surely militated against the use of both marginal cost and average cost of the marginal firm, especially in view of the typically very wide cost differentials in Soviet industry between firms, and even between production lines within a single firm. Exceptions were made by way of imposing turnover taxes on producer goods in cases where the pressure of demand was especially heavy, usually because of obvious mutual substitutability of producer goods with very different average production costs, as in the case of fuels. But these exceptions only helped "prove the rule"—at least until the Price Reform of 1966–67.[8]

At this point may we digress briefly to comment on the doctrinal foundation of Soviet price-setting practice? It is frequently asserted that the doctrinal foundation of average-cost pricing is the Marxian labor theory of value (or law of value), and that indeed this instance is perhaps one of the best examples of the domination of Soviet reality by doctrine (or dogma). Does not the fact that prices are typically set roughly proportional to average cost (*sebestoimost'*), which in turn is resolvable almost entirely into wage cost, indicate that the law of value—according to which prices are proportional to socially necessary labor inputs—is generally observed, often in contravention to other price-setting norms? There is no gainsaying that since the early forties, when Stalin proclaimed, contrary to his earlier view, that the law of value "operates" in the Soviet economy, setting prices in some relation to *sebestoimost'* has been explained in Soviet sources with reference to this Marxian law. But the practice of setting prices according to industrywide average cost antedated the rediscovery of the law of value by at least a decade and was the basis for the first comprehensive industrial price revision in 1936! Indeed, there is no evidence that the price-setting practices that emerged at the beginning of the Plan Era were intentionally based on any first principles drawn from the corpus of Marxist theory. Rather, they responded to the pragmatic and pressing requisites of running a shortage economy with a rapidly developing system of materials allocation and of centralized direction of enterprises. In a sense, the pervasive fact of "deficitness"— helped by an ideological hostility to free markets and free prices, to be

8. Cf. Bergson (supra n. 5), pp. 162ff. A lengthy treatment of average-cost pricing in the USSR is to be found in Haffner (supra n. 5), pp. 85–104.

sure — imposed its logic in the form of physical rationing, which in turn required and got physical targets and physical planning in general. Average-cost pricing was a rather logical corollary. That this happened to accord with the technocratic biases of the engineers and the antimarket biases of the political leaders surely smoothed the way to the establishment of a command economy. But there seems to have been no doctrinal blueprint to be followed in regard to prices (or much else), as one gathers from, say, Hutchings' research on the historical origins of the Soviet industrial price system.[9] The explanation of average-cost in Marxian terms came later by way of rationalization of the existing practice. Of course, with time, certain economists and philosophers established a vested intellectual interest in the law of value or some other Marxian price-setting formula, and their voluminous outpourings on the subject, especially since 1956, may well have found resonance in the consciousness of Soviet men of affairs, always eager (as are their counterparts everywhere) to grasp for doctrinal legitimation of their pragmatic stances.[10]

The desideratum of stable prices

Authoritative Soviet sources frequently characterize the goal of Soviet price policy as one of combining stability with flexibility, a formula that price controllers the world over would probably accept in principle, no less for its vagueness than for its content. The difficult problem is how to combine the two, or rather how to compromise between the two.

In a major programmatic address delivered less than a year after the completion of the Price Reform, the chairman of the SPB stressed the distinction between stable and frozen prices. The latter phrase was used by him pejoratively to denote controlled prices that remain rigidly unaltered in the face of conditions that require their revision. He warned of this danger and stressed that the reformed economic system called for "flexible prices that reflect in good time changes in the production

9. R. F. D. Hutchings, "The Origins of the Soviet Industrial Price System," *Soviet Studies* 13, no. 1 (July 1961): 1–22. Bergson gives more weight to the doctrinal significance of the labor theory than is suggested here (Bergson, p. 172). It is interesting to note that under not dissimilar circumstances, even if with a very different ideological and theoretical background, the National Socialist regime in Germany during World War II adopted an industrial price-control formula that first rested on the individual firm's average production cost, and later on industry average cost. See Erich Preiser, *Bildung und Verteilung des Volkseinkommens*, 2d ed. (Göttingen: Vandenhoeck & Ruprecht, 1961).

10. A classic critique of the Stalinist invocation of the law of value in the Soviet economy from the standpoint of a Western Marxist is Ronald Meek's *Studies in the Labor Theory of Value* (London: Lawrence and Wishart, 1956).

and sale of output."[11] On the other hand, stable prices in his terminology are prices that permit of the needed flexibility while at the same time eschewing excessively frequent or unjustified movement.

In current Soviet usage, price stability seems to comprise two different things. First, it stands for stability of the general price level over the short and medium term. (Over the long term, the general price level is not expected to remain stable; rather, it is expected to decline as labor productivity rises.) This of course presupposes, *ceteris paribus,* that average wages will rise less rapidly than productivity — a relationship that is indeed a major objective of Soviet policy, especially again since 1968,[12] but one that appears to be not much more easily realized in the Soviet economy than in less authoritarian ones to the west.[13] Second, and perhaps more important, "stability" pertains to the avoidance of price drift, the tendency for prices to move upward in an unauthorized manner under conditions of the general seller's market. To this end the authorities constantly insist on the observance of what in Soviet jargon is usually called "state discipline" in regard to prices, which means that all concerned must (a) adhere to the lawfully set individual prices (and the relevant technical and commercial specifications for the commodities), or (b) in the absence of set prices, as would frequently be the case with new or unique products, abide by the rules governing the computation and determination of such prices.

What are the reasons for preferring stability of prices? Probably one reason is the mere existence of an ongoing price-setting and price-enforcing bureaucracy, which may be expected to accentuate — wittingly or

11. V. K. Sitnin, "Usilenie roli optovykh tsen v povyshenii effektivnosti obshchestvennogo proizvodstva," in *Sovershenstvovanie planirovaniia i uluchshenie ekonomicheskoi raboty v narodnom khoziaistve* (*Materialy Vsesoiuznogo ekonomicheskogo soveshchaniia*), ed. A. V. Bachurin et al. (Moscow, 1969), pp. 303ff. The volume contains proceedings of the All-Union Conference on Perfecting Planning and Improving Economic Work in the Economy, which met in Moscow on 14–17 May 1968. It seems to have been very much of an "establishment" conference, with many leading politicians, planners, and administrators reporting and in attendance. Sitnin's report contains one of the best presentations of SPB's policy and intentions as of that time.

12. For relevant developments since 1968, see Gertrude E. Schroeder, "Recent Developments in Soviet Planning and Incentives," U.S. Congress, Joint Economic Committee, *Soviet Economic Prospects for the Seventies* (Washington: US GPO, 1973), pp. 11–38.

13. Just why this should be the long-term goal is not at all clear. It seems to have been that under Stalin the objective escaped his grasp except during the very unusual conditions of the last years of his life. If I am not mistaken, Khrushchev was less concerned with it, but it reappeared in the Brezhnev-Kosygin period, and (as noted in the text) was translated even into short-term wage-productivity rules in 1968, and further institutionalized in 1972. One should assume that under Soviet conditions of planning and management of the economy short- and medium-term wholesale price stability is much more important than long-term stability, let alone long-term decline. I resist the temptation to speculate here about the reasons for the long-term goal.

unwittingly—the objective of stable prices in the minds of the system's directors. Of more substance is the likely fear that inflation of wholesale prices of producer goods as well as consumer goods may, with time, force up retail prices, which is of course what did happen in Soviet history in 1935, in 1947, and in regard to livestock products in 1962—to mention just the more conspicuous instances. There is little doubt that any significant rise in retail prices is currently viewed as politically undesirable; witness the repeated public protestations by Soviet leaders to the effect that retail prices will be held stable, and possibly even reduced in the long run. Such protestations were emphatically made, for example, at the time of the 1966–67 Price Reform, which included some considerable increases in wholesale prices. Lastly, strong evidence of the unwillingness of the authorities to raise retail prices in the face of a cost push is to be found in the enormous subsidies currently being paid out by the treasury to keep down prices of meat, dairy products, and other goods, as well as house rents. But it is not to be assumed that further significant increases in such subsidies in the wake of a rise in wholesale prices will be viewed with equanimity.

Turning to planning, price changes cause considerable inconvenience in the carrying out of the five-year plan. Thus, "a proposal has even been put forth that prices should remain unchanged throughout the quinquennium for purposes of compiling the annual plans, although the only argument advanced is that, if prices change, it is supposedly impossible to set up a basis for planning or to assign any tasks to branches and enterprises."[14]

A more serious (and peculiarly Soviet) difficulty arises with the one-year plans. Since each firm's OYP specifies sales targets and other financial flows, any price changes after the drafting of the firm's OYP should ideally be followed by a recalculation of planned sales values and other financial flows of the given enterprise, of every affected enterprise, and of the corresponding accounts of the state budget. This is well-nigh impossible, leading to unanticipated effects on plan fulfillment and windfall financial gains and losses to the firms and to the budget. A succinct description of a particular case is worth quoting:

> Recently, prices for steel pipe were considerably reduced. The production plan of the steel industry should have been consequently lowered by a certain amount. And accordingly, those branches that consume this good should have increased their payments into the state budget on account of savings [in the purchase cost] . . . of

14. E. V. Komarova, "Plan i tseny," *Ekonomika i organizatsiia promyshlennogo proizvodstva,* 1972, no. 1, p. 104. In the same paragraph the author stresses that "growth rates laid down in national economic plans are computed on the basis of physical indicators and constant prices. Things go so far that the ministry does not know in what prices the branch's plans are drawn up: those of the last or current year, actual or plan prices."

the pipe. Instead, the following happened: prices for steel products had been lowered, but it turned out to be extremely complicated to distribute this reduction by [individual] buyers. And so there arose bargaining, which by all rights would have taken place before the price reduction. In the end, both the steel industry and the state budget suffered losses.[15]

This difficulty has been approached by means of three devices. (1) In order to be incorporated in the OYP of the following year, a price change must be announced no later than May 1. (2) Otherwise, buyers continue to pay the old price for the duration of the plan year while the seller receives the new price, the difference being paid (or absorbed) by a "fund for the current regulation of prices" administered by the SPB. (3) So-called stepped prices may be laid down years in advance, so that both sellers and buyers can anticipate price changes in good time.[16]

Lastly, price stability concerns also the prevention of price drift, the successful attempts by enterprises to raise prices above the levels that are stipulated in the authorized price lists (*preiskuranty*) or are implied in the various regulations and norms that govern the decentralized setting of prices by the producers themselves (usually nominally with the concurrence of the buyers, though this is often only an ineffectual formality). In the eyes of the authorities, price drift not only represents contravention of laws, regulations, and norms, but also has undesirable consequences of both a distributive and allocative kind. In short, price drift is unintended inflation.

Price drift and inflation

One should distinguish two methods by which enterprises attempt to obtain higher prices: (1) "outright violation," violating existing fixed prices or the commercial and technical specifications pertaining thereto, i.e., by breaking the law; and (2) by themselves setting — when permitted — relatively high prices for new products, i.e., products for which fixed prices did not previously exist. The latter method need not involve any illegal manipulation; existing legal provisions may permit the setting of relatively high prices for new products — and, as we shall see, may even

15. Komarova, p. 103. Cf. A. Komin, deputy chairman of the SPB, in *Planovoe khoziaistvo* (hereinafter *PKh*), 1972, no. 2, p. 121; N. Grigor'ev, "Plan i tseny," *Ekonomicheskaia gazeta* (hereinafter *EG*), 1971, no. 46, p. 7. Grigor'ev also complains of the inadequacy and lack of up-to-dateness of the official price lists. A good description of the problems for the annual enterprise plans caused by price revisions is to be found in A. Komin, "Nekotorye voprosy sovershenstvovaniia planovogo tsenoobrazovaniia," *Den'gi i kredit,* 1970, no. 1, pp. 20–22. The author stresses that the aim of timely flexibility in regard to prices does not fit in with the existing methodology of plan construction. The result can be that new prices go into effect only a year later than intended.

16. On stepped prices see *infra*, text at n. 75.

encourage this much in the interests of stimulating technical progress and innovation. But not infrequently there seems to be an element of illegality in the obtaining of relatively high prices for new products, either because of the padding of cost estimates which underlie the determination of such prices or by spurious classification of products as new when they are only unsubstantially so. The second method — inflation by dint of real or pretended innovation — is the more interesting case for present purposes because it throws into high relief the dilemma of the authorities stemming from the conflict of two major sets of goals: price stability with its political and distributive implications, on the one hand, and the desiderata of economic efficiency and progress, on the other. The dilemma is of course not at all peculiar to the USSR but is inherent in any price control situation under any politico-economic system, although the specific institutions of the Soviet system surely affect the methods employed in its resolution and their relative success.

As for outright violations, judging by the Soviet literature their incidence seems to be very high, though naturally there is no way of arriving at any quantitative estimates. There hardly appears a major published statement by a leading price controller without complaining of this phenomenon and calling for better "state discipline" in regard to prices. From time to time the press carries descriptions of particular cases and mention of the punishments meted out. Central administrative attention to the problem of outright violation seems to have intensified since the formation of the SPB in 1965, and especially since 1969 (judging by the press, at least) following a special resolution of the USSR Council of Ministers on this question, which, among other things, also enlarged the SPB's powers of supervision and enforcement of controlled prices.[17] One-time audits of prices charged by industrial enterprises were conducted in the RSFSR in July 1970, and in the whole USSR in 1971.[18] There seem to be two significant weaknesses in the supervision and enforcement procedure, however. First, the one-time audits just mentioned were conducted by the enterprises and their respective ministries themselves[19] — and, to be sure, a subsequent spot check in the case of the 1970 audit by the SPB showed that many cases of price violation had not been revealed in the course of the original audit. Second, in the many specific instances reported in the press, the typical penalty is simply the confiscation of the illicit increment in the enterprise's profit attributable to excessive prices. Only oc-

17. Interview with A. T. Kuznetsov, deputy chairman of SPB, in *EG*, 1963, no. 3, p. 9. The interview was in anticipation of the All-Union Conference of Price-Formation Personnel, which apparently was to devote considerable attention to the problem of violations. See also *EG*, 1969, no. 24, p. 9, and *PKh*, 1971, no. 7, pp. 42ff., for major articles on price audit and enforcement.

18. *EG*, 1971, no. 23, p. 8, and *EG*, 1971, no. 25, p. 10. The latter only announces the 1971 price audit; it is not known whether the audit actually took place.

19. Same sources as in n. 17.

casionally, in what apparently are unusually grave instances, are the guilty individuals punished.[20]

That the outright price violations have some allocative and distributive significance has already been noted. Yet one may doubt the gravity of their impact on either the static efficiency or the longer-term progressiveness of the Soviet economy. Of greater importance, especially from the standpoint of progressiveness, would seem to be the price drift of the second kind, that associated with the introduction of new products. The Soviet press and literature carry frequent complaints of unjustifiably high prices on new (not to speak of pseudo-new) products. ("Unjustifiably" here refers to the price-determining regulations in force.) That the practice is very widespread is not to be doubted. While it affects consumer goods at retail as well as producer goods in general and capital goods in particular, some industries clearly contain better opportunities for this kind of price manipulation than do others, and the machinery and equipment industries are foremost in this regard. Most of the published complaints of excessive prices — and correspondingly excessive profitability — of new products pertain to machinery and equipment.

So far as the known facts are concerned, we now fortunately possess a very useful, concise analysis by Becker in regard to machinery prices during 1950–70.[21] Becker begins by noting the striking contradiction be-

20. For example, see *EG,* 1971, no. 23, p. 8, lower panel. Note such reports as the following: "In [1971 and 1972], every third enterprise checked in Kazakhstan had violated state price discipline [including retail prices, and possibly only with regard to goods that are price-controlled at the republic level]. . . . The republic now has 261 commissions for price and marketing control" (*Kazakhstanskaia pravda,* 15 May 1973, as summarized in *ABSEES,* Oct. 1973, p. 15). An outstanding case was the discovery of widespread price-control violations in the furniture factories under the USSR Ministry of Forest and Woodworking industries, where some goods were sold at "willfully arbitrary" (*proizvol'nye*) prices and some enterprises claiming fulfillment of sales plan for 1969 in fact, after price correction, missed them by wide margins (*Sotsialisticheskaia industriia,* 23 May 1970, p. 2). It is interesting to note in this connection that furniture was one of only four commodity groups that fulfilled, or bettered, the output target of the Eighth Five-Year Plan. In the case of furniture the target was in *rubles* and the claimed fulfillment was just 100 percent. Of the three other commodity groups, one — apparatuses, automation equipment, and parts — with a claimed fulfillment of 117.5 percent, also had a target expressed in rubles. See my "From the Eighth to the Ninth Five-Year Plan," in *Analysis of the USSR's 24th Party Congress and 9th Five-Year Plan,* ed. Norton T. Dodge (Mechanicsville, Md., 1971), p. 56. Curiously, Soviet law seems to be ambiguous as to whether the buyer has the right to collect the amount by which he is overcharged owing to an illegal price. Nor does it provide for sanctions against entities other than the producing enterprise (e.g., the ministry or a research institute) that may have had a hand in setting an illegal price. Cf. V. V. Laptev et al., *Pravovye problemy rukovodstva upravleniia otrasl'iu promyshlennosti SSSR* (Moscow, 1973), pp. 353–55; E. Liberman, "Neobkhodimo sobliudat'gosudarstvennuiu distsiplinu v ustanovlenii i primenenii tsen," *Sovetskaia iustitsiia,* 1969, no. 23, pp. 14–15. The above-mentioned ambiguity perhaps reflects an assumption — not unnatural in a command economy — that the price is a matter of relations between the producing enterprise and higher authorities rather than between enterprises.

21. Abraham S. Becker, *Ruble Price Levels and Dollar-Ruble Ratios of Soviet Machinery in the 1960s* (R-1063-DDRE) (Santa Monica: Rand Corporation, Jan. 1973).

tween the fact that the official Soviet index of wholesale prices ("industry level") for the "machinery and metalworking" (MMW) branch declines almost monotonically during the period, and the numerous complaints of rising machinery prices in the same period. He then finds that the MMW price index is a sample index with fixed weights that takes little or no account of new products. Since the prices of "old" machines are subject to occasional reduction, the downward movement of the index is explainable by the method of its construction. On the other hand, new machinery and equipment are constantly put into production and sold at allegedly relatively high prices, so that a more comprehensive index of machinery prices (however it might be constructed in view of the rapid turnover in the commodity mix) might well show a rise for the period. On the basis of quite sketchy evidence, recognized by him as such, Becker estimates that machinery[22] prices may have risen 25 percent from 1958 to 1970, and specifically as follows: 7 percent in 1959, 2 percent per year to 1966, none in 1967, and 1 percent per year from 1968 to 1970. It is of course hard to tell to what extent the inflation in machinery prices is attributable, not to lawful price increases, but to illegal bending of price-setting rules by the producers and other violations. Yet Soviet sources do give a strong impression that to a large extent this is the case, abetted by the impotence of the buyer in a seller's market to successfully oppose such practices and by the inability of the price-controllers to adequately monitor so complex an industry as machine building, with a very large, varied, and rapidly changing product mix.

In sum, by dint of outright violations or thanks to various legal exceptions and loopholes, when the administrative controls fail to function, Soviet prices are prone to rise. The buyer's countervailing power is typically low compared with that of the seller, nor need he even have much incentive in opposing price increases.[23]

The Price Reform of 1966–67

This is a major landmark in the history of Soviet price formation. The new prices had been in preparation since the beginning of the 1960s and were supposed to have been introduced on several early occasions (1963, 1965), but the task was delayed by disagreements of both theoretical and practical kinds, by the change in leadership in 1964, and by the

22. Becker points out that it is not clear whether munitions are included under "machinery" either in this estimate or in the official Soviet price index.

23. The buyer's weakness and apathy in the face of price increases is of course frequently mentioned in Soviet sources. For a particularly trenchant statement see L. V. Braginskii, "Voprosy khozraschetnoi otvetstvennosti," *Finansy SSSR,* 1974, no. 3, p. 40, and for an authoritative one see Sitnin (supra n. 11), p. 309.

enormity of the job itself.[24] At last, on 1 October 1966 and 1 January 1967, new price lists went into effect for light industry, and on 1 July 1967 for heavy industry. (Retail prices were not affected at the time.) These price lists have since been extensively supplemented and revised – most recently in the case of ferrous products as of 1 January 1972, light industry and much of machine-building as of 1 January 1973, and railroad rates as of 1 January 1974 – although the principles of the 1966–67 Reform apparently still stand, by and large. While the new principles allow us to speak of a price *reform* rather than a mere price recalculation or *revision* (*peresmotr*), it would be too much to claim that the Soviet price structure was radically altered as a result. Wholesale prices of industrial products remain very largely set by central or republican price boards specially charged with this task, and, with some significant exceptions that will be mentioned later, are not subject to determination by the mutual agreement of seller and buyer. No concerted attempt is made to bring the fixed prices to equilibrium levels, and materials and equipment are subject to about the same degree and rigor of central allocation (rationing) as before. Whether under these circumstances prices are now better measures of the relative scarcity of individual goods (in a static-efficiency sense) is not immediately apparent to the outside observer, although they may be better on other scores.

A good discussion of the 1966–67 Price Reform is to be found in Schroeder's article, while the quantitative changes in the prices of commodities and commodity groups are conveniently brought together in a note by Minnich.[25] Hence, the summary to follow will be brief.

As in the case of previous across-the-board price recomputations, the 1966–67 Reform aimed to eliminate both the losses and the very high profits that had characterized many enterprises and some whole industries (in the case of losses, notably the coal industry.)[26] In this regard the reform introduced two novel features, however. First, average profit

24. Regarding attempts at price revision between 1960 and 1964 see Morris Bornstein, "The 1963 Soviet Industrial Price Revision," *Soviet Studies,* 15, no. 1 (July 1963): 43–52; his "Soviet Price Theory and Policy" in U.S. Congress, Joint Economic Committee, *New Directions in the Soviet Economy,* Part I (Washington: US GPO, 1966), esp. pp. 73–74; and Haffner (supra n. 3), pp. 284ff.

25. Gertrude E. Schroeder, "The 1966–67 Soviet Industrial Price Reform: A Study in Complications," *Soviet Studies,* 20, no. 4 (April 1969): 462–77; Barbara S. Minnich, "Materials on the Soviet Price Reform of July 1967," *ASTE Bulletin,* 10, no. 2 (Fall 1968): 12–19. The actual 1966–67 price lists apparently have not been published for general use, contrary to the practice in some previous price revisions. It has been said that altogether 717 price lists for industrial products were issued as part of the Price Reform; of these, 200 had been confirmed by the SPB at the union level, 387 by price boards at the republic level, and 130 by ministries and departments (*vedomstva*), *Ekomonicheskaia gazeta,* suppl. *Khoziaistvennaia reforma v SSSR* (Moscow, 1969).

26. It was said that the Price Reform reduced the number of industrial enterprises working at a loss by one half, accounting for only 4 percent of sales, A. N. Komin, *Problemy planovogo tsenoobrazovaniia* (Moscow, 1971), p. 84.

margins were very considerably widened in order to accommodate the simultaneously introduced "payment for funds"—i.e., interest on fixed and working assets, typically at 6 percent per annum, regarded as a use of profits and not as a cost—and transfers of profit to the three incentive funds established by the 1965 Economic Reform. Second, the profit margin—typically still a markup on average industrywide production cost (*sebestoimost'*) rather than the difference between it and an independently established selling price—is now computed in a new way. It will be recalled that previously profit was computed as a modest markup on *sebestoimost'*, some 3–5 percent at the time of price setting. Now, in accordance with the shift in theoretical conceptions toward a Marxian "production price," the profit margin (still a markup on industrywide average cost) is computed to be normally 15 percent of the value of fixed plus circulating assets per unit of output for the *industry* as a whole.[27]

While the shift in the course of the 1966–67 Reform from a cost-related to a capital-related markup has received a good deal of attention, it is less well known that it referred primarily to the profit margin for whole industrial branches or commodity groups and not for individual commodities, especially where the product mix is a varied one. In the calculation of the markup for individual commodities a two-step approach was typically used: first, the total desired profit of the branch or commodity group was computed as above; next, this total was distributed to commodities in proportion to *sebestoimost'* or standard value added (*normativnaia stoimost' obrabotki*) or some other category of this kind.[28] This is to say, a kind of compromise was effected with the very real practical difficulty of determining the capital intensity of a given commodity if the industry (or branch) produces a large assortment.[29] Yet there may be some—if unconscious—efficiency payoff to this compromise as well. To

27. The proportionality factor was generally taken to be 15 percent; but in some industries, notably coal, where the price increase was large, it was reduced to avoid an even greater price increase. The economic rationale of such exceptional treatment is of course dubious. It may be added that in these industries the rate of interest on capital investment was correspondingly scaled down. Note the use of an objective criterion here, too. The price received by the individual firm for its product is composed of industrywide average cost plus a mark-up derived from industrywide capital intensity. Thus both the firm's own management and its superior and controlling authorities compare the firm's performance with the general industry standard.

28. See Komin, p. 79. The author is deputy chairman of the SPB and the book clearly represents the Board's official standpoint. See also B. M. Kosminskii, *Sebestoimost' v planovom tsenoobrazovanii* (Moscow, 1972), pp. 29–31, who states that 80 percent of all prices, accounting for 65 percent of gross output of industry (with the extractive industries mostly excepted), were set by the compromise method. In the course of the recomputation of prices in the iron and steel industry, which went into effect on 1 Jan. 1972, the markup for individual commodities was computed in proportion to *labor* cost (*PKh*, 1972, no. 2, p. 141).

29. The economic—and insoluble—problem here is of course that of allocating overhead among joint products.

the extent that product prices have an allocative role for the enterprise through bonuses to management, and insofar as management may have much greater possibility of deploying labor and materials for the production of alternative products than of varying the total investment in the plant, setting the markup on individual goods in relation to the former rather than to the latter makes sense from the standpoint of efficient rules of managerial behavior.[30]

Another well-known feature of the 1966–67 Reform is the introduction of differential rent as one of the components of price in some industries (mainly extractive ones), in which the average cost of production varies greatly from firm to firm. In these industries, a price geared to the average cost of the industry, or even for a region, would leave some firms with very high profits and others with large losses to be made up by the budget. The traditional Soviet answer to this problem has been to set prices individually for each firm, so as to cover its costs and provide a small profit (*raschetnye tseny,* "accounting prices"), and to sell the good at a nationally or regionally uniform price to buyers, so as to equalize *their* cost conditions. The price equalization is performed by an intermediary organization. This practice turned out to be unsatisfactory for a variety of reasons, which will not be spelled out here.

Although the "accounting prices" still remain in effect in some industries, the new solution is to set the price of the product considerably above the average cost for the industry (or region), though below the cost of the marginal firm(s). Thus, the marginal firm(s) still have to be subsidized, but the now even larger profits of the low-cost producers are at least partly captured by a kind of royalty payment to the budget for each unit produced, the "fixed payment" – so called because it remains constant per unit of the product for each firm for some period of time. Economic rent is the subject of a separate essay in this volume; there is no need for me to delve deeper into this matter. Suffice it to say that in principle the solution is new in Soviet practice only as regards industry, for it is analogous to the long-standing Soviet practice of collecting rent in agriculture, though with a technical difference. In agriculture, rent has been collected by varying procurement or purchase prices, setting them lower (per unit of farm product) in the lower-cost regions and higher in the higher-cost regions. The difference between the prices is the difference in the implicit rent. In industry under the new arrangement, price received by all firms is nominally uniform, but out of it the firms pay "fixed payments" of varying amounts (including zero) per unit product.

---

30. See the discussion of this point by Bertrand Horwitz, *Accounting Controls and the Soviet Economic Reform of 1966* [sic], American Accounting Association, Studies in Accounting Research No. 4 (Evanston, Ill., 1970), ch. 9, where he draws interesting parallels with intrafirm arrangements in the United States. For similar reasons, Komin, pp. 80–81, would relate profitability to wage cost alone.

The higher the "fixed payment," the lower the net unit revenue to the producer, so that the price to the seller is actually not uniform as between sellers. Thus, the new method of collecting differential rent in industry, like the traditional method in agriculture, presumably entails those allocative inefficiencies that we generally associate with non-uniform product prices (insofar as average unit revenue at all enters into calculations for allocative purposes, as it probably does in many cases). A lump-sum annual payment of economic rent would conform better to the requisites of allocative efficiency,[31] "second best" conundrums apart. In any case, the chief objective of the new fixed-payment charge in Soviet industry would seem to be the prevention of undue accumulations of profits and liquid funds in enterprise hands (and the alternative of large subventions to high-cost firms) rather than the enhancement of allocative efficiency as understood elsewhere.

The introduction under the 1965 Economic Reform of an interest charge—"payment for funds"—on the value of assets in the enterprise has already been noted. In this case, too, the purpose seems to be less broadly allocative than administrative; namely, as an incentive against asset hoarding. Yet, given its moderate level (6 percent, and sometimes lower) and the general insensitivity of the Soviet enterprise to cost, the antihoarding significance of the interest charge can be doubted.

A curious detail is that apparently some attention was given in the course of the 1966–67 Price Reform to the relation of the new internal prices of certain materials to prices in major Western markets. To my knowledge such concern had not been openly expressed at the time of any previous wholesale price revision since the start of the Plan Era. Thus Komin:

> A necessary stage in the justification of [the new] price levels is comparison with prices of similar products abroad and on the world market. It should be noted that not enough attention is given to this in actual price setting. Comparison with world prices is a necessary element of the economic analysis of the levels of cost and price. If [specific] internal prices are above world prices, then it is necessary to inquire into the reasons.[32]

He goes on to discuss this relation for various commodity groups. Finding that internal Soviet prices for products of extractive industries tend to be above world prices, he adds:

> The problem of bringing the prices of products of extractive indus-

---

31. This point is well made by Robert W. Campbell in his "Price, Rent, and Decision-making: The Economic Reform in Soviet Oil and Gas Production," *Jahrbuch der Wirtschaft Osteuropas,* 2 (Munich: Olzog, 1971): 249ff.
32. Komin (supra n. 26), pp. 127–28.

tries closer to world prices can be solved primarily by lowering costs via increased labor productivity.[33]

Komin offers no explanation of the implied desideratum that internal prices be close to world (i.e., Western) prices, nor any indication of the exchange rate at which the comparison is or should be made. Yet in view of past Soviet practice it is significant that the question is posed at all.[34]

With one exception, external prices do not at this time determine in any direct way the internal wholesale prices of either importables or exportables,[35] a condition that does not contribute to efficiency in resource allocation for well-known reasons.[36] Yet, at a time of considerable inflation in the outside world it does help maintain — occasionally with the help of subsidies from the budget, to be sure — the prized stability of internal wholesale prices.

Distributive and allocative effects of prices

As mentioned, the combined effect of the 1965 Economic Reform and the 1966–67 Price Reform may have been to increase the distributive

33. Komin, p. 128.

34. By sketchy appearances, the question seems to have been raised particularly in regard to nonferrous metals. Thus, for no obvious reason, a major descriptive work dealing with post-1967 prices mentions, with a transparent tone of approval, that prices on nonferrous metals "have been brought considerably closer to those in capitalist markets," and follows the statement with figures that show that the ratio of lead to zinc prices in the USSR was reduced (presumably by the 1967 reform) from 2.1 to 1.2, which compares with the same ratio (date unspecified) of 1.02 in the United States (K. N. Plotnikov and A. S. Gusarov, *Sovremennye problemy teorii i praktiki tsenoobrazovaniia pri sotsializme,* Moscow, 1971, p. 409). Similarly a monograph on the economics of the nonferrous industry states, also for no obvious reason, that "prices for rare metals (selenium, tellurium, gallium, etc.) have been brought closer to world prices" and follows this up with a table showing Soviet prices for nine nonferrous metals before and after the 1967 change and New York or London prices of 1968. The range of the Soviet:Western price ratios (post-reform) is over 3:1. S. A. Pervushin et al., *Ekonomika tsvetnoi metallurgii SSSR* (Moscow, 1970), pp. 377–79. I am grateful to Murray Feshbach for drawing my attention to this source.

35. Cf. Mitrofanova in *PKh,* 1973, no. 9, pp. 90–97, where this absence of a direct link in the USSR is contrasted with the current practice in nearly all the other East European countries. The exception is imported machinery that has no domestic analogues; this carries domestic prices equal to foreign prices multiplied by special conversion rates set by the SPB (*PKh,* 1973, no. 2, p. 81).

36. In the event, it manifests itself in the frequent difficulty of inducing enterprises to pay due attention to production for export where the products have relatively low internal prices, particularly in view of the quality requirements for export. Cf. G. M. Zhukovskii, "O stimulirovanii proizvodstva eksportnoi produktsii," *Ekonomika i organizatsiia promyshlennogo proizvodstva,* 1972, no. 6, pp. 243–48, and A. D. Leznik, "Ekonomicheskoe stimulirovanie produktsii dlia eksporta," ibid., 1971, no. 4, pp. 183–89. Cf. also N. Smeliakov (former head of Amtorg), "Delovye vstrechi," *Novyi mir,* 1973, no. 12, p. 220: "The material, administrative, and other responsibility [by enterprises] for export deliveries render exporting unpopular under our conditions. . . . At the end of the sixties, after additional incentives had been introduced, we expected numerous suggestions [for exports] to be initiated by [enterprise directors]. However, there were only a few such cases. Things have changed little to date."

effect of wholesale prices or, more accurately, of changes in prices. In any case, taking into account both the original economic reform and subsequent amendments, an industrial enterprise and its staff (especially managerial staff) stand to gain in the following respects from higher product prices:

(a) Improvement in the performance record in what are now the chief overall success indicators: sales, profit, profitability (in relation to assets), and—now again—value of gross output;[37]
(b) Relaxation of the constraint that the absolute amount of profit may impose on the formation of incentive funds;
(c) Increase in the labor-productivity indicator, which is measured in relation to gross value of output;
(d) Eligibility for higher wage withdrawals from the Gosbank, which are geared to gross output.

No doubt other ways in which higher prices are advantageous to the Soviet enterprise—and, more to the point, personally beneficial to its management—could be cited. In sum, we should expect attempts by enterprises to obtain higher prices for their products, and there is ample evidence that they do so on a very large scale indeed.

It should be noted that higher product prices per se are advantageous to the enterprise and its management—insofar as they raise value of gross output, value of sales, labor productivity, etc.—quite apart from the effect on profit. Despite some early indications to this effect, profit did not emerge from the 1965 Economic Reform as a leading synthetic success indicator, and its relative importance has been declining through the successive "perfectionings" of the reform. Its chief importance—not a minor one, to be sure—now seems to lie in that it feeds the various enterprise incentive funds; it is thus a necessary condition for the payment of bonuses, etc., and may limit them if the absolute amount of profit is insufficient. If the absolute amount is sufficient, though, additional profit is surrendered by the enterprise to the treasury, as already noted. It follows that the enterprise is often much less sensitive to cost than to product price. A reduction in cost increases profit; an equivalent increase in sales revenue thanks to higher prices does the same *and* much more for the enterprise and its management. For the Soviet director a kopek saved is worth much less than a kopek earned.

More than that: frequently the expenditure on equipment or materials is not even a charge on the cost of production or a subtraction from potential profits, as in the case of equipment and supplies for capital invest-

37. Cf. V. Kirichenko in *PKh*, 1970, no. 5, p. 9. V. Ashkinadze (ibid., p. 91) makes the point that enterprises are sometimes driven to raise prices by pressure to fulfill overambitious sales plans.

ment that is financed by the budget or the bank, development that is financed out of the ministry's "fund for the assimilation of new technology," and other forms of extramurally financed or subsidized activity. In such cases the buyer has virtually no pecuniary concern with the price of the equipment or material. Lastly, as has been well documented in the literature, the Soviet firm may even have a perverse interest in higher input prices, because cost increases can often be "passed through" to higher product prices, to the benefit of the firm's success indicators and the personal gain of its staff.[38]

Under such conditions the task of the price controllers is a difficult one indeed. No wonder then that one of the more daring proposals to be advanced in responsible quarters in the USSR in recent years has lately come from just this quarter. Writing in early 1974, the director of the research institute of the SPB has proposed that the automatic capture of the uncommitted portion of enterprise profit (the "free remainder") by the fisc be superseded by the division of profit between the enterprise and the fisc in a certain predetermined proportion:[39]

> Then every worker would know that from each ruble of accounting (*raschetnoi*) profit of the enterprise, from each ruble's worth of unexpended materials, electricity, etc., so many kopeks will go into the material incentive fund [i.e., for bonuses]. . . . The price increment for higher product quality and the discount for product obsolescence would then become palpable for every employee, which in turn will strengthen the stimulating force of price.

38. An exception to the general picture of cost insensitivity on the demand side may occur at the "project making" (engineering design) stage of capital investment. There is supposedly effort made to hold down both the capital cost and per-unit materials cost of the project; consequently, prices of equipment and materials are presumably "active" in shaping the designers' choices. We do not know enough about decision making at this stage; but we do know from many accounts in the Soviet literature that the designers' cost estimates are subject to very large "overruns," so that decisions taken in the course of project making are presumably not definitive and final.

39. Iu. Iakovets, "Tsena — vazhnyi ekonomicheskii rychag," *EG*, 1974, no. 8, p. 13. The title, "price is an important economic instrument," is itself significant in this connection. Some months earlier there appeared an article by Vs. Sitnin (not to be confused with Vladimir D. Sitnin, chairman of the SPB since its formation in 1965) constituting a strong plea for the supersession of the "free remainder" arrangement by a structure of proportional or progressive profit taxes in groups of raising incentives in enterprises for earning profits and reducing costs ("Raspredelenie pribyli i effektivnost' proizvodstva," *Voprosy ekonomiki* [hereinafter *VE*], 1973, no. 9, 22–31). Sitnin supports his case with reference to similar schemes already in effect or under consideration in other East European countries. He also points to the experiment, in effect since mid-1970, in the Ministry for Apparatuses, Means of Automation, and Control Systems, whereby the ministry shares additional profits with the budget; however, the author finds this experiment to be rather inconclusive, owing to some of its particular features. On the experiment see K. Rudnev (the minister), "Puti povysheniia effektivnosti raboty otrasli," *Kommunist*, 1972, no. 11, pp. 26–38.

This proportion must be firmly guaranteed to the enterprise in order to produce the incentive effect. The author of the proposal states that such a system has already been adopted with regard to the quality supplements to prices in the case of products that earn the certificate (*attestat*) of highest quality, which was introduced in 1971.[40] Should the replacement of profit capture by a profit tax succeed in making enterprises significantly more cost conscious, the buyer's interest in observing fixed prices may increase, although this would depend on the tax schedule as well as on the many other factors that today contribute to the lack of cost and profit sensitivity. On the other hand, a heightened profit consciousness may also raise the seller's incentive to violate price limits. Still, it would seem to be a step in the right direction if the use of prices by the SPB as an instrument variable (the "flexibility" part of the formula) is to be at all effective.

Returning to the existing situation, we must bear in mind the motivational asymmetry: the buyer's concern with a price increase (or simple overcharge) is likely to be much less intense than the seller's interest in obtaining the price increase, quite apart from the asymmetry in physical terms owing to the usual difficulty of obtaining supplies as contrasted with the relative ease of disposing of them. That this situation amounts to a potential (and potent) engine of inflation need hardly be stressed, and any significant relaxation of controls is likely to have just this effect. Therefore, insofar as the authorities may deem it advisable to relax controls for instrumental purposes, they not only must proceed with caution so as to contain the inflationary tendencies within acceptable bounds, but will find the instrumental use of prices almost always more effective in controlling the behavior of the producer/seller than of the buyer/user (within the state sector). Judging by the evidence of the post-1965 period, the authorities appear to have learned both of these lessons.[41] As already noted, they have chosen to use prices instrumentally primarily in the two areas where producer resistance has traditionally been rather effective

40. On quality certification see Schroeder, (supra n. 12), pp. 20–22. On the problem of quality generally see also Martin C. Spechler, "Decentralizing the Soviet Economy: Legal Regulation of Price and Quality," *Soviet Studies*, 22, no. 2 (Oct. 1970): 222–54.

41. Thus, in his definitive study of economic decision making in Soviet metal-fabricating industry, David Granick writes (with reference to the pre-1965 period) that "prices for new [machinery] products are kept low because . . . it is believed that prices which are too high would penalize the adoption of new technology. Doubtlessly this is true in many cases, but one might hazard the guess that Soviet pricing principles have been established in terms of a miscalculation as to the location of the main resistance to new products: prime attention is given to overcoming consumer rather than producer resistance. There has been some movement over time away from this emphasis . . . but it still remains basic." Granick, *Soviet Metal-Fabricating and Economic Development: Practice versus Policy* (Madison: Univ. of Wisconsin Press, 1967), p. 235. Despite the shift in emphasis noted in the text, the notion that low prices on new types of equipment spur technical progress remains very much alive in the Soviet literature.

in thwarting administrative measures to raise firm behavior to more acceptable levels — namely, product innovation, especially in the machine-building industries, and quality improvement in all other industries.

Instrumental use of prices

The use of price as an "economic lever" toward ends such as the ones just listed is not an entirely new idea in Soviet history.[42] But the stress placed on it since 1965 in official pronouncements, and in the press and literature in general, seems to be of a new order. It echoes similar themes that had received much publicity in other East European countries some years earlier (e.g., in East Germany, where "lever" — *Hebel* — has been a favored term). Now it is also cloaked with the meliorative term "flexibility."

The policy was adumbrated in Kosygin's report to the Central Committee Plenum on the Economic Reform of 1965:

> Prices are also [i.e., in addition to "reflecting socially necessary outlays" and feeding incentive funds] called upon to play a large role in solving problems relating to the improvement of product quality and the rational durability and reliability goods. Therefore, price setting on new and better articles must take into account both the additional expenses of the producers and the economic effect which will be obtained by the users in using the better products. In such a case, producers will have a greater incentive in improving their output, while users will find it economically advantageous to use it.[43]

The ensuing Resolution of the CC CPSU and CM USSR, dated 4 October 1965, devoted a lengthy section to prices, echoed Kosygin's remarks on this subject, and spoke of price supplements (*nadbavki, doplaty*) to compensate producers for the additional expenses required to introduce newer and better products and to give them additional incentive to do so. In anticipation of things to come, it related these measures to the setting of new industrial standards.[44] We find a substantial development of these ideas in the SPB chairman's important report to the 1968 Conference,[45] to which we will have occasion to refer yet again, and officially sanctioned anew in the Resolution of the CM USSR on

---

42. Thus, *constant* 1926/27 prices were apparently manipulated on some occasions, when the firm's chief success indicator was gross output in constant prices, to affect the product mix. For an indication of such in connection with the rearmament effort on the eve of World War II, see my note, "A Small New Light on 1926/27 Prices," *ASTE Bulletin*, 9, no. 2 (Fall 1967): 30–31.

43. *Pravda*, 28 Sept. 1965, p. 3.

44. *Resheniia partii i pravitel'stva po khoziaistvennym voprosam*, vol. 5, 1962–1965, pp. 681–83.

45. Sitnin (supra n. 11).

". . . Improving Wholesale Prices on Products of Heavy Industry . . . in 1971–1975."[46]

Lastly, if they are to have some effect on enterprise behavior, the incentives associated with price differentials should be substantial—and they are. Up to 70 percent of the additional profit realized from lawfully established wholesale-price supplements for higher-quality goods can be transferred to the producing enterprise's incentive funds.[47] In the case of quality supplements to retail prices, which may remain in effect for up to two years, their incentive feature is that up to 15 percent of the value of the supplements can be set aside in special accounts for the payment of bonuses to *individuals* directly partaking in the planning and the startup of production (*razrabotka i osvoenie*) of the higher-quality consumer goods.[48] In both cases the size of the incentive payments is a function of sales, and not of the technical or design work alone. There must be buyers.

The instrumental use of price is of course a form of control (guidance) of the economy. Like much traditional Soviet planning it is microeconomic control, but unlike the traditional kind, it operates with value variables and not with quantity (physical) variables. It does not rely on direct orders; rather, it depends on indirect effects transmitted through a cost-profit calculus and the incentive structure, though with a large admixture of administrative control (as is of course inevitable with microeconomic guidance). The contrast is also organizational. Quantitative directives are within the competence of Gosplan, Gossnab, the State Board of Standards, etc. Prices are within the competence of the SPB and the territorial structure of price-setting organs below it.[49] But there are also serious limits to the SPB's competence owing to the very nature of price. Every price is a ratio in which the numerator is in the money unit and the denominator is in a physical unit. This denominator—the physical specification of the good—is often within the competence of another department, such as the State Board of Standards. Since prices and technical standards frequently have to be set simultaneously, a great deal of coordination between the SPB and the State Board of Standards (and

46. *Resheniia*, vol. 8, 1970–Feb. 1972 (Moscow, 1972), p. 537: "to increase the role of prices in the stimulation of technical progress and the raising of product quality, and to create the economic conditions which will promote the timely replacement of old products by new, the raising of the motivation of enterprises to produce and to utilize new and more efficient equipment and materials, and to end the production of obsolescent articles." Almost identical formulations are found in other official texts and in many articles.

47. *PKh*, 1973, no. 10, p. 6. Legal regulations in *EG*, 1969, no. 27, p. 10.

48. Ibid., p. 8. Originally limited to one year, the duration of the quality supplements to retail prices (at least in light industry) was extended to two years by decision of SPB in mid-1974 (*EG*, 1974, no. 27, p. 16).

49. Regarding the administrative structure see Haffner (supra n. 3), pp. 162ff., and V. N. Ershov, "Sovershenstvovanie gosudarstvennogo upravleniia tsenoobrazovaniem," *Sovetskoe gosudarstvo i pravo*, 1971, no. 5, pp. 62ff.

possibly other departments) is required. Price control necessitates quality control from above.[50] If one or the other authority delays action in a specific case, the producing and transacting units in the economy may be stymied, for no transaction can lawfully take place if the good in question does not have a lawfully set price.[51]

In general, delay in the setting of prices by the appropriate bodies is a frequent occurrence, according to many complaints in the literature. The delays are most likely to affect new goods and special, one-time jobs; hence, in these cases there is special reason to delegate the determination of prices to entities on the operating level. Thus, only half a year after the completion of the 1967 Price Reform the chairman of the SPB wrote, looking ahead:

> It is necessary to give some thought to how [to avoid undue delays] one could broaden the powers of enterprises in setting specific prices, while preserving the mechanism of centralized direction of price formation. We see the way out in working out a set of economically justified standards (*normativy*) of costs and profit margins by types of product. With such — systematically reexamined — standards the enterprises would be able to determine prices for their changing product assortments, while conforming to the government's policy in regard to prices and their existing level.[52]

The problem of "new technology"

The problem of "new technology" — of technical modernization and renovation of product capacity, technological progress, ability to produce technically up-to-date equipment, ability to operate it successfully, and related matters — goes back to the dawn of Soviet history. There is no need to recount the story here. Suffice it to note that despite all the economic and technical progress of the past half century, the problem does not seem to have waned in importance or urgency in the minds of the Soviet leaders. Lately, it has been linked with the so-called technology gap vis-à-vis the West, with national goals of military power and ideological prestige, with the stepped-up purchases of Western equipment and know-how, and with the overall objective of rapid economic progress at home. At the same time the depletion of internal reserves for the traditional "extensive" form of economic growth since the beginning of the seventies has added urgency to technical progress. In terms of economic performance, the problem of "new technology" is tied up with the allegedly unsatisfactory payoff from the massive Soviet effort in

50. This much is of course true of price control under any economic system.
51. *Resheniia*, vol. 7, p. 381.
52. Sitnin in *EG*, 1968, no. 6, p. 11.

research and development, the long-standing and deeply ingrained resistance to product innovation at the factory level, and other difficulties of a systemic character.

Crucial to the understanding of this complex of problems is an appreciation of the role that the Soviet machine-building industry (MB) plays in the process of innovation. This role is rather different from the role played by the corresponding industry in a developed Western country. It is much less active—one might even say passive. The industry's objective—as with all Soviet industries—is to fulfill its plan, and the same is true of every firm or association in it. The firm (association) is virtually assured of takers for its products to the limits of its capacity. It does not have to search out markets, invent new types of equipment or new uses for old types, or engage in a competitive struggle for markets. It is little concerned with the production and commercial problems of its customers, does not usually try to anticipate them, and has little interest in supplying follow-up services and technical advice. (These shortcomings have attended, for instance, the introduction of computers in the Soviet economy.) Typically, the MB firm does not have its own research and development facilities, while the research institutes have concerned themselves little with production problems and even less with the problems of marketing their brainchildren. Thus, innovation and technological progress in regard to its products and to its own processes are not actively sought by the MB firm; they are largely foisted on it from above (planning authorities) or from the side (research and development institutes). Hence, the chronic difficulty of making MB firms adopt the production of new types of machinery and abandon the production of obsolete types.[53]

In contrast, the role that Western MB firms play in technical progress and innovation is a much more active one, thanks to competition, the search for markets and consequent attention to customers' needs, and the direct involvement in research and development by many firms. In fact, in the West, individual MB firms are major generators and diffusers of technical progress and innovation. This contrast between the dynamic roles of the Soviet and Western MB industries is certainly overdrawn and oversimplified. There are important exceptions to the rule on both sides. But it seems to be accurate *grosso modo*. What is more, it comes close to the image that Soviet authorities have of their own MB industry. Con-

53. There is a sizable Western literature on the problem of innovation in the Soviet economy (not to mention the enormous Soviet one). Among the most useful works is Eugène Zaleski et al., *Science Policy in the USSR* (Paris: OECD, 1969), especially part V (by R. Amann, M. J. Berry, and R. W. Davies). Very helpful also is Granick, esp. pp. 232ff. Certain aspects were treated by me in Grossman, "Innovation and Information in the Soviet Economy," *AER* 56, no. 2 (May 1966): 118–30.

sequently, remedial measures have to a large extent focused on injecting greater dynamism and initiative into the operations of the Soviet machine-building industry; in other words, they have focused on shaping the behavior of the equipment *producer.*

Typically, the remedial measures have comprised the Soviet syndrome of directives, controls, sanctions, subsidies, and—increasingly in recent years—monetary incentives to persons who are or might be directly involved in the process of technical advance and innovation. To be sure, the user of new technology has also been subject to directives and controls (such as the rather ineffectual "plans for new technology" imposed annually since 1948 on enterprises),[54] but because he is weaker than the producer, and in any case has less reason to resist the appearance of the new machine, the user has been less subjected to lures of pecuniary advantage and personal monetary reward than the producer.

In regard to pricing, the problem (as under price control in any economic system) has centered on those items of machinery and equipment for which there are yet no established prices and whose average unit cost, the basis of such a price, is difficult to determine. This group includes new types of machinery and equipment intended for "serial" production, one-time (*razovye*) articles, and experimental items. In such cases the authorities face a number of difficulties in arriving at a price for the machine:

(a) There may be little precedent in regard to price, average unit cost under conditions of normal production is yet uncertain, and such cost information as may be already available is under the control of the producer, who is not disinterested in the outcome.[55]

(b) The facts just mentioned under (a) are likely to considerably protract the procedure of price setting by the central (or republic) authorities, and thus slow down and often block the whole process of innovation.

(c) Given the many impediments and disincentives faced by the innovator in the Soviet economy, only a relatively high price on the new article (direct subsidies apart) can typically provide sufficient pecuniary incentive to induce the enterprise to proceed and persist with product innovation. But this has inflationary implications.

(d) As already repeatedly noted, the countervailing power of the buyer is too weak to arrest such an inflationary push. Nonetheless, if his price-

---

54. See Grossman, ibid.
55. Thus, in the similar case of Poland, "the prices of the means of production are mostly based on cost estimates submitted by enterprises. . . . all estimates are inflated by at least 30 percent. The higher levels of the hierarchy are not able to scrutinize the estimates properly . . ." *Zycie gospodarcze,* 15 April 1973, pp. 1, 8; here quoted from summary in *ABSEES* (Glasgow), 4, no. 1 (39), p. 202.

elasticity of demand for the new machine is something less than zero, then (it is often stated) the high prices of new equipment may deter him from buying it, to the detriment of technical progress.[56] (In so arguing, Soviet sources frequently imply that technical progress is an end in itself almost regardless of its cost.)

(e) Moreover, such an inflation feeds on itself in the long run, in that the high-priced innovations of today will become the obsolescent machines of tomorrow, which will require replacement by the novelties of the future. Yet, if today's new machine starts its life with a high price, and therefore a large profit margin, which later widens some more as unit cost declines over time (and the price remains constant), the innovation of the future will have to contain an even wider profit margin, and a correspondingly higher price, if its production is to begin in due time replacing today's machine. And if not, then again the process of innovation is hampered.

The early solution (and not only in regard to new *machinery*) was to decentralize the actual setting of prices on new and one-time products to the level of the producer (or his proximate superior, such as a ministry and later a *sovnarkhoz*) for the sake of administrative speed and economic flexibility. These were, and still are, the "provisional" (*vremennye*, often rendered as "temporary") prices. However, to limit the inevitable tendencies for inflation and self-serving abuse under conditions of a pervading and chronic seller's market, three constraints have been attached to the procedure: (1) the prices are to be determined by mutual agreement between seller and buyer (or their proximate superiors); (2) they are to be cost-bound prices with a very narrow profit margin (usually 3–5 percent); and (3) they are to be in effect for a short period of time only (e.g., six months to one year), before they are superseded by permanent prices determined (or at least approved) by the competent price-controlling authority.

Just when provisional prices first appeared on the scene is not clear—one suspects rather early in Soviet history—but it is known that on the eve of the Second World War they were already formally in effect,[57] and with some procedural modifications they remain in existence to the present. They came to be very widely applied. For instance, we are told that in 1964 as much as one-third of all "serial" production of MB was sold

56. The "contradiction" between the interests of the producer of new equipment and those of its potential user (and, hence, the cause of technical progress) has been a recurring theme in the Soviet price literature. Cf. two authoritative statements straddling in time the Economic Reform of 1965: Sh. Ia. Turetskii, *Ocherki planovogo tsenoobrazovaniia v SSSR* (Moscow, 1959), pp. 174–76; and Sitnin (supra n. 11), pp. 308–9. In the absence of a usable microeconomic theory it is indeed difficult to resolve this kind of "contradiction."

57. Hutchings (supra n. 9), p. 18, where a 1941 Soviet source is cited.

at such prices.[58] But the experience proved unsatisfactory, and its wide extent has only served to intensify the criticism.

The most common complaint is that provisional prices tend to be unduly high. It seems that this result has been in part legitimated by the regulations themselves, which defined the relevant cost as the unit of the first year or two of "serial" production, which naturally tends to be relatively high; and in addition some of the initial expenses were allowed to be amortized over as little as a year or two. Thus, in cases in which production costs decline over time, the actual profit margins often widen considerably (which in turn reduces the producers' interest in switching to yet newer products in the future). But the procedure also has given ample scope for cost padding and other abuses by the producers, while the necessary concurrence by the buyers in fact meant very little, owing to the condition of the seller's market.[59] To make things worse yet, the high provisional prices have tended to be perpetuated by being officially confirmed as permanent prices, because the authorities simply have lacked the ability to inquire properly into most individual cases. No wonder, therefore, that the practice has spread widely — it has been highly attractive to the producer, and the producer holds sway.

At the same time and paradoxically, a common complaint has been that provisional prices are sometimes too low, in the sense that the permissible profit margins are too narrow to induce producers to put new articles into production in place of the old ones.[60]

Another difficulty has been that provisional prices are determined only when production is ready to begin, i.e., after the stage of research and development, so that neither the potential producer nor (especially) the potential users have a price that they can include in their calculations. Further, it has been pointed out that provisional prices do not take the user's conditions into account, i.e., they are not demand prices and do not fully reflect the user's economic rent. (The last point is of course more consistent with the charge that the prices are too low than that they are too high.) Lastly, they often cause identical articles produced by different enterprises to carry different prices.

58. P. S. Mstislavskii, M. G. Gabrieli, and Iu. V. Borozdin, *Ekonomicheskoe obosnovanie optovykh tsen na novuiu promyshlennuiu produktsiiu* (Moscow, 1968), p. 9; *Tekstil'naia promyshlennost'*, 1968, no. 7, p. 19. The Soviet literature on provisional prices, and especially on their irrationalities and their abuse, is by now very large; for a convenient list of their shortcomings see Mstislavskii et al., p. 9.

59. Thus, Sitnin mentions that at the end of 1968 and the beginning of 1969 the SPB refused to register 23 percent of the 1,000 provisional prices submitted to it for registration because they had been overstated, although the buyer's concurrence had been nominally obtained in these cases. (supra n. 11, p. 309). One wonders what proportion of the other 77 percent, though passed by the SPB, might have also been padded.

60. Cf. Granick (supra n. 41), p. 235; his information pertains to the pre-1965 years.

Not surprisingly, therefore, the Resolution on the 1965 Economic Reform called for restricting the scope of application of provisional prices (though it did not specify how),[61] and much of the attention of the SPB since 1967 has gone into supplanting them with something better.

But before turning to the new pricing procedures, let us note that as of the beginning of 1961 there has been in effect a financial instrument for the purpose of holding down the provisional prices of new products in certain industries. This is the Fund for the Assimilation of New Technology (*fond osvoeniia novoi tekhniki*).[62] At first restricted in application to a limited number of branches of industry, its application was extended in 1964 to other branches, so that a large part of civilian industries came to be covered by its provisions thereafter. The funds exist at individual ministries (formerly at *sovnarkhozy*) and are fed by levies on the overall production costs of the individual enterprises. The purpose is to subsidize design, development, and start-up expenses and thereby to exert a downward effect on new-product prices, though of course by dint of some small increase in the costs and prices of products in the given branches generally.[63] Whatever its economic logic, the Fund has not proved to be very successful on its own terms.[64] Nevertheless, the position of the SPB has consistently been and continues to be that the Fund is necessary in order to hold down what would otherwise be unacceptably high prices on new equipment, while such shortcomings as it may have are remedied by further regulatory and normative measures.[65]

New equipment pricing since 1969

Immediately after the completion of the 1966–67 Price Reform, the SPB turned its attention to a thorough revision of procedures governing the setting of prices on new products.[66] To our knowledge, the first major

61. *Resheniia,* vol. 5, p. 638.

62. The phrase can also be rendered as ". . . New Equipment."

63. Concise descriptions of the Fund can be found in Zaleski (supra n. 53), pp. 478–79, and Louvan E. Nolting, *Sources of Financing of Stages of the Research, Development, and Innovation Cycle in the U.S.S.R.* (U.S. Department of Commerce, Bureau of Economic Analysis, Foreign Economic Reports no. 3, Sept. 1973), pp. 29–30. In 1968 the Fund accounted for 16 percent of all the financing of new technology in industry (Nolting). Both sources also speak of other funds used to subsidize the development and production of new equipment.

64. For critiques of the Fund in Soviet sources see L. Maizenberg, in *VE,* 1970, no. 6, p. 6; Komin, *Problemy,* pp. 151–52; and A. A. Vilkov in V. P. D'iachenko, *Obshchestvenno neobkhodimye zatraty truda, sebestoimost', i rentabel'nost'* (Moscow, 1963), pp. 197–213.

65. Cf. Sitnin, in *EG,* 1968, no. 6, p. 11; Komin, in *EG,* 1974, no. 11, p. 10, where he advocates, inter alia, that profit margin be added to the sums disbursed from the Fund to an enterprise in order to induce greater resort to the Fund.

66. Cf. L. Maizenberg, p. 4, and in *EG,* 1969, no. 1, pp. 24–25. Even earlier the SPB began to tighten up on provisional prices. In 1966 their application was limited to goods whose

measure to emerge from these efforts was a directive (*Instruktivnye ukazaniia*) pertaining to prices on one-time (i.e., custom-built) articles, issued by the SPB on 23 December 1968.[67] The calculational rules laid down by the directive did not deviate greatly from the old ones governing provisional prices, except for the significant change of widening the profit margin from 5 to 10–20 percent over expected unit cost. The main attention of the directive was focused on the definition of one-time products in order to minimize the common abuse of pricing serial products as though they were custom-ordered.

More important practically and conceptually much more innovating was the measure promulgated by the SPB on 23 June 1969 under the title of Methodology for Determining Wholesale Prices for New Producer Goods and Equipment (*Metodika opredeleniia optovykh tsen na novuiu produktsiiu proizvodstvenno-tekhnicheskogo naznacheniia,* hereinafter the 1969 Methodology).[68] The conceptual novelties, albeit not consistently applied, included what the Western economist would recognize as supply and demand prices, economic rent, its division between seller and buyer, and a marginalist approach to its determination.

The 1969 Methodology classified all new products within its purview into three groups. Group I comprises those items which are intended to replace, or at least to be mutually substitutable with, equipment already in production and operation. Group II consists of items that are similar to existing ones but differ from them in regard to some technical and economic parameters (such as horsepower rating, hourly capacity, etc.). Although the 1969 Methodology and the subsequent Soviet literature treat the two groups as mutually exclusive, this would not seem to be necessarily the case. The point is important because the two groups are subject to completely different methodologies. Finally, Group III comprises products (equipment) that are so different from any already produced in the USSR as to fall outside the first two groups.

---

production was new to the USSR as a whole (not just to the given enterprise or ministry) and which are "truly new." The term of their legal existence was shortened. Compulsory registration of provisional prices with the SPB was introduced. The SPB was to check cost calculations and the claimed novelty of the product. "Thanks to these measures the number of provisional prices set by ministries and departments fell sharply." Komin, *Problemy,* pp. 150–51.

67. *EG,* 1969, no. 1, pp. 24–25.

68. Summary in *EG,* 1969, no. 31, p. 11. Komin, *Problemy,* pp. 156ff., essentially reproduces its provisions. See also Michael J. Lavelle, "The Soviet 'New Method' Pricing Formulae," *Soviet Studies,* 26, no. 1, (Jan. 1974): 81–97. Note should be taken of SPB's Directives of 31 Aug. 1972 regarding the setting of prices on experimental prototypes and prototype batches of new producer goods and equipment intended for serial production. *EG,* 1972, no. 39, p. 22.

Group I. Here price is to be somewhere within a range defined by a "lower limit" and an "upper limit" — respectively akin to our concepts of supply and demand price. The method requires, first, selection (presumably by the producer) of an extant piece of equipment which will serve as the standard of comparison for the new product, the so-called basic product. The lower limit then is said to be that price at which the *producer* is indifferent between the proposed new article and the basic article. (What if the prospective producer of the new item does not already manufacture anything that can reasonably serve as such a standard of comparison? The literature seems to bypass this possibility.) More precisely — though this is not exactly the same thing — the lower limit is defined as the expected unit cost of the new item during the *second* year of serial production plus the prescribed profit margin for the given branch of industry (and sometimes certain other adjustments). Development expenses and the extra cost of the first year of serial production are to be covered by the above-discussed Fund for the Assimilation of New Technology and from other sources. The upper limit is computed according to a rather complicated formula[69] — omitted here as not essential for present purposes — which aims to arrive at combined savings in terms of capital outlays and capitalized current costs on a user's part if he opts for the new piece of equipment in lieu of the basic one. What is more, the 1969 Methodology apparently provided that in the event of multiple uses for a limited supply of the product it is the use with the lowest effect — i.e., the marginal use — that defines the upper limit.[70] In other words, the upper limit is intended to be that level of price at which the purchase and use of the new piece of equipment is equally advantageous with those of the basic article, at the margin. The upper limit is thus a kind of demand price (if the only alternative for the buyers is acquiring the basic piece of equipment).

The difference between the upper and lower limits is designated as the "economic effect" obtainable from the displacement of the basic item by the new item, which is to be divided between the producer and the buyer. The economic effect is thus in a sense the difference between demand price and supply price, or economic rent. This economic rent of course supposes that the only alternative in both production and use to the new piece of equipment is the basic one. It is therefore smaller than the rent that might emerge if other alternatives were admissible and if the rent that might already attach to the basic item were also taken into account.

As an incentive to switch production from the basic product to its replacement, the producer is to receive some part of the economic effect

69. For the formulae see the works of Komin (supra n. 26) and Lavelle, cited in the preceding footnote.
70. *PKh*, 1973, no. 8, p. 10.

in the sales price of the new product; while the part of the economic effect that goes to users—in the form of a differential between the price and the (higher) demand price—is thought of as the portion that is captured by society at large. Accordingly, the economic effect is to be divided not quite evenly; the 1969 Methodology anticipated that 30–50 percent would go to the producer, and 50–70 percent to the user and "society." In the event, the last two seem to have done rather better than that: "in the case of most new goods the producer gets no more than 10–12 percent of the economic effect."[71]

It would take us too far afield to assess fully these methodological provisions.[72] Surely the attempt to relate the price to the economic rent of the new equipment is a most significant departure from the traditional Soviet approach to price formation. Somewhat less novel but nonetheless also significant is the attempt to relate the premium to the producing enterprise to the economy's benefit from the innovation. Given the structure of individual incentives, this comes close to scaling managerial bonuses according to the economy's benefit from the innovation. (Direct premia to inventors and innovators have for some time now been scaled according to the presumed economic effect of the new technology.) There is thus to be found in this instance both a major step toward greater economic rationality and a further affirmation of the principle of material incentive—not an uncommon concomitance during the post-Stalin decades.

At the same time, the method in regard to Group I raises some questions. The binary comparison with some "basic" item is a clumsy one; at the very least, it provides scope for self-serving arbitrariness by interested parties. Further, the method depends on a great deal of information from potential users. Can they be correctly identified in all cases? Can the marginal use be determined? Do the potential users have any significant incentive to cooperate in providing data? Are they usually in a position

71. A. Koshuta (deputy chairman of SPB) and Iu. Borozdin, "Sovershenstvovanie metodiki opredeleniia tsen na novuiu produktsiiu proizvodstvenno-tekhnicheskogo naznacheniia," *PKh,* 1973, no. 8, p. 11. However, the producer may be doing better than these percentages suggest, for the described procedure (and that of parametric price setting, to be discussed presently) "sometimes serve[s] as the excuse for unjustified price increases." Kosminskii (supra n. 28), p. 23.

72. It may be remarked that the method of setting the price between lower and upper limits, as here described, was anticipated in some detail by Mstislavskii et al. (supra n. 58). They spoke of reconciling by means of the price three contradictory interests: those of the producer, the consumer, and society (pp. 15ff). The work set out to develop certain basic principles (including upper and lower limits of price) laid down in a document entitled "Basic Guidelines for a Methodology to Determine Wholesale Prices of New Types of Industrial Output with Reference to Its Technical-Economic Parameters," confirmed by Gosplan on 27 May 1965. Unfortunately the text of the latter document is not available. Soviet sources suggest that its impact was small because of its "academic" character (A. Komin in *PKh,* 1968, no. 4, p. 7).

to do so even if they would? Is there really such a thing as a demand price for a piece of equipment under Soviet conditions? How meaningful are the parameters – prices, depreciation rates, "normative recoupment periods" – of the formula, if the notion of an "economic effect" of an innovation is to be taken really seriously? There are problems with the formula itself, too. Finally it should be noted that the resulting price is not an equilibrium price, being deliberately set below the demand price.

Group II. For new pieces of equipment which differ from existing ones only in some clearly identifiable technical parameter(s) (Group II), we encounter not only a completely different approach but also seemingly quite different objectives. In this case, a mathematical relation is established (by means of regression analysis or the like) between price and the relevant technical parameters, on the basis of the existing types or sizes of equipment. The price for the new item is then computed from the equation. Clearly, the advantage of this approach is its relative simplicity, objectivity (in the sense used earlier in this chapter),[73] and – not least – minimization of leeway in price setting for the producer. But in going from Group I to Group II the 1969 Methodology suddenly abandons the concept of the economic effect of the innovation. The ostensible justification is that the new products in Group II are not mutually substitutable with existing items; yet it is difficult to suppose that this would be invariably the case.[74] Perhaps underlying the distinction is the notion that a Group II product is different from the extant kindred products merely in terms of some technical parameters; it does not incorporate technological progress as such. This being the case, there is supposedly no need to encourage its production and its acceptance in competition with the others. But is it always so?

Group III. The concept of the economic effect seems to be also absent in the Methodology's treatment of price setting in Group III, the case where the new equipment has no present substitutes or analogues with different technical parameters. Here, the familiar cost-plus method was reaffirmed, the profit margin now being the standard one for the given industrial branch (instead of the mere 5 percent previously).

The 1969 Methodology also legitimated a method for automatically

73. However, it does not eliminate all arbitrariness. There is still choice to be made between alternative sets of technical parameters as independent variables in the price relations, not to say allotting the given product to Group I, II, or III.

74. A lengthy discussion of the parametric method of price setting is to be found in Komin, *Problemy,* pp. 161ff. See also Kosminskii (supra n. 28), pp. 36ff and 97ff, and Iu. Borozdin, "Parametry, sebestoimost' i tseny mashin" *PKh,* 1971, no. 6, pp. 29–35, for critical discussions of the parametric method of price setting.

revising the prices of new products in the future, the method of so-called stepped (*stupenchatye*) prices. The approach seems to rest on the following premises. The unit cost of any piece of equipment is bound to decline in the future thanks to learning by doing. This ought to be accompanied by price reductions, for two reasons: first, to forestall the emergence of excessive profit on the part of the producer (it being assumed that he can continue to sell at the original high price, perhaps not an unrealistic assumption under Soviet conditions); and second, the same excessive profit will constitute a disincentive to the producer to switch production to some newer piece of equipment that may appear in the future. Alternatively, as we have seen earlier in the chapter, the newer piece of equipment would have to carry a very large profit margin in order to win out over the (then) old machine in the *producer's* eyes.

The standard answer is that the price of the old machine has to be gradually reduced as its cost of production declines and as it becomes increasingly obsolete. But how to accomplish this? What should the two prices be? How can the price authorities diagnose the situation in time? How to warn the producer sufficiently beforehand to switch over to the new machine, and how to alert the potential users of their prospective opportunities? Finally, how to avoid upsetting the annual plan (as already discussed) by changing the price without sufficient notice to the planners?

The preferred solution is the *stepped price,* a price that is predetermined at the time of its original confirmation to decline by "steps," that is, by stated amounts on set future dates. At first glance, the solution combines the virtues of flexibility, promotion of innovation, prevention of excessive profits, certainty for all concerned, and—not the least— administrative convenience.[75] It has a major defect: the great difficulty

---

75. The chairman of the SPB, V. K. Sitnin, has been consistently advocating stepped prices since at least his assumption of the office in 1965 (see *Pravda,* 12 Nov. 1965, and nearly every one of his later published statements). A major article on the subject, from the official standpoint, is Iu. Borozdin, "Planirovanie stupenchatykh optovykh tsen v promyshlennosti," *VE,* 1970, no. 5, pp. 74–85. See also K. N. Plotnikov and A. S. Gusarov, *Sovremennye problemy teorii i praktiki tsenoobrazovaniia pri sotsializme* (Moscow, 1971), pp. 469–75. Keith Bush points out that the idea was originally broached by Turetski in the early 1930s ("The Impending Introduction of Stepped Wholesale Prices?" Radio Liberty Dispatch, 21 May 1971). It is possible though that in its most recent incarnation the idea of stepped prices has been influenced by East German thought and practice. A so-called industrial price regulation system was introduced in East Germany in 1968 whose essence is the automatic lowering of price by the producer when his profitability for the article reaches the set upper limit. The price is reduced to effect the pre-set lower limit of profitability. The scheme has certain advantages, among them administrative convenience. But compared with the Soviet variant it would seem to entail some disadvantages, such as uncertainty for users and planners and possibility of abuse by sellers. Brief descriptions and analyses of the scheme can be found in Manfred Melzer, "Preispolitik und Preisbildungsprobleme in der DDR," *Vierteljahreshefte zur Wirtschaftsforschung,* 1969, no. 3, pp. 338ff.; and Hans Böhme, "Dynamische Preisbildung in der sozialistischen Planwirtschaft der DDR," *Jahrbücher für Nationalökonomie und Statistik,* 3 183, nos. 3–4 (Aug. 1969): 228ff.

of determining the steps correctly some years in advance, for this would require fairly accurate prediction of the movement of most of such crucial variables as the unit cost of production, other relevant costs, and especially the prospective course of technology as it affects the development of advanced substitutes for the given machine. Moreover, the stepped-price approach overlooks the fact that substitution need not take place by means of single pieces of equipment; whole processes, whole industries may replace the old ones. Lastly, one should not expect the producers to welcome a device that guarantees lower profits at periodic intervals. All in all, it is not surprising that only very few stepped prices have been actually established as yet.[76] Nonetheless, they continue to be vigorously advocated by the authorities.

The 1969 Methodology has now been superseded by one under the identical title, confirmed by the SPB on 26 April 1974. At this writing, only a summary of the 1974 Methodology is available[77] and a definitive appraisal is not yet possible. It seems that in principle the 1974 Methodology follows that of 1969, and that the chief modification is in the attempt to strengthen the link between the higher price for the new product and the pecuniary gain to the producing enterprise and its management. In this respect it is in line with what (in our opinion) has been the general trend in the Soviet economy since 1965, namely, a growing emphasis on personal material incentive in eliciting proper performance from economic agents in general and managerial and other technical personnel in particular. The 1974 document aims to enlist the pecuniary interest of the enterprise by separating the incentive element in the price of a new product from the price *sensu stricto* and calling it a "supplement" (*nadbavka*) to the lower-limit price. At first glance the operation is meaningless. However, it takes into account the fact that the distributive consequences of a price supplement are formally different from those of the profit contained in the price itself. The additional profit, as already mentioned, often is simply captured by the treasury; the supplement, how-

76. Thus Koshuta in *Sotsialisticheskaia industriia,* 4 Aug. 1970, p. 2: "We are trying to [introduce]. . . stepped prices. But so far there are no more than about ten articles for which such prices have been established." The new price lists for MB products introduced on 1 Jan. 1973 were said to contain an increased number of stepped prices; however, writing in 1973, Koshuta and Borozdin (supra n. 71), p. 14, stated: "owing to lack of necessary coordination in the mechanism of planning and price-setting, stepped prices have not yet been accorded a sufficiently wide application." As a curiosity, it may be noted that stepped prices have lately been in effect for deliveries of electronic components from Bulgaria to the Soviet Union (private information obtained in Bulgaria by the present writer in Sept. 1973).

77. *EG,* 1974, no. 30, p. 22. For the sake of brevity we are not taking up separately in this chapter the stimulation of higher quality (other than new equipment) through price, but for an insight into the official approach, the reader may refer to the latest measures by the SPB as summarized in *EG,* 1974, no. 27, p. 16. The situation before 1969 is skillfully depicted and analyzed by Spechler (supra n. 40).

ever, can be directly applied to feed the various enterprise incentive funds. The size of the supplement is governed by a schedule, where it depends on the ratio of the upper-limit price to the lower-limit price, with the proviso that it cannot exceed 50 percent of the "economic effect."

Concluding remarks

The problem that we have been considering is a problem in price control: how to prevent prices from rising, unduly by microeconomic means, without simultaneously stifling such impetuses to innovation as emanate from administrative direction of the economy, on the one hand, and from the spontaneous initiative of the operating levels, on the other. It is a question of trade-offs. The problem is certainly not peculiar to the Soviet economy; it is bound to exist in some form or other in any economy under price control.[78] But in the Soviet case the problem of balancing inflation and innovation confronts certain specific dimensions and institutions. For one thing, technological progress and innovation rate extremely highly in the regime's schedule of priorities, while the stability of the wholesale price level (and in the long term even its reduction) also receives great attention, at least at this historical juncture. Second, price control is not regarded, as often is the case in other countries, as a temporary expedient *faute de mieux,* but as a permanent integral feature of the economic system. There is no next "phase" around the corner on which to stake an automatic revitalization of technological progress. And third, the setting of the problem is that of a highly centralized command economy, in which technological advance and innovation have long been—perhaps as much by default as by design—the prerogatives of the central planners and administrators.

The command economy continues to rest on personal material rewards. Indeed, if there is a new element in the picture, especially since 1965, it is the reassertion of individual material incentive as a means for eliciting proper performance by all economic agents, from the humblest peasant to the general director of an "association." The enhancement of material rewards has its minuses. It grates on ideological sensibilities, for both domestic and foreign purposes. (In regard to the last point, one must not be misled by the simultaneous stress on *moral* incentives in the official pronouncements of the regime's spokesmen. In reality everything points the other way, and if words seem to contradict deeds, their pur-

---

78. Cf. the gingerliness with which the U.S. Cost of Living Council in its day approached the problems posed by new (and, of course, pseudo-new) products, e.g., *Cost of Living Council News,* 12 Sept. 1971.

pose is more to soothe the soul than to guide the brain and brawn.) It causes difficulties for the incomes policy and in the labor market. It mutes the official condemnation of the many self-serving activities that are now so deeply imbedded in Soviet society, such as bribery, corruption, peculation and speculation, and even "honest" labor but on one's own account. It spawns group interests and interest groups. Yet, as Western society knows only too well, the emphasis on material rewards has its functional sides. It tends to attenuate the conflict between individual and group interests and social goals. And it affords to the authorities the possibility of using powerful indirect instruments—the "economic levers" of communist parlance—to further the attainment of their objectives.

The growing place of material incentives since 1965, together with the revision of wholesale prices in 1966–67, has indeed enlarged opportunities to activize prices for specific ends—though, to be sure, within the setting of what is still essentially the traditional Soviet command economy. In this chapter we have attempted to trace the course of such policies and measures since 1965, the year that saw both the launching of the limited Economic Reform (since, much diluted) and the establishment of the State Price Board. It is thus not surprising that the authorities would choose to employ their now more potent price instrument precisely in the areas where administrative methods have been notoriously inefficacious; namely, in regard to technical progress and innovation, and to the quality of products in general. Moreover, given the inequality between the seller's and the buyer's powers, the price instrument is more effective when applied to the seller than to the buyer, which is where it is now primarily applied.

It should be emphasized that the use of the price tool is not only selective and limited to specific areas of the economy, but is primarily a supplement to the existing structure of administrative controls over resource use. It is not intended to replace them; instead, it is designed to strengthen them. To forestall abuses and contain the very strong inflationary tendencies, the price tool is subject to tight control in regard to both price itself and the physical dimensions of the good. What we encounter here once again is the familiar Soviet syndrome of incentive and coercion, of the carrot and the stick. Moreover, because the controls are exercised along several dimensions (price, quality, standards, allocation, planning, etc.) the mix of administrative dramatis personae who get into the act is a rather complex one.

It may be said that the constructive use of prices to promote innovation and quality is nothing new; this much often was accomplished de facto by the provisional prices, in existence since the thirties. True. The differ-

ence is that now the constructive use of the price instrument is legitimated
— "price flexibility" has become a positive value in the official language —
while the excessive and abusive features of provisional prices are now to
be more effectively suppressed. Furthermore, the greater tribute to personal material incentives since 1965 means that a *smaller* concession in
price to the producer may now have a greater impact on personal reward
and, hence, a larger leverage on enterprise behavior.[79] Phrased differently,
it may now be possible to produce effects in desired directions, such as
innovation, at lesser cost in terms of inflation (which is now also more
strictly monitored), but with greater distributive consequences for better
or for worse. The trade-off is a three-way affair — between innovation (or
quality), inflation, and distributive desiderata.

Also not atypical of Soviet experience is the way in which conceptual
advances have been incorporated in the new methods, especially in one
portion of the 1969 Methodology (and its successor of 1974), as discussed
in this chapter. Insofar as microeconomics as we know it is primarily
a calculus of rational choice, and insofar as the Soviets face up more and
more to the logic of things in a framework that transcends mere technological relations, quite naturally they rediscover or rehabilitate economic concepts of which Stalinist theorizing was conspicuously deprived.

Two observations of some interest might be offered here, though. The
first is that these conceptual advances are happening within an institutional matrix that remains highly conservative (highly centralized and
hostile to spontaneous economic forces), and within a rather traditional
intellectual environment as well. Second, the conceptual advances are
finding their way into practice, not so much because of imperatives of
rational resource allocation as because of the requirements of distributive
equity — namely, to calibrate material incentives in some proportion with
the economic benefit derivable by society from the innovation (or —
though more tenuously — higher quality). It may be retorted that the distributive effects will surely lead to corresponding allocative results. But
this is not always so, since the primary push for innovation and higher
quality still comes from the upper reaches of the administrative hierarchy,
where the given distributive patterns do not hold, and where the rationale
need not be based on a strictly economic (as contrasted with, say, technological) calculus. The practical adoption of more or less rational economic concepts out of *distributive* considerations is not uncommon in
recent Soviet history. It has occurred in regard to techniques of rational
allocation of capital (where the need to scale innovators' premia was a

79. On the key significance of material incentives in stimulating innovation on the level
of the producing enterprise see the interesting remarks by Iu. Borozdin, a leading expert
on new equipment prices, in *PKh*, 1973, no. 1, p. 72.

significant, though not sole, desideratum), the introduction of rent in mining and other activities ("fixed payments"), the yet very timid appearance of land rent, and so forth.

The constraints imposed by anti-inflationary preferences of the regime have been referred to several times in this chapter; we will not repeat them at this point. But something more should perhaps be said regarding the distributive dimension of the problem. Generally speaking, the current tendencies in regard to the distribution of income (and wealth) appear to contain a potential for social and economic difficulties. That this is without doubt so in regard to the seemingly large and widespread illicit incomes (to which we have already alluded), which must have an unequal impact among various social, economic, and regional elements of the population, need hardly be argued. But the various licit rewards that have been introduced or enlarged thanks to the increasing emphasis on material incentives—further magnified and distorted by the abuses to which they are so often subjected—must also mold income distribution in ways that at once distort the labor market (and it is a market) and raise serious social problems. One need only mention the so-called Shchekino method (by which some of the economized wages of eliminated redundant workers are transferred to the remaining workers in the given plant), by dint of which intraplant productivity is bought at the expense of interplant inequalities of pay.[80] Similarly, further attempts to use the price tool and other instruments to push innovation and higher quality, by progressively enhancing material rewards to managerial and technical personnel, may also run up against difficulties on distributive grounds.[81]

Just how effective, not to say efficient, the recently developed price instruments are, it is yet difficult to tell. We have had occasion in this chapter to raise a good number of questions on this score. The modification that was introduced in April 1974, described above, surely suggests that the authorities are still seeking, by trial and error, to find the linkage between price and material incentive that will bring about an acceptable set of marginal trade-offs between innovation and higher quality of goods, on the one hand, and price stability and distributive equity, on the other. In view of the well-known systemic obstacles to innovation and to quality improvement, it is legitimate to ask whether such an acceptable set of

80. The fullest Western discussion of the Shchekino method and its implications is by Jeanne Delamotte, *Shchekino, entreprise soviètique pilote* (Paris: Editions ouvrières, 1973); on distributive implications see esp. pp. 181–84.

81. As early as the economic conference of May 1968 a strong warning regarding the distributive consequences of economic reform (and presumably also the types of incentive measures discussed in this chapter) was sounded by no less an authority than B. M. Sukharevskii, deputy chairman of the State Board for Labor and Wages; see Bachurin et al., *Sovershenstvovanie planirovaniia* (supra n. 11), p. 317.

marginal trade-offs is at all reachable within the existing policy constraints on all sides.[82]

82. Interesting in this connection is the seemingly growing problem of "overcorrection" in the stimulation of new technology by the price instrument. In essence, what happens in such cases is that the enterprises respond to the pecuniary incentives by producing machinery of a degree of complexity and sophistication that exceeds the requirements of most potential buyers. The problem was repeatedly cited to the author by Soviet pricing specialists during interviews in Moscow in Sept. 1974. Cf. A. Koshuta and L. Rozenova, "Effektivnost' novoi tekhniki i zainteresovannost' predpriiatiy v ee osvoenii," *VE*, 1974, no. 8, pp. 46–57. Both authors are members of the SPB staff. The effect is inflationary in a sense. It should be noted that the chairman of the SPB, V. K. Sitnin, was not reappointed to his position when the new USSR Council of Ministers was constituted in June 1974. Of the 105 positions on the Council of Ministers, only the chairmanships of the SPB and of the State Board of Labor and Wages have remained unfilled to our knowledge to date (Oct. 1974). Efforts to spur innovation by means of the price instrument have been attempted as well in a number of other East European countries; see the symposium *Tseny i stimulirovanie nauchno-tekhnicheskogo progressa v sotsialisticheskikh stranakh* (Moscow, 1973). The volume includes several useful chapters on Soviet experience and the recent measures, some of which, incidentally, were anticipated in such countries as Czechoslovakia and the German Democratic Republic. At least in the latter case, however, the problem of stimulating innovation by price measures "remains unsolved" according to some observers. Kurt Erdmann and Maria Haendcke-Hoppe, "Plansystem der DDR im Umbau," Forschungsstelle für gesamtdeutsche wirtschaftliche und soziale Fragen, *Analysen*, 1974, no. 4, p. 6.

7

Disguised Inflation in the Soviet Union: The Relationship between Soviet Income Growth and Price Increases in the Postwar Period

Aron Katsenelinboigen

University of Pennsylvania

First of all we should define the concept of inflation. In the West, with its market economy, the term is usually synonymous with a rise in prices. This, in fact, is true. However, inflation is not only a rise in prices. It is a process in which there arises an incompatibility between the paid-out sums of money and the rise in prices. The increased quantity of money depreciates and this depreciation has a feedback (secondary effect) on the economy which may be tantamount to the destruction of the money mechanism.

Some Western economists are prone to consider that there is inflation in the USSR because there is a rise in prices and a depreciation of money. However, they do not take into consideration that the interrelationship between government and enterprises is based on a principle in which a rise in prices is meaningless to the enterprise, since that rise is made up for by planned government subsidies. Under these conditions, feedback is inoperative so that one cannot speak of an inflationary process.

The foregoing conditions give rise to a contrasting opinion: that there are no inflationary processes in the USSR whatsoever. At a time when the Western nations are gripped by inflation, such an opinion may give birth to the illusion that a socialist economy, in general, can prevent inflation. However, as was shown above, there are inflationary processes in the USSR. They encompass only some areas of the economy, primarily the area of consumer goods. Thus, the inflationary process in the USSR takes

The author wishes to express his heartfelt gratitude to Professors Janet Chapman, Gregory Grossman, and Herbert Levine for their attention and critical comments, and for their help in preparing this chapter for publication. I would also like to express my gratitude to Thomas Fallows who translated it.

place in a very peculiar manner because the government attempts to disguise it in any way possible.

In order to reach equilibrium in an economic system, the aggregate of incomes received by consumers, after deduction of taxes and voluntary savings, must equal the value of goods and services available. This is a simple condition of balance. Yet it can be met in various ways. In theory, or, in more precise terms, if one ignores the many important factors in an economy's development, such as the psychology of the participants, it is not important how the equilibrium is reached. But in practice, when one must take human psychology into account, one can no longer ignore the question of what means should be used in reaching equilibrium. In this chapter we shall consider only one of the available means for reaching such an equilibrium—the role of income as a means of stimulating workers to increase labor productivity and to change occupation or place of work. For simplicity, the discussion below concerns only how labor can be stimulated to increase productivity. We shall examine only the situation when there is a labor shortage and when the intensification of labor's effort without the pressure of unemployment is a critical issue. The account will be illustrated by examples from the Soviet postwar experience.

The problem

Workers can be stimulated by increases in either money or real wages. Generally, it is more effective to raise money wages since this relates earnings directly to work (of course, on condition that prices are more or less stable). When real wages rise through a fall in prices there is no direct stimulus for increasing productivity, since the worker cannot understand how his own activity will influence a price decrease in the future. Needless to say, money wage increases may well be differentiated by the different effects on different workers. Yet the fall of prices affects everyone. Of course, one could regulate the reduction of prices for various products in order to secure a greater increase of real wages for certain worker income groups which have relatively high demand for articles whose relative prices fall. But all of these measures stimulate an increase in labor productivity only indirectly.

Although a rise in nominal wages has certain advantages, it can create substantial difficulties. Therefore a great deal of care is required when this economic instrument is used. For example, an increase of money wages can even lead to a loss of output for workers, when we consider the effect of substituting leisure for consumer goods. This is particularly important to keep in mind when a worker is employed in the production of goods in more than one place. In this situation, the effect of substitution can reveal itself in a rather more complicated way. In an organization where the worker receives a large income, he can increase output. But at the same time, he can reduce output at another of his jobs, preferring leisure to additional labor. This kind of effect apparently took place in agriculture between the late 1960s and early 1970s. The increase of incomes at collective farms (kolkhozes) stimulated a rise in agricultural output. But at the same time, the output of kolkhoz workers on their private plots fell, since they did not want to work more intensively, even there. As a result, it seems that the total production of certain crops fell. This had been unexpected, for it was always believed that a rise of income would stimulate an increase in output. We shall consider in greater detail below a more typical situation in which the growth of money wages promotes an increase of labor productivity.

The ideal situation would be a rate of increase in money wages which effectively stimulates labor, but which at the same time is equal to or below the rate of increase of output.[1] In this situation one may combine all the advantages of the rise of money wages with the increase (or maintenance) of real wages. However, money wages can rise more rapidly than the increase in the output of consumer goods. In order to reach equilibrium here between the aggregate of incomes and the available quantity of consumer goods, it is necessary to overcome certain difficulties. New problems arise here which are related to the introduction of taxes, the stimulation of savings, and the rise of prices. We shall consider in slightly greater detail one of the reasons which gives rise to a rate of growth of income higher than the rate of growth of output. We shall also examine the conditions under which such an excess rate of growth of income can be successfully realized.

It is well known that in order to use material means to stimulate a person into increasing the volume of his activity, it is necessary to offer him some minimum amount; a worker will not react to a smaller amount. At the same time, however, owing to physiological restrictions, a person can increase the volume of his activity only by a limited amount. Under the above conditions, the increase in incomes will not always precisely correspond to the increase in output: the increase of output can be smaller. As has been noted, an introduction of higher taxes, a stimulation of savings, and a rise of prices can, in principle, make up for the gap between the rate of increase in income and the rate of increase in output. Thus here we encounter a process in which it becomes necessary, because of re-

---

1. For the time being, we assume for simplicity that the increase in output is in the form of consumer goods which will rapidly cover the rising income. Things become more complex when a worker is stimulated into raising his productivity and he also produces means of production, since they can be converted into consumer goods only with a certain lag. Finally, it follows for us to single out the situation when a worker is stimulated into increasing the output of collective consumption goods which cannot be used directly for stimulating the worker. In this situation, an increase in output does not cover the expanded fund of workers' incomes, even with a lag.

strictions on human psychology, to use simultaneously both accelerators (an increase of incomes) and braking devices (increased taxes, savings, and prices).

Here one might suggest an analogy with the complex chemical processes in which it is necessary to use simultaneously both a catalyst and an inhibitor. The reason for this simultaneous use of both inhibitors and catalysts frequently lies in the very nature of the chemical process. Catalysts can proceed too rapidly, and so inhibitors are needed in order to slow down the process to the desired speed. One of my Moscow friends graphically compared this case in economics and chemistry with the lash and reins the horseman uses.

When money wages rise, prices are the most important means to reach equilibrium. This is due to the fact that the tax system is fairly conservative and the growth of savings is limited because of restrictions on the interest rate. Inflationary processes arise in this situation. If prices increase slowly, the worker has time to receive a greater quantity of consumer goods for his higher wages. To put it more simply, if the worker maintains his faith in money, inflation performs the role of the inhibitor, and the process of developing production will, in general, be more effective. In other words, mild inflation becomes a factor which contributes to the growth of the economy.

Perhaps this explanation of the role of mild inflation in stimulating economic growth contributes a new element to the number of explanations presented in economic literature in describing the influence of mild inflation. It seems to me that in the West, along with the maintenance of such an economy, there has been an improvement of the welfare of the population, and an improvement of skills of workers for whom the pressure of unemployment is not very sharp; for all the above, it is even more necessary that productivity be raised by increasing wages. Thus, the use of an increase of wages as a means for stimulating a rise in production requires a corresponding economic policy, one which is related to the system of taxes, savings, and prices. All these economic parameters have definite social implications insofar as they hurt the workers in their role of consumers; the population reacts with great pain to an increase in taxes, prices, and the like.

When a policy of increasing production by raising wages is conducted, it is necessary to be clear about the resulting social difficulties and not be limited to half-measures. Fearing the social consequences of their policy of using inhibitors, politicians have at times attempted to disguise these difficulties; these were efforts to create an illusion of social equilibrium. These activities have only a local effect, yet they can ultimately lead to even sharper social conflicts. In practice, if inhibitors are not deployed to the necessary degree when wages are rising, an accumulation of free money will ensue. After reaching a certain volume, the free money can

become an unstable mass. Out of this emerges the danger of galloping inflation. Mild inflation turns into galloping inflation, with all its accompanying social consequences, if the increase of prices is inadequate.

Thus an attempt to use economic methods in achieving an increase in
production requires a special and well-thought-out social-economic
policy. Economists can describe in precise detail only a few aspects of
the processes which occur here and have only a few recommendations to
offer to politicians. Social scientists, on the other hand, can offer many
more insights to government officials. But on the whole, the decision-making process requires that political leaders be very skillful. If there are no
experienced politicians armed with the most up-to-date knowledge of
economics and the social sciences, the use of economic methods in
managing the economy can lead to sharp social conflicts. In order to
deal with these conflicts leaders sometimes turn from economic to administrative methods in managing the economy.

We shall examine all the above from the experience of the development of the Soviet Union in the postwar period. In the goal of stimulating
labor to greater productivity, various economic policies were undertaken
during this period, including even the corvée and labor-camp systems.
In practice, not even the slightest kind of an economic machinery was in
operation here.[2] The relation between economic and extra-economic

2. According to the accepted Marxist social-economic doctrine, a consistent shift of
formations takes place. Each of these formations has its characteristic economic structure.
Corvée is a structure characteristic of feudal society. It is therefore awkward, from the
Marxist standpoint, to discuss the fact that an essentially feudal structure functions in the
socialist epoch. Structural formations in society arise because a specific mode of functioning generally corresponds to the existing conditions. Analyzing the development of social-
economic systems from the standpoint of goals and conditions of their development, it is
possible to see how in every concrete historical situation a synthesis of the various structures occurs. These structures can appear or disappear, depending on how social goals and
conditions change. From this point of view, one can say the following: In conditions when
an extraordinary task comes to the fore, when important resources are scarce, and when the
level of development is low, one could claim that it is expedient to use such management
mechanisms as slavery and serfdom. If the private economy remains, the worker can either
refuse to hand over his produced article or produce less. Although we shall not dwell at
length on the conditions which demand slavery or corvée, we can note the specific advantages of the corvée and quitrent systems. Under the quitrent system, the laborer owns his
own product and turns over a part of that product, in one form or another, to the lord. On
the other hand, under corvée, the laborer must carry out direct obligations; the product of
his activity clearly does not belong to him. Moreover, it is easier to pressure the serf into
fulfilling obligations on the lord's estate than it is to seize the product of the serf's labor. The
corvée system provides for a small allotment of land left to the laborer in order to keep him
alive. Therefore, one cannot generalize to claim that quitrent is more effective than corvée.
Everything depends on the conditions underlying the two structures. One may assume that
under the conditions created in the 1930s, the introduction of corvée in the form of kolkhoz
production was one of the most convenient means of confiscating agricultural output in order
to carry out a policy of rapid industrialization. (An entirely separate question, however, is
whether such rates of industrialization were necessary.) As far as the slave structure is
concerned, it too can be used in the Soviet Union. Through the use of the labor-camp system, an enormous project of opening up new regions was undertaken.

methods of government was not identical in various sectors of the Soviet economy. In the following we shall examine those sectors where economic stimuli played a significant role (above all in industry). Yet even in these sectors, equilibrium between incomes and the available quantity of consumer goods was established in various ways, with a greater or lesser use of extra-economic means.

The year 1953 represents a watershed. It is well known that after Stalin's death, the immediate goals for the development of Soviet society changed. This was expressed in the rejection of the policy of trying to achieve world supremacy, which would be realized by the outbreak of a new world war. More attention began to be devoted to the production of consumer goods. By virtue of this, the proportion between economic (wages, prices, taxes) and administrative methods (commands) changed. The great need for the overwhelming predominance of administrative methods of management lost its former importance; the role of economic means of management gained in strength.

It is important to note that even though the role of economic methods of management increased after 1953, at the same time it became apparent that the Soviet system was inadequately prepared for a consistent and effective use of these methods.

The period from 1947 to 1953

In those sectors of the national economy where economic methods were used during the period under review, the accent nevertheless fell on administrative means, organically supplemented by demagoguery. In concrete terms, this took place in the following manner. Wage rates and salary scales within enterprises were fixed. It seems that in 1948 the Council of Ministers even promulgated a special decree which prohibited an increase in salary scales and wage rates. I became familiar with this matter from the following sources. In 1951 I wrote a book (my *kandidat* dissertation) on the organization of labor and wages in the Soviet economy. This dissertation in part analyzes the system of paying foremen. It indicated that the practice of paying foremen, in which the foremen receive less wages than the skilled workers, had been revived after a period before World War II, when the government condemned the practice. It was suggested that the foremen's salary scale be raised. For critical review, I had given my study to officials at the Department of Labor and Wages of the Moscow Automobile Factory named for Likhachev (at that time named for Stalin). The officials replied that my dissertation contained great political errors. Among the errors, they noted the dissertation's advocacy of an increase of foremen's wages. The call for higher wages for the foremen clashed with the decree of the Council of Ministers, signed personally by Comrade Stalin, which specifically prohibited an increase of salary scales and wage rates. If a pieceworker increased his productivity, his earnings would rise for a period, but would gradually return to their former levels.

Such a revision of norms for piece-rate workers, who form the majority of those employed in industry and construction,[3] was carried out in the first quarter of every year. Since the so-called "experimental-statistical" norms (norms based on past performance, as contrasted to norms determined scientifically on the basis of machine capacity, time-motion studies, etc.) were the prevalent form, a mild revision of piece rates was guaranteed. During this period the gap between basic wage rates and earnings was very high in several branches of the economy. The gap was supported artificially by the important percentage by which norms were overfilled. E. L. Manevich's dissertation very thoroughly analyzed the above situation in the organization of the wage system and the system of norms. The results are partially published in his work *Zarabotnaia plata i ee formy v promyshlennosti SSSR* (Moscow, 1951).

Although hourly workers (*povremenshiki*) received a fixed basic tariff rate, their total earnings were not fixed. This is explained by the fact that this category of workers received bonuses, depending on the outcome of their activity. It was rather simple to regulate their wages. Since so many conditions had to be met before one could receive a bonus, it was always possible to find a pretext to reduce bonuses by claiming that a certain condition had not been satisfied or had not been met completely. In 1950 and 1951 there were months when the size of bonuses in general was reduced by 25 percent, in accordance with a decree of the Soviet of Ministers. I know of this from personal experience at the Frezer factory in Moscow during those years. Thus the bonus fund was regulated in such a manner as to prevent increases in earnings of time-workers. Their activity gained in intensity, yet their wages remained the same. This occurred with the help of annual increases in planned output through the process known as "planning from the achieved level" (*planirovanie ot dostignutogo*).

Constraints on the level of workers' money wages could not adequately serve to maintain equilibrium between workers' incomes and the available quantity of consumer goods. The explanation here lies in the fact that the fund of wages rose throughout the country, as a result of significant increases in the size of the work force. The number of workers increased faster than the output of consumer goods and services.

Under these conditions, the government resorted to taxes, in order to

3. According to figures compiled by A. G. Aganbegian and V. F. Maier in *Zarabotnaia plata v SSSR* (Moscow, 1959), pieceworkers formed by 1959 around three-quarters of all workers in industry and around 90 percent of all construction workers (p. 149).

preserve equilibrium between the level of income and available consumer goods. For demagogic purposes, however, the government officially announced this as a system of loans for which laborers would "voluntarily" sign up each year. At the same time, and also for demagogic reasons, under conditions of widespread shortages of consumer goods, prices for these goods were marked down annually.[4]

The policy conducted during this period had its own foundations. In order to expand military power, it was necessary to raise labor productivity. The output of consumer goods had to be held at a low level. In this situation, it was dangerous to raise money wages in order to stimulate productivity increases. If prices and taxes were not raised simultaneously, it would lead to an accumulation of free money, with all its accompanying negative consequences. Furthermore, systematic and significant increases of prices and taxes reflect very negatively on a country's ideology, especially for a socialist country. This is why, in the postwar period to 1953, it was easier to coordinate a harsh militarization policy with the administrative method of raising labor productivity.[5]

The period after 1953

As we have noted above, after 1953, material methods of production were strengthened in the Soviet Union. This was expressed in the noticeably higher rates of increase of money wages. We can illustrate by citing materials showing the increase in the average money wage throughout the economy. (It should be kept in mind, of course, that the increase in the average wage also reflects *structural changes* in the economy. This is shown in Table 7.1.)

The rise in money wages had three main causes: (1) the practice of simultaneously revising norms and piece rates on a mass basis was discontinued; (2) the minimum wage was increased systematically; and (3) wage and salary rates were increased for workers in the leading branches of the economy and in the remote regions of the country. We cannot single out the role of each individual cause, yet they all tremendously influenced the increase of money wages. We consider these causes in greater detail below.

(1) In 1957, in accordance with the decree of the Councils of Ministers

4. Particular prices fell for liquor, especially for vodka. For example, in the decrease of prices in 1949, prices for vodka fell by 28 percent, for liqueurs by 25 percent, and for grape and berry wine and for cognac by 15 percent. *Pravda*, 1 March 1949.

5. This is how this situation is described in "scientific terms" in a very interesting work by two well-known Soviet economists: "The Soviet State in the postwar period conducted a policy of reducing retail prices. Therefore, factors lying on the side of money and which are related to a change in the scale of prices no longer determined the movement of money wages. Factors lying on the side of labor and which flow directly from the economic nature of socialism rose to the forefront" (Aganbegian and Maier, p. 86).

Table 7.1. Increase in average monthly wage, USSR, 1950 to 1970.

Years	Average wage	Increase within five-year period	
		Rubles	Percent
1950	64.2	7.6	11.8
1955	71.8	8.8	12.3
1960	80.6	15.9	19.7
1965	96.5	22.5	26.4
1970	122.0		

Source: Narkhoz 1922–72, p. 350.

entitled "On the Change in the Procedure for Revising Output Norms," a different practice was introduced to revise output norms. Norms were to be revised according to the degree to which technical and organizational measures, related to the reduction of labor intensity, had been put into practice.

Naturally, one should not take this decree literally. Since workers' money wages increase, on the average, according to the plan, there is no need for a massive campaign for a revision of norms. At the same time, up to the present, wages have often been viewed in the main as a means for establishing levels of living, as a means for directly stimulating better activity. Norms are revised in order to bring de facto wages closer to planned wages. Since the norms continue to be predominantly experimental-statistical norms up to this time,[6] it is rather easy to implement this kind of wage manipulation.

(2) In the last twenty years, the minimum wage has risen very significantly. In 1947 the minimum wage was set at 20–22 rubles a month (in current money units). One of the first measures of the government after 1953 was an increase of wages for the poorly paid categories of workers. Yet even in 1957 the minimum wage was set at 27 rubles.[7] The minimum wage was raised by steps. Presently in the Soviet Union, measures setting the minimum wage at 70 rubles a month are being carried out in accordance with the current five-year plan.

(3) In the period since 1953, salary scales and wage rates for workers and employees of the coal industry, construction, public health, and the like have been raised repeatedly, in agreement with the corresponding decrees of the Central Committee of the Communist Party and of the Council of Ministers. At the same time, the income of kolkhoz workers

6. As A. Volkov, President of the State Committee of the Council Ministers for Labor and Wages, says, basic wage rates will be increased in the transition to new conditions in workers' pay taking place in the Soviet Union in 1974. An increase in the share of basic rates to 70–75 percent of earnings must promote a fundamental improvement in the establishment of labor norms. Volkov notes that the experimental-statistical rates still prevail at many enterprises (*Pravda,* 10 April 1974).

7. Aganbegian and Maier, pp. 220–21.

has risen significantly. Pensions and scholarships also increased sharply. Since the literature on the Soviet economy has devoted a substantial amount of attention to these matters, we need not discuss them here. There is no doubt but that these measures had the effect of increasing the workers' material incentives and that they played a role in raising the effectiveness of production. However, the introduction of economic methods for stimulating the workers and the increase of money incomes require that a flexible policy be carried out in the sphere of prices, taxes, etc. At the same time, the economic policy being implemented is perhaps inadequately flexible. Though money incomes were increased during the post-1953 period, taxes on wages were curtailed.[8] The annual "voluntary" loans, which served as a disguised form of tax, were abolished. Yet all this only further increased the already expanded amount of cash paid out to labor.

We shall examine in more detail what happened with prices. At this moment we shall not touch on the official price statistics, which record the slight official changes in consumer goods prices. Within this period official price changes, whether increases or decreases,[9] were small. The official price increases, however, essentially failed to keep pace with the growing disparity between the increase of cash incomes and the volume of consumer goods. At the same time, de facto prices rose in the following way. Prices for separate kinds of food, clothes, furniture, automobiles, etc., increased under the guise of an improvement in the quality of these goods. Slight changes in the style of the articles caused a noticeable increase in the price.[10] The rise of prices, which consumers usually interpret with a great deal of alarm, was made less apparent to the con-

8. It is well known that there were even plans to eliminate the taxes on wages entirely. We shall not go into a detailed review here of the reasons for these proposals. Rather, we will note only that these plans display economic illiteracy, since taxes on wages play an important role in coordinating wages, as the price of labor, with the quantity of goods which the worker will consume. For more on this, see my work, written jointly with S. M. Movshovich and Iu. V. Ovsienko, *Vosproizvodstvo i economicheskii optimum* (Moscow, 1972).

9. Official and unofficial prices rose for the most important "ideological" product— liquor. This increase also was directed in the struggle against "fire water" (zelenyi zmei), the influence of which rose to threatening heights. If we recall the reduction of prices for wine and liquor prior to 1953, the perniciousness of Stalin's methods of management becomes even more obvious, and we see the far-ranging negative consequences of Stalin's methods, which corrupted the people.

10. Leonid Brezhnev's remarks in the Report of the Central Committee of the CPSU to the Twenty-Fourth Congress of the Communist Party of the Soviet Union confirmed the available facts in regard to the artificial increase of prices: "The great and complex task of satisfying the market with articles of mass consumption must be resolved under a stable level of state retail prices and, to the extent to which the essential economic preconditions have been created, with reduced prices for individual goods. It follows that we should decisively suppress an excessive increase in prices, intensify control over the setting of retail prices and rates for services, and harshly call to account those directors of enterprises and of economic organs who attempt to circumvent the state-established order" (*Kommunist*, 1971, no. 5, p. 72).

sumer as a result of the currency conversion carried out in 1960. In this currency reform, one new ruble was made worth ten old rubles and all prices and wages were thus reduced by seven-eighths. With this overall reduction of commodity prices to 10 percent of their former level, prices could be raised rather imperceptibly. Consumers out of habit continued to think in terms of the old rates.[11]

Another way in which prices can increase is related to the so-called "washing out" of inexpensive goods (the disappearance of these items from the stores). Official statistics provide no figures on these goods. But on the basis of personal observations and the observations of my colleagues, it is possible to assert with adequate confidence that the process of "washing out" inexpensive goods took place throughout these years. This is particularly evident even in the unusual case of television sets, where prices dropped for certain types of television units.[12] At the same time, however, inexpensive, small-screen television sets, which earlier had prevailed, gradually disappeared from the market. In their place, relatively more expensive television sets with larger screens went on sale (although the prices for these, I repeat, were reduced!). The process of "washing out" of cheap goods also affected meats, macaroni products, and other such items.

However, the increase of prices which was taking place (with an inadequate output of consumer goods) was unable to make up for the rise in the population's cash income. All this led to an artificial increase in the aggregate of free money. Whereas between 1950 and 1960 the sum of savings deposits increased annually (on the average) by 905 million rubles, it rose by 3,569 million rubles annually from 1960 to 1970, and by 7,300 million rubles annually from 1970 to 1973.[13] In 1973, savings banks held 68.6 billion rubles.[14] One may suppose that another 25 percent or so lies in the population's hands, "stuffed under the mattress" (*v chulkakh; v kubyshkakh*).

The surplus of free money is to some extent explained by the fact that the population does not want to buy poor-quality consumer goods, espe-

11. The currency revaluation led to an artificial redistribution of income for various groups within the population. Thus expenses rose sharply in the service sector, since many services are rendered for tips. (If you don't give a tip, you can be deprived of services.) If a tenant ordered a repairman from the housing administration for a small repair before 1960, for example, he would give the repairman a ruble. Soon after 1960, he would give the repairman the same ruble tip, even though the ruble was now worth ten times its earlier value. The same story occurred at the open (kolkhoz) market, where vegetables were sold for the same price in kopecks after 1960 as they had been before 1960.

12. This is defined to a large extent by the fact that military considerations in the radio industry dictate the increase of television production. In peacetime, however, the military capacities cannot be applied exclusively for military purposes and for the production of producer goods which are used for the output of producer goods.

13. *Narkhoz 22–72*, p. 373; *Pravda*, 26 Jan. 1974.

14. *Ibid.*

Table 7.2. Inventories of goods in retail and wholesale trade and in industry, and deposits in savings banks (in millions of rubles).

Years	Inventories	Total deposits	Ratio of inventories to deposits (percent)
1950	9,821	1,853	530.0
1960	24,483	10,909	224.4
1970	45,693	46,600	98.1
1971	48,298	53,215	90.8
1972	49,707	60,732	81.8

Source: Narkhoz-22–72, pp. 373, 401; Narkhoz-72, pp. 561, 590.

cially clothing and footwear.[15] The basic reason for the presence of "free money," however, lies in the scarcity of goods; such accumulation of "free money" is not motivated by precautionary or speculative desires for liquidity. In this we should note that the relationship of the total inventories to the sum of deposits in savings banks (not counting money in the hands of the population) has been steadily decreasing. Table 7.2 shows clearly that, whereas the ratio of inventories to the sum of deposits in savings banks stood at 530% in 1950, that percentage fell to 81.8% by 1972. Thus the aggregate expansion of money in savings banks, not counting the money "stuffed under the mattress," has already noticeably exceeded the aggregate of commodity reserves.

It goes without saying that, speaking in general, the above movement cannot be regarded as negative. To criticize it one would have to determine the national ratio between inventories and savings. It is not possible for us to calculate this norm. In any case, however, it is possible to say that, insofar as this ratio has shown a sharp tendency to decrease and lately forms an amount smaller than 100 percent, we should regard this relation with a great deal of caution. It threatens the existence of the commodity-money mechanism for distributing consumer goods and can lead to the introduction of rationing. Indeed, in times of panic, the people can bring out their "free money" and begin to hoard commodities. This can lead to a shortage of commodities available in the stores, the emergence of a black market, galloping price increases, etc. There is a possibility of a panic in the Soviet Union, since consumers fall easy prey to all kinds of rumors. They have no real information on measures which are being drawn up to change prices, the money system, etc. In this regard, several years ago when the threat of panic appeared, the Soviet

15. Thus, since 15 April 1974, a clearance sale of several types of clothes, footwear, and fancy goods has been in progress, with prices lowered to roughly half their former level. The sale has reached a total sum of one billion rubles (*Pravda,* 17 April 1974).

press printed refutations to the rumors which claimed that bank notes were about to be changed.

Of course, the picture we have drawn is only a possibility, since the state holds the levers for preventing a disruption of the commodity-money mechanism. The basic lever is to pump money gradually out of the population by increasing the price of consumption goods faster than incomes rise. However, the increase in total deposits held in savings banks indicates that the accumulation of free money continues.

The state can find a solution to this situation either by freezing savings bank accounts, as was done in the time of the Second World War, or reducing the value of savings, as was done during the financial reform of 1947.

Thus, the fact that the movement of incomes in the Soviet Union, both immediately before the war and in the first decade after the war, proceeded in basic agreement with the movement of prices (in the sense that reserves of "free money" were not created) gave birth to the opinion that in the planned economy there can be no galloping inflation in peacetime and that galloping inflation can threaten only a capitalist economy.

However, the material examined above indicates that the Soviet Union today is undergoing a suppressed inflationary process which can, in principle, give birth to galloping inflation in peacetime. In this we are dealing with a variety of suppressed inflation, which could be called "disguised inflation." The term "disguised inflation" reflects the fact that the state, afraid of laying bare the difficulties in the economy, disguises the rise of prices. At the same time, in order to overcome the arising difficulties, the state increases to an even greater degree the aggregate of free money, thereby creating the preconditions for galloping inflation.

Of course, the Soviet state, since it concentrates in its own hands incomparably more power over the separate spheres of society than do the Western states, is better able to prevent this inflation, or to suppress it more rapidly. But at the same time, we should note that the threat of galloping inflation can also become the object of a sharp political struggle within the present Soviet leadership and can make for the triumph of the conservative forces. Indeed, insofar as the threat of galloping inflation is hard to overcome without detriment to the savings of the population, since this requires creation of a flexible social-economic mechanism capable of securing the increase of the output of consumer goods, administrative methods for solving this problem may appear very tempting. And in the struggle, this gives an advantage to those groups in the Party which are still vividly conscious of Stalin's time and do not cease to recall that under Stalin prices were falling and the power of the country was growing and the people were satisfied and the world trembled before the Soviet Union. And if it was necessary to remove free money from circulation (as was done during the financial reform of 1947, or during the period when there were subscription loans), the people met this with enthusiasm.

8

Price Formation Models and Economic Efficiency

Alan A. Brown

University of Windsor

Joseph A. Licari

Occidental College

I. Introduction

We may distinguish, in a broad sense, between quantity-guided and price-guided economic mechanisms based upon the general dominance of one or the other type of message unit. Although a centrally planned economy may generally be considered a member of the quantity-guided class, this is not to imply that price information is either nonexistent or neutral in a centralized system. In fact, prices represent an important class of information even within such a system. The purpose of this study is to examine the informational content of centrally determined prices in Hungary on an empirical level and to indicate the impact that the quality of price information can have on the performance — actual and perceived — of a planned economy.[1] Our implicit concern in this chapter is with static allocational efficiency under planning to the extent that prices influence the allocation of resources, either directly, through the permissible reaction patterns of microeconomic agents to price messages, or indirectly through the planned allocation established by the central authorities in response to perceived constraints and feasible alternatives.[2]

1. In the limit, questions of pricing ultimately come down to questions of "how society should be ordered and what each person should be allowed to do" (Alchian, p. 5). Given our concern here solely with centralized mechanisms in Hungary, such questions have been implicitly answered, albeit with some variation possible in the latter regard. The intriguing cultural and political consequences of these answers remain outside the scope of this study. (For full citations, see the references listed at the end of the chapter.)

2. Again let us recognize the variation in "plannedness" (Levine 1971) that occurred over the period 1949–1967. Nonetheless, the economic mechanism in Hungary on the eve of the New Economic Mechanism still retained its predominantly centralized character. For

In our examination of pricing under planning, we will not be concerned with the traditional detailed procedures for computing commodity prices, since these have been well-documented elsewhere.[3] Our focus, instead, will be the description of alternative formalized models for centralized price formation and the use of these models to evaluate the economic characteristics of official prices. The following section will first describe interrelationships between prices and planning, and the particular roles performed by price information within a centralized economic system. We then present alternative price formation models that have emerged in the recent East European literature and use those models to determine empirically the degree of distortion of official prices in Hungary. These distortions are also shown to introduce a significant bias into the measurement of economic structure, a measurement which is crucial to the construction of the central plan. Lastly, the pricing models are employed to compute a measure of the change in aggregate economic efficiency in Hungary during the early sixties.

II. Prices and Planning

The three roles of prices

The evaluation of any system of prices must be predicated upon both an explicit understanding of the economic model within which they are to function and an explicit description of the roles they are to perform in it. In his classic article on the Soviet price system, Bornstein carefully identified three roles that prices perform to varying degrees in all economic systems, and therefore even in a planned economy of the Soviet or Hungarian type. They are: (1) measurement (for control and evaluation); (2) allocation; and (3) income distribution. (Bornstein 1966, p. 65).

The allocative role of prices in a decentralized economic mechanism is well known in both Eastern and Western economic circles. What is not generally appreciated is the allocative role, implicit or explicit, of prices under central planning. Even in the Soviet-type centrally planned economy (CPE) prices do influence the allocation of resources. For instance, on a macroeconomic level, planning decisions are generally made through macrobalances in value terms; and on a microeconomic level, enterprise targets are often specified in value or aggregate terms, which allow unpredictable flexibility for managerial determination if the specific input and output mix is based on the existing commodity price struc-

---

a factor productivity approach to the measurement of comparative aggregate static efficiency, see Bergson 1971.

3. See Balassa (1959, pp. 92–119) for details of the Hungarian procedures.

ture, supply elasticity, and incentive system.[4] Planners, therefore, require prices since there is a feedback from measurement to allocation.[5]

As for distribution, prices have played both explicit and implicit roles in CPEs. There has been a relatively free labor market, and wage rates have been influenced by the combined influences of supply and demand. In addition, an important source of rural income has been the sale of agricultural products produced on private plots on collective-farm markets. These factors have determined the explicit distribution of money income. The distribution of real income differs from that of money income because of the use of a complex system of indirect taxes (turnover taxes) and subsidies to establish retail prices of consumer goods (see Bornstein 1966, pp. 89–92). The net result is that distortions in the structure of retail prices – some goods sell above resource cost and some below – create implicit transfers of real income which have a substantial impact on the real standard of living. In all CPEs, prices have served as a major social policy instrument for shaping the distribution of real income through implicit grants.

The general quality of centrally determined prices

To evaluate the quality of centrally determined prices we may briefly refer to Bergson's two ideal standards of valuation.[6] The *efficiency standard* requires that the prices of any two commodities be inversely proportional to the corresponding marginal rates of transformation or, equivalently, directly proportional to their marginal costs. Prices conforming to the efficiency standard are appropriate for appraising production potential. The *welfare standard* requires that the prices of any two commodities be directly proportional to the marginal utilities of these commodities to consumers, or, where collective preferences are relevant, to the marginal rate of substitution between these commodities for the planners. Valuation based on the welfare standard is in order when the concern is to measure comparative levels of welfare. As Bergson states: "The efficiency and welfare standards are independent. Either may be realized without the other. However, the community ideally may produce a 'bill of goods' which is 'optimal' from the standpoint of welfare. If so, prices will correspond at the same time to both standards."[7]

Price formation mechanisms in CPEs are effectively divorced from

4. For an excellent, concise description of the allocative role of prices under central planning, see Bornstein 1966, pp. 66–68.

5. Of course, in a purely quantity-guided centralized system, without planning in terms of value aggregates, this feedback from measurement to allocation would be effectively severed.

6. Details are given in Bergson 1961, pp. 25–41, and 1953, pp. 42–54.

7. Bergson 1961, p. 31. Of course, prices in a system of perfectly competitive markets, functioning in a classical environment, simultaneously meet both standards.

real scarcity considerations and so fail to satisfy the conditions of either ideal standard. "[P]rices are not an autonomous force determining production, resource allocation, and consumption. Instead, prices are manipulated by the central authorities as one of various instruments intended to accomplish their planned goals" (Bornstein 1962, p. 64). Traditional accounting practices in CPEs ignored differential rent on land, as well as interest charges on fixed assets and working capital. Official prices tended therefore to undervalue raw materials and equipment relative to wages and thus encouraged an excessive use of material inputs relative to labor. Relative costs among products and industries quite naturally deviated arbitrarily from rational economic considerations and therefore from the efficiency standard.[8]

Further, the failure of centrally determined prices to satisfy economic criteria was exacerbated by the separation of prices into several disconnected domains. In particular, industrial wholesale prices were insulated from retail prices by a complicated array of turnover taxes, and domestic prices in general were divorced from foreign prices. The state budget served as the central device for correcting financial discrepancies caused by these price distortions. In this dual price system, relative prices of two goods in the industrial wholesale price structure need not be identical to those in the state retail price structure: retail prices were used to manipulate consumer purchases (equate supply and demand) and wholesale prices were adjusted according to different criteria (e.g., to manipulate profitability rates in goods production).[9] This arbitrariness of price formation was accepted as long as the control or allocative role of prices was subordinate to the distributive or social policy role. Obviously, as the old system moves toward decentralization, the relative importance of the various roles shifts and traditional methods of price formation become increasingly dysfunctional to the further development of the economy. The full impact of the wisdom behind Béla Csikós-Nagy's comment that "it was a mistake of some Marxian economists . . . to suppose that macro-economic laws could be enforced only in a battle against micro-economic laws" then comes to be agonizingly felt.[10]

8. The economic consequences of these deviations are neatly catalogued in Marczewski 1971, pp. 109–10.

9. See also Bornstein 1966, p. 70.

10. Czikós-Nagy 1968, p. 9. Along the same line of thought is the following comment from the Yugoslav economists, Maksimovic and Pjanic (1968): "It was long the assumption of Marxists that the economic mechanism of socialism would operate with the sort of parameters typical of the natural sciences: production units would merely be technical and organizational components of the system, and the distribution of available labour would be calculable as a technological relationship. This belief has not been borne out by the practical experience of socialist countries, which has shown that rational calculation requires a determinate system of prices; a much wider field is thus left to economic laws than had originally been thought" (p. 185).

III. Alternative Price Formation Models

Apparent weaknesses in the system of central price determination sparked a candid reappraisal of pricing procedures which began in the early 1960s. In the ensuing discussions, Hungarian economists have played a leading role, quite naturally, since the relatively greater interest in meaningful decentralization in Hungary has placed a higher opportunity cost on the maintenance of distorted price structures. A number of alternative price formation models have been put forward as preferred bases for computation of prices. One may argue, however, that all of these models suffer from the dominance of the Marxian view of prices as objective phenomena—prices are calculable from production data only—to the exclusion of the Western subjective interpretation of prices (see Grossman 1960, p. 14). This cost interpretation of value can at best satisfy only the efficiency standard since it ignores the influence of demand and therefore of preferences in the formation of prices.[11] The pricing models emerging in eastern Europe are then best interpreted as attempts to move planned economies closer to their production possibilities locus by developing a price structure that is more reflective of relative marginal resource costs and by employing this improved information set on both macroeconomic and microeconomic levels in resource use decisions.[12] Of course, by focusing on cost as the determinant of prices, these pricing models are quite consistent with both classical theory and long-run neoclassical theory, where value is independent of utility considerations.

These price formation models, which are formal attempts to establish an economically meaningful structure of prices, are in fact based on the same assumptions that underlie Bergson's Adjusted Factor Cost Standard:[13]

(1) All commodity prices resolve fully into charges for primary factors, particularly labor, land, and capital.

(2) For capital there is a net charge corresponding to the average internal return of this factor in the economy generally, and an allowance for depreciation of a conventional sort.

(3) The charge for land, "rent," corresponds on the average to the differential return to superior land.

(4) "Wages" are at a uniform rate for any occupation and as between occupations differ on the average in accord with differences in productivity and disutility.

11. Marczewski (1971, p. 109) notes that recent price reforms in East Germany still fail to account for demand influences.

12. For a discussion of the Soviet price debate, see Bornstein 1966, pp. 69–73.

13. These assumptions are adapted from the full set given in Bergson 1953, p. 42.

(5) Similar principles apply in the case of the relation of wages to form labor income.

(6) Commodity prices are uniform in any given market area.

Typically, however, the models ignore rent and focus exclusively on labor and capital as sources of value.[14] Also, unless the input-output tables are pre-adjusted for differential turnover taxes and subsidies, the models tend to ignore the dual price problem. Hejl, Kyn, and Sekerka (1967, p. 62) have argued that the socialist price structure problem is composed of two parts: (1) the mutual relation between wholesale and retail prices through a system of indirect taxes and subsidies (the dual price problem); and (2) the relations between prices of different products (the relative price problem). It is essentially the latter aspect of the pricing question that is addressed by the proposed formal models.[15]

A. *Formalized pricing models*

The East European pricing models begin with the standard Marxian assumption that every price consists of three basic components: material costs (c), wages (w), and profits or all nonwage value added (z). Thus:

$$P = c + w + z.$$

While socialist economists agreed that surplus product (z) should be included in prices in some uniform way rather than the arbitrary traditional procedures, it was necessary to choose among several alternative rules for this inclusion. Each rule in turn forms a core of a new price base.

A formidable analytical problem arises in implementing any rule, since material costs c and, under certain rules, surplus value z must themselves be computed at new prices simultaneously with the recomputation of a particular commodity price in order to make the computation of a new price base internally consistent. To take into consideration the interdependencies between prices and resource costs, Marxian value theory has been fused with the Western input-output framework to make the pricing models operational. Of course, this means that the models suffer from all the limitations associated with the assumptions behind that technique: linear production functions (constant returns to scale), no factor substitution (constant production coefficients), and absence of joint products, among other assumptions.

Work on the use of the new pricing models in Hungarian planning began in the late 1950s. By the early 1960s, the Hungarian National

14. Brown (1971) has shown that while rent may be a minor portion (2–5 percent) of total factor income in eastern Europe, it may have a much greater marginal impact on revaluation procedures than this implies.

15. The only major exception is the limited Czechoslovak attempts in the mid-1960s to address both problems simultaneously. See Sekerka et al. 1970.

Price Board was developing a price model based on an input-output table.[16] The theoretical foundation of this and related models was due primarily to András Bródy, and Sándor Ganczer pioneered its early applications.[17] Related work (to be discussed below) was also under way at the same time elsewhere in eastern Europe but particularly in Czechoslovakia. Let us now briefly review the essential properties and formal definitions of the alternative price formation models that have emerged in eastern Europe. We are not concerned so much with choosing among them as with the different interpretations of the quality of actual Hungarian prices and of the composition of the structure of the Hungarian economy, discussed below in this chapter.

B. *The general model*[18]

Actual prices of products in CPEs have been based on material costs evaluated at prevailing prices, wage costs, and the so-called accumulation (i.e., profits and taxes or subsidies). The ratio of accumulation to other elements of value varies from one sector to another in no relation to any kind of cost concept. The basic purpose of all price models is to allocate this nonwage component of value according to some economically justifiable criteria. This changes all relative prices. In order

16. The existence of a "special 'price model' elaborated by the Hungarian National Price Board for the calculation of prices" is mentioned by T. Morva (1962, pp. 243–48).

17. Bródy's primary theoretical work is contained in Bródy 1962, 1964, and 1965. This line of development culminated in his magnum opus (1970), in which he attempted a full reinterpretation of traditional Marxian value theory in terms of contemporary linear economic theory. Kornai 1967, chs. 16 and 17, also gives a useful theoretical description of the basic pricing models. Ganczer gives results of early applications of the price adjustment models based upon the price formation models (this relationship will be clarified below) in Csikós-Nagy et al. 1965, and Ganczer 1965 and 1966. Further results were published in the UN's (1967) *Macro-economic models.*

18. The general model and all particular models flowing from it are members of the class of equilibrium prices, where equilibrium is defined in relation to the satisfaction of a system of equality constraints on national income and/or its components. Alternatively, we could speak of shadow prices which are optimally derived, based upon maximization of an objective function subject to the satisfaction of a system of inequality constraints on resource and product availability. While these prices are economically preferred as indices of scarcity, both Bródy (1965, p. 58) and Ganczer (1966, pp. 57–58) recognize that practical limitations make their operational importance limited in the foreseeable future. In particular, early work by Kornai and his collaborators at the Institute of Economics suggested that systems of shadow prices may not be stable under normal circumstances, owing to the discontinuous nature of the underlying mathematical model. Recent results presented by Simon (1970) suggest, however, that under certain conditions relative shadow prices may be less sensitive to changes in resource constraints and in the objective function than first thought. To use Bornstein's useful distinction (1966, pp. 71–72), our focus in this chapter will be the models advocated by the "surplus product markup school" rather than the "opportunity cost school," since it is only the former that can now have any practical significance in planning or research.

to revalue material costs of production at the new prices and at the same time revalue the existing capital stock which is also priced at the prevailing, irrational prices, all models utilize an input-output framework to consider the various interdependencies between costs and prices.

Following the conventional Leontief notation, total output for the i-th sector is given by

$$X_i = \sum_{j=1}^{N} x_{ij} + Y_i, \, i = 1, \ldots, N, \tag{1}$$

where X_i is the total output of sector i in physical units,

  x_{ij} is the output of i-th sector employed in production in j-th sector,
  Y_i is the output of i-th sector directly satisfying final demand.

The dual of this relation is

$$P_i X_i = \sum_{j=1}^{N} P_j x_{ji} + W_i + Z_i, \, i = 1, \ldots, N, \tag{2}$$

where P_i is the unit price of output of i-th sector,

  W_i is the wage bill of i-th sector,
  Z_i is the accumulation (nonwage value added or profit) of i-th sector.

By conventional accounting procedures, Z_i is computed as the residual necessary to satisfy the accounting identity

$$Z_i = P_i X_i - \sum_{j} P_j x_{ji} - W_i \tag{3}$$

and all commodities are priced at official or prevailing rates.

The fundamental shortcoming of this scheme is the arbitrary nature of the residual Z_i, which represents nonwage elements in pricing. This residual is arbitrary as long as prices employed in the computations fail to reflect accurately the opportunity costs of resource use. To provide a more rational basis for valuing individual commodities, and total and sectoral output, it is necessary to establish a more meaningful basis for calculating the level of allocation among sectors of Z_i, the nonlabor return. This is, in fact, the focus of all pricing schemes to be developed.

There are in principle three simple ways of viewing the residual Z_i:

  (i) Z_i reflects a return to all (noncapital) material inputs used in production in sector i;
  (ii) Z_i reflects a return to direct labor used in production in sector i;
  (iii) Z_i reflects a return to capital (fixed and working) employed in production in sector i.

If we limit these relationships for practical purposes to direct proportionalities, we can define Z_i as[19]

$$Z_i^* = \alpha \sum_j P_j x_{ji} + \beta W_i + \gamma \sum_j P_j K_{ji}, \tag{4}$$

where K_{ji} is the output in physical units of j-th sector employed as fixed or working capital in i-th sector, and α, β, γ are proportionality constants.

Combining this rule for the formation of the residual with the dual equation (2), we have

$$P_i^* X_i = (1 + \alpha) \sum_j P_j^* x_{ji} + (1 + \beta)\, W_i + \gamma \sum_j P_j^* K_{ji}, \tag{5}$$

where P_i^* is the new unit price for i-th sector based upon the general markup rule for generating surplus product. The interdependence between commodity prices is apparent in equation (5), since the new price for sector i (P_i^*) is a function of the new prices of all other sectors j (P_j^*). Consequently, all new prices must be calculated simultaneously.

If we state the full system of equilibrium relations (5) in matrix notation, we have:

$$P^* X = (1 + \alpha)\, P^* \overline{X} + (1 + \beta) W + \gamma P^* K, \tag{6}$$

where P^* is an N-element row vector $\{P_i^*\}$,
$\quad X$ is an $N \times N$ matrix $\{x_{ij}\}$,
$\quad\quad (X_{ii} = X_i)$
$\quad \overline{X}$ is an $N \times N$ matrix $\{x_{ji}\}$,
$\quad W$ is an N-element row vector $\{W_i\}$,
$\quad K$ is an $N \times N$ matrix $\{K_{ji}\}$.

If we further restate (6) in terms of conventional technical coefficients, we obtain

$$P^* = (1 + \alpha)\, P^* A + (1 + \beta)\, W^* + \gamma P^* K^*, \tag{7}$$

where A is an $N \times N$ matrix $\{a_{ji}\}$ and $a_{ji} = x_{ji}/X_j$,
$\quad W^*$ is an N-element row vector $\{w_i\}$ and $w_i = W_i/X_j$,
$\quad K^*$ is an $N \times N$ matrix $\{K_{ji}^*\}$ and $K_{ji}^* = K_{ji}/X_j$.

Obviously, $P^* A$, W^*, and $P^* K^*$ are, respectively, the material costs, wages, and capital charges required for one unit of production at P^* prices. The prices P^* "cover costs of materials and form income as a sum of three components: the first is proportional to cost of materials,

19. Bornstein's choice of the term "surplus product markup school" follows directly from this relation.

the second to capital, and the third to wages. Prices defined by equation (7) are therefore called *three-channel prices.*[20] This three-channel model will be the basis for all specific models to follow.

Equation (7) highlights our earlier comments regarding the nature and limitations of all centralized price formation models. The price vector P^* is obviously a function only of factor costs; there is no direct role for demand to influence the formation of these prices. Nonetheless, the fact that (7) represents an attempt to distribute accumulation based upon economically meaningful criteria should make such prices better measures of resource costs than official prices based on arbitrary rates of profit. Prices P^* should then be closer to Bergson's efficiency standard, thus providing an improved basis for measuring production potential on macro and micro decision levels. Measurement of welfare, however, by these or prevailing prices remains questionable.

Equation (7) contains N unknown commodity prices and three unknown parameters (α,β,γ). If we specify each parameter exogenously, then equation (7) can be solved analytically for the new vector of commodity prices P^* consistent with the stipulated markup pattern:

$$P^* = (1 + \beta)W^* [I - (1 + \alpha)A - \gamma K^*]^{-1}. \tag{8}$$

In practical application, however, it is desirable to impose an additional constraint on the new prices P^*.[21] These may be institutional or policy constraints, such as stability of the consumer price index or overall stability of the price level. Two types of constraint dominate in the literature:[22]

(a) *The value of the consumption fund under the new and prevailing price systems should be the same:*

$$P^*C = PC, \tag{9a}$$

where C is an N-element column vector of consumption in physical units.

The underlying rationale is that since wages are the same under both systems, the aggregate real value of workers' consumption should remain fixed. This is equivalent to keeping the consumer price index constant as relative prices are adjusted. This is not to say that reform of the price structure could not be linked with a

20. Sekerka et al. 1970, p. 186. See also pp. 185–87.
21. Analytically, this is equivalent to imposition of a normalizing condition or the selection of a numéraire. See Sekerka et al. 1970, p. 192.
22. A third type of constraint, that the value of total output in the new price system remain unchanged, i.e., $P^*X = PX$, has received limited investigation by Yugoslav economists. See Sekulic and Grdic 1972. The logic behind this constraint appears less clear than behind the two alternatives discussed below.

change in the absolute level of real consumption. "However, a separate analysis is needed to determine the extent of the modification and the type of complementary measures to be taken in the field of wages and income policy" (Ganczer 1966, p. 59). In any case, the constraint based on the consumption fund assumes that the adjustment of relative prices may change the price level of the nonconsumption components and, consequently, the overall price level of national income or net material product. The consumption fund constraint has been favored in both Hungarian (Ganczer 1965, 1966) and Czechoslovak (Levine 1971) applications of the pricing models.

(b) *The value of aggregate output (i.e., final demand or net material product, NMP) under the new and prevailing price systems should be identical:*

$$P^*Y = PY. \tag{9b}$$

Since wages are the same under both systems, this constraint is equivalent to keeping the total nonwage value added constant, and merely reallocating it among sectors according to specified rules. This constraint maintains a constant final demand price index, but of course all relative prices are allowed to change. Computed prices based upon the aggregate output constraint also allow changes in the relative weights of the main expenditure categories or components of the NMP, including consumption. While changes in the consumer price index may be objectionable on policy grounds, for purposes of economic analysis a maintenance of constant NMP would permit more meaningful intertemporal and cross-country comparisons.

Of course, the addition of either constraint to the basic system of price determination (equation 7) necessitates the inclusion of an additional degree of freedom to prevent the full system from being overdetermined. Practically, this means that any one of the three proportionality constants can be taken as an additional unknown, along with the vector P^*, and values for the $N+1$ unknowns of the new price system can be determined simultaneously from equation (7) and either equation (9a) or equation (9b). It is in fact variations in the exogeneity and endogeneity of α, β, and γ that are the fundamental sources of difference in the particular pricing models we shall now discuss.

1. *Value prices.*[23] In this price system, the full nonwage value-added component, or "accumulation," in every branch of the economy is made

23. See Balassa 1959, p. 99; Bornstein 1966, p. 71; Šik 1967, p. 245; Ganczer 1966, p. 56; Sekerka et al. 1970, p. 189; Hejl et al. 1967, p. 62; and Bródy 1970, p. 73.

proportional to the cost of wages in that sector. Hence, it does not take into account the opportunity cost of capital. With reference to our general model in equation (7), value prices correspond to the case where $\alpha = 0$, $\gamma = 0$; and β is to be endogenously determined. Bródy has shown that value prices will lead to efficiency decisions regarding resource use only under conditions of simple commodity production (no investment).[24]

2. *Cost or averaged value prices*.[25] In the second type of price system, accumulation is proportional to prime costs — both material costs and direct wages. Then $\gamma = 0$, and $\alpha = \beta$; therefore, there is again only a single parameter to be determined endogenously within the model. In averaged value prices, the rate of profit is the same for all commodities and is equal to $\alpha/(1 + \alpha)$. These prices are generically related to commodity prices computed in the Western input-output literature. Leontief, in his pioneering study of the American economy, computed (1941, pp. 189–94) a system of commodity prices based on a given vector V of unit value added by sector v_i:

$$P^* = V[I - A]^{-1}.$$

This price vector is analogous to averaged value prices, given α_0:

$$P^* = (1 + \alpha_0)W[I - A]^{-1}.$$

However, the unit value-added vector does not necessarily imply a constant ratio of wage to nonwage value added for all sectors.[26]

3. *Production prices*.[27] In the third price system, accumulation is taken as a fixed fraction of the capital used in a given sector, but simultaneously capital is also revalued according to the price adjustment of the respective producing sectors where the various types of capital originated. This means that the nonwage residual in each sector of the economy becomes proportional to the fixed assets and working capital tied up in that sector. Thus, we are interpreting the nonwage value added solely as an imputed capital cost. As a result, the rate of return on capital in all sectors is the same. In terms of equation (7), $\alpha = 0$, $\beta = 0$, and γ is the uniform rate of return on capital, which is to be determined endogenously, subject to equation (9a) or equation (9b). Following Bródy, "under idealized conditions of expanded reproduction, it is production

24. See Bródy 1970, p. 73. Here Bródy introduces the concept of "properly orienting" prices, meaning that the relative resource use levels of alternate processes will be correctly reflected in the relative costs of inputs, based on the given structure of commodity prices.

25. See Bornstein 1966, p. 71; Ganczer 1966, p. 56; Sekerka et al. 1970, pp. 190–91; Hejl et al. 1967, p. 62.

26. The Leontief formulation of averaged value prices has recently been used in a study by Fontela (Fontela et al. 1972).

27. See Balassa 1959, p. 100; Bornstein 1966, p. 71; Šik 1967, pp. 246–47; Šekerka et al. 1970, p. 191; Hejl et al. 1967, p. 63; and Bródy 1970, p. 76. In the Hungarian literature these are sometimes referred to as "producer type-variant 'a'." See Ganczer 1965, pp. 68–69.

prices rather than value prices that should orient technological decisions" (1970, p. 76). Interestingly, Watanabe and Shishido (1970), in their recent study of the Japanese price structure along Leontief lines, used a price model analogous to production prices.

4. *Two-channel prices.*[28] In the fourth price system, nonwage value added is divided into two parts, one of which is allocated among sectors in proportion to the revalued capital stock in that sector, and the other is allocated among sectors in proportion to wage costs. Thus, this price model involves both a rate of return on capital and a rate of surcharge on wages; it is, in short, a mixture of the value-type and the producer-type prices. Now $\alpha = 0$, but depending on the relative magnitudes of β and γ, there are a number of variants in this type of price system. Usually, β is given exogenously as β_0 (e.g., according to the proportion of fringe benefits to wages), while γ is endogenously determined.

One may offer three theoretical justifications for the part of surplus product apportioned according to wages. First, one may argue that the true opportunity cost of labor to enterprises is higher than the wage bill and a proportionate increase would reflect various fringe benefits, or other labor-related costs, not included in wages and salaries paid directly to employees. As Esze and Nagy have argued in favor of two-channel prices: "Here [with the wage-related portion of accumulation] we think about that part which accrues to the workers as indirect transfer, including the amount spent to train new workers. This part is, strictly speaking, not a net income of society, but — from the viewpoint of society — as much the cost of labor as wages" (quoted by Bródy 1970, p. 78). Bródy claims that government-financed social costs of "reproducing manpower" (health services, education, training) amount to roughly 20–30 percent of wages (1970, p. 77). Ganczer has used a somewhat higher figure of 35 percent (1966, p. 57). A second justification of the two-channel prices refers to the economy as a whole; e.g., linear programing calculations have indicated that shadow wages are "unequivocally" higher than actual wages. These estimates are also clustered around a 30 percent excess over actual wages (Simon 1965, pp. 90–91). Third, Bródy has suggested an interpretation based on human capital concepts. The portion of surplus product proportional to wages is, in this view, an imputed return to human capital, not reflected in direct wages.[29] Quite naturally, then, to

28. See Bornstein 1966, p. 71; Šik 1967, pp. 246–47; Bródy 1970, pp. 76ff.; Hejl et al. 1967, p. 63; and Sekerka et al. 1970, pp. 189–91. Two-channel prices include "producer type-variants 'b' and 'c'" in the Hungarian literature. See Ganczer 1965, pp. 68–70.

29. Bródy (1970, pp. 82–83) presents an interesting case for the relativity of pricing models to historical stages of development. The two-channel model is then peculiarly relevant to the stage after substantial capital accumulation, where both physical and human capital are important sources of surplus product.

the degree that human capital provides a greater contribution to the surplus than physical capital, two-channel prices will approach value prices.

In any event, value and production prices, respectively, represent the two extreme limits for two-channel prices: the first, when $\gamma = 0$, implies that all surplus should be proportionate to wages; the second, when $\beta = 0$, implies that all surplus should be imputed to capital. Between the two extreme bounds, depending on the actual value of β_0, there is an infinite number of possibilities for the two-channel price system.[30]

5. *Income prices.*[31] In the fifth type of price system, no distinction is made between wages and other accumulation. All value added (wage and nonwage) is allocated according to capital employed in each sector. Thus, $\alpha = 0$, $\beta = -1$, and γ is endogenously determined. Less attention has been given this model in Hungary than elsewhere in eastern Europe.

C. Price adjustment models

From an operational standpoint, the above models have two basic shortcomings. First, they ignore the fact that the available interindustry data are expressed as value aggregates based on official prices, not in physical units. Second, they fail to recognize explicitly the existence of a given price structure. What we need to do, then, is to develop procedures for adjusting official prices based upon the price formation models and available interindustry data in monetary units. This leads us to a series of price adjustment models, directly analogous to the above series of price formation models.

The key to making the pricing models operational is a set of price adjustment coefficients (p_i) — one coefficient for each sector of the economy — that indicate the extent to which prevailing sectoral prices diverge from given definitions of factor cost. For sector i, we have

$$p_i = \frac{P_i^*}{P_i}. \tag{10}$$

The price adjustment coefficient can thus be interpreted as the ratio of the sector price based on redefined factor cost to the official sector price.

By equation (5), the factor cost price P_i^* is defined by

$$P_i^* X_i = \sum_j P_j^* x_{ji} + W_i + Z_i^*. \tag{11}$$

30. A form of two-channel model was employed for computing fixed and bounded prices under the New Economic Mechanism. See Portes 1970, pp. 308–9.

31. Sekerka et al. 1970, p. 188; Hejl et al. 1967, p. 63; and Maksimovic and Pjanic 1968, p. 190.

Given equation (10), this becomes

$$p_i P_i X_i = \sum_j p_j P_j x_{ji} + W_i + Z_i^*. \tag{12}$$

Now let $X_i^* = P_i X_i$ be the total value of sector i output at official prices, and $x_{ji}^* = P_j x_{ji}$ be the value of output of sector j used in production in sector i at official prices. Thus equation (12) becomes

$$p_i X_i^* = \sum_j p_j x_{ji}^* + W_i + Z_i^*. \tag{13}$$

By equation (4), along with equation (10), the general factor-cost definition of nonwage value added Z_i^* is

$$Z_i^* = \alpha \sum_j p_j x_{ji}^* + \beta W_i + \gamma \sum_j p_j k_{ji}, \tag{14}$$

where $k_{ji} = P_j K_{ji}$ is the value of output of sector j used as capital (fixed or working) in sector i at official prices.

In general, then, the three-channel model in terms of price adjustment coefficients becomes

$$p_i X_i^* = (1 + \alpha) \sum_j p_j x_{ji}^* + (1 + \beta) W_i + \gamma \sum_j p_j k_{ji}. \tag{15}$$

For all N sectors:

$$pX^* = (1 + \alpha) \, p\overline{X}^* + (1 + \beta) W + \gamma p\overline{K}, \tag{16}$$

where

p is an N-element row vector $\{p_i\}$,
X^* is an $N \times N$-matrix $\{x_{ij}^*\}$,
$\overline{X}^*$ is an $N \times N$-element matrix $\{x_{ji}^*\}$,
W is an N-element row vector $\{W_i\}$, and
$\overline{K}$ is an $N \times N$-element matrix $\{k_{ji}\}$.

Let us note two things regarding equation (16). First, it is a direct analog to equation (6); with the replacement of capital and output data in physical units by those in value units, the vector of unknowns becomes a vector of price indices, not absolute prices. Second, it implies that the relative distribution of wages among sectors is an acceptable approximation of the opportunity cost of labor, the underlying assumption being that labor is sufficiently mobile or that relative wages reflect relative labor productivities.[32]

32. Of course, in the two-channel case, an adjustment is made for indirect labor charges accounting for a portion of accumulation.

For convenience, let us restate equation (16) in terms of unit production, capital, and wage coefficients in value terms based on official prices:

$$p = (1 + \alpha) \, pA^* + (1 + \beta) \, \overline{W} + \gamma p \overline{K}^*, \qquad (17)$$

where

A^* is an $N \times N$-element matrix $\{a_{ji}{}^*\}$ and $a_{ji}{}^* = x_{ji}{}^*/X_j{}^*$,
$\overline{W}$ is an N-element row vector $\{\overline{W}_i\}$ and $\overline{W}_i = W_i/X_i{}^*$, and
$\overline{K}^*$ is an $N \times N$-element matrix $\{k_{ji}{}^*\}$ and $k_{ji}{}^* = k_{ji}/X_j{}^*$.

Equation (17) is of course a direct analog to equation (7). That the new price variable is indeed a price index can be seen by examining the representative term $p_i a_{ji}{}^*$:

$$p_i a_{ji}{}^* = \frac{P_i{}^*}{P_i} \frac{P_i x_{ji}}{P_j X_j} = \frac{P_i{}^* x_{ji}}{P_j X_j}.$$

Thus, the term $p_i a_{ji}{}^*$ indicates the value of output of sector i in adjusted prices, consumed per unit value of output of sector j in original prices. By analogy, since p_i is given by

$$p_i = (1 + \beta) \sum_j p_j a_{ji}{}^* + (1 + \beta)\overline{W}_i + \gamma \sum_j p_j k_{ji}{}^*,$$

the price adjustment coefficient for sector i represents the total value of factor inputs or total factor cost in the new system of prices per unit value of output of sector i in official prices. But this is equivalent to the ratio of unit value at new prices to unit value at official prices, or $P_i{}^*/P_i$, which is of course the definition of p_i given in equation (10).

To complete the general price adjustment model, equation (17) must be combined with a normalization condition restated in terms of unit values at official prices and price adjustment coefficients. By analogy to equations (9a) and (9b), we have two possibilities:

(a) *Constant consumption:* $pC^* = 1$, (18a)

where C^* is an N-element column vector $\{C_i{}^*\}$ and $C_i{}^* = P_i C_i / \sum_i P_i C_i$.

(b) *Constant national income:* $pY^* = 1$, (18b)

where Y^* is an N-element column vector $\{Y_i{}^*\}$ and $Y_i{}^* = P_i Y_i / \sum_i P_i Y_i$.

Vectors of price adjustment coefficients can be obtained for any of the above definitions of factor costs by solving equation (17) and either equation (18a) or equation (18b), with appropriate definitions of the values of the proportionality constants α, β, and γ.[33] In production, two-channel, and income price systems, nonlinearities exist due to the combined endogenous nature of γ and the simultaneous revaluation of capital at the new prices[34] (see equation 17). Iterative procedures must be employed to obtain numerical approximations to the equilibrium values of the unknown price coefficient vector and γ. A general solution algorithm developed at the International Development Research Center, Indiana University, is described in detail in Brown, Hall, and Licari (1973). Additional discussion of approaches to solution of the price adjustment models is given in Hejl et al. (1967, pp. 75–76).

The price adjustment coefficients computed by the above procedures are indices which indicate the deviation of actual prices from some alternative scheme of factor-cost pricing. The degree to which the price adjustment coefficients deviate from a value of unity is an indication of the degree to which actual prices fail to conform to the implied definition of factor costs.[35] As such, they provide a means of recomputing socialist prices on the basis of a theoretically more satisfactory concept of resource costs.

But the price adjustment models measure distortions in prices *only* from the view of costs, not welfare. Given a particular definition of factor cost, the corresponding price adjustment coefficients provide a basis for better measuring production potential to the extent that the linear production functions in the model approximate the actual production relationships existing in the economy. But no explicit role exists for price adjustments to reflect deviations from relative rates of substitution based on either consumer or planner preferences.

By measuring distortions from the viewpoint of production potential, not welfare, adjusted prices are analogous to Bergson's Adjusted Factor Cost Standard (AFCS) for revaluation of national income data of socialist economies.[36] Both the AFCS and adjusted prices would correspond to average cost if factor prices were uniform across sectors and reflected average relative factor productivities in the economy as a whole. Assuming constant returns to scale as a suitable approximation to the prevailing technology, both also meet the requirements of the Efficiency Standard

33. For an alternative development of the concept of price adjustment coefficients in the context of the price formation models, see Sekerka et al. 1970, p. 193.

34. Solution of the model is itself not a simple task. Only in the cases of value and averaged-value prices are analytical solutions available.

35. The price adjustment coefficients here refer to deviations of official prices from equilibrium prices. Alternatively, one could compute an analog adjustment coefficient as the ratio of shadow price to official price, which would indicate the deviation of prevailing prices from optimal scarcity prices. For an illustration of this latter approach, see Simon 1970. The former approach remains of much more practical significance, owing, among other things, to the calculational difficulties with shadow-price schemes.

36. See esp. Bergson 1961, pp. 26–41, and 1953, pp. 43–52.

for optimal measurement of production potential. Nonetheless, their relationship to the Welfare Standard remains uncertain unless additional information regarding relative consumer or planner preferences is available. The obvious superiority of the price adjustment models is their capability to account for the simultaneous effects of a price change in one sector upon the structure of prices and costs in every sector of the economy and by so doing to arrive at an internally consistent set of synthetic equilibrium prices.

D. *Use of adjusted prices*

The price adjustment models are concerned with the empirical problem of estimating factor-cost prices that are more consistent with the Efficiency Standard than are prevailing prices. They are addressed solely to the question of reaching the production possibility frontier through improved valuation and abstract entirely from the broader question of optimality where marginal rates of transformation in production must be equated to marginal rates of substitution in consumption. Nonetheless, in providing a mechanism for improved measurement of production potential, adjusted prices have an important role to play both in the reform of official price structures and in the measurement and study of economic performance in socialist economies.

Price adjustment models have already been employed in the design of price reforms in eastern Europe. The early work in Hungary in the late 1950s was instrumental in the design of the 1959 price reform:

> The price system which came into effect on 1 January 1959 was derived with the help of the inverse matrix obtained from the input-output table for 1957. The introduction of the new price system had the immediate effect of revealing hidden profits in certain branches of the economy which arose from discrepancies between costs of production and former prices. Later a 300 × 300 table of commodities was inverted: this table was not complete, but the typical inputs and outputs of each branch was represented. The resulting inverse showed the degree of interdependence between commodities with sufficient accuracy to permit qualitative judgments about the consequences of price changes in commodities upon one another (United Nations 1968, p. 91).

A two-channel adjustment model based on the 1962 Czechoslovakian input-output table provided the guiding framework for the wholesale price reform that went into effect in Czechoslovakia on 1 January 1967.[37]

---

37. See Hejl et al. 1967 and Sekerka et al. 1970, p. 201. Šik (1967, pp. 262–64) gives an excellent verbal description of the actual price adjustment process and the role of price adjustment coefficients in price reform.

Similarly, a 1962 Yugoslav input-output table and a two-channel adjustment model were used in designing the 1965 Yugoslav price reform (Sekulik and Grdic 1972). In fact, Šik (1967, p. 262) has argued that price adjustment models can be an important guide even in the decentralized formation of prices under market influences.[38]

The East European price models can also be of vital importance in empirical research and ultimately in planning itself. The fundamental problem facing studies of the structure and performance of socialist economies is the extent to which conclusions, even if reached through valid analysis, may be biased by the distorted prices underlying the aggregates being analyzed. Prices are weighting systems used in answering questions of structure, growth, and structural change. Since prevailing prices are poor measures of the real drain on production potential, they will invalidate the answers suggested by the data.

The major objective of the price adjustment models is to provide a separate set of price adjustment coefficients for each alternative definition of factor cost. When combined with official statistics, these coefficients give a sophisticated mechanism for adjusting the price basis underlying the valuation of various national economic aggregates and subaggregates to reflect more adequately their actual factor costs. Thus, they make possible more reasonable weighting systems which should improve evaluation of the country's economic performance. Improvements in interpretation and understanding of socialist experiences must be predicated on improving the underlying price basis of the aggregates. This improvement in economic measurement can in turn have an impact on the efficiency of the planning process through the mutual intimate interaction of centrally established plans and perceived structure and performance of the economy.[39]

In sum, although the pricing models described in this chapter are of a rather formal nature, they have important applications in both planning and empirical research. Socialist economies have become increasingly concerned about the efficiency of their system of administration, particularly since inefficiencies represent sacrificed growth. The computation of price adjustment coefficients based on the above schemes provides a mechanism for determining an appropriate combination of price changes which ought to be better measures of the drain on production potential and hence a better set of signals to guide (centralized or decentralized) decisions about resource use. These price models then can be of immense practical significance generally in planning, and particularly in the design of price reforms.

38. The idea here is that adjusted prices can serve as norms for the guidance of market prices.
39. This indirect allocational role of prices through feedback of measurement on central allocation and control decisions was discussed earlier.

IV. Price Distortions under Planning

We now turn to an examination of the quantitative degree of distortion in centrally determined prices in Hungary relative to our formal definitions of factor-cost pricing. We will focus on the three pricing models with the strongest theoretical basis — value, production, and two-channel prices — and will examine the structure of price adjustment coefficients computed for each. The normalizing condition in all cases will be constant national income or more specifically net material product (equation 18b), although studies have shown that the choice of constraint has only a second-order effect on the computed coefficients.[40]

All calculations are based on reconstructed Hungarian 13-sector input-output tables (see the Appendix to this chapter and Brown and Walker 1973). All transactions data were "expressed at domestic, factory sales (producer's) prices [for a given year] . . . and include any turnover tax added to the basic price of a commodity. These values are equivalent to purchaser's prices less transport costs and the trade margin, which are treated as separate inputs purchased by the consuming sector from the transport and trade sectors" (Brown and Walker 1973, pp. 20–21). Measured distortions are thus best interpreted in relation to prevailing purchaser's prices net of transport costs and the trade margin. In addition, imports are consistently treated as noncompetitive with domestic production, as in the standard procedure in Hungarian input-output accounting.[41]

A. *Price distortions in Hungary, 1959–1968*

Price adjustment coefficients for value, production, and two-channel pricing for 1959, 1964, 1966, and 1968 are presented in Tables 8.1,

40. Walker's comprehensive study (1971) of the operational properties of the price adjustment models includes important sensitivity analysis regarding the impact of constraint choice, aggregation level, and inclusion of economic rent on the computed price adjustment coefficients. All impacts appeared to be of second-order importance as compared with the primary impact of price adjustment itself in relation to official prices. Differences between coefficients based upon the consumption constraint varied 1–5 percent from those based upon the national income constraint (pp. 115–19). However, the former led to a general upward bias in all coefficients since the average price level was not held invariant. Inclusion of rent in agriculture also had a modest effect on the calculations. Variations seldom reached 10 percent; as expected, coefficients for agriculture and sectors closely tied to agriculture rose with inclusion of rent (pp. 127–30) but the change amounted at most to 17 percent. As for aggregation effects, coefficients computed from 13-sector and 7-sector tables differed by only 1–3 percent (pp. 131–33). As a result of these sensitivity experiments, it appears that inferences drawn from price adjustment calculations based upon the national income constraint, exclusive of rent, and a 13-sector table are not likely to be significantly biased by the particular conditions of the analysis.

41. This is not to imply that standard tables can be directly employed in adjustment calculations. On the contrary, major modifications of the tables are required, particularly in the treatment of imports and amortization funds. For details see Ganczer 1965, p. 73; Brown, Hall, and Licari 1973, pp. 21–22; and Walker 1971, pp. 85–87.

Table 8.1. Price adjustment coefficients for value prices.

Sector	1959	1964	1966	1968
Basic and energy industry	0.86	0.90	0.88	0.90
Machinery industry	0.86	0.80	0.88	0.91
Chemical industry	0.72	0.70	0.74	0.85
Light industry	0.65	0.71	0.78	0.99
Food industry	0.95	0.93	0.93	1.11
Other industry	0.98	0.99	0.98	—
Private industry	1.05	1.22	1.21	0.96
Total industry[a]	(0.83)	(0.83)	(0.86)	(0.96)
Construction	1.11	1.07	1.10	0.99
Agriculture	1.28	1.39	1.29	1.27
Transport-communication	1.07	1.25	1.23	1.14
Domestic trade	0.88	1.08	1.00	0.70
Foreign trade	0.89	1.07	1.06	0.56
Sundry activities	0.56	1.01	1.00	—
Imports (adapted rates)	0.87	0.86	0.89	0.97
Amortization	0.88	1.00	1.03	0.98
β (wage markup)	0.72	0.86	0.82	0.80

Source: 1959 and 1964 coefficients are from IDRC data bank; 1966 and 1968 coefficients are given in Walker 1973.

Notes: All coefficients are computed from current price input-output tables. *a.* This figure is a weighted average of the individual industry sectors.

8.2, and 8.3. Let us examine first the adjustment coefficients for value prices in Table 8.1. In 1959, average industrial prices were overvalued: value prices were 17 percent below official prices, with chemicals and light industrial goods much more overpriced (value prices being about 30 percent below official prices) than other industrial products.[42] The trade sectors were also overpriced, but somewhat less than industry. Not surprisingly, agricultural products were greatly underpriced (about 30 percent), reflecting the traditional development strategy of planned economies: underpricing of agricultural relative to industrial products is used as a device to transfer the agricultural surplus to the state to finance investment.[43] Construction and transportation-communications were also underpriced, but less than agriculture. As for sundry activities, this sector is quite small and its statistics questionable. Imports at adapted rates (which means a revaluation of imports at equilibrium exchange rates) seemed to be overvalued according to the 1959 adjustment coefficient. This paradox is easily resolved when one recognizes that imports

42. For a more granular analysis of 1959, with industry disaggregated into 19 sectors, see Walker 1973.

43. The use of such price distortions as a method of capital accumulation in a planned economy is the basis of the analysis in Jonas.

were initially evaluated not at domestic prices but at foreign prices, translated into forints at the purchasing power parity of the forint (adapted
rates), to account for import subsidies. Thus, while the price adjustment
coefficients suggest that in 1959 import prices should have been 13 percent lower, if the domestic price of imports had been set according to
foreign prices at official exchange rates, they would have been valued
approximately 7 percent below equilibrium factor costs.[44] The computed
wage markup (β) of 0.72 simply implies that accumulation, the nonwage
element in value added, amounted to 72 percent of wages; conversely,
wages accounted for 58.1 percent of value added in 1959.

Now let us consider the profile of price distortions over time. The
average overpricing in industry remained fairly constant until the introduction of the New Economic Mechanism (NEM), but it declined dramatically to only 4 percent in 1968. It appears that the price reform was
effective and the economy took a long stride toward rationalization of
industrial prices. There remained, however, a considerable dispersion
around the average. For instance, food industry, which had been relatively overpriced (about 5 percent in 1959), became overpriced (11 percent by 1968), while chemicals were still underpriced in 1968, although
the earlier price distortion (about 30 percent) was about halved. Underpricing in construction was practically eliminated by 1968. However,
downward bias in the transport-communication sector remained; it increased greatly between 1959 and the mid-1960s, and in 1968, in spite
of substantial improvement, it was still greater than in 1959. The general
gains in nonagricultural sectors do not seem to be matched in agriculture.
Agricultural output appears to be consistently underpriced (by about
30 percent) over the entire period. Overpricing seems to have worsened
in the domestic and foreign trade sectors, where price distortions were
11–12 percent in 1959, but rose to 30–46 percent in 1968. While the adjustment coefficient for imports at adapted rates approached unity, the
equivalent coefficient at domestic prices rose to approximately 1.20,
indicating that at official exchange rates imports would have been even
more underpriced in 1968 than in 1959. The wage markup profile suggests
a higher nonwage contribution to value added after 1959.

Price adjustment coefficients based on production prices are given in
Table 8.2. The general structure of distortions both between sectors and
over the period is surprisingly similar to that found under value pricing,
despite the very different definition of factor costs underlying production
prices. Again, average industrial prices appear overpriced by 15–20
percent in 1959 and show dramatic improvement in rationality by 1968,
when the distortion has all but disappeared. And as with value prices, the
general dispersion around this average behavior is also considerable in

44. For details, see Walker 1973, p. 20, and Brown and Walker 1973, pp. 41–43.

Table 8.2. Price adjustment coefficients for production prices.

Sector	1959	1964	1966	1968
Basic and energy industry	0.93	0.99	1.03	1.02
Machinery industry	0.85	0.76	0.89	0.91
Chemical industry	0.77	0.76	0.83	0.94
Light industry	0.61	0.64	0.70	0.91
Food industry	0.98	0.98	0.92	1.10
Other industry	1.03	1.00	0.95	—
Private industry	0.79	0.89	0.95	0.77
Total industry[a]	(0.84)	(0.84)	(0.88)	(0.97)
Construction	0.97	0.91	0.97	0.87
Agriculture	1.21	1.38	1.17	1.18
Transport-communication	1.71	1.75	1.80	1.43
Domestic trade	1.00	1.18	1.29	0.92
Foreign trade	1.32	1.41	1.47	0.51
Sundry activities	0.44	0.78	0.78	—
Imports (adapted rates)	0.89	0.87	0.92	0.98
Amortization	0.81	0.94	0.96	0.90
γ (return on capital)	0.12	0.13	0.13	0.12

Source: 1959 and 1964 coefficients are from IDRC data bank; 1966 and 1968 coefficients are given in Walker 1973.

Notes: All coefficients are computed from current price input-output tables.   *a.* This figure is a weighted average of the individual industry sectors.

production prices. Chemicals and light industry show reductions in upward price bias from 30–40 percent in 1959 to less than 10 percent in 1968. Again, the food sector illustrates a contrary trend, as prices in this sector moved from close agreement with production price concepts of factor costs to a 10 percent undervaluation in 1968. The inference that agricultural prices failed to undergo a restructuring, in any way approximating the gains in the structure of industrial prices, is also supported by the production price adjustment coefficients. Agricultural output still appeared to be about 20 percent undervalued in 1968, approximately the same figure as in 1959.

The primary difference between production and value prices is the imputation in the former of the full surplus to capital rather than to labor. This is vividly reflected in comparative adjustment coefficients calculated for particular sectors under both schemes. Basic industry is a relatively capital-intensive sector; therefore, its price adjustment coefficient is consistently higher under production prices — in 1968, the figures are 1.02 versus 0.90 — where capital intensity has a positive impact on price. On the other hand, private industry is relatively labor-intensive; reallocation of accumulation in proportion to capital means a relatively low factor-cost price for this sector, and that is precisely what is implied by the lower adjustment coefficient under production prices. Therefore, official prices in private industry are relatively high if accumulation is distributed in proportion to capital. To a much lesser extent, a similar argument may be advanced in the case of agriculture. It is also relatively labor-intensive so that its measured distortion is smaller (its price adjustment coefficient is closer to unity) in the case of production prices. As expected, the variation is most pronounced in the very capital-intensive transportation and communication sector. Prices in this sector are greatly underpriced in relation to the capital assets of these sectors, as much as 40–70 percent. Reallocation of accumulation according to capital assets would dramatically increase the value added generated in this sector. The greater dispersion observed in production price coefficients suggests that official prices more closely reflect relative labor-intensity rather than relative capital-intensity. This is perfectly consistent with accounting practices during this period, which tended to ignore grossly the opportunity costs of capital. Until 1964, no charges were levied on enterprises for capital held, and beginning in 1964, enterprises were assessed only a 5 percent charge (Skikszai 1969, pp. 258–59). Our results show that, if all accumulation had been imputed to capital, the average rate of return on capital throughout the period would have been 12–13 percent.

Turning to the case of two-channel prices shown in Table 8.3, we see a basic confirmation of general sectoral and time patterns observed earlier. Since two-channel prices are merely a weighted average of value and production prices, this is to be expected. Between 1959 and 1968, overvaluation in industry dramatically declines, while agriculture, transportation and communication, and the trade sectors all retain major distortions from consistent factor-cost pricing concepts. Note, however, that with the partial imputation of accumulation to labor, the imputed average return to capital falls below 10 percent.

The nature of distortions of official prices from any of the alternative factor-cost concepts discussed above and their implications for sectoral development policy can be seen even more clearly by examining movements in relative prices between sectors or the sectoral terms of trade. For sectors i and j, the official terms of trade are

$$t_0 = \frac{P_i}{P_j},$$

while under a factor-cost adjustment it becomes

$$t_a = \frac{P_i^*}{P_j^*}.$$

Table 8.3. Price adjustment coefficients for two-channel prices.

Sector	1959	1964	1966	1968
Basic and energy industry	0.90	0.95	0.96	0.99
Machinery industry	0.85	0.78	0.89	0.91
Chemical industry	0.75	0.73	0.79	0.92
Light industry	0.63	0.67	0.74	0.93
Food industry	0.96	0.96	0.93	1.10
Other industry	1.00	1.00	0.96	—
Private industry	0.92	1.02	1.06	0.82
Total industry[a]	(0.84)	(0.84)	(0.88)	(0.97)
Construction	1.04	0.98	1.02	0.90
Agriculture	1.24	1.38	1.22	1.21
Transport-communication	1.41	1.55	1.55	1.35
Domestic trade	0.94	1.14	1.16	0.86
Foreign trade	1.11	1.28	1.29	0.53
Sundry activities	0.50	0.88	0.87	—
Imports (adapted rates)	0.88	0.87	0.91	0.97
Amortization	0.85	0.97	0.99	0.92
β (wage markup)	0.35	0.35	0.35	0.20[b]
γ (return on capital)	0.06	0.07	0.06	0.09

Source: 1959 and 1964 coefficients are from IDRC data bank; 1966 and 1968 coefficients are given in Walker 1973.

Notes: All coefficients are computed from current price input-output tables. *a.* This figure is a weighted average of the individual industry sectors. *b.* The assumed markup on wages in 1968 is below that of previous years to reflect changes in pricing policy with the introduction of the New Economic Mechanism. See Portes 1970, pp. 308–9.

It follows then that the ratio of the factor cost to the official terms of trade is given by

$$\frac{t_a}{t_0} = \frac{P_i^*}{P_j^*}\frac{P_j}{P_i} = \frac{P_i^*/P_i}{P_j^*/P_j} = \frac{p_i}{p_j}.$$

Thus, the ratio of price adjustment coefficients indicates the change in relative prices with factor-cost pricing. If this ratio is greater than 1, it indicates that official prices are distorted in favor of sector *j;* if less than 1, they are distorted in favor of sector *i;* if equal to 1, they are in the same proportion as the defined factor-cost prices. These ratios of adjusted official relative prices are given in Table 8.4 for the four years and all three price models. For convenience, industry is taken as sector *j* in all cases; the indexes then measure distortions in relative prices between other sectors and industry.

Examination of these figures clearly discloses the priority accorded industry in official pricing policy, regardless of the price model. The

Table 8.4. Deviations in relative prices from factor-cost base, normalized to industry prices.

Year and price model	Industry	Const.	Agric.	Trans.	Domestic trade	Foreign trade	Sundry	Import	Amort.
1959									
Value	1.00	1.34	1.54	1.29	1.06	1.07	0.68	1.05	1.06
Production	1.00	1.15	1.44	2.04	1.19	1.57	0.52	1.06	0.96
Two-channel	1.00	1.24	1.48	1.68	1.12	1.32	0.60	1.05	1.01
1964									
Value	1.00	1.26	1.65	1.49	1.29	1.28	1.24	1.06	1.20
Production	1.00	1.06	1.62	2.08	1.43	1.71	0.98	1.08	1.12
Two-channel	1.00	1.17	1.64	1.85	1.36	1.52	1.04	1.03	1.15
1966									
Value	1.00	1.28	1.50	1.43	1.16	1.23	1.16	1.04	1.19
Production	1.00	1.10	1.33	2.04	1.46	1.67	0.88	1.04	1.09
Two-channel	1.00	1.16	1.39	1.76	1.32	1.47	0.99	1.03	1.12
1968									
Value	1.00	1.03	1.32	1.19	0.73	0.58	...	1.01	1.02
Production	1.00	0.90	1.22	1.47	0.95	0.53	...	1.01	0.93
Two-channel	1.00	0.93	1.25	1.39	0.89	0.55	...	1.00	0.95

All figures in this table represent the ratio of relative prices between a given sector and industry at factor cost to the same relative prices at official prices. A value above unity indicates a distortion of relative prices in favor of industry; a value below unity indicates an opposite distortion in the sectoral terms of trade.

terms of trade index are generally greater than 1, indicating that industrial prices were more overvalued than those of the sector with which it is being compared. Distortions are greatest in the terms of trade between industry and agriculture, and industry and transportation and communication, but there seemed to have been significant improvements by 1968. In the former case, the bias toward industry was reduced from 50 percent in 1959 to around 25 percent in 1968; while, in the latter case, the reduction was from 70 percent to 40 percent. The figures for agriculture of course highlight the conscious policy use of downward biased terms of trade for agriculture to finance investment. Interestingly, the relative prices between imports at adapted rates and industry remained essentially undistorted throughout the period, indicating that the parity price of imports involved the same general degree of distortion from factor-cost concepts as industrial prices. We should also note that the distortions in relative prices between industry and construction shifted during the period from an initial bias in favor of industry to an eventual bias in favor of construction. This is a reflection of the greater rationalization of industrial prices over this period; by 1968, construction was more overvalued than industry.

What have we discovered to this point regarding price distortions under planning in Hungary? Regardless of the factor-cost model chosen, certain general observations emerge. First, in the late 1950s, distortions permeated the entire structure of prices. Hungarian industrial prices exceeded valuation based on factor-cost pricing by 15–20 percent on the average, with greater overpricing in chemicals and light industry. At the same time, agricultural output was undervalued by about 30 percent, and transportation and communication services by as much as 70 percent. The structure of Hungarian prices was then quite consistent with the traditional development strategy of planned economies, where underpricing in agriculture and overpricing in industry were instruments of state policy for financing investment programs through forced saving in agriculture.

Second, during the period from 1959 to 1968, industrial prices became significantly rationalized according to factor-cost pricing, with the greatest improvements in chemicals and light industry. It is not unlikely that the improvement in the structure of industrial prices was considered part of the necessary groundwork for the introduction of the New Economic Mechanism. At least initially, however, major distortions remained in other sectors, especially in agriculture and in transportation and communication, where undervaluation of the order of 20 percent persisted. The limited data suggest the existence of other important distortions in the structure of prices. This is undoubtedly a reflection of the limited flexibility of prices during the early years of the new system, where most prices were either fixed or bounded by various constraints.

This picture of price distortions under planning in Hungary is quite consistent with other Hungarian data.[45] The first quantitative estimates of these distortions for Hungary were given by Balassa (1959) for a limited number of products for the mid-1950s (p. 120, n. 79). These were crude figures that did not represent general equilibrium adjustments. Yet the estimated distortions from both value and production price concepts followed the now familiar patterns. Output of the light industrial, chemical, and food sectors was overvalued by 10–30 percent, while that of construction and electrical energy sectors was undervalued by 10–50 percent. Ganczer later presented (1965, p. 74, and 1966, p. 62) some summary data computed from the 1961 input-output table based upon value, averaged-value, production, and two-channel price adjustment models. In that year, agriculture was undervalued by 25–50 percent and transport and communications by 10–50 percent, while industrial output was overvalued about 16 percent. Distortions were greatest for production prices, since these accentuated the failure to take into account the opportunity cost of capital.[46] However, the use by Ganczer of a constant consumption normalizing condition and his exclusion of variable capital from capital figures in general, and roads and bridges from capital stock in transportation in particular, make detailed comparisons with our results somewhat suspect. An interesting piece of additional information provided by Ganczer's results, though, is that prevailing prices, at least in 1961, were closest to averaged-value pricing. This is consistent with the fact that traditional pricing procedures in Hungary amounted to equating price roughly to average material and labor content plus a small markup, generally proportional to these prime costs. Finally, we should note the linear programing results of Simon (1970, p. 213), using 1961 input-output data. His computed ratios of average shadow prices to domestic prices showed sectoral patterns very consistent with price distortions found under the above equilibrium pricing

45. As for other East European countries, we have only sporadic information. The pattern of distortion of the Yugoslav price structure in the early 1960s was found to be quite similar to that in Hungary. Independent price adjustment studies by Sekulic and Grdic (1972) for 1962 and services and Brown, Hall, and Licari (1973) for 1964 show undervaluation in agriculture and services and overvaluation in industry. However, distortions computed for 1964 appeared much smaller than for either Yugoslavia in 1962 or Hungary in 1964. In contrast, results for Czechoslovakia are consistently the reverse of the Yugoslav and Hungarian patterns. The data of Hejl, Kyn, and Sekerka for both 1962 (Hejl et al. 1967) and 1966 (Sekerka et al. 1970) show agriculture and service sectors to be consistently overvalued and industrial sectors to be generally undervalued in official prices. Whether this relative inflation of consumer prices in Czechoslovakia during this period was imposed by conscious policy or supply-and-demand conditions in those markets is not addressed by the authors.

46. Production prices give the greatest weight to capital in computing factor cost, since the full surplus is viewed as an imputed return to capital.

schemes. Undervaluation of agriculture with reference to optimal scarcity prices was about 50 percent, of transport and communication about 10 percent, and of energy and minerals between 10 and 70 percent; while overvaluation of industrial output ranged from 40 percent in oil, chemicals, and textiles to less than 10 percent for processed food and wood products. While these programing results confirm the general pattern and magnitudes of distortions in the structure of official prices during this period, we have already noted the additional uncertainty in their particular values due to difficulties in their computation.[47]

B. *Are observed price distortions "optimal"?*

The above analysis leaves the question open whether the observed distortions in centrally determined prices can be justified in some way on economic grounds, or whether these price distortions are irrational under all conditions. The entire question of price rationality is itself somewhat arbitrary, since it presupposes the choice of some reference point as a basis for judgment.[48] In the conventional Western literature, this reference point is the operation of perfectly competitive markets where prices are equated to marginal costs. Since Hotelling's work in the 1930s, it has become standard procedure to argue that rational pricing means marginal cost pricing. Shortfalls in revenues where there are increasing returns can be covered by lump-sum taxation, which will leave undisturbed the optimal marginal conditions of equilibrium that follow from pricing at marginal cost. In a related case, Bergson (1953, pp. 49–50) has argued that commodity taxes in planned economies may actually be a device for improving rather than distorting the rationality of the price structure, if the taxes move pricing procedures toward marginal cost concepts by correcting the underlying distortions in official factor prices.

It has become increasingly recognized that, except for the unacceptable Pigovian poll tax, any tax imposed to raise revenues for the state will unavoidably affect some price. As Baumol and Bradford (1970, p. 265) put it: "Any level of tax revenue which the government is determined to collect, whether as a means to make up a deficit resulting from a marginal cost pricing arrangement or for any other purpose, must in practice produce some price distortion." In its most general context, the optimal pricing problem becomes a "second-best problem."

Recent work by Baumol and Bradford (1970), Lerner (1970), and Dixit (1970) has shown that "prices which deviate in a systematic manner from

---

47. Of course, an important contribution of Simon's study is the indication that these difficulties may not be as severe as first believed in the studies of Kornai and others.
48. Bornstein has argued this (1962, pp. 97–98).

marginal costs will be required for an optimal allocation of resources, even in the absence of externalities" (Baumol and Bradford 1970, p. 265). One must here talk in terms of "optimal nonmarginal cost pricing" or "optimal deviations" from marginal cost pricing, which is tantamount to the design of a system of optimal excise or commodity taxes. In its simplest form, the Baumol-Bradford theorem yields a system of optimally discriminatory prices consistent with a revenue constraint, where proportional deviations from marginal cost vary inversely with the price elasticity of demand:

$$\frac{P_i - MC_i}{P_i} = \frac{1 + \lambda}{\lambda} \frac{1}{E_i}, \tag{19}$$

where

P_i is the retail price of commodity i,
E_i is the price elasticity of demand for commodity i,
λ is the Lagrangian multiplier (a constant).

By this relation, only if all elasticities are the same will prices proportional to marginal costs be optimal. In general, optimal use of commodity taxes will require unequal deviations from marginal costs.

Now let us relate these ideas directly to socialist pricing practices. The centrally determined price of any commodity can be taken as its full average factor cost (AC) plus a markup (m) which includes both profit and a turnover tax:

$$P = AC + m \tag{20}$$

By equation (19), if all prices are to be optimally divergent from marginal costs:

$$\frac{AC + m - MC}{AC + m} = \frac{1 + \lambda}{\lambda} \frac{1}{E},$$

which yields as the optimal markup:

$$m = \frac{AC\left[\frac{1 + \lambda}{\lambda} \frac{1}{E} - 1\right] + MC}{1 - \frac{1 + \lambda}{\lambda} \frac{1}{E}}. \tag{21}$$

For the case of constant returns (MC = AC)

$$m = \frac{AC}{\frac{E}{k} - 1} \quad \text{where } k = \frac{1 + \lambda}{\lambda}, \tag{22}$$

and the optimal proportional markup is

$$\frac{m}{AC} = \frac{1}{\frac{E}{k} - 1} = \frac{k}{E - k}.$$ (23)

This relationship indicates that an optimal markup structure would have higher markups, the lower the price elasticity of demand.[49]

In the absence of detailed turnover tax data and profit rates for various commodities, one can only speculate on the relevance of this perspective on price distortions in Hungary. Certainly, the reliance on indirect taxes is not in itself a necessary source of nonoptimality in the broader sense we now recognize. The measured price distortions do represent deviations from consistent concepts of factor-cost pricing, which are generically related to marginal cost pricing ideas. However, we must recognize that rational pricing can require deviations from marginal cost procedures, if commodity taxes are to be employed as the primary mechanism for raising governmental revenue. Whether or not the actual pattern of price distortions in Hungary meets these new requirements of optimal non-marginal cost pricing must await further study.

V. Prices and the Measurement of Economic Structure

We have already argued earlier that there exists an implicit allocational role for prices even in centrally planned economies, since the measurement of economic aggregates is used to gauge macroeconomic performance and design central plans. The question then arises, to what extent distortions in the official structure of prices introduce a bias into this feedback from measurement of the structure of inputs and outputs that can derive from price distortions. To keep the analysis manageable, we will focus on 1964 data and will compare the results for official prices and production prices.[50]

A. *The structure of output*

First let us examine the structure of total output for each sector. Data for both official and production prices as shown in Table 8.5, with separate sectoral shares computed, are based upon only domestic production or domestic production plus imports. The effect of repricing on the per-

49. A similar analysis was presented by Bryson (n.d.) in an unpublished paper.
50. To say this is not to imply that 1964 was "a most typical year." In retrospect, though, it certainly emerges as an acceptable reference point for illustrating the degree of measurement distortions possible.

Table 8.5. Composition of total output by sector, 1964 (percent).

Sector	Official prices		Production prices	
	Dom. Prod.	Dom. Prod. & Imports	Dom. Prod.	Dom. Prod. & Imports
Basic	14.0	12.4	13.9	12.2
Machinery	15.1	13.3	11.6	10.2
Chemicals	6.0	5.3	4.6	4.0
Light	13.1	11.6	8.4	7.3
Food	11.9	10.5	11.7	10.2
Other	2.5	2.2	2.5	2.2
Private	0.8	0.7	0.7	0.6
Industry	(63.5)	(56.1)	(53.3)	(46.8)
Construction	9.2	8.2	8.4	7.4
Agriculture	16.9	15.0	23.4	20.6
Transport	4.8	4.2	8.4	7.3
Home trade	4.0	3.6	4.8	4.2
Foreign trade	0.8	0.8	1.2	1.1
Sundry	0.7	0.6	0.6	0.5
Imports	—	11.6	—	12.2
Total	100.0	100.0	100.0	100.0

Source: IDRC Data Bank.

ceived structure of sectoral output is seen to be considerable and similar in the two cases. In the case of domestic production only, the share of total industry falls from 63 to 53 percent. Within industry, the basic sector contributes 14 percent of total output under both price structures, while the contribution of light industry falls from 13 percent to 8 percent and that of machinery falls from 15 to 12 percent. On the other hand, with revaluation, the share of agriculture rises from 17 to 23 percent. Similarly, the contribution of transportation almost doubles, to over 8 percent.

The pattern of changes in sector shares in final demand and its components is shown in Table 8.6. For consumption, the revalued share of light industry is seven percentage points lower; as a percentage of food it is approximately the same; and of agriculture, it is six percentage points higher than when measured at official prices. Shifts in fixed investment are less pronounced, although the share of machinery falls almost five percentage points. The impact on inventory change is important in several sectors: there is a six-percentage-point fall in light industry's contribution to inventory adjustments, and a two-percentage-point fall in the machinery industry's contribution, while those of basic industry and agriculture rise four percentage points each. The agricultural sector is also seen to contribute four percentage points more to exports, and the food sector two percentage points more; but light and machinery industries

Table 8.6. Composition of domestic final demand by sector, 1964 (percent).

Sector	Consump-tion	Invest-ment	Change in stock	Exports	Final demand
		A. At official prices			
Basic	4.3	4.6	29.8	12.2	7.7
Machinery	5.1	27.3	14.9	32.2	17.8
Chemicals	4.3	0.5	12.6	8.2	4.9
Light	17.2	1.1	22.9	21.6	15.0
Food	25.8	0.1	10.4	14.5	16.2
Other	2.6	0.8	0.0	0.0	1.4
Private	2.8	0.0	0.0	0.1	1.3
Construction	1.8	57.5	0.0	0.0	13.9
Agriculture	18.5	4.4	6.4	7.2	11.7
Transport	4.7	2.2	0.5	1.5	3.1
Home trade	10.8	0.9	1.6	0.0	5.2
Foreign trade	0.2	0.7	0.9	2.4	0.9
Sundry	2.0	0.0	0.0	0.0	0.9
Total	100.0	100.0	100.0	100.0	100.0
		B. At production prices			
Basic	4.2	4.9	33.4	13.8	8.0
Machinery	3.8	22.8	13.0	28.4	14.3
Chemicals	3.2	0.4	10.8	7.2	3.9
Light	10.7	0.7	16.5	15.8	10.0
Food	24.6	0.1	11.6	16.3	16.7
Other	2.5	0.8	0.0	0.0	1.4
Private	2.4	0.0	0.0	0.1	1.2
Construction	1.6	57.3	0.0	0.0	13.3
Agriculture	24.9	6.7	10.1	11.4	17.0
Transport	8.1	4.1	1.0	3.0	5.7
Home trade	12.4	1.1	2.1	0.0	6.5
Foreign trade	0.3	1.0	1.4	3.0	1.4
Sundry	1.5	0.0	0.0	0.0	0.8
Total	100.0	100.0	100.0	100.0	100.0

Source: IDRC Data Bank.

provide six and four percentage points less, respectively. For final demand as a whole, the share of industry falls from 64 to 55 percent, while that of agriculture rises from 12 to 17 percent. Not surprisingly, the role of industry, both in total production and in final demand, is adjusted sharply downward when official industrial prices (which have an upward bias) are adjusted. The reverse is seen to be the case for agriculture.[51]

51. Similar results are shown for Hungary in 1961 by Ganczer (1965, p. 77, and 1966, p. 65) and for Yugoslavia in 1964 by Brown, Hall, and Licari (1973, pp. 38–41). Changes in sector output and net material product due to repricing are shown for Czechoslovakia in 1966 in Sekerka et al. (1970, pp. 195–200), although we have noted earlier that the patterns of distortions differ from those observed in Hungary and Yugoslavia during the same general period.

B. *The structure of inputs*

Let us now turn to the input side of production and examine the changes in the perceived pattern of inputs that emerge upon revaluation of official data. Table 8.7 shows the distribution of value added between sectors under official and adjusted factor-cost prices. The pattern of wages is of course invariant since the price adjustment procedure assumes pre-

Table 8.7. Value added by sector, 1964 (percent).

Sector	Accumulation, percentage of total	Wages, percentage of total	Value added, percentage of total	Ratio of accumulation to value added	Ratio of wages to value added
	A. At official prices				
Basic	13.5	9.8	11.6	57.8	42.2
Machinery	19.3	10.6	14.9	64.4	35.6
Chemicals	9.5	1.9	5.7	83.1	16.9
Light	22.4	8.7	15.5	71.8	28.2
Food	13.6	2.8	8.2	83.0	17.0
Other	2.4	2.2	2.3	51.0	49.0
Private	0.4	1.7	1.0	18.4	81.6
Industry	(81.1)	(37.6)	(59.2)	(68.1)	(31.9)
Construction	6.2	12.2	9.2	33.4	66.6
Agriculture	5.7	33.6	19.7	14.3	85.7
Transport	0.5	7.9	4.2	5.5	94.5
Home trade	5.1	7.1	6.1	41.4	58.6
Foreign trade	0.8	0.5	0.6	58.0	42.0
Sundry	0.7	1.0	0.9	38.5	61.5
Total	100.0	100.0	100.0	49.7	50.3
	B. At production prices				
Basic	14.3	9.8	11.8	55.6	44.4
Machinery	7.1	10.6	9.0	36.6	63.4
Chemicals	3.1	1.9	2.4	57.8	42.2
Light	3.9	8.7	6.5	27.9	72.1
Food	4.7	2.8	3.6	59.2	40.8
Other	2.0	2.2	2.1	43.3	56.7
Private	0.1	1.7	0.9	3.0	97.0
Industry	(35.1)	(37.6)	(36.5)	(44.4)	(55.6)
Construction	1.7	12.2	7.3	10.7	89.3
Agriculture	33.0	33.6	33.4	45.7	54.3
Transport	21.4	7.9	14.1	69.9	30.1
Home trade	8.0	7.1	7.5	48.8	51.2
Foreign trade	0.7	0.5	0.6	53.9	46.1
Sundry	0.1	1.0	0.6	9.7	90.3
Total	100.0	100.0	100.0	46.2	53.8

Source: IDRC Data Bank.

vailing wage rates to be acceptably rational.[52] However, dramatic shifts occur within accumulation. The noneconomic official pricing policy is reflected in a drop in industry's share from 81 to 35 percent upon revaluation based on factor-cost concepts. Upward distortions in official accumulation data are particularly pronounced in the machinery, light, and food industrial sectors. The shifts are just as dramatic in agriculture and transportation, but in the opposite direction. Under production prices, agriculture's contribution to the net surplus rises from 6 to 35 percent, and transportation's share increases from less than 1 to 21 percent.[53] The ratios also presented in Table 8.7 further highlight the extent of industrial overaccumulation, and perceived underaccumulation in transportation and agriculture, due to official pricing policy. A very different view of the sources of real surplus or profit is obtained if we shift our attention from the distribution at official, distorted prices to adjusted factor-cost prices.

Price distortions even affect the perceived distribution of fixed and working capital among sectors. This is illustrated in Table 8.8. These

52. This assumption is based on the fairly flexible labor markets.

53. Since production prices distribute accumulation according to the adjusted value of capital in each sector, this price adjustment model may overcompensate for underpricing in a very capital-intensive sector like transportation. Nonetheless, the general pattern of effects illustrated by these data is indicative of the relationship between factor-cost price adjustments and shifts in relative sectoral shares.

Table 8.8. Composition of capital stock by sector, 1964 (percent).

Sector	A. At official prices		B. At production prices	
	Fixed capital	Variable capital	Fixed capital	Variable capital
Basic	89.4	10.6	87.6	12.4
Machinery	59.5	40.5	61.3	38.7
Chemicals	83.5	16.5	84.7	15.3
Light	72.1	27.9	77.0	23.0
Food	62.4	37.6	58.3	41.7
Other	64.1	35.9	59.5	40.5
Private	100.0	0.0	100.0	0.0
Industry	(75.8)	(24.2)	(75.4)	(24.6)
Construction	58.1	41.9	54.8	45.2
Agriculture	72.0	28.0	67.4	32.6
Transport	96.9	3.1	97.2	2.8
Home trade	27.8	72.2	29.8	70.2
Foreign trade	6.8	93.2	7.4	92.6
Sundry	50.6	49.4	52.5	47.5
Total	74.3	25.7	72.9	27.1

Source: IDRC Data Bank.

data show that the importance of fixed capital is relatively greater in machinery and light industries, but relatively less in basic and food industries, as well as in agriculture and on the average in all producing sectors, than shown by official data.

A more comprehensive view of the factor-intensity of production is given in Table 8.9 with reference to final demand. Results at production prices show that consumption goods use less capital and labor, although they generate a larger share of accumulation than it would appear that they do at official prices. On the other hand, investment goods and inventories, as well as exports, become more labor-intensive and more import-intensive upon revaluation. Overall, official prices understate both the import-intensity and labor-intensity of commodities entering final demand.

The final look at the nature of input distortions is presented in Table 8.10. Here we show the factor-intensity of production by producing sec-

Table 8.9. Primary inputs and factor-intensity of final demand, 1964 (ratios).

Primary inputs and factors	Consump- tion	Invest- ment	Change in stock	Exports	Final demand
	A. At official prices				
Imports	0.1405	0.1512	0.1988	0.1872	0.1582
Amortization	0.0979	0.1131	0.1097	1.0986	0.1021
Accumulation	0.3518	0.3437	0.4002	0.4097	0.3677
Wages	0.4097	0.3920	0.2913	0.3046	0.3720
Total primary inputs	1.0000	1.0000	1.0000	1.0000	1.0000
Fixed capital	2.1802	1.8209	1.8667	1.7907	1.9802
Variable capital	0.8706	0.4958	0.5134	0.5547	0.6842
Total capital	3.0508	2.3167	2.3801	2.3454	2.6644
Total labor[a]	18.8543	14.9749	12.7983	13.5949	16.2818
	B. At production prices				
Imports	0.1439	0.1731	0.2375	0.2263	0.1745
Amortization	0.0895	0.1155	0.1169	0.1063	0.1005
Accumulation	0.3672	0.2845	0.3144	0.3170	0.3346
Wages	0.3994	0.4270	0.3312	0.3504	0.3905
Total primary inputs	1.0000	1.0000	1.0000	1.0000	1.0000
Fixed capital	1.9819	1.7022	1.8637	1.8327	1.8793
Variable capital	0.8464	0.4887	0.5580	0.6086	0.6975
Total capital	2.8284	2.1908	2.4216	2.4412	2.5768
Total labor[a]	18.3767	16.3100	14.5483	15.6409	17.0883

Source: IDRC Data Bank.

a. Man-years per million forints of output.

Table 8.10. Primary input and factor-intensity of production by sector, 1964 (ratios).

Sector	Imports	Amortization	Accumulation	Wages	Fixed capital	Variable capital	Total capital	Labor	Capital-labor ratio (millions of forints) per man-years)
					A. At official prices				
Basic	0.2230	0.1770	0.3348	0.2653	2.5468	0.3690	2.9158	9.5656	0.305
Machinery	0.1984	0.0929	0.4415	0.2672	1.3486	0.5413	1.8899	11.2413	0.168
Chemicals	0.3002	0.0935	0.4460	0.1603	1.4508	0.2976	1.7484	6.8302	0.258
Light	0.1801	0.0541	0.5141	0.2517	0.9847	0.3264	1.3110	12.9157	0.102
Food	0.1594	0.0768	0.3920	0.3719	1.9674	0.8075	2.7749	17.7003	0.157
Other	0.1104	0.1111	0.3655	0.4130	2.2338	0.8280	3.0618	15.5233	0.197
Private	0.1098	0.0493	0.2737	0.5671	0.9642	0.4828	1.4470	22.7722	0.064
Industry	(0.1913)	(0.0894)	(0.4283)	(0.2908)	(1.5328)	(0.5240)	(2.1068)	(13.0497)	(0.161)
Construction	0.1315	0.1112	0.3154	0.4419	1.6682	0.3989	2.0671	15.9169	0.131
Agriculture	0.0807	0.0827	0.1775	0.6591	2.7056	1.0593	3.7649	31.7925	0.118
Transport	0.1049	0.3442	0.1230	0.4279	7.6394	0.3704	8.0098	16.1279	0.497
Home trade	0.0501	0.1209	0.3423	0.4866	2.3738	2.6278	5.0016	23.1889	0.216
Foreign trade	0.0765	0.2221	0.2873	0.4141	4.8900	1.6964	6.5864	13.5158	0.487
Sundry	0.1102	0.0562	0.3815	0.4522	1.0268	0.3824	1.4092	15.5430	0.091
Overall	0.1582	0.1021	0.3677	0.3720	1.9802	0.6842	2.6644	16.2818	0.164

B. At production prices

Basic	0.2374	0.1681	0.3258	0.2687	2.1529	0.3565	2.5094	9.6900	0.259
Machinery	0.2726	0.1139	0.2642	0.3493	1.4700	0.5650	2.0350	14.6970	0.138
Chemicals	0.4178	0.1161	0.2539	0.2122	1.6198	0.3358	1.9556	9.0439	0.216
Light	0.2976	0.0798	0.2270	0.3957	1.3408	0.4070	1.7478	20.3055	0.086
Food	0.1711	0.0735	0.3756	0.3798	1.9551	0.9375	2.8926	18.0789	0.160
Other	0.1156	0.1038	0.3688	0.4117	1.9824	0.8583	2.8407	15.4740	0.184
Private	0.1304	0.0522	0.1768	0.6407	0.9284	0.4329	1.3613	25.7253	0.053
Industry	(0.2445)	(0.1020)	(0.2999)	(0.3536)	(1.7030)	(0.6070)	(2.3100)	(15.8682)	(0.146)
Construction	0.1512	0.1141	0.2512	0.4835	1.5396	0.3952	1.9349	17.3055	0.112
Agriculture	0.0614	0.0561	0.4054	0.4770	2.1151	1.0076	3.1226	23.0101	0.136
Transport	0.0632	0.1849	0.5068	0.2452	3.7261	0.1767	3.9028	9.2408	0.422
Home trade	0.0447	0.0963	0.4458	0.4132	1.7137	1.7200	3.4337	19.6888	0.174
Foreign trade	0.0569	0.1473	0.5030	0.2929	2.9434	0.9306	3.8740	9.5577	0.405
Sundry	0.1484	0.0675	0.2050	0.5792	1.1549	0.4239	1.5788	19.9094	0.079
Overall	0.1745	0.1005	0.3346	0.3905	1.8793	0.6975	2.5768	17.0883	0.151

Source: IDRC Data Bank.

tor. Official Hungarian prices in 1964 considerably understate the import-intensity and wage-intensity of industry in general, and of machinery, chemicals, and light industry in particular. At official prices, however, the import-intensity and wage-intensity had an upward bias in agriculture and trade, and the import-intensity in transportation was also overstated. As for relative factor-intensity, the overall production technology of the Hungarian economy in 1964 was more capital-intensive at official prices than at factor-cost prices. Capital-labor ratios were generally overstated at official prices, except in agriculture and the food industry.

VI. Changes in Economic Efficiency

We may now consider how the price adjustment models may be used to measure changes in aggregate economic efficiency.[54] While analogous to the measurement of efficiency based on time series data and production function analysis, rates of change in efficiency based upon price adjustment are disaggregated into separate annual rates between periods. They then provide a more granular view of productivity effects over time.

To see how we might proceed to employ pricing models to measure aggregate changes in productivity, let us first introduce a distinction between transactions data in any year t in current prices and data in any year t in constant prices of year T ($T \geq t$): $P_i^t x_{ij}^t$ is the value in current official prices of output of sector i employed in production in sector j in year t; $P_i^T x_{ij}^t$ is the value in constant year T official prices of output of sector i employed in production in sector j in year t.

Further, let

$$p_i^t = \frac{P_i^{t*}}{P_i^t}$$ be the price adjustment coefficient of sector i in year t.

We then have

$$\sum_i P_j^T x_{ij}^t + W_j^t + Z_j^t,$$

as the factor cost of sector j output in year t in constant year T official prices;

$$\sum_j P_i^T x_{ij}^t + P_i^T Y_i,$$

as the expenditure value on sector i output in year t in constant year T official prices.

54. The use of these models to measure efficiency was clarified through a number of discussions with Dr. Douglas O. Walker of the United Nations.

Upon correction for distortions in official prices by means of price adjustments, these relations become

$$\sum_i p_j^T P_j^T x_{ij}{}^t + W_j{}^t + {}^T Z_j{}^t,$$

the factor cost of sector j output in year t in constant year T adjusted prices and ${}^T Z_j{}^t$ is defined by the particular pricing model chosen;

$$\sum_j p_i^T P_i^T x_{ij}{}^t + p_i^T P_i^T Y_i{}^t,$$

the expenditure value on sector i output in year t in constant year T adjusted prices.

Further, we can obtain these two adjusted aggregate totals:

$$E_t = \sum_i p_i^T P_i^T Y_i^t,$$

the expenditure on actual final demand in year t in constant year T adjusted prices;

$$F_t = \sum_j (W_j{}^t + {}^T Z_j{}^t),$$

the total value added or factor cost in year t in constant year T adjusted prices.

Upon reflection it will be obvious that E_t can be interpreted as the year T cost to produce the actual year t final demand vector, and F_t can be interpreted as the year t cost to produce the year t final demand vector, where all costs are measured with reference to adjusted year T prices. It follows then that we can define a useful aggregate efficiency index as

$$e_t = \frac{E_t - F_t}{E_t}.$$

Here, e_t is the proportionate change in efficiency between years t and T. A positive e_t indicates a higher overall efficiency of resource use in t; a negative e_t, the reverse. Computing the first differences in e_t will then indicate the proportionate gain in efficiency between years t and $t-1$ with reference to the base year T. A positive first difference shows a rise in total productivity, and a negative first difference a fall between the relevant years.

To illustrate the use of these procedures, we have applied them to Hungarian data for 1959 to 1964 at constant 1964 prices. Results are presented in Table 8.11. The figures for $e_t - e_{t-1}$ effectively summarize the movements in overall efficiency over the period. The pattern of these figures seems generally independent of pricing model selected. We see

Table 8.11. Measurement of aggregate efficiency.

	1959	1960	1961	1962	1963	1964
		A. Expenditures on final demand at 1964 adjusted prices (E_t)				
Value	134,339	144,350	147,443	153,526	164,238	174,387
Two-channel	133,463	143,639	147,028	153,322	163,127	174,387
Producer	132,913	143,174	146,750	153,166	163,039	174,387
		B. Total factor costs at 1964 adjusted factor costs (F_t)				
Value	142,092	146,434	145,241	153,933	166,740	174,387
Two-channel	138,191	143,005	143,896	151,453	164,250	174,384
Producer	135,494	140,619	142,945	152,473	162,523	174,385
		C. Proportionate excess of expenditures over factor costs in 1964 adjusted prices (e_t)				
Value[a]	−0.0577	−0.0144	0.0148	−0.0026	−0.0214	0.0000
	(0.0433)	(0.0292)	(−0.0174)	(−0.0188)	(0.0214)	
Two-channel[a]	−0.0354	0.0044	0.0213	0.0055	0.0068	0.0000
	(0.0398)	(0.0169)	(−0.10158)	(0.0013)	(−0.0068)	
Producer[a]	−0.0194	0.0178	0.0259	0.0111	0.0031	0.0000
	(0.0372)	(0.0081)	(−0.0148)	(−0.0080)	(−0.0031)	

These figures are computed from constant 1964 base input-output data. a. Figures in parentheses are the first differences in e_t: $e_t - e_{t-1}$.

the strong growth performance of 1959–1961 reflected in substantial, though falling, gains in productivity: about 4 percent between 1959 and 1960 and 1 to 3 percent between 1960 and 1961. The retardation of the early 1960s is seen in a generally stagnant or falling productivity, with changes between 1961 and 1964 ranging from 0 to 2 percent.[55] When one recognizes the large leakage of real savings during the early 1960s into excessive inventories and uncompleted investment projects, the picture of movements in systemic efficiency emerging from the above data is quite consistent with the events.

VII. Concluding Remarks

In this chapter, we have attempted to examine the extent and impact of distortions in official prices based on alternative definitions of factor costs. To a major extent, the official price structure is used as an active instrument to further various social and economic policy objectives. Nonetheless, in seeking to achieve a range of objectives through pricing policy, CPEs have accepted a set of prices which failed to reflect accurately either relative resource costs or relative marginal preferences. The direct and indirect allocational effects of these divergences caused the Hungarian CPE to operate considerably within its technologically feasible production set.

The distortions found in Hungary during the period 1959–1968 were generally consistent with the traditional development strategy of other CPEs. Overpricing of industrial products and underpricing of agricultural output were two sides of the device to extract the agricultural surplus, control consumption, and support the ambitious investment plan. By 1968, however, there appears to have been a distinct move toward rationalization of the industrial price structure, as measured divergences between official prices and prices based on alternative pricing models fell toward zero. In fact, some of the groundwork was prepared earlier in the 1960s—for instance, with the institution of a direct charge on capital. However, prices in agriculture, transportation, and other service sectors failed to show a similar move to rationalization over the period. That the structure of centrally determined prices as it existed in the mid-1960s was an unsound basis for decentralization of decision making seems obvious if we examine the extent of prevailing price distortions.

With the birth of the New Economic Mechanism in 1968, market forces were in principle allowed to mold the formation of prices for the

55. Since these figures relate only to the relative capacity of the system to transform inputs into outputs, they do not necessarily correlate with movements in growth rates themselves. The latter depend on changes in stocks and flows of resources, as well as on the efficiency with which they are employed.

purposes of guiding the newly decentralized production decision-making structure. Nonetheless, the new system could not set aside overnight the legacies of the CPE. The concentration of production within large units was encouraged during the period of central planning. These market imperfections still severely limit the improvement in resource allocation that can be realized through the operation of free markets; prices formed under the influence of strong market power by individual enterprises are themselves likely to deviate sharply from efficiency concepts.[56]

Another legacy that restricts the pace at which rationalization of prices can proceed is the traditional use in CPEs of implicit transfers — differential taxes (primarily on manufactured consumers goods) and subsidies (mainly on food, transportation, and other services) — to redistribute real incomes. The architects of the NEM inherited a price system in which subsidized goods represented a much larger portion of the expenditures by the poor than by the rich, while heavily taxed goods were mainly consumed by the upper income groups. Elimination of these distributional devices requires a concomitant system of compensating measures to prevent a very significant deterioration in the living standard of the poor. There is then a need for a shift in social policy instruments from implicit to explicit transfers of income. This shift must be a process of slow substitution; the institution of a more direct incomes policy will have to be combined with the attempt to rationalize consumer prices under the New Economic Mechanism.[57]

Appendix: Data Sources

All computations in this study are based on standard input-output flow data augmented by capital stock matrices. Hungarian input-output tables have been published annually since 1959, although levels of aggregation and sectoral definitions do vary between tables. An attempt was made at the East Europe Project of the International Development Research Center (IDRC) to reconcile the tables prior to analysis.

56. These factors certainly contributed to the retention of central control over many prices through either central price setting or constraining bounds, even under the New Economic Mechanism. See Portes 1970, pp. 308–9. This also implies that the pricing models discussed in this chapter will retain an important role in price formation even with the shift to market mechanisms, since that very shift will be carefully guided and monitored.

57. The fact that price reforms result in maldistribution of income, unless appropriate countermeasures are introduced, was spelled out by Edward Gierek, when he became new First Secretary of the Polish United Workers Party: "This crisis has been brought on by ill-considered . . . policies. Measures will be taken to offer material improvement to families with the lowest incomes and the most children who, as a result of recent price changes, suffered the most" (see Brown and Licari 1972, p. 16).

The *current price* tables were obtained from the following sources:

1959: *A Magyar Népgazdaság Ágazati Kapcsolatainak Mérlegei,* 1959 (Budapest: Központi Statisztikai Hivatal, 1961).
1964: *A Magyar Népgazdaság Ágazati Kapcsolatainak Mérlegei, 1959–1964* (Budapest: Központi Statisztikai Hivatal, 1966).
1966: *A Magyar Népgazdaság Ágazati Kapcsolatainak Mérlegei, 1964–1966* (Budapest: Központi Statisztikai Hivatal, 1968).
1968: *A Magyar Népgazdaság Ágazati Kapcsolatainak Mérlegei, 1965–1968* (Budapest: Központi Statisztikai Hivatal, 1970).

The coefficients of the tables for 1959–1964 in *constant 1964 prices* were given in *A Magyar Népgazdaság Ágazati Kapcsolatainak Mérlegei, 1959–1964* (Budapest: Központi Statisztikai Hivatal, 1966). A detailed discussion of the reconstruction of full tables from these official sources is given in Alan A. Brown and Douglas O. Walker, *Hungarian input-output tables: description, reconstruction and price adjustment,* Working Paper No. 20 (Indiana Univ., International Development Research Center, March 1973).

Except for value prices, all repricing schemes also require capital data disaggregated by sector. Detailed fixed-capital figures are less available than input-output flow data, but useful series can be constructed from various official sources that supplement the sporadic information on capital stock in the annual yearbooks. The best source for fixed-capital data is a periodic publication of the Central Statistical Office, *Statisztikai Időszaki Közlemények.* Several volumes of this series in the mid-1960s were devoted to long-term series of capital stock, retroactively calculated from 1950 in constant prices. Since the late 1950s, detailed fixed-capital balance sheets have also been published which show a breakdown of beginning and ending stock for consecutive years for various productive and nonproductive sectors or branches of the economy. On variable capital the information is more sparse. For the period as a whole, variable-capital stock figures can be only estimated for highly aggregated sectors of the national economy. (For sources and references, see A. A. Brown and D. Walker, *Hungarian input-output tables.*)

References

Alchian, Armen. 1967. *Pricing and society.* Occasional Paper 17. London: Institute of Economic Affairs.
Balassa, Béla A. 1959. *The Hungarian experience in economic planning.* New Haven: Yale Univ. Press.
Baumol, William J., and David F. Bradford. 1970. "Optimal departures from marginal cost pricing." *American Economic Review* 60, no. 3 (June): 265–83.
Bergson, Abram. 1953. *Soviet national income and product in 1937.* New York: Columbia Univ. Press.
———. 1961. *The real national income of Soviet Russia since 1928.* Cambridge: Harvard Univ. Press.
———. 1971. "Comparative productivity and efficiency in the USA and the USSR." In *Comparison of economic systems,* ed. Alexander Eckstein. Berkeley: Univ. of California Press. Pp. 161–218.

Boehme, Hans. 1968. "East German price formation under the New Economic System." *Soviet Studies* 19, no. 3 (Jan.): 340–58.

Bornstein, Morris. 1962. "The Soviet price system." *American Economic Review* 52, no. 2 (March): 64–103.

————. 1966. "Soviet price theory and policy." In *New directions in the Soviet economy*, Joint Economic Committee. Washington: US GPO. Pp. 63–98.

Bródy, András. 1962. "The unicity of prices of production and of the average rate of profit." In *Input-output tables: their compilation and use*, ed. O. Lukacs. Budapest: Akadémiai Kiadó.

————. 1964. "Három Árrendszerre." *Közgazdasági Szemle*, no. 12: 1426–36.

————. 1965. "Three types of price systems." *Economics of Planning* 5, no. 3: 58–66.

————. 1970. *Proportions, prices and planning.* Amsterdam: North-Holland Publishing Company.

Brown, Alan A. 1971. "Hungary." Paper presented at the Conference on Measurement of Aggregate Output and Productivity in Eastern Europe, Yale Univ.

————, Owen P. Hall, and Joseph A. Licari. 1973. *Price adjustment models for socialist economics: theory and an empirical technique.* Studies in East European and Soviet Planning, Development and Trade, no. 18. Bloomington: Indiana Univ., International Development Research Center, June.

———— and Joseph A. Licari. 1972. "Models of implicit grants in East European price systems." Windsor Univ. Working Paper no. 14. Paper presented at the Joint Institute of Comparative Urban and Grants Economics, Univ. of Augsburg, Aug.

———— and Douglas O. Walker. 1973. "Hungarian input-output tables: description, reconstruction and price adjustment." Working Paper no. 20. Bloomington: Indiana Univ., International Development Research Center, March.

Bryson, Philip J. "Reformed command pricing in Eastern Germany: coincidental rationality?" Mimeographed. No date.

Csikós-Nagy, Béla. 1968. *Pricing in Hungary.* Occasional Paper 19. London: Institute of Economic Affairs.

————, Sándor Ganczer, and Lászlo Rácz. 1964. "Az elsö termékrendszerü ármodell" (The first price model based on input-output tables). *Közgazdasági Szemle*, no. 1.

Dixit, Avinash K. 1970. "On the optimum structure of commodity taxes." *American Economic Review* 60, no. 3 (June): 295–301.

Fontela, E., L. Solari, and A. Duval. 1972. "Production constraints and prices in an input-output system." In *Input-output techniques*, ed. Anne F. Carter and András Bródy. Amsterdam: North-Holland Publishing Company. Pp. 242–60.

Ganczer, Sándor. 1965. "Price calculations in Hungary on the basis of mathematical methods." *Economics of Planning* 5, no. 3: 67–79.

————. 1966. "Price calculations and the analysis of proportions within the national economy." *Acta Oeconomica*, pp. 55–68.

Grossman, Gregory A. 1960. "Introduction." In *Value and plan*, ed. Gregory Grossman. Berkeley: Univ. of California Press. Pp. 1–16.

Hejl, Lubos, Oldrich Kyn, and Bohuslav Sekerka. 1967. "Price calculations." *Czechoslovak Economic Papers* 8:61–81.

Holesovsky, Vaclav. 1971. "The double-channel aberration in East European price formulas." *Yearbook of East-European Economics* 2:329–42.

Jonas, Paul. "The nature of the price system in a 'classic' Soviet-type economy." Mimeographed. No date.

Kornai, János. 1967. *Mathematical planning of structural decisions.* Amsterdam: North-Holland Publishing Company.

Leontief, Wassily W. 1941. *The structure of American economy, 1919–1939.* New York: Oxford Univ. Press.

Lerner, Abba P. 1970. "On optimal taxes with an untaxable sector." *American Economic Review* 60, no. 3 (June): 284–94.

Levine, Herbert S. 1971. "On comparing planned economies." In *Comparison of economic systems,* ed. Alexander Eckstein. Berkeley: Univ. of California Press. Pp. 137–60.

Maksimovic, I., and Z. Pjanic. 1968. "Price problems in Yugoslav theory and practice." In *Economic development for eastern Europe,* ed. Michael C. Kaser. London: Macmillan. Pp. 185–95.

Marczewski, Jean. 1971. "The role of prices in a command economy." *Soviet Studies* 23, no. 1 (July): 109–19.

Morva, T. 1962. "Price examination by the chessboard table of the social product." In *Input-output tables: their compilation and use,* ed. O. Lukacs. Budapest: Akadémiai Kiadó.

Portes, Richard D. 1970. "Economic reforms in Hungary." *American Economic Review* 60, no. 2 (May): 307–13.

Sekerka, Bohuslav, Oldrich Kyn, and Lubos Hejl. 1970. "Price systems computable for input-output coefficients." In *Contributions to input-output analysis,* ed. Anne P. Carter and András Bródy. Amsterdam: North-Holland Publishing Company. Pp. 183–203.

Sekulic, Mijo, and Gojko Grdic. 1972. "Using input-output analysis for Yugoslav price and currency reform." In *Input-output techniques,* ed. Anne P. Carter and András Bródy. Amsterdam: North-Holland Publishing Company. Pp. 233–41.

Šik, Ota. 1967. *Plan and market under socialism.* White Plains, N.Y.: International Arts and Sciences Press, Inc.

Simon, György. 1965. "Ex-post examination of macro-economic shadow prices." *Economics of Planning* 5, no. 3: 80–93.

———. 1970. "Trends and stability of economy-wide shadow prices." In *Contributions to input-output economics,* ed. Anne P. Carter and András Bródy. Amsterdam: North-Holland Publishing Company. Pp. 204–17.

Szikszai, Béla. 1969. "Changes in the price system and in the price mechanism in Hungary." In *Planning and markets,* ed. John T. Dunlop and Nikolay P. Fedorenko. New York: McGraw-Hill. Pp. 254–60.

United Nations. 1967. "Hungary: application of price formation models in the analysis of major proportions of the economy." In *Macro-economic models for planning and policy making,* by the Economic Commission for Europe. Geneva: United Nations. Pp. 134–60.

———. 1968. *Problems of input-output tables and analysis.* Series F., no. 14.

von Mises, Ludwig. 1951. *Die Gemeinwirtschaft.* Originally published in 1922; later published in an expanded translation as *Socialism: an economic and sociological analysis.* New Haven: Yale Univ. Press.

Walker, Douglas O. 1971. "Socialist price-formation models and input-output analysis: a study of Hungary, 1959–1964." Ph.D. dissertation, Univ. of Southern California.

———. 1973. *Socialist price formation models and the Hungarian economy.*

Studies in East European and Soviet Planning, Development and Trade, no. 19. Bloomington: Indiana Univ., International Development Research Center, June.

Watanabe, Tsunchiko, and Shuntaro Shishido. 1970. "Planning applications of the Leontief model in Japan." In *Contributions to input-output analysis,* ed. Anne P. Carter and András Bródy. Amsterdam: North-Holland Publishing Company. Pp. 9–23.

9

Price Formation Models and Price Policy in Hungary

Morris Bornstein

The University of Michigan

The elaboration of price formation models, such as those discussed in the chapters by Francis Seton and by Alan A. Brown and Joseph A. Licari in this volume, began in the mid-1950s as part of a broad attempt to rationalize and modernize the economies of the USSR and the East European countries after the death of Stalin. The political leaders reappraised national policies affecting the rate and pattern of economic growth, living standards, and external economic relations. At the same time, with official encouragement, economic theorists and administrators reexamined, in technical journals and conferences, the mechanisms and techniques of economic control. These discussions covered many topics, including, along with the reform of the price system, the use of mathematical techniques, such as input-output and linear programming; investment criteria; the decentralization of economic management through changes in administrative organization, enterprise performance indicators, and the extent of central allocation of material inputs; and new approaches to managerial and worker compensation intended to provide stronger incentives for cost reduction, quality improvement, the adaptation of production to customer demand, and innovation in both production processes and product design.

The main thrust of the discussions on the price system was a search for "more objective" criteria for price formation, in place of the prevailing "administrative" approach which had evolved in the USSR and had subsequently been copied in the East European countries.[1]

This chapter draws on research supported by The University of Michigan Comparative Economics Program, under a grant from the Ford Foundation, and on information obtained during a research trip to Hungary arranged with the assistance of the International Research and Exchanges Board. Their aid is gratefully acknowledged.

1. For a more extensive account of the Soviet price reform debate, which was followed by similar discussions in the East European countries, see Morris Bornstein, "The Soviet Price Reform Discussion," *Quarterly Journal of Economics* 78, no. 1 (Feb. 1964): 15–48.

First, it was asserted that—with some possible exceptions, such as substitute fuels—producer (i.e., wholesale) prices should be set according to some common standard formula incorporating cost and profit elements. (Final retail prices, however, might differ from such producer prices because of taxes intended to adjust demand to supply, or subsidies designed to implement income distribution objectives.)

Second, it was agreed that the components and justification for the common standard had to be found in Marxian value theory. According to this theory, the value of a commodity is composed of three parts: (1) the value of past labor embodied in the materials and that portion of the plant and equipment (as measured by depreciation charges) used up in producing the commodity; (2) the value of current labor for which workers receive compensation in the form of wages (their "product for themselves"); and (3) the value of current labor for which workers are not compensated ("surplus value" for the employer in capitalism, or "product for society" in socialism). Various "price formation models" (hereinafter, PFM's) were proposed, all providing that price should cover all three elements, but differing about the basis for the surplus product markup to be added to the two cost elements in order to reflect the full "value" of the commodity.

Third, it was expected that the winning formula chosen from the several competing versions would serve as the basis for a comprehensive reform embracing all wholesale prices of producer goods (excluding agricultural procurement prices), which would require several years to prepare and implement.

This study has two main sections. The first considers, from the viewpoint of economic theory, some of the problems and implications of using PFM's to measure "distortions" in prevailing (usually officially set) prices, as proposed by Brown and Licari. The second section examines, from the viewpoint of economic policy, the extent to which the Hungarian pricing authorities should have been, or were, guided by PFM's during and after the 1968 price reform in that country. A brief third section presents a few summary conclusions.

I. Price Formation Models as Theoretical Standards

The chapter by Brown and Licari in this volume has several objectives:

1. to explain various PFM's—all "cost-plus" or "surplus product markup" pricing schemes—proposed by Soviet and East European economists;
2. to compare the prices yielded by three of these schemes with officially established prices in Hungary;

3. to show differences in the economic structure of Hungary when measured at official prices compared with those generated by one of these PFM's ("production prices"); and

4. to measure changes in aggregate productivity in Hungary in terms of three of the PFM's.

To accomplish these tasks, Brown and Licari express the several PFM's in conventional Leontief notation and then present a number of computations for 1959, 1964, 1966, and 1968 based on a reconstructed 13-sector input-output table for Hungary. Through these computations and comparisons, they seek to measure the "distortions" of official prices.

Brown and Licari stress that they attempt to measure "distortions" only in regard to an "efficiency standard" and not also by a "welfare standard." The former refers to production potential and requires that the prices of any two commodities be inversely proportional to the corresponding marginal rates of transformation, or be directly proportional to their marginal costs. The latter requires that the prices of any two commodities be directly proportional to the marginal utilities of these commodities to consumers or, where more relevant, the marginal rates of substitution of the state authorities. Let us consider first the extent to which PFM's are suitable yardsticks for the efficiency standard, and second the implications of neglecting the welfare standard.

To measure "distortions" in regard to the efficiency standard, Brown and Licari presumably require some measure of factor cost equivalent to marginal cost. However, as an alternative, they turn to Bergson's adjusted factor cost standard (AFCS), which is described as requiring the following:

1. All commodity prices resolve fully into charges for primary factors, particularly labor, land, and capital.
2. For capital there is a net charge corresponding to the average internal return of this factor in the economy generally, and an allowance for depreciation of a conventional sort.
3. The charge for land, "rent," corresponds on the average to the differential return to superior land.
4. "Wages" are at a uniform rate for any occupation and as between occupations differ on the average in accord with differences in productivity and disutility.
5. Similar principles apply in the case of the relation of wages to farm labor income.
6. Commodity prices are uniform in any given market area.

But in fact Brown and Licari use neither marginal-cost prices nor Bergsonian AFCS prices to evaluate "distortions" in the official Hungarian prices. Instead, they turn to various PFM's suggested in the Soviet and East European literature, namely:

1. "Value prices"—in which the surplus of nonwage value added is allocated in proportion to wages.
2. "Cost or averaged value prices"—in which the surplus is allocated in proportion to the sum of materials costs and wages.
3. "Production prices"—in which the surplus is allocated in proportion to the amount of fixed and working capital.
4. "Two-channel prices"—a combination of (1) and (3).
5. "Income prices"—in which all value added (wages and nonwages) is allocated according to the capital employed in each sector.

Of these five PFM's, Brown and Licari designate three—"value" (1), "production" (3), and "two-channel" (4)—as having "the strongest theoretical base," and they select these to calculate alternative yardsticks by which to measure the deficiencies of official Hungarian prices, through comparisons with sectoral price levels obtained from their 13-sector input-output table. These PFM's are used to judge official prices on the ground that sectoral price levels generated by these formulae correspond to, or reflect, factor cost, or at least "a theoretically more satisfactory concept of resource costs."

However, none of the three preferred PFM's truly corresponds to either a marginal cost criterion or Bergson's AFCS. First, as Brown and Licari themselves note, a "rent" charge for land is excluded from all of them. Second, of the three PFM's selected as "theoretically strongest," one is the "value" PFM and another is the "two-channel" PFM which rests in part on the "value" PFM. This choice is puzzling in light of the observations by Brown and Licari that the "value" PFM ignores the opportunity cost of capital (whereas a capital charge is explicitly mentioned in Bergson's AFCS), and that even the Hungarian economist Bródy, in his sophisticated mathematical reinterpretation of Marxian value theory, rejects "value" prices as incapable of leading to efficient decisions except under unrealistic and inapplicable simplifying conditions.

Thus, one hesitates to accept the conclusion of Brown and Licari that "the measured price distortions do represent deviations from consistent concepts of factor-cost pricing, which are generically [?] related to marginal cost pricing ideas."

Another property claimed for the PFM yardsticks is that they yield "an internally consistent set of synthetic equilibrium prices" where ". . . equilibrium is defined in relation to the satisfaction of a system of equality constraints on national income and/or its components" (footnote 18).

If "equilibrium" merely requires internal consistency—and specifically does not also require that prices be "scarcity" prices equating supply and demand without formal or informal rationing—then could not one also label the actual official prices as "equilibrium" prices since they too yielded a set of statistically consistent (national income or input-output) accounts?

This raises a second problem—the conscious neglect of the welfare standard and considerations of demand. The PFM's with which Brown and Licari concern themselves explicitly ignore demand, and the underlying preferences and incomes, in the formation of prices. As Brown and Licari put it, the PFM's address themselves only to the "relative price problem" of relative intersectoral (producer) price levels. They ignore the "dual price problem" of the relationship between wholesale and retail prices and why they may differ because of indirect taxes and subsidies arising from differences between the preferences of the political authorities and those of households, income distribution objectives, and so forth.

I, for one, find it hard to think of price formation without considering demand. To ignore demand in price formation is like cutting with a one-bladed scissor, or clapping with one hand. PFM's which explicitly neglect demand presumably assume administrative rationing to compensate for the absence of scarcity prices. Although this is a convenient—and in centrally planned economies, not unrealistic—assumption, such PFM's can hardly provide an "optimal" pricing criterion by which to evaluate shortcomings of officially established prices.

For this purpose, the programming models of the "opportunity cost school" would be superior to the PFM's discussed in this chapter. The reasons are that the former—unlike the latter—consider both desired outcomes and resource and product constraints, and that they yield scarcity prices. It is true that, as Brown and Licari observe (footnote 18), there are computational problems in calculating shadow prices, but these may not be so serious as previously thought. If some of these computational problems can be solved satisfactorily, the resulting prices should not only be superior to those generated by PFM's as measures of the "distortions" of official prices, but also could help in efforts to relax administrative rationing and increase market relations in the production sectors of centrally planned economies.

II. Price Formation Models and the 1968 Hungarian Price Reform

This section discusses in turn the nature and magnitude of price adjustment coefficients calculated for Hungarian prices by Brown and

Licari, the Hungarian economic and price reforms of 1968, a comparison of actual 1968 prices with "ideal" "two-channel" prices, and the flexibility of the Hungarian price mechanism.

Price adjustment coefficients for Hungarian prices

From each of the PFM's representing a particular conception (or more aptly, construction) of "value," it is possible to derive a corresponding "price adjustment model" (PAM) to show the difference between actual prevailing sectoral price levels and those generated by the particular PFM. In each case, in the procedure followed by Brown and Licari, the resulting "price adjustment coefficients" (PAC's) express the ratio of the calculated sectoral price levels to the prevailing sectoral price levels. Thus, if the PAC is greater than 1.0, the calculated price level exceeds the actual price level, and that sector is considered (relatively) "underpriced." If the PAC equals 1.0, the calculated and actual sectoral price levels are identical, and the latter is deemed to be "correct." If the PAC is less than 1.0, the actual sectoral price level exceeds the price level derived from the PFM, and that sector is regarded as "overpriced."

By means of a 13-sector input-output table, Brown and Licari calculated such PAC's for Hungary in 1959, 1964, 1966, and 1968, for three PFM's: "value prices," "production prices," and "two-channel prices" (their Tables 1, 2, and 3). In view of the important conceptual differences between the PFM's for "value prices" and "production prices," one might not expect that the corresponding PAC's in these tables would prove to be so close in regard to both the direction and the extent of "distortion" of official prices. On the other hand, since the "two-channel" PFM is conceptually only a weighted average of the first two PFM's, the similarity of its PAC's to theirs is not surprising.

Essentially the same picture emerges from all three sets of PAC's. According to the calculations for 1966 — when the 1968 price reform was already being prepared — all branches of industry except private industry had PAC's less than 1.0 and their output therefore is classified by Brown and Licari as "overpriced," with the most severe "overpricing" in the chemical and light industries. On the other hand, sales by the agricultural, transport-communications, and domestic and foreign trade sectors are considered "underpriced," with PAC's above 1.0.[2]

According to the PAC's calculated for 1968, the price reform of that year almost entirely eliminated "overpricing" for industry as a whole, chiefly through reductions in "overpricing" in the chemical, light, and food branches. In the case of the food industry, the correction even in-

2. In their calculations for domestic trade in 1966, the "value" PAC is 1.00, but the "production" PAC is 1.29 and the "two-channel" PAC is 1.16.

volved a shift from "overpricing" to "underpricing": for example, the "two-channel" PAC rose from 0.93 in 1966 to 1.10 in 1968. In contrast, the reform shifted the domestic and foreign trade sectors from "underpricing" to "overpricing." "Underpricing" was reduced significantly for the transport-communications sector, whose "two-channel" PAC went from 1.55 in 1966 to 1.35 in 1968. However, there was no significant change in the substantial "underpricing" of agriculture, whose "two-channel" PAC was 1.22 in 1966 and 1.21 in 1968.

In short, according to the PAC calculations of Brown and Licari, the 1968 Hungarian price reform may be praised for reducing "overpricing" in industry, but criticized for not correcting "underpricing" in agriculture and for "over-correcting" by shifting some sectors from "overpricing" to "underpricing" or vice versa.

1968 economic and price reforms

To what extent does this appraisal of the 1968 price reform correspond to the aims and perceptions of the Hungarian pricing authorities concerning the reform?

The 1968 price reform was part of, and must be assessed in the light of, the broader economic reform which introduced the New Economic Mechanism (NEM). The main features of the NEM were as follows:[3]

1. Central administrative specification of enterprise production and sales programs was abandoned, and enterprises were permitted to determine their production patterns on the basis of contracts with buyers.
2. Central administrative allocation of material inputs was also ended, with a few exceptions.
3. One-year operational plans were eliminated, and the five-year plan became the chief orientation for economic development and the "steering" of the economy.
4. Centrally fixed wage scales were terminated, but average wage levels of enterprises were severely restrained.

3. Studies of the 1968 economic reform and its subsequent development include István Friss, ed., *Reform of the Economic Mechanism in Hungary* (Budapest: Akadémiai Kiadó, 1969); Ottó Gadó, ed., *Reform of the Economic Mechanism in Hungary: Development 1968–71* (Budapest: Akadémiai Kiadó, 1972); Richard D. Portes, "Economic Reforms in Hungary," *American Economic Review* 60, no. 2 (May 1970): 307–13; Béla Balassa, "The Firm in the New Economic Mechanism in Hungary," in Morris Bornstein, ed., *Plan and Market: Economic Reform in Eastern Europe* (New Haven, Conn.: Yale University Press, 1973), ch. 10; David Granick, "The Hungarian Economic Reform," *World Politics* 25, no. 3 (April 1973): 414–29; William F. Robinson, *The Pattern of Reform in Hungary: A Political, Economic, and Cultural Analysis* (New York: Praeger Publishers, 1973); and Tamás Morva, "Planning in Hungary," in Morris Bornstein, ed., *Economic Planning, East and West* (Cambridge, Mass.: Ballinger Publishing Co., 1975), ch. 9.

5. Central allocation of investment funds was replaced in part by self-financing from profits, but central supervision of investment activities remains strong.
6. The chief objective of enterprise activity is pursuit of profit, and incentives for managers and workers are linked to profit through profit-sharing schemes.
7. Separate "foreign-trade multipliers" for the CMEA and world-market trading areas were introduced to link domestic and foreign prices and thereby influence domestic production in response to the pattern of foreign trade. However, the system of taxes and subsidies on exports and imports, involving "price-equalization funds," was retained.
8. A price reform adjusted relative producer prices and introduced greater flexibility in price formation.

Although the reform sought through these measures to expand decentralized decision making at the enterprise level in response to (domestic and foreign) market forces, a considerable degree of centralized control was retained—some of it informal rather than formal. The country is small, Party control remains strong in all spheres, in many branches production is concentrated in a few firms, and in 1972 the 50 largest enterprises were formally put under close central supervision.

The fundamental aim of the 1968 price reform was to establish a system of prices which would take into account three basic factors:[4]

1. Cost: This criterion approaches price from the standpoint of the producing firm, which, as a rule, should not be expected to sell at a loss and to which the price should provide some surplus for profit-sharing and self-financing of investment.
2. Judgment of the market: This criterion considers price from the standpoint of the consumer. According to it, price cannot be divorced from the utility which the consumer (in the case of exports, the foreign buyer) attributes to the product.
3. State policy: Societal preferences—articulated by the political authorities—sometimes overrule individual preferences and call for a different pattern of production, consumption, and income distribution than market processes would generate. These state preferences may be imposed through direct administrative orders, or in a market setting through the use of taxes, subsidies, and transfer payments of various kinds.

4. Béla Csikós-Nagy, "The New Hungarian Price System," in Friss, ed., *Reform of the Economic Mechanism in Hungary*, p. 147; Béla Csikós-Nagy, "Anti-Inflationary Policies: Debates and Experience in Hungary," in *Anti-Inflationary Policies: East and West* (Milan: CESES, 1975), p. 150.

Only the first of these criteria is reflected in the "factor-cost" prices calculated by PFM's, whereas the second and third criteria are likely to call for "deviations" of actual prices from those calculated according to any of the PFM's.

A key political constraint on the 1968 price reform was that neither the level nor the structure of retail prices should be significantly altered, since such changes would lead to demands for adjustments in wages, agricultural prices, and transfer payments, and create (or intensify) opposition to the NEM.

The main features of the 1968 price reform may now be reviewed briefly in the light of these objectives and constraints.

1. As Table 9.1 shows, the producer price level for industry as a whole was increased by only 5.6 percent, although there was considerable dispersion around the average. For example, within heavy industry, energy prices were reduced by 15 percent, coal prices by 9.7 percent, metallurgical prices by 5.2 percent, and chemical prices by 4.1 percent, while prices were raised 5 percent for the engineering branch and 9 percent for building materials. For light industry as a whole, the increase averaged 14.5 percent, but included an increase of 17.5 percent for textiles and a decrease of 16 percent for clothing, reflecting the shift from turnover taxes to capital charges and profits taxes.

The 1968 price reform was claimed to approach "production-type

Table 9.1. Price indices for industrial production, by branch and industry, January 1968 (January 1967 = 100).

Mining	99.5
Coal mining	90.3
Crude oil and natural gas production	108.6
Electric energy	85.0
Metallurgy	94.8
Engineering (machinery, equipment, instruments, metal products)	105.0
Building materials	109.0
Chemicals	95.9
Heavy industry, total	100.1
Wood processing	113.5
Paper	111.7
Printing	120.7
Textile	117.5
Leather, fur, and shoe	143.7
Textile clothing	84.0
Miscellaneous industries	105.3
Handicraft	96.3
Light industry, total	114.5
Food processing	111.4
Socialist industry	105.6

Source: Hungarian Central Statistical Office (HCSO), *Statistical Yearbook 1968* (Budapest: HCSO, 1970), pp. 92–93.

prices" because (a) a 5 percent charge on assets was introduced; (b) the rate of profit was expressed as a percentage of the value of assets; (c) taxation of enterprise profits was related to the proportions between the value of assets and the size of the wage bill; and (d) nonrepayable budget grants were partly replaced by self-financing out of retained profits.

However, the profit rates provided by the new prices varied by branch for two main reasons. First, the price levels and therefore profitability of industries heavily engaged in exports had to be determined in the light of international prices (and the "foreign-trade multipliers" linking them to domestic prices). Second, in some cases, especially in light industry, the supply-demand relationships expected in the market dictated relatively higher prices and profits. Thus, the price changes shown in Table 9.1 provided profit rates (in relation to assets) of 6.5 percent for industry as a whole, but ranged from 1.6 percent for mining to 9.6 percent for light industry. Even more striking was the variation in profitability for product groups and individual commodities within branches — again because of domestic and/or foreign market conditions calling for prices different from the cost-plus-uniform-markup prices generated by PFM's.[5]

2. In 1968 state agricultural procurement prices were raised 9.3 percent on the average, including 12.1 percent for plant products and 7.3 percent for animal products.[6]

3. Despite the increase in both industrial producer prices and agricultural procurement prices, neither the level nor the structure of consumer prices was significantly altered, for the political reasons already mentioned. Table 9.2 shows the modest changes in retail prices in 1968 compared with 1967.

5. Csikós-Nagy, "The New Hungarian Price System," pp. 145–46.
6. Hungarian Central Statistical Office (HCSO), *Statistical Yearbook 1968* (Budapest: HCSO, 1970), p. 196.

Table 9.2. Consumer price indices, by product group and consumer group, 1968 (1967 = 100).

	Workers and employees	Peasants
Food	100	99
Clothing	100	100
Miscellaneous industrial commodities	98	97
Heating and lighting	99	99
Services	104	104
Total	100	99

Source: Hungarian Central Statistical Office (HCSO), *Statistical Yearbook 1968* (Budapest: HCSO, 1970), p. 335.

Actual 1968 prices vs. "two-channel PFM prices

How do these price changes under the 1968 price reform compare with those implied by the PFM's? Because of differences in valuation, classification, and aggregation schemes, it is not possible to compare these official price statistics with the PAC calculations by Brown and Licari discussed above. However, the Chairman of the National Board for Prices and Materials, Béla Csikós-Nagy, has compared the 1968 prices with "ideal" prices constructed according to a "two-channel" PFM which incorporates production costs plus a 12 percent markup on wages plus a 10 percent markup on the value of assets.[7]

The results for producer prices, shown in Table 9.3, indicate that— judged by the standard of this PFM—the price levels set in 1968 for heavy and light industry and construction were too high, the level for freight transport correct, and the levels for agriculture and the food industry too low. However, Csikós-Nagy stresses, the producer prices adopted in 1968 had to differ from the input-(only)-based prices of the PFM in order to take into account domestic and foreign demand factors and national economic policy.

Because the 1968 reform raised state agricultural procurement prices more than industrial producer prices, it narrowed the gap between them

7. Csikós-Nagy, "The New Hungarian Price System," pp. 136–40.

Table 9.3. Relationship of 1968 producer price level to "ideal" two-channel price level,[a] selected branches ("ideal" price level = 100).

Heavy industry	110
Light industry	115
Food industry	94
Industry, total	106
Construction	106
Agriculture	83
Freight transport	100

Source: B. Csikós-Nagy, "The New Hungarian Price System," in István Friss, ed., *Reform of the Economic Mechanism in Hungary* (Budapest: Akadémiai Kiadó, 1969), p. 137.

a. See text for definition of "ideal" price level.

Table 9.4. Relationship of 1968 price levels of industrial and agricultural sales to "ideal" two-channel price level,[a] by category of price ("ideal" price level = 100).

	Industrial sales	Agricultural sales
Consumer prices	114	84
Producer prices, including taxes	106	83
Producer prices, excluding taxes	53	57

Source: Csikós-Nagy, "The New Hungarian Price System," p. 138.

a. See text for definition of "ideal" price level.

somewhat. Yet, as Table 9.4 shows, in relation to the "ideal" two-channel formula mentioned above, industrial sales are still "overpriced" and agricultural sales are still "underpriced" if the comparison is made either at consumer prices or at producer prices including taxes. On the other hand, if taxes are excluded, industrial and agricultural sales are both "underpriced" to approximately the same (large) degree. In this sense, though deviating from their "ideal" price levels, the industrial and agricultural price levels might be considered at last to have been brought into balance with each other.

Finally, Table 9.5 shows the relationship of the 1968 consumer price level to the "ideal" two-channel price level for a number of product groups. The considerable variation of actual price levels above and below the "ideal" price level once again reflects both market factors and state income distribution policies.

Table 9.5. Relationship of 1968 consumer price level to "ideal" two-channel price level,[a] selected product groups and items ("ideal" price level = 100).

Light industrial goods	132
Building materials	126
Tobacco and spirits	120–150
Engineering products	118
Meat, dairy, baked, preserved foods	70–90
Electric energy	82
Transport and communications	74
Coal	55
Housing rents	30

Source: Csikós-Nagy, "The New Hungarian Price System," p. 140.

a. See text for definition of "ideal" price level.

Price flexibility

In addition to adjusting relative prices, and linking Hungarian and foreign prices, the 1968 price reform sought to make the price system more flexible in response to market forces by introducing four categories of price regulation:

1. "Fixed" prices: These are set centrally at a specific level, i.e., a single amount in forints.
2. "Maximum" prices: A ceiling price is set, but sellers are permitted to charge less if they wish.
3. "Limit" prices: Ceiling and floor prices are set centrally (usually 4–15 percent apart), but sellers may adjust prices between these limits.
4. "Free" prices: Prices in this category are set through negotiations between buyers and sellers.

Table 9.6 shows the estimated relative importance of the four price control categories, by major type of transactions, after the 1968 price reform. Most raw materials were put in the "fixed" and "maximum" categories. Although over three-fourths of interproducer sales of finished goods were placed in the "free" price category, control of these prices was effectively exercised through the close regulation of the prices of the raw and semifinished materials constituting inputs into finished goods, and through strict supervision of wage expenditures at all levels of production.[8] Agricultural procurement prices remained under close control. Because a relatively stable retail price level—increasing no more than 2–3 percent per year—is considered a cornerstone of Hungarian eco-

8. See Peter Wiles, "The Control of Inflation in Hungary, Jan. 1968–June 1973," *Economie Appliquée* 27, no. 1 (1974): 119–47.

Table 9.6. Relative importance of price control categories, by major type of transaction, 1968 (percent of total sales).

Types of transactions	Price control category			
	Fixed	Maximum	Limit	Free
Interproducer sales of raw and semifinished materials	30	40	2	28
Interproducer sales of finished goods	3	16	3	78
State agricultural procurements	60	–	30	10
Household consumption expenditures[a]	20	30	27	23

Source: Csikós-Nagy, "The New Hungarian Price System," pp. 148–51.
a. Excluding rents, passenger transport, and postal services.

nomic policy, all key items of mass consumption were assigned to the tighter control categories, and only about one-fourth of household consumption expenditures (chiefly fashion items and imported goods) were put in the "free" price category.

At the time of the 1968 reform, its designers hoped (1) that the share of the "limit" and "free" categories in total sales would steadily increase; (2) that prices in the "maximum" and "limit" categories would often be below the ceiling; and (3) that in the "free" category supply and demand forces would lead to price decreases as well as increases. However, in the years following 1968 none of these hopes was realized to a significant degree, because of inflationary pressures of domestic and foreign origin.[9] As a result, progress in expanding the coverage of the "free" price category has been much slower than expected.[10] Furthermore, various forms of official guidance of "free" prices were introduced, including rules for cost calculation and guidelines for distinguishing "fair" vs. "unfair" levels of profit above costs so calculated.

Hence, with some exceptions (such as the prices of petroleum and products made from it), neither the level nor the structure of Hungarian prices has changed notably since the 1968 price reform.

III. Conclusions

Because they must take into account (1) both domestic and foreign demand factors and (2) state policies regarding the development of the economy and the distribution of money and real income, the Hungarian pricing authorities have found the prices constructed by PFM's to be incomplete and inadequate guides to price formation. As Seton notes in his chapter in this volume, "value," "production," and "two-channel" PFM's can perhaps claim to provide "diagnostic" prices which somehow describe social relationships by characterizing the respective contributions of labor and capital. However, because the PFM's neglect utility, demand, and scarcity, their results cannot be used to steer production and consumption.

This limitation of PFM's has increasingly been recognized, as the progress of the Hungarian debate on the price system indicates.[11] The first stage in this debate occurred during the late 1950s in the context of a

9. See Wiles, "The Control of Inflation in Hungary," and Csikós-Nagy, "Anti-Inflationary Policies."

10. In 1968, it was expected that the share of the "free" category in consumer expenditures would rise from 23 percent in 1968 to 50 percent in 1975, but the actual figure is estimated at 35–38 percent. Csikós-Nagy, "Anti-Inflationary Policies," p. 154.

11. Béla Csikós-Nagy, "Two Stages of the Hungarian Debate on Prices," *Acta Oeconomica* 1, nos. 3–4 (1966): 255–65; and Csikós-Nagy, "Anti-Inflationary Policies," pp. 157–58.

command economy in which production and prices were both centrally fixed and producer prices served chiefly an accounting, rather than an allocative, function. As a result, this stage of the debate focused on a search for the most appropriate formula for calculating "value" in some "uniform" way within a Marxian framework.

In the second stage, during the 1960s, the debate turned to the development of a price system compatible with the greater use of the market contemplated by the NEM. The debate therefore shifted from "a price system based on inputs" and whether prices should "arbitrarily" deviate from "value," to questions of "use value, marginal value, scarcity, competitive prices, equilibrium prices, market prices, etc.," not considered by PFM's.

The third stage of the debate, in the 1970s, has emerged because of the failure to achieve the greater flexibility in the price mechanism envisioned in the 1968 price reform. This new stage focuses on three main issues: (1) how excessive domestic pressure on prices can be reduced by proper monetary and fiscal measures; (2) how external pressure on prices, from inflation abroad, can be offset by a foreign exchange policy which adjusts the "foreign-trade multipliers" linking domestic and foreign prices; and (3) how to overcome official fears of inflation so great that they prevent even necessary and modest price movements.

Thus, the third stage is concerned largely with macroeconomic issues, in contrast to the microeconomic emphasis of the second stage. However, as in the second stage, PFM's are no longer the center of interest.

10

Soviet Wages under Socialism

Janet G. Chapman

University of Pittsburgh

Wages in the planned socialist systems have more economic content, or, at least, more market content, than some other types of socialist prices. While the demand for labor is determined by plans, there is considerable freedom of occupational choice on the supply side. Thus, while, like other prices, wages are determined centrally, the differential wage system as directed to workers has an important allocative function. The relative wage system is also the major determinant of income distribution, a matter of particular political importance in a socialist state. As wages form the main source of household income, the level of real wages is an important element in the determination of the distribution of national income between personal consumption and other uses. This chapter focuses on Soviet wages in the postwar period. The nature and major roles of wages in the USSR are discussed first. In Section II the main features of the two postwar wage reforms are outlined. New data on the size distribution of Soviet wages and salaries are presented in Section III. Section IV discusses the shape of the earnings distribution, a Soviet theory of why a lognormal distribution is typical of and appropriate to socialism, and a Western theory of why the Pareto tail does not fit socialist distributions. The relative emphasis in this chapter on the distribution question is justified by the new availability of Soviet data on this sensitive but increasingly important issue.

I am indebted to Asatoshi Maeshiro, Gene Gruver, and Douglas Gray for assistance on some statistical concepts, and to Mr. Gray for the computations underlying Table 10.1. For helpful comments on an early version of this chapter I am indebted to the participants in the conference, particularly Janusz G. Zielinski, and to Abram Bergson, Arnold Katz, Frederic Pryor, and Peter Wiles. The work was aided by grants from the American Council of Learned Societies and the National Science Foundation.

I. The Nature and Role of Soviet Wages

Soviet wages are set centrally, and wage differentials are based on the socialist principle of payment according to contribution. As suggested above, the wage system is primarily directed toward workers rather than management. In theory the focus in establishing relative wages is on the nature of the work rather than on demand for the products of the labor. But the more sophisticated economists bring in, on the back of Marx's stipulation that the work should be socially necessary, the concept of "social utility." The simple notion that labor payment should be based on the quantity and quality of the work is replaced by the notion of the complexity or social utility of the work. "Complex labor, being more effective from the point of view of the national economy should be valued more highly than simple labor" (Kunel'skii 1972, p. 116).[1] In practice, demand and relative scarcities of different kinds of labor clearly play an important role.

In establishing relative wages, the Soviet wage setters start, as Leonard Kirsch (1972, ch. 1) puts it, by deliberately setting what Western economists call "pure wage differentials" (but which in a market economy can only be approached theoretically and *ex post*). The pure differentials which make up the Soviet wage structure are: skill (including responsibility) differentials, expressed for wage earners in the graded skill scales and for salaried workers in occupational salary scales and the related job qualification manuals; differentials for conditions of work — intensity, arduousness, danger, night work; interindustrial differentials, based on the importance of the industry; geographical differentials; and on-the-job incentives — piecework, bonuses, etc. Demand is usually explicitly recognized only with reference to the interindustrial differentials which reflect planners' priorities, but demand in relation to supply plays a role in all aspects of the wage differentials, both as centrally determined and as resulting from wage drift.

The establishment of wages, as of other prices, at the center means that changes in the wage structure are undertaken only periodically and sometimes at long intervals. The wage reform begun in 1956 was the first general revision of the wage structure since the early 1930s. Inevitably there will be a certain rigidity in the structure of wages. Some flexibility, however, is built into the Soviet procedures for wage determination. In general, the basic wage and salary rates and the general rules concerning incentive pay are set centrally, while piece rates and performance norms are set at the enterprise level. This gives enterprise

---

1. Full citations are given in the references at the end of this chapter.

management some discretion over earnings and provides some flexibility to correct for errors in the rate structure and to adapt to changing conditions between central revisions of rates. This leads to what might be called wage drift, which historically has been significant, especially in the prewar and war years.

The wage system has been heavily relied on as the major means for the allocation of the labor force in the period up to World War II and again in the postwar period. While demand for labor by occupation, skill level, sector, and region is established in the plans, the differential wage system is directed to inducing workers to take the planned jobs and to increase their level of skill and qualification, as well as to work harder. During the war years, restrictions were imposed on labor movement, and direct allocation of labor was used in addition to the wage system. Direct allocation of labor and most restrictions on freedom of occupational choice were dropped formally in 1956, probably earlier in practice. The major qualifications to this freedom are (i) the assignment of graduates of vocational-technical schools, specialized secondary schools, and higher educational institutions to their first jobs and (ii) the considerable Party control over upper-level appointments.

During the prewar years, the very rapid growth of industry required large and rapid shifts in the structure of the labor force and an increase in skilled workers and technical personnel. The most notable shift was that from agriculture to industry and construction.[2] Real incomes were initially lower in agriculture and money wages rose substantially outside agriculture between 1928 and the mid-1930s. Though the real nonagricultural wage fell, the decline in peasant income to the early 1930s was apparently greater. However, collectivization created such a push from the countryside that it is difficult to tell how much of the very large gross in- and out-migration and the substantial net migration to the cities was in response to income differentials (see TsUNKhU 1936, p. 7).

In the nonagricultural sector the wage reform of 1931–1933 reversed an earlier policy stressing egalitarianism and appears to reflect a belief that differential wages were necessary to industrialization. The skill scales were widened and the rate structure was revised in favor of the heavy industries. The widening of skill differentials was intended to encourage workers to upgrade their skills and presumably reflected both the shortage of skilled workers and the increasing supplies of raw peasant labor. The relatively greater rise in rates in heavy industry reflected planners' priorities. As is known, between 1928 and 1935 a drastic change in the ranking of industries by relative levels of average earnings took

2. In a country like China, where labor is surplus in relation to the capacity to expand industry, and agriculture is highly labor-intensive, such structural shifts should be more moderate and the need for a strong differential wage system weaker.

place, with relative rises in the rankings of heavy industries and relative declines in the consumer goods industries (TsUNKhU 1936, and Chapman 1970, p. 47). Such changes in relative wages must have played an important role in the allocation of labor. It is true that it is difficult to quantify this. A preliminary and unsophisticated attempt to measure the relationship between changes in employment and changes in relative earnings among Soviet industries between 1928 and 1935 shows little correlation.[3] But this is based on total employment by industry and ignores the crucial question of skill levels and quality of labor. The higher level of wages in the priority industries should have served to attract the more skilled and better workers to them and to have given the employers the ability to pick and choose among applicants. The fact that Soviet managers did compete for labor by raising wages (whether through gaining official approval for a raise in rates or through manipulating norms, piece rates, and the grading system) indicates that managers as well as the planners believed wages were important in attracting and keeping the better workers.

There is no doubt that there occurred a significant increase in the level of education and skill of the Soviet labor force. While much of this must be attributed to the expansion of education and training and the fact that education has been free (with the exception of war years), the success of the training programs might well have been less without the stimulus of the higher incomes and status accompanying jobs requiring additional education.

The importance of allocative efficiency has been heightened in the postwar era. Labor has become scarcer, for the labor force is increasing only very slowly. Most of the able-bodied population has already been drawn into the labor force so that increments to the labor force are limited virtually to youths reaching working age, and the birth rate has been declining. While there is still a large labor force in agriculture, it is difficult to draw on this rapidly because some of the younger and better

3. The rank correlation for 18 industries between (a) changes in employment between 1928 and 1935 and (b) the level of wages in 1935 is only .23. The calculations are based on data in TsUNKhU 1936. The data refer to large-scale industry and may be distorted because of the increase in the proportion of total employment accounted for by large-scale industry over this period and differential increases in this respect among industries. The results are strongly affected by one industry—the garment industry—where the rise in employment was the greatest (possibly largely because of changes in scale) and the rise in wages smallest. Excluding the garment industry, the rank correlation rises to .42 (Chapman and Shun Hsin Chou [forthcoming], ch. 5). Efforts to measure the extent to which relative wage changes influence the structure of employment by industry have not been very conclusive for either the socialist or market economies. See, e.g., Galenson and Fox 1967, and O.E.C.D. 1965. In part, this is no doubt due to the aggregative nature of the data and perhaps to deficient measuring techniques. See Hamermesh and Portes 1972 for a criticism of such studies and for an application of more sophisticated econometric techniques to a study of the Hungarian labor market during 1951–1967.

educated, who are most likely to leave the farms, are needed there if agricultural productivity is to increase and also because of urbanization costs. There is evidence, too, of considerable maldistribution of labor with actual or potential surpluses in some occupations and places, and acute shortages in others (Feshbach 1966). At the same time, a very large part of the planned growth in output during the current plan period depends on increased labor productivity. The increase in specialization of both production and individuals means that getting the right people into the right jobs is more difficult and more important than in the prewar years. Presumably finer allocation tools are required. With the abolition of the wartime restrictions on labor mobility and freedom of occupational choice, the wage system again became the primary labor allocation mechanism and the wage reforms begun in 1956 were intended to make this more efficient.

Wage differentials have been directed primarily to the workers and have been little used as signals for managers to economize on labor costs. Emphasis on meeting output goals and cost-plus (planned) pricing mean that there is little incentive to economize on labor costs, while taut planning and supply problems provide incentives to have more labor on hand than would otherwise be necessary. This is reinforced by the policy of no unemployment and the requirement that the manager must find an employee another job and get the consent of the union before firing him. Attitudes here appear to be changing, particularly in the light of the increasing scarcity of labor. The spirit of the economic reforms launched in 1965 with greater emphasis on profits implies greater attention to costs. One of the more significant trends in current Soviet wage policy seems to be an increased effort to direct wage differentials at management and to make management more sensitive to labor costs.

In its allocation function as directed to workers, the Soviet wage system has certainly been far from perfect. One problem seems to be that in fact it was relied on too heavily, or was not adequately supported by other mechanisms. Complaints have been made about poor planning of labor requirements and poor coordination of education and training with manpower needs. Youths directed to their first jobs have often been directed to jobs they have not trained for and apparently many youths avoid obeying the directives or leave before their tour of duty is over. A major shortcoming has been the absence of an employment service to assist in matching available workers with available jobs.

While efficiency has become more important, so too has equity. Given the level of development already achieved in the Soviet Union, the question of the transition from socialism to full communism arises. Even if full communism remains a distant utopia, it is increasingly recognized that in the competition between the systems, the Soviet system will ultimately be judged in terms of the level of living of the population and the extent of equity in distribution. Rabkina and Rimashevskaia (1972, p. 61) say the distribution of income has "enormous significance as one of the criteria of the economic successes of the country."[4] Under socialism, equity continues to be viewed as equal pay for equal work. But the trend is now seen as a movement to greater equality as the differences between the skill and educational levels of the workers, and the differences between the requirements of different jobs, are seen to be decreasing.

On the macro level, major policy goals of wage policy have been to restrain the level of personal consumption in the interest of increased communal consumption, investment, and defense; to prevent the inflation in the consumer market that the first policy is likely to lead to; and to increase participation in the labor force. During the prewar and war years, control over the level of money wages was inadequate, and money wages rose much faster than productivity. With the failure of money wage policy, resort was to rationing (late 1928 to early 1936 and mid-1941 to late 1947) and to raising retail prices. Real wages, as a result, fell during the early 1930s and again during the war and only regained the 1928 level in the early 1950s (Chapman 1963), while labor productivity rose, with the probable exception of the early war years, throughout the period. Control over the wage bill has been more successful during the postwar period. More moderate rates of increase in money wages, combined with substantial reductions in retail prices between 1948 and 1954, have led to a significant increase in real wages since 1948. This real-wage increase has still lagged behind gains in labor productivity, though by considerably less than previously.

The very low level of real wages which prevailed until at least the late 1950s was undoubtedly an important factor in the large increase in participation in the labor force, particularly among wives, which took place, and to the extraordinarily high level of participation. Over 90 percent of the able-bodied population of working age were in the labor force in 1970 (*State Five Year Plan . . . 1971–1975*, p. 88). The high participation rate of women, at the same time, is clearly a factor in the present demographic problem of a declining birth rate and slowly growing labor force. With the postwar improvements in real wages, the possibility may arise of decreasing participation in the labor force by some people, such as low-paid wives of well-paid husbands, youths, and pensioners. But lowering real wages to counteract such a tendency, if it arises, no longer seems a feasible alternative. The present Soviet leadership appears to have a commitment to improve the welfare of the popu-

---

4. Shutov (1972, p. 6) makes the point concerning level of consumption.

lation. The Polish experience of 1970, where dissatisfaction with real-wage policies led to the loss of power of the Polish Communist leadership, will surely serve as a restraint.

Macro considerations will ordinarily place some restraints on micro wage policies, since changes in relative wages are more readily accomplished through increases in the wages of some persons, rather than through reducing anyone's wage. This may be seen, for instance, in plans to implement wage reform over a period of years, rather than all at once.

II. The Wage Reforms

The first central overhaul of the wage system as a whole since the early 1930s was begun experimentally in 1956. It was introduced industry by industry and sector by sector. It was completed in industry, construction, and some other branches during 1960 and in the remaining "material branches" and in science during 1961. It was extended to the other non-material or service sectors during 1964 and 1965. A minimum wage of 27–35 rubles a month for workers in industry, construction, transportation, and communications was established in January 1957. From 1959 on, a minimum monthly wage of 40 rubles was introduced as the reform was put into effect in each industry or sector. This reform has been adequately described elsewhere (Chapman 1970; Kirsch 1972), so only a few main points need be made here.

The basic purposes of this reform were to restore central control over the wage structure and to improve the incentive and allocative efficiency of the wage system. This meant creating a structure of basic wage and salary rates which conformed to current conditions and a system in which the basic rates played a major role in earnings differentials. The varieties of incentive provisions which had developed, and generally loose but widely varying performance norms, meant that the basic rate had become a relatively insignificant determinant of relative earnings. The aims were to make the basic wage structure more consistent and to provide for equal pay for equal work — but with differentials for the importance of the industry. The wide variety of existing wage scales (even within an industry) was reduced, the wage scales were simplified and made more uniform, and the spread of basic rates generally was reduced. For instance, in ferrous metallurgy, the new spread in basic wage rates for production workers was set at 3.2 : 1, compared to earlier spreads of 3.3–4.1 : 1; in the machinery and several other industries the new spread was set at 2 : 1 compared to the former spreads in the machinery industry of 1.9–3.6 : 1. In the light and food industries, the new spread was 1.8 : 1

while formerly the spread ranged from 1.9 to 2.6 : 1 (Aganbegian and Maier 1959, p. 135; Maier 1963, p. 148). Differentials for conditions of work and for geographic location were made more explicit and more uniform.

Incentive provisions were made more uniform and incentive earnings were to play a smaller role. There was some reduction in the use of piecework, and progressive piecework was virtually abolished. Greater emphasis was placed on the bonus system, for pieceworkers as well as for time workers, but limits were placed on the amount of bonus that could be earned. Limiting incentive earnings was designed to preserve the importance of the centrally determined basic rate structure and of central control. Another important consideration was the desire to limit inflationary pressures. This was reinforced by tightened control over enterprise expenditures of the wage fund.

A more equal distribution of earnings was an aim of this reform, but an aim only made explicit in 1959 when the 40-ruble minimum wage was announced. The effect of the reform was a substantial reduction in differentiation, the extent of which will be considered in the next section.

The USSR is currently in the midst of a second major wage reform. This might be dated from the increase in the minimum wage by 50 percent to 60 rubles a month for all wage earners and salaried employees simultaneously on 1 January 1968. Adjustments were made for those at rates up to 70 rubles, but otherwise wages and salaries above the minimum remained unchanged. An exception was a raise in rates of machine-tool operators which was a response to an acute shortage of and high turnover among machine-tool operators. The next obvious stage was revision of the rates and salaries for those above the minimum wage level. This was to be done in connection with a further rise in the minimum wage to 70 rubles. This was carried out in the construction and construction materials industries in 1969. The major completion of the second wage reform was scheduled for the period 1971–1975 and is outlined in the Ninth Five Year Plan.

While the previous reform was put into effect sector by sector, the current reform is being put into effect primarily on a region-by-region base, starting with the North, Siberia, and the Far East. This timing means that wages will be raised first in the areas where the labor shortages and turnover problems are most acute. It also has the advantage of avoiding the wide varieties in interindustry pay which prevailed within a given region during the course of implementation of the earlier wage reform and which added to the problem of excessive labor turnover (Chapman 1971, p. 13).

In the terminology of the current plan, the minimum wage will be raised to 70 rubles and the wages and salaries of "middle-paid" workers will be raised. The definition of "middle-paid" workers appears to encompass those with basic wage and salary rates up to 200–230 rubles (Kunel'skii 1972, p. 72; Kostin 1973, p. 11). This would appear to include a large proportion of the labor force. The plan specifically provides for a rise in the wage and salary rates "above all" for skilled workers, engineers, and other specialists and for preferential rises in the branches that determine technical progress.

The wage scales for wage earners, many of them extremely curtailed as a result of the 1968 rise in the minimum wage, will for the most part be widened. However, the new range will generally be narrower than that of wages established in the 1956–1960 reform. In a number of industries, the new ratio of the basic rate in the highest grade to that in the lowest grade is to be 1.6 to 1.7, compared with ratios of 1.8 to 2.0 established for the same industries during 1956–1960; in underground coal mining the new ratio is to be 1.9 compared with the earlier 3.75; and in ferrous metallurgy the reduction in this ratio is from 3.2 to 2.1 (Chapman 1970; Kostin 1973, pp. 14–15). The range of salary rates is also being reduced. The highest managerial salaries are apparently being held at the former level, while salaries for managers of less important enterprises as well as for technicians, engineers, and other technical, professional, and managerial personnel are being raised.[5]

Incentives are being emphasized more than in the earlier reform. There will be more use of piecework and bonuses. Limits are apparently being retained on the total amount of bonus that can be earned by managerial and other salaried personnel, and for wage earners there are limits on the amount of bonuses that can be paid from the wage fund, but no limits on the amount of bonus wage earners can be paid from the incentive fund (Schroeder 1972, p. 35; Kostin 1973, p. 24). Much effort has been devoted to the attempt to make monetary incentives more effective in terms of improved performance and productivity.

In line with the principle of equal pay for equal work, the wage structure is to be made more consistent and uniform. Many more occupations are evaluated in terms of skill level on the basis of the nature of the work process and fewer on the basis of the specific industry in which the work is performed. Differentials for conditions of work and the regional differentials are being increased. The increase in the differential for night-shift work is connected with a goal of increasing the number of shifts worked.

Egalitarianism is still frowned on, but there is a new commitment to

5. Kostin 1973; Pak 1973; Batkaev 1973; Kunel'skii 1972. That the higher managerial salaries are not so far being raised is indicated in the scale of manager salaries in the machinery industry in Kostin 1973, p. 18, as compared with the earlier range reported in Maier 1963, p. 158.

equity. The sharp rise in the minimum wage in 1968 was announced on the eve of the celebrations of the fiftieth anniversary of the Revolution as fulfilling the Party's pledge to narrow the gap between the low and highly paid workers and to secure the wellbeing of all workers (Smirnov 1967). The level of the minimum wage, it has been explained, is determined in relation to the cost of a minimum adequate standard of living (Kunel'skii 1968, p. 20; Kunel'skii 1972, pp. 62–64). Raising the minimum wage was also seen as a step toward "eliminating poverty." What seems to be new here is the concept of establishing a floor of income below which no Soviet family should have to subsist. And indeed, the current plan, while stipulating increased differentiation of wages, promises to establish children's allowances for families with a per capita income below 50 rubles a month.

The wage system is still directed primarily toward the workers, but there seems to be some evidence that this reform more than earlier ones is directed also to management. The reform in the system of economic management and incentives of 1965 creates a rather different setting for wage reform than prevailed in 1956. Some of the features of the wage reform may be seen as reflecting efforts to make the wage system more consistent with the economic reforms and to make management more conscious of labor costs and of the increasing scarcity of labor.

It seems quite possible that the 1968 rise in the minimum wage and the further rise in progress may be intended to make labor more expensive and management more aware of the cost of labor. In the late 1960s, Liberman and Kantorovich were advocating making labor more expensive as a means of inducing management to weed out inefficient and/or superfluous employees (Chapman 1970, p. 128). More recently a Soviet economist has argued thus:

> The possibility of introducing new machines, as for technological progress generally, depends on the relationship of the cost of the machines to the outlay on wages of the workers replaced by the machines. . . . A relatively low level of wages deters the introduction of new techniques, especially in branches and sectors where low-paid manual labor prevails. Raising the wages of low-paid workers serves to widen the economic limits for the introduction of new machines.

He points out that over 40 percent of the workers in industry are engaged in manual labor (Sarkisian 1972, pp. 126–27). A major potential for raising labor productivity is the mechanization of many of these jobs performed by manual labor.

How operational this will turn out to be at the enterprise level remains a question in view of the continued emphasis on physical planning of inputs and laxity regarding costs and wage-fund allocations. It is also unclear what effect raising wages has on relative costs of labor and capital, since capital also has become more expensive with the introduction of a capital charge and the upward industrial price revisions of recent years. So far as the planning level is concerned, it might be noted that the suggestion has been made that the very high real cost of labor in the remoter regions (taking into account both premium wage levels and the necessary development of infrastructure) indicates that only the most capital-intensive processes are justified in such areas.

A clear effort to provide management with an incentive to pay more attention to labor costs may be seen in the Shchekino system, launched experimentally in the Shchekino Chemical Combine in October 1967. This system allows the enterprise to retain for a specified number of years any amount of the wage bill saved by reducing employment and permits such savings to be used to increase the wages of those remaining on the payroll. In principal, this compensates them for additional duties or responsibilities they take on. This system with various modifications has been widely adopted. As the deputy head of the State Committee on Labor and Wages says, the Shchekino experience has left the realm of the experimental and has become a norm of economic life (Pak 1973, p. 20).

In the economic reform, profitability and productivity have replaced gross output and cost reduction as success criteria. Strangely, the rules for profit retention for the enterprise's incentive fund and social-cultural fund are related to the size of the wage fund, which diminishes the incentive to economize on labor costs. But, in addition to the Shchekino movement, other measures have been taken which tend to enhance management's interest in productivity. (1) Increasingly, increases in the wage fund and in the incentive fund are tied to increases in labor productivity, and penalties have been instituted for permitting the average wage to rise faster than productivity (Schroeder 1972, p. 35; Schroeder 1973, pp. 30–32). (2) The level and growth of labor productivity have been added as two of the major indicators to be used in determining the category an enterprise falls into for purposes of establishing the level of managerial salaries. These indicators, which continue to include size of enterprise, level of output, variety and quality of output, etc., are intended to reflect the responsibility required of the management of an enterprise of the given category.[6] (3) Provisions have also been made for raising wage

6. Details of the revised indicators for some industries have been published in Gosudarstvannyi komitet Soveta ministrov po voprosam trud i zarabotnoi platy, *Biulleten'*, various issues, 1973.

rates above the centrally set industry level in enterprises where the level of productivity exceeds the industry norm.[7]

The current wage reform seems to make somewhat more provision for flexibility in adapting to local conditions and to allow the enterprise somewhat more discretion in wage matters than did the previous reform. There seems to be a fair amount of leeway at the enterprise level for developing variations on the Shchekino system and for establishing criteria for bonus payments. The salary range for a given occupation is being widened, which gives the manager more leeway in matching the salary to the individual's qualifications, and management has the right to pay especially highly qualified engineers and other technical personnel up to 30 percent above the centrally established scale for the occupation without ministerial approval (Kunel'skii 1972, p. 185; Pak 1973, p. 19). There will, at the same time, be more of a check on the proper classification by management of engineers and other professional staff according to occupation and salary, since there are to be periodic certifications of such employees by special certification commissions (*Vestnik statistiki* 1973, no. 12, pp. 69–70).

As Emily Clark Brown points out, "a major difficulty in efforts to achieve the most effective and rational use of the labor force is the surprising lack of adequate statistics" (Brown 1974, p. 171). The current reform could be drawn up on the basis of better information and knowledge, though there are still strong deficiencies. There have been extensive studies of labor, wages, work motivation, and the like by Soviet economists and sociologists since the late 1960s. In addition to attempts to improve the wage system itself, various measures have been or are being taken to support the wage system. These would include moves toward locating industries where labor is available or suitable jobs for particular groups or sexes are lacking and improvements of living conditions as well as monetary incentives in Siberia, the Far East, and the Far North. Probably the most significant of these measures is the introduction of a comprehensive employment service in 1966 for the first time since the employment service was abolished in the 1930s. It is still apparently not very well developed but it is surely a significant trend (see Brown 1974).

III. Changes in the Size Distribution of Soviet Earnings, 1946 to 1970

Information has recently become available on trends in the size distribution of Soviet wages and salaries since 1946. First it will be neces-

7. Details on such provisions for a number of industries are in Gosudarstvennyi komitet Soveta ministrov po voprosam trud i zarabotnoi platy, *Biulleten'*, 1973, no. 3, pp. 3–8; no. 6, pp. 3–8; no. 7, pp. 17–19.

sary to describe this information, as it involves some academic sleuthing. In the postwar years (as a result of heightened interest in wage and income distribution), periodic censuses of the size distribution of wages and salaries similar to those made in the 1920s and early 1930s have been resumed by the Central Statistical Administration. These require detailed reporting by all state enterprises and institutions on the number of wage earners and salaried workers employed, and the total wage fund. In addition, for those who worked the full month, their distribution by wage and salary grade and their distribution by total earnings is reported. Wage earners and salaried workers in all state enterprises and institutions include most of the civilian labor force, including employees of state farms; excluded are the military, members of collective farms, members of cooperatives, individual artisans, domestic servants, and (probably) employees of the Communist Party. The censuses are for the month of March and have been made in 1946, 1956, 1959, 1961, 1964, 1966, 1968, and 1970.[8]

The data from the recent censuses are not published as were the data of the censuses of the 1920s and 1930s. What has been published are a few useful summary measures, such as decile ratios, statements of the changes in the proportions of the labor force with earnings above or below a certain level, some details for a small portion of the census, and pictures of the distributions without numbers or any clues to scale such as those shown in figs. 10.1, 10.2, and 10.3. However, one source provides clues which enable us to reproduce what appear to be reasonably close approximations to the entire distribution (Rabkina and Rimashevskaia 1972). These clues are (1) a time series equation permitting the calculation of the means of the distributions for the period 1946 to 1968, (2) a regression equation for computing the value of the decile ratios over the same period (actually, two alternate equations; in one the decile ratio is a function of time, in the other a function of the mean; Rabkina and Rimashevskaia 1972, p. 250), and (3) the statement, with some evidence, that the distribution closely approximates the lognormal. The properties of the lognormal distribution are such that the entire shape of the distribution is known if the two parameters, the mean and the standard deviation, are known. The standard deviation can be computed from the decile ratio (Rabkina and Rimashevskaia 1972, pp. 244–45; Aitchison and Brown 1957). It is then possible to calculate the ruble values of the mode, the median, the deciles, or any other desired percentiles. The resulting derived distributions will be referred to as "computed theoretical distributions."

8. More than one source reports that these censuses were begun in 1956, though data for 1946 have been used. Possibly the 1946 census is not entirely comparable to the more recent ones.

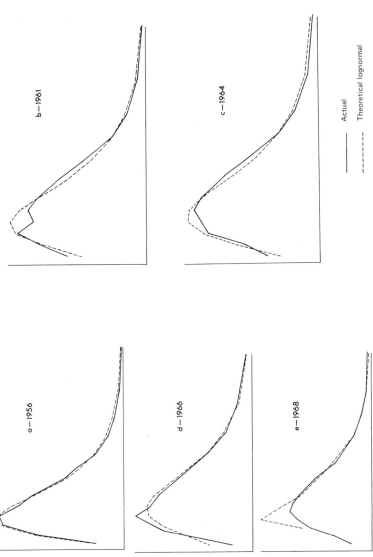

Figure 10.1. Distribution of Soviet wage earners and salaried workers by level of earnings, actual and theoretical, March 1956, 1961, 1964, 1966, 1968.

Source: Rabkina and Rimashevskaia, *Osnovy differentsiatsii zarabotonoi platy i dokhodov naseleniia,* 1972, pp. 138, 139, 194.

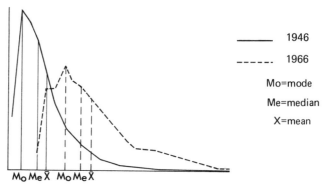

Figure 10.2. Distribution of Soviet wage earners and salaried workers by level of earnings, actual, March 1946 and 1966.

Source: *Sotsialisticheskii trud*, 1968, No. 10, p. 128.

Key results of this exercise are shown in Table 10.1. The upper portion of this table shows the ruble values of the computed mean, mode, and selected percentiles (counting from the low end up) of the distributions. The lower portion of Table 10.1 shows the decile and quartile ratios and the ratios between the median (P_{50}) and selected percentiles. Ratios of this latter type were introduced by Lydall (1968) as an illuminating and convenient way of comparing distributions of varying reliability among

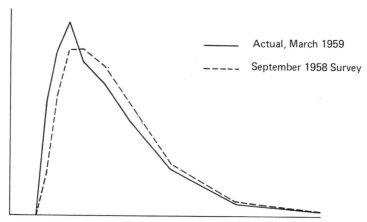

Figure 10.3. Distribution of Soviet wage earners and salaried workers by level of earnings in March, 1959, and according to the sample survey of September 1958.

Source: N. M. Rimashevskaia, *Ekonomicheskii analiz dokhodov rabochikh i sluzhashchikh,* 1965, p. 61.

Table 10.1. Computed theoretical distribution of Soviet wages and salaries, 1946 to 1970.

	1946	1956	1959	1961	1964	1966	1968	1970
	Rubles per month at indicated point in the distribution							
Mean	46.02	67.02	75.02	80.88	90.54	97.61	105.24	113.45
Mode	19.16	38.99	46.94	52.84	62.63	69.84	77.64	86.08
P_{10}	12.92	25.93	31.37	35.48	42.45	47.69	53.44	59.75
P_{25}	20.53	37.32	44.02	49.01	57.33	63.50	70.20	77.49
P_{50}	34.36	55.95	64.17	70.18	80.07	87.30	95.09	103.48
P_{75}	57.52	83.89	93.53	100.50	111.84	120.04	128.80	138.18
P_{90}	91.40	120.74	131.25	138.80	151.02	159.83	169.21	179.21
P_{95}	120.80	150.34	160.96	168.60	180.98	189.91	199.43	209.60
	Ratio between earnings at indicated percentiles of the distribution							
				Reported				
P_{90}/P_{10}	7.24	4.4	4.2	—	3.7	3.26	2.7	3.2
				Computed				
P_{90}/P_{10}[a]	7.09	4.66	4.19	3.92	3.56	3.36	3.17	3.00
P_{75}/P_{25}	2.80	2.25	2.12	2.05	1.95	1.89	1.83	1.78
P_{95}/P_{50}	3.52	2.69	2.51	2.40	2.26	2.18	2.10	2.02
P_{90}/P_{50}	2.66	2.16	2.04	1.98	1.89	1.83	1.78	1.73
P_{25}/P_{50}	.60	.67	.69	.70	.72	.73	.74	.75
P_{10}/P_{50}	.38	.46	.49	.50	.53	.55	.56	.58

Source and Methods: See the text.

a. Computed from the regression formula for the decile ratio. The other ratios are computed from the computed ruble values shown in upper part of the table.

many countries. These various ratios provide a relatively clear means of describing a distribution or any part of it. They usually involve some interpolation, but they avoid the more serious problem of estimating total earnings in the open-ended extremes of the distribution, necessary for measures such as the Gini coefficient. The years included in Table 10.1 are those of the March censuses from which data were included in the Rabkina-Rimashevskaia equations (the last being 1968) and also a projection to 1970. The table includes, in addition to the computed decile ratio, the reported decile ratio based on the actual data of the given year.

Two further measures based on the actual data have been published for certain years. One is the ratio of the average earnings of the highest paid 10 percent of the wage earners and salaried workers to the average earnings of the lowest paid 10 percent. This ratio is reported to have been 8:1 in 1956, 5.8:1 in 1959, and 5:1 in 1968. The ratio between average earnings of the highest paid 25 percent to the average earnings of the lowest paid 25 percent is reported to have been 4.5 in 1956 and 3.2 in 1968 (Kunel'skii 1972, p. 69; Mstislavskii 1961, p. 86).

So far as reliability is concerned, we have three sets of problems. The first is the extent to which the actual Soviet distributions are accurately characterized as lognormal. An impression of the extent to which the actual distributions correspond to the lognormal may be gained for five of the seven years from the graphs provided by Rabkina and Rimashevskaia (1972), shown in fig. 10.1. They also present measures of the "coefficient of similarity" between the actual and theoretical distributions. This measure indicates the proportion of the total area under the curves which is common to both curves. With the total area taken as 100, this coefficient is as follows: 1956, 96.1; 1961, 95.1; 1964, 96.0; 1966, 95.7; 1968, 91.6.[9] The major deviations from lognormality are in 1961 and 1968. How accurately and completely the graphs portray the actual distribution remains a question. How accurately they could be drawn depends on the fineness of the class intervals in which the basic data are available, particularly at the extremes. I understand that the bottom class interval is fairly large—containing at least 1 percent of the total and perhaps considerably more—but that the information for the upper class intervals is considerably finer, with the top interval containing well under 1 percent of the population.[10]

The second problem concerning reliability is the question of how closely the theoretical distributions computed as described come to actual distributions of the March censuses. It will be clear that since the key parameters are derived from time series regressions and the rest of the distribution from the characteristics of the lognormal distribution, we have very much smoothed results. These may not give a very true picture for any given year. We are told by Rabkina and Rimashevskaia that the mean computed from their regression equation deviates from the actual by only 0.1 to 1.0 ruble, except in one year when the deviation is 2.9 rubles, and that the decile ratios computed from either of their alternate regression equations differ from the actual by only one or two tenths of a unit (1972, pp. 250–51). Actual decile ratios based on the March censuses have been published for all census years except 1961. These indicate a sharp drop in 1968, while the computed decile ratios smooth this out with the effect of showing a somewhat smaller but more continuous decrease in the ratio over the whole period (Table 10.1). The first decile of under 54 rubles computed for 1968 is very low in relation to the minimum wage of 60 rubles a month established at the beginning of that year. Persons with earnings below the minimum wage rate could include regular full-time workers at the minimum wage rate who fail to

9. The coefficient is computed by comparing the two frequency distributions—the actual and the theoretical—and by taking for each class interval the smaller of the two frequencies and adding. Rabkina and Rimashevskaia 1972, pp. 193, 195.

10. Conversation with N. E. Rabkina, May 1974. In their examples, some of which are based on real (though partial) data, Rabkina and Rimashevskaia show 1.7 to 5.0 percent in the lowest earnings class, but 0.5 or 0.2 percent in their top class (1972, pp. 73, 166–69, 223).

meet performance norms, apprentices, and part-time (full month) workers. But it is most unlikely that these could have amounted to over 10 percent of employment. Many workers with basic wage rates at the minimum level earn more than the minimum. This raises additional doubts about the 1968 computed distribution. Some further scraps of information about the actual data are compared with the computed theoretical results in the Appendix. These suggest that we are generally in the right ball park, though perhaps rather far off for 1968.

The third set of questions concerning reliability relates to the nature and coverage of the March censuses and the relation of the March census data to the regularly published series on average wages. The March census data cover only persons who worked the full month of March. Full-month employment would usually be full-time employment, but persons employed part-time for the full month, including dual job holders, would be included. Dual job holders present something of a problem, since, apparently, a person working full-time in, e.g., enterprise A with earnings of 150 rubles and quarter-time in enterprise B with earnings of 50 rubles would show up in the statistics not as one individual with earnings of 200 rubles but as two individuals, one with earnings of 150 rubles and one with earnings of 50 rubles. It is not known how extensive part-time first and second job work is. This was offered by Dr. Rabkina as one explanation for the relatively large open-ended lowest wage class interval. From the point of view of the distribution of earnings by individuals this would cut off some of the highest earners at the upper end of the distribution and add to the number of earners at the bottom of the distribution.

The earnings reported are supposedly total pre-tax earnings from the establishment where the individual was employed for the full month. Earnings would include the basic wage or salary, piece rate earnings, any supplements to the basic wage for night shifts or dangerous work, regional supplements, overtime earnings, and bonuses. However, there is some question whether all bonuses are included. If treatment of bonuses in the March census reports was the same as in the regular monthly reports on which the average annual earnings data are based, not all bonuses are included and the treatment of bonuses may have varied over the period (see the Appendix below). It is not known whether the value of items like work clothing provided in kind by the enterprise is included. It is unlikely that the value of the use of official cars and similar "perks" of office are included.

The computed mean for March earnings (which we know to be close to the actual mean of March earnings) is lower than the average monthly earnings based on reports for the entire year and regularly published in the annual statistical handbooks (see Table 10.2 in the Appendix).

While one might expect earnings of persons employed the full month to be higher than earnings of all, there is apparently a difference in reporting between the March census data and the annual average data. The annual data do not count dual job holders twice, while evidently the March data do. Also, some types of payment may be included in the wage bill from which the annual data are computed that are not counted in the reports on earnings of individuals in March. March earnings might be below the annual average if new performance norms are introduced early in the year or even simply if earnings rise more or less continuously throughout the year. Bonus payments may be made monthly and quarterly, but year-end bonuses are probably largest and these would not be caught in March earnings. There is some evidence that bonuses tend to be proportionately larger at higher levels of wage and salary rates (Kunel'skii 1972, pp. 111, 198; Kirsch 1972, pp. 94–98). If this is so, it is possible that the data of the March censuses understate the degree of differentiation of annual earnings.

While some doubts must be kept in mind about the reliability of the data and the calculations, they are based on a complete census and are the best we have. Soviet economists appear to use the March census data with considerable confidence and have not subjected them to the kinds of criticisms they have made of the sample surveys of household budgets.

What do these data show? They show a remarkable degree of inequality in earnings distribution in 1946 and a very substantial decrease in inequality since then. We unfortunately do not know whether 1946 represents the peak of the trend toward inequality of the prewar and war years. The 1946 distribution may have been affected by war-related changes in the composition of the labor force, such as an increase in the proportion of women, of men below the draft age and draft rejects, and of older men. Since rationing was still in effect in 1946, the real impact of this degree of differentiation is not altogether clear. On the one hand, rationing tends to reduce the inequities of different incomes, since rubles beyond the cost of the ration are spent at higher prices and are in that sense worth less. On the other hand, the "perks" of office of the better paid in the form of access to official cars and the like, and of preferential access to consumer goods at a time when many goods were in short supply and no automobiles could be privately owned, would tend to sharpen the real differentiation.

Between 1946 and 1956 the decile ratio (reported) declined from 7.24 to 4.4. The sharpness of this decrease comes as something of a surprise. It has been argued that the bread allowance granted in September 1946 to lower-paid workers to compensate them for price increases made in preparation for the abolition of rationing must have led to a substantial reduction in wage differentiation (Galenson 1963; Chapman 1970, pp.

9–12; Yanowitch 1955 and 1960). Kirsch (1972, p. 183) thinks this has been exaggerated. The question may remain unsettled as the trends between September 1946 and 1956 are not very clear (Chapman 1970, pp. 9–12).

Since 1956, wage policy has been more explicit and more information is available about policy. The distribution of earnings is affected by numerous factors in addition to wage policy per se. The impact of the various stages of the wage reform seem in broad outline to be shown in the data in Table 10.1. The time sequence of the wage reform is reflected interestingly in the bimodality of the distribution of wages and salaries in 1961 (fig. 10.1b). The first wage reform had been completed in the material branches but the 40-ruble minimum wage and the rest of the reform were not introduced in the service branches until 1964–1965. By 1966, when the first wage reform had been completed in the entire economy, the decile ratio (reported) had declined from 4.4 in 1956 to 3.26. While earnings at all levels increased, the increase was significantly greater at the lower than at the upper levels. The increase in the first decile (computed theoretical) was 84 percent, while the increase in the ninth decile (computed theoretical) was 32 percent, and the difference between mode, median, and mean decreased (Table 10.1).

The impact of the 50 percent increase in the minimum wage of January 1968 is seen in the sharp reduction in the reported decile ratio from 3.26 in 1966 to 2.7 in 1968. The computed theoretical distribution for 1968 misses this sharp drop in differentiation. Note also that the curve of the actual distribution of earnings in 1968 shows a higher mode and considerably less concentration at the mode than the theoretical distribution (fig. 10.1e).

The reported (but not computed) decile ratio for 1970 reflects the temporary nature of the sharp reduction in differentiation of 1968 and the beginnings of adjustment of wage and salary rates at levels above the minimum. As indicated above, the information so far available on the new wage scales suggests that the spreads will be wider in many industries than those prevailing immediately after the increase in the minimum wage to 60 rubles in 1968, but generally narrower than those introduced during the first postwar wage reform. Clearly, the second phase of the second wage reform will increase differentiation of earnings over the 1968 level. Whether the resulting differentiation will be greater or smaller than that prevailing in 1966 will become clear only as the reform is completed.

One author, Kunel'skii, presents data on the relation between the minimum wage and the average wage indicating that the current five-year plan implies a slight increase in this ratio. The ratio of the average wage to the minimum is reported to have been 3.6:1 in 1955, 3:1 in 1960,

2.4:1 in 1965, and 2.1:1 in 1970 and is expected to be 2.1:1 in 1975. He nevertheless appears to expect the trend toward decreasing differentiation to continue. He forecasts that the ratio between the average earnings of the highest paid and lowest paid deciles will decrease from 5:1 in 1968 to 4:1 in 1975 and that the ratio between average earnings of the top and bottom quartiles will decrease from 3.2:1 in 1968 to 3:1 in 1975 (Kunel'skii 1972, p. 69).

We do not know how current differentiation of wages and salaries for all wage earners and salaried workers compares with that prevailing before World War II. Data for wage earners in industry only indicate that differentiation in 1959 was still somewhat greater than in 1934, but that by 1961 it was less than in 1934. The decile ratio of earnings of industrial wage earners was 3.17 in 1934, 3.38 in 1956, 3.28 in 1959, and less, perhaps substantially, then 2.8 in 1961.[11] The quartile ratio (P75/P25) for industrial wage earners was 1.82 in 1934, 1.85 in 1956, 1.84 in 1959 (Mozhina 1961, pp. 20, 21, 24) and was 1.67 in 1961 (Raitsin 1969, p. 35).

Comparisons with other countries make even more striking the extraordinarily high degree of differentiation in Soviet earnings in 1946 and the very impressive decrease in differentiation since then. Soviet differentiation of wages and salaries in 1946 was substantially greater than the differentiation prevailing in the United States recently and probably for several decades. U.S. data for 1972 for earnings of nonagricultural wage earners and salaried workers who worked full-time the full year indicate a decile ratio of 4.48, compared with the Soviet decile ratio (reported) in 1946 of 7.24. The Soviet distributions of 1956 and 1959, however, seem fairly comparable to this 1972 U.S. distribution. Other ratios of the 1972 U.S. distribution which can be compared to the computed Soviet ratios in Table 10.1 are these: P75/P25: 2.16; P95/P50: 2.64; P90/P50: 2.12; P10/ P50: 0.47.[12] Clearly by the 1960s, however, Soviet wage and salary

11. The ratio of average earnings of the top paid 10 percent to average earnings of the bottom paid 10 percent was 2.8 in 1961 (Bliakhman 1964, p. 154), and the decile ratio would be smaller, since it compares the lowest earnings of the highest-paid 10 percent to the highest earnings of the lowest-paid 10 percent.

12. The U.S. data are computed from the U.S. Department of Commerce, *Current Population Reports,* Series P-60, no. 90, Dec. 1973, Table 60. The coverage seems to be about as comparable to the March Soviet data as is possible, but there are some incomparabilities. The U.S. data refer to total earnings of those who were employed as wage and salary workers whose employment for the longest period in the year was as wage and salary workers, while the Soviet data exclude any earnings other than wages and salaries. The U.S. data exclude all persons in agriculture, while the Soviet data include those on state farms and exclude those on collective farms. It is not clear how the Soviet full-month employment (which can include part-time work) compares with the U.S. full-time, full-year employment. Among all American persons who worked full time for the full year 1972, the decile ratio of total earnings was 5.04 (same source, Table 54). The tendency in the U.S. has been for some widening of differentials in earnings and in wages and salaries since about 1950. See Peter Henle, "Exploring the Distribution of Earned Income," *Monthly Labor Review,* Dec. 1972.

distribution had become considerably more nearly equal than that prevailing in the United States today.

When one looks at industrial wage earners alone, it was apparently not until the early 1960s that the Soviet distribution became as nearly equal as that in the U.S. in 1958 and 1964 (Chapman 1970, pp. 120–22).

In comparison with other East European socialist countries, wage and salary differentiation was considerably wider in the USSR in the late 1950s and early 1960s. Since 1966, however, Soviet wage and salary differentiation seems, on the basis of decile ratios, to be about as small as in Poland and Yugoslavia, though still greater than in Hungary, Rumania, Czechoslovakia, and Bulgaria. Brzeski (1972) reports the decile ratio for Polish full-time wage and salary earnings in the socialized sector to have been 3.55 in 1955, 3.15 in 1960, 3.19 in 1965, and 3.23 in 1970. A comparable decile ratio of 3.2 can be computed for Yugoslavia in 1966 from the official statistics (*Statistički Godišnjak Jugoslavije* 1967, p. 271). Decile ratios of wage and salary earnings in the state sector in 1970 in other socialist countries were as follows: Bulgaria 2.4 (1967); Czechoslovakia 2.4 (and the same in 1959); Hungary 2.6 (and 2.5 in 1960); and Rumania 2.3 (Wiles 1974).

Pryor, in his cross-country analysis of earnings differentials in East and West, finds that wage differentiation tends to increase as the size of the country increases and to decrease as the level of development or per capita GNP rises. He found that the inequality in Soviet wage and salary distribution in 1959 appears to have been greater, while that prevailing now would appear to be smaller, than would be expected on the basis of the size of the USSR and its level of per capita income (Pryor 1973, pp. 80–86, and personal correspondence of 31 March 1974).

What is the explanation of the very significant reduction in inequality of earnings which has taken place? I have argued previously that the primary explanation for the decrease in wage differentials was the adaptation of the wage structure to the relatively more plentiful supply of skilled workers and relatively less plentiful supply of unskilled workers and to the decrease in differentiation in skill and productivity. This latter is the result of the increased level of education, technological advance, and the increased quantity and improved capital with which the less skilled work. The situation was one in which efficiency and equity considerations were on the whole complementary rather than in conflict (Chapman 1970, pp. 101–10). This situation may be continuing. Plausible efficiency-type explanations can be offered for the large relative increase in lower-level earnings. These would include efforts to maintain the high rate of participation in the labor force in the light of a higher level of real wages; the increased demand for workers in the consumer goods and services industries where pay and prestige have traditionally been low; difficulties in filling the unattractive heavy manual jobs which no one likes, particularly the young, who have developed higher expectations; the greater relative scarcity of labor; and the desire to have management economize on redundant labor. At the same time, the substantial increase in the minimum wage which has taken place and the increasing commitment to setting a floor under family income may well also reflect a strong social policy. Possibly equity considerations have led to a reduction in inequality of earnings greater than called for by efficiency considerations.

IV. The Shape of the Soviet Earnings Distribution

A number of studies have found that the distribution of wages and salaries in many countries tends to be approximately lognormal over a substantial portion of the distribution, but with a longer Pareto-type tail. And Lydall (1968) and Pryor (1973) have found this Pareto tail does not appear to be characteristic of socialist distributions. Rabkina and Rimashevskaia (1972) present empirical evidence that the distribution approximates lognormality in the USSR and offer a theoretical explanation for this. I shall describe and comment on this and then raise some questions concerning Lydall's explanation of why the Pareto tail is not found in socialist distributions.

Much of the empirical evidence concerning the lognormality of the Soviet earnings distribution has been discussed in the preceding section. It includes the graphs showing the closensss of fit of the theoretical lognormal to the actual March earnings distributions, shown in fig. 10.1. Rabkina and Rimashevskaia show a number of similar graphs based on distributions from separate segments of the economy and different periods and tell us that study of data from many censuses and surveys of the economy as a whole, of separate branches and regions, and sometimes of individual large enterprises indicate the same general moderately right-skewed, lognormal-type distribution.

Exceptions exist, they admit, but these generally seem to have explanations. The explanation given above for the bimodality of the 1961 distribution seems reasonable. Another bimodal distribution is shown for wages in the coal industry, and the explanation is the difference in rates between underground and surface mining.[13] But the point they make is that there is a basic tendency which reflects socialist wage principles for the distribution to tend toward lognormality. They illustrate this by reference to the similarity of the shape of the distribution of industrial

13. Rabkina and Rimashevskaia 1972, pp. 137–38. In 1962, basic wage rates were 61–230 rubles in underground coal mining and 49–156 rubles in surface mining (Chapman 1970, p. 142).

wages in 1930, 1961, and 1968, in spite of the many changes in wages and other policies over this long period and in spite of the 1965 economic reforms.[14] They also find the lognormal distribution the most useful model for forecasting changes in wage distributions and in the average wage, a major purpose of much of their work.

The theoretical explanation of why wages under socialism should be distributed lognormally offered by Rabkina and Rimashevskaia is similar to the mathematical probability model, but is related to the socialist principle of payment according to work and to the nature of work. Payment of labor should be according to the complexity (*slozhnost'*) of work in its broad sense or to its social utility. Complexity of labor is based on a number of factors, and the crucial idea is that these different factors tend to have cumulative rather than simply additive effects. Additional training after a certain length of experience will have a greater effect than the training without the experience, and the effect is progressive. Similarly, with conditions of work taken as an element of complexity, they say that if work in arduous or dangerous conditions requires a greater expenditure of labor, then for the skilled worker the volume of additional labor will be greater than for the unskilled — not because greater strength is required, but because the strength of the more skilled has a different value. When the different elements of complexity of work are combined, the effect is not a simple sum, but a product. And additional elements of complexity acquired by a worker over time are likely to be proportional to the level of complexity already achieved. Given that this is the case, wage payments should follow the same law, both statically and dynamically. That is, differences in wages for different work should be proportional to the differences in complexity of work, and wage increments of an individual reaching a higher level of complexity in his work should be proportional to his previous wage (pp. 80–84).

The principles on which Soviet wages are based are essentially of this nature. That is, differences between wage rates in a given scale increase in percentage steps between grades and differentials for working conditions, and bonuses are calculated as a proportion of the basic rate (pp. 83–84).

This explains why the socialist earnings distribution should be skewed to the right, but does not explain why the distribution should be specifically lognormal. To explain this they postulate that the distribution of the labor force among jobs, if one imagines a continuous grading of

14. Rabkina and Rimashevskaia 1972, pp. 78–79. Additional evidence that wages tend to change exponentially and to be distributed lognormally is offered in diagrams showing that an exponential function provides a better fit than a linear function for the changes in the mean and median over time (pp. 85–86). These diagrams are not very clear, but suggest that there may have been a break in trend which would "explain" the curvature, but which might be represented as well by two linear functions.

jobs from the simplest to the most complex, follows the normal, Gaussian distribution. As an example, they point to the fact that in the very large machinery industry, where most wage earners are on a six-grade wage scale, the average grade has fluctuated for many years around grade 3 to 3.5 and the number of wage earners in higher and lower grades decreases comparatively evenly on both sides. The concrete job structure in an enterprise, sector, or the whole economy will be determined by the structure of production, but there are many factors which determine where an individual will end up in this structure and, they suggest, these factors are independent of one another. Numerous independent variables are conditions for a normal distribution. The factors they mention as relevant and independent are individual abilities, preferences for one kind of work over another, factors relating to time and place of birth, conditions of upbringing and development, state of health, family situation, and so on and so forth. They indicate that they made a special experiment in constructing a continuous grading of jobs according to skill and are satisfied that if all existing wage and salary scales were combined, the distribution of workers by grade on this unified scale would be symmetrical and approximately normal (pp. 104–7). Note that what is supposed to be normally distributed here is not individual abilities but the distribution of individuals among jobs requiring different levels of skill.[15] The idea seems to be that the distribution of individuals among jobs of varying levels of skill or complexity is normal, but that the degree of social utility contributed by the individual rises progressively from the simpler to the more complex jobs in the scale and is, and should be, paid accordingly, so that the distribution of earnings is lognormal (pp. 114–15).

These authors do not present the evidence on which they conclude that the Soviet distribution on the unified skill scale is normal. Their assumption that the factors which determine where an individual will end up on the skill pyramid are random and independent is surely questionable. The close correlation between family occupation and education, the individual's level of education, and the importance of this combination of interdependent factors as a determinant of the individual's place in the job pyramid has been widely remarked. The correlation between family background and level of education and subsequent occupation may be less strong in the USSR because of free education and student stipends, but it remains, even so, a problem clearly recognized there. Rabkina and Rimashevskaia admit that if the assumption about the normal distri-

15. Their concept appears to combine elements of demand for productive services with elements of supply of personal attributes. See Reder 1969, pp. 227–29, for a discussion of the importance of the distinction between characteristics relative to demand for labor and supply characteristics of individuals.

bution over the skill scale doesn't hold, the lognormal model "doesn't work" (*ne rabotaet*) (p. 115).

The theoretical explanation may not be altogether convincing, but the empirical evidence for at least approximate lognormality of the earnings distribution in the USSR is rather convincing. Rabkina and Rimashevskaia suggest that this is typical also of other socialist countries. Brzeski finds the Polish earnings distribution over the period 1955–1970 is "strikingly close" to the lognormal.[16] However, Jan Michal, with reference particularly to Czechoslovakia but also to Hungary, finds that "socialist distributions deviate substantially from lognormality" (Michal 1972, p. 5; Michal 1971, p. 10, and figs. 3 and 4). Pryor (1973) finds the distribution of earnings less differentiated in the socialist than in the market economies and attributes this to the system, and Lydall (1968) stresses the absence of a Pareto upper tail in the socialist distribution of eastern Europe.

Lydall (1968) offers a theoretical explanation for the Pareto upper tail, a theory which he claims also provides an explanation for the absence of such a tail in the socialist countries of East Europe. He explains the Pareto tail in terms of the principle of hierarchy within large organizations. Salaries are based on position within this hierarchy. His model, briefly, says that the salary at any given level in the hierarchy will be a function of the number of employees and their salaries directly supervised in the next lower level and indirectly supervised in subsequently lower levels. The manager's salary will be a function of the total number of employees in the hierarchy and of their pay. In Lydall's terminology, such relative salaries are based on "responsibility," a conceptually distinct criterion from "ability." An aspect of responsibility that must be compensated is the "worry" the responsibility entails (Lydall 1968, pp. 125–29).

He offers two explanations of why the Pareto tail does not seem to be characteristic of socialist countries. The first is that it is official policy in these countries to pay salaries according to ability rather than according to responsibility, following Marx's formula that under socialism labor should be paid according to its quantity and quality. The second is that "communist managers have been given much less responsibility than managers in capitalist countries, since the task of a manager has been to carry out the plan laid down for him. In such a situation there is less reason for paying a manager a higher salary because he controls more men or materials, since there is less scope for him to exercise his initiative." He suggests that the economic reforms, if pursued vigorously,

16. Brzeski 1972, p. 28, citing J. Kordas and Z. Stroinska, *Statystyczne metody analizy rozkladu plac i dochodow ludnosci* (Statistical methods of analyzing the distribution of wages and incomes of the population) (Warsaw: GUS, 1971), p. 49.

would increase managerial responsibility and that this might lead to a Pareto distribution (p. 130).

There is considerable merit to Lydall's second explanation, but the first just doesn't hold. Responsibility is definitely taken into account in measuring the quantity and quality or, in more recent terminology, the complexity of work and in setting salary scales. Lydall's hierarchic principle in fact comes quite close to describing the way in which the Soviet managerial salary structure is constructed. The Soviet managerial salary structure is built up from the lowest level, that of the foreman. The foreman's salary is set in relation to the wage rates of the most highly skilled workers he supervises. The senior foreman's salary is set in relation to that of the foreman, and it is stipulated how many foremen he must supervise to be classified as a senior foreman. And so on, up the scale to the manager. Within the enterprise salaries of heads of sections and departments are higher for the more important sections and departments (e.g., technical) than for the less important sections and departments (Kunel'skii 1972, p. 195).

In addition to the consideration of levels of responsibility within the enterprise, managerial salaries are differentiated between industries and between enterprises within the same industry. Enterprises in each industry are graded into several categories (typically four to seven) for purposes of setting the level of pay of managerial personnel. Detailed criteria with a system of weights for summing them up are established for the purpose of determining the salary-level category of each enterprise. Similar, though generally fewer, categories are established for departments and shops of an enterprise. These indicators are intended to reflect the size of the enterprise, the value of output, the extent of the assortment, the complexity of the products and of the production process, the level of technology, and now also the level and growth of labor productivity. All of these are relevant to determining the level of responsibility, in the sense Lydall means it, of managerial personnel. And the higher up the managerial ladder, the greater is the salary differentiation among enterprises. Upper-level executive salaries are thus finely differentiated on the basis of responsibility. It is reported that about half of all centrally established salary rates are rates for executive personnel although these personnel amount to only 5 to 15 percent of all engineering, professional, and managerial personnel (Kunel'skii 1972, p. 205).

At the end of the 1956–1960 wage reform in industry, among enterprises of category I (where the highest salaries prevail) the interindustry range of director's salaries was 1 : 3.5. The intraindustry range varies among industries. In the machinery industry the basic salary of the director of a category I enterprise was 2.6 times that of the director of a category VII enterprise. In a category I enterprise in this industry, the director's basic salary was 4.7 times the technician's salary, while in a category VII enterprise the director's salary was 2.4 times the technician's salary (Maier 1963, pp. 157–59). The overall spread in manager salaries at this time was from a basic salary of 80 rubles a month in the lowest-category milk and cheese factory to about 410 rubles in the highest-category coal mine, a ratio of 1 : 5.1. Counting maximum bonuses of 40 percent in the food industry and 60 percent in heavy industry, maximum earnings would range from 112 rubles to 656 rubles, a ratio of 1 : 5.9 (Dolgopolova and Shakhmagon 1963, pp. 153, 207; Maier 1963, p. 157).[17]

This suggests that Lydall's model is at least as appropriate to a bureaucracy such as a socialist economy or the civil service as to modern large Western corporations. Indeed, the Soviet spread of managerial salaries is much narrower than those prevailing in Western private industry, especially in the United States, and the Soviet distribution does not seem to have a Pareto tail. This would presumably also be true of the U.S. civil service to which the hierarchic principle seems applicable. A rough, preliminary comparison suggests that the U.S. civil service salary ranges are fairly comparable to the Soviet salary ranges for engineering, professional, and managerial personnel in industry.[18] If managerial salaries are determined on the hierarchic principle, then the question is this: Which has to be explained—the narrow range of Soviet and U.S. civil service pay scales, or the wide range of Western private enterprise pay scales?

We have no trouble explaining the limited range of U.S. civil service salaries. In a democracy there are limits on the level of salaries the taxpayers are willing to tolerate. Besides the general aversion to taxes,

17. As indicated, the current reform will mean a narrowing of managerial pay ranges because of restrictions on raising salaries of the "highly paid." Possibly it will be found necessary to remove these restrictions and raise managers' salaries in the more important industries and enterprises. Kunel'skii (1972, p. 184) suggests that a more flexible regulation of pay of managerial personnel should be established for those enterprises and combines with production indicators which substantially exceed those established for category I. Presumably he means their pay should be raised.

18. Differences between government administration and the management of an individual enterprise make it somewhat difficult to match civil service ranks with Soviet industrial jobs of approximately equivalent levels of responsibility. For the exercise, let us assume that the U.S. civil service executive levels III to V (leaving two higher levels to correspond to ministerial positions above the Soviet manager), with salaries of $36,000 to $40,000 a year, are equivalent to the Soviet industrial manager. These American civil service executive salaries are 5.2 to 5.5 times the civil service starting rate for engineers (GS5). The executive salaries were established in 1969; the GS schedule used was effective as of January 1972 (U.S. Civil Service Commission 1971, pp. 19–44). The top Soviet enterprise manager's salary exceeded the lowest Soviet engineer's salary by about 5.1 times in the early 1960s. The proposal before Congress to raise executive salaries will increase the U.S. civil service spread.

there is undoubtedly a widely pervasive feeling among the bulk of the population that there are limits to the amount to which some individuals should be valued above others.

In Soviet socialism the population does not have this power of the vote. But a basic tenet of Marxism and justification for the power of the leadership is the goal of equality. Equality during the socialist phase, it is true, is equal pay for equal work. But there must be strong egalitarian sentiments and limits to the extent of the difference in valuation of their work which the population finds acceptable and, hence, which the leadership finds politically feasible. Lydall's argument that Soviet managers have less responsibility may play a role as well. And in a system where enterprises are not allowed to fail, one might add that Soviet managers face less risk than Western managers.

Then, too, when a single hierarchy exists, as in the USSR but not in the United States, those at the top can set their salaries above all others and need not be concerned that someone at the top of another hierarchy may outdo them.

Appendix: Relation of the Theoretical to the Actual Distributions

Relationship of the theoretical distributions to the actual March distributions

According to Rabkina and Rimashevskaia (1972, p. 250), the computed mean deviates from the actual within limits of 0.1 to 1.0 ruble, except for one year when the deviation is 2.9 rubles (see Figure 10.1). The computed mean ranges from 46 rubles in 1946 to 105 rubles in 1968. The authors present diagrams indicating a fairly close relationship between the actual and computed decile ratios and report that the difference between the computed and actual decile ratios is of the order of one-tenth to two-tenths of a unit (p. 251). The comparison of the computed with the reported actual decile ratios in Table 10.1 confirms this, except for 1968. (The reported decile ratios for 1946 and 1966 are from Loznevaia 1968, p. 129; for 1959 from Rimashevskaia 1965, p. 43; for 1956, 1964, 1966, 1968, 1970 from Sarkisian 1972, pp. 125–26, 133.) The distributions are shown in Figures 10.2 and 10.3.

A number of relationships between the 1946 and 1966 actual distributions, as well as some relationships for each of these distributions, are presented in Loznevaia (1968), the source of fig. 10.2. These are compared with our computed results in Table 10.2.

It is from the above reported relationships, laborious measurements of the curves in fig. 10.2, and some data on percentage changes in the proportions in various class intervals that Peter Wiles and Stefan Markowski (*Soviet Studies*, April 1971, p. 503) worked out the distributions for these two years. Our computed results correspond fairly well with their's.

Table 10.2.

Reported	Computed
Mode 46 = .38 Mean 46	Mode 46 = .416 Mean 46
Median 46 = .762 Mean 46	Median 46 = .747 Mean 46
Mode 66 = .674 Mean 66	Mode 66 = .716 Mean 66
Median 66 = .897 Mean 66	Median 66 = .894 Mean 66
Mean 66 = 2.2 Mean 46	Mean 66 = 2.12 Mean 46
Median 66 = 2.5 Median 46	Median 66 = 2.54 Median 46
Mode 66 = 3.9 Mode 46	Mode 66 = 3.64 Mode 46
1st decile 66 = almost 4 1st decile 46	1st decile 66 = 3.7 1st decile 46
9th decile 66 = 1.89 9th decile 46	9th decile 66 = 1.75 9th decile 46

Various other relationships based on the actual data are compared with our computations in Table 10.3. (The 1956/1964 comparisons are from Rabkina and Rimashevskaia 1966, p. 125; the others are from Sarkisian 1972, p. 133.)

For certain years there is evidence concerning the number of persons with earnings below a certain level against which we can check some of our computations for the lower end of the distribution. It is reported that in 1956 the number of wage earners and salaried workers with earnings below 30 rubles a month was 5.1 million, or slightly over 10 percent of all, and in 1961 was 2.1 million or about 3.2 percent of all (Bromlei 1966, p. 7; *Narkhoz-60*, p. 633; *Trud-68*, p. 22). One would then expect the first decile in 1956 to be close to or below 30 rubles; the calculated first decile is 25.93 and the second decile is 33.77 rubles. The computations for 1961 indicate 5 percent had earnings below 29.21 rubles and 6 percent had earnings below 30.65 rubles, somewhat above what Bromlei's actual figures would suggest. For 1968 the computed first decile of 53.44 rubles seems low, considering that the minimum wage was 60 rubles for all wage earners and salaried workers from 1 January 1968. Full-month earnings for a worker at the minimum wage rate who works full-time may fall below the minimum if performance norms are not met. Earnings of full-month part-time workers, and of a dual job holder in his second, part-time job might well be below the minimum wage, and so might earnings of apprentices. Even allowing for these, it seems unlikely that over 10 percent earned less than the minimum wage. Rabkina and Rimashevskaia in a 1966 article assume that 1 percent of the workers would have earnings below the minimum in forecasting changes in wage distribution (1966, pp. 126, 129) but in a hypothetical example in their 1972 book (pp. 230–32) they assume that 5 percent would have earnings below the minimum wage. Presumably this upper revision is based on their familiarity with the actual data. It is reported that in 1970, when the minimum wage was still 60 rubles, of those

Table 10.3.

Reported	Computed
Median 64 = almost 1.35 Median 56	Median 64 = 1.358 Median 56
1st decile 64 = 1.45 1st decile 56	1st decile 64 = 1.637 1st decile 56
9th decile 64 = 1.215 9th decile 56	9th decile 64 = 1.251 9th decile 56
Mean 61 = 2.48 1st decile 61	Mean 61 = 2.28 1st decile 61
Mean 64 = 2.35 1st decile 64	Mean 64 = 2.13 1st decile 64
Mean 70 = 1.79 1st decile 70	Mean 70 = 1.90 1st decile 70

workers at wage and salary rates between 60 and 70 rubles, actual earnings of half were within this range, while earnings of the other half were above 70 rubles (Kunel'skii 1972, p. 68). The numbers earning below the minimum wage are likely to be greater when the minimum is first established than in subsequent years (Rabkina and Rimashevskaia 1972, p. 232).

The evidence presented here seems to suggest that the computed theoretical distributions provide an approximation to reality, but that the computed figure for any given decile or year cannot be relied on heavily. Caution is particularly in order for years like 1968 in which a sudden change in wage policy is made, or for years during which major wage reforms are being carried out piecemeal by branch or region.

Relation of the computed March average earnings to average annual monthly earnings

The computed means for full-month March earnings are compared with average annual monthly earnings of all wage earners and salaried workers regularly reported in the annual statistical handbooks in Table 10.4. Two annual series are shown which differ primarily in the treatment of bonuses, as will be explained. The March average is below but fairly close to the averages in both annual series in every year. An exploration of the possible reasons for this divergence may provide a further basis for evaluating the reliability of the March distribution

Table 10.4. Average earnings, wage earners and salaried workers, national economy, USSR.

Year	Average annual earnings (rubles per month)		March earnings, full-month (rubles per month)
	Old series	New series	Computed
1945	43.4	—	—
1946	47.5	48.1	46.0
1955	71.5	71.8	—
1956	73.4	—	67.0
1957	76.2	—	—
1958	77.8	—	—
1959	79.0	—	75.0
1960	80.1	80.6	—
1961	83.4	83.9	80.9
1962	86.2	86.7	—
1963	87.6	88.2	—
1964	90.1	90.8	90.5
1965	95.6	96.5	—
1966	99.2	100.2	97.6
1967	103.0	104.7	—
1968	—	112.7	105.2
1969	—	116.9	—
1970	—	122.0	113.4

Sources: Annual, old series: *Trud-68*, pp. 137–38; Annual, new series: *Narkhoz-68*, p. 555; *Narkhoz-22-72*, p. 350; March earnings: Table 10.1.

data. The difference might be attributable to differences in coverage and definition of the two sets of statistics, or to seasonal and other factors affecting earnings over the year.

The annual series are based on monthly reports by all state enterprises and institutions on the average wage paid their wage earners and salaried workers. This is calculated by dividing the *wage fund* by the average number of *registered employees*. It is not clear that the dividend and the divisor represent exactly the same universe. The registered employees are those who registered at (and whose labor books are held by) the employing enterprise. Those registered who are absent on business trips, on vacation, or on sick and maternity leave are counted. Nonregistered employees of a given enterprise (excluded from the calculation) are mainly (a) persons with more than one job who hold their primary job and are registered at another enterprise, and (b) persons employed five days or less per month on work not directly related to the enterprise's basic production responsibility and students engaged in practice work. Evidently, however, earnings of the nonregistered employees are included in the wage fund, though payments to students in practice work have been excluded since 1966 (*Trud v SSSR* 1968, p. 329; Schroeder 1972, pp. 291–93).

The wage fund, the dividend of the calculation, as defined in the old series, includes all regular wages and salaries paid in accordance with established rates and scales (including piecework earnings, differentials for work conditions, regional supplements, overtime), all regular bonuses paid in connection with the operation of the established wage and salary system, all supplemental wage payments (such as severance pay) provided by law, vacation pay, and the retail value of free housing and other in-kind payments required by law to be provided in some cases. For enterprises operating under the rules of the economic reforms of 1965, bonuses connected with plan fulfillment paid to salaried workers are no longer considered part of the wage fund, but are (along with some bonuses for wage earners) accounted for under a separate "incentive fund"; these bonuses are added in separately in calculating the average wage for the period 1965 through 1967 in the old series. The following kinds of payment are not included in calculating the average wage of the old series: one-time bonuses paid from special funds (e.g., bonuses for victory in socialist competitions), bonuses for creating and introducing new technology, rewards for discoveries, inventions, and suggestions, bonuses for saving on fuel, for collecting scrap, and for using waste materials, and bonuses from the enterprise "director's fund" that existed prior to the 1965 reforms (Schroeder 1972, pp. 291–95). Also excluded are payments from the social security system to those registered employees who are absent on sick or maternity leave (*Trud-68*, p. 329). The new series, introduced in 1968, includes "payments from the incentive fund (except for one-time assistance grants) and one-time and other bonuses not included in the wage fund" (*Narkhoz-68*, p. 555; *Narkhoz-72*, p. 789), presumably including bonuses from the pre-1965 director's fund as well as from the post-1965 incentive fund. It is still not clear whether all bonuses are included.

The March census differs from the annual series on the employment side in that it includes only persons who worked the full month. I understand also that in the March census a dual job holder is counted twice, with his earnings from each job reported separately (conversation with Dr. Rabkina, May 1974). This differs from the rule for the annual series, which records a dual job holder only once at the enterprise where he is registered, but which includes his earnings at the second enterprise in the average wage for that enterprise and for all enterprises combined. This would clearly tend to make the March average lower than the annual monthly average.

The March series purportedly covers total earnings, but no details on the coverage appear to have been published. Since the March census is concerned with the size distribution of earnings, one would assume that the enterprise is supposed to report for each employee working the full month only amounts specifically earned by that employee. That is, the reports should be based on records for individual employees rather than on total wage payments and total employment. The purpose of the March census suggests that all kinds of bonuses should be included. But we cannot be certain that this is the case. If the definition of bonuses to be included is the same as in the annual series, presumably it is the definition of the old series which applied (at least until 1968) and this excludes more kinds of bonuses than the new series.

If there were no difference in coverage between the annual series and the March series, except for the exclusion from the latter of persons who worked less than the full month, what relationship might be expected between the March and annual average monthly earnings? Presumably full-month earnings would be above the earnings of all employed, at least in the same month. March earnings would be lower than average annual monthly earnings if earnings rise more or less continuously throughout the year. It is likely that the introduction of revised performance norms at the beginning of the year means earnings grow more slowly during the early months than later in the year. Various other seasonal factors may be at work. The timing of bonus payments, in particular, may be significant in explaining the difference between March and average annual monthly earnings. Bonuses may be paid monthly and quarterly, but there is reason to believe the year-end bonuses are the largest. Kostin (1973, pp. 36–37, 39) refers to the "thirteenth wage," and bonuses for winning socialist competitions are for the year's performance.

This discussion suggests that there are probably reasonable explanations for the differences, which are really rather small, between the average full-month March earnings and the average annual monthly earnings.

The two features of the March data that raise some concern about how accurately they portray wage and salary distribution are (a) the double counting of dual job holders, which means one individual with relatively high earnings is recorded as two individuals with lower earnings, and (b) the possibility that some kinds of bonuses are excluded, particularly since there is reason to believe that bonuses tend to be proportionally higher for those at the upper end of the wage and salary scales. If it is only the year-end bonuses which are excluded (because of the month of the census) this latter problem remains, but it is much less serious than if other types of bonuses are excluded. Both of these features suggest that the March data may somewhat understate the degree of differentiation in earnings.

References

Aganbegian, A. G., and V. F. Maier. 1959. *Zarabotnaia plata v SSSR* (*Wages in the USSR*). Moscow, Gosplanizdat.

Aitchison, J., and J. A. C. Brown. 1957. *The lognormal distribution.* New York: Cambridge Univ. Press.

Batkaev, R. 1973. "Razvitie tarifnoi sistemy (Development of the wage rate system)." *Sotsialisticheskii trud* (*Socialist Labor*), 1973, no. 10, pp. 28–37.

Bliakhman, L. 1964. *Proizvoditel'nost' i oplata truda v period razvernutogo stroitel'stva kommunizma* (*Productivity and labor payment in the period of the building of communism*). Leningrad: Lenizdat.

Bromlei, N. Ia. 1966. "Uroven' zhizni v SSSR 1950–1965 gg (The level of living in the USSR, 1950–1965)." *Voprosy istorii* (*Problems of History*), no. 7, pp. 3–17.

Brown, Emily Clark. 1974. "Continuity and change in the Soviet labor market." In *The Soviet Economy*, 4th ed., ed. M. Bornstein and D. Fusfeld. Homewood, Ill.: Richard D. Irwin.

Brzeski, Andrzej. 1972. "Income distribution under socialism: Poland, 1950–1970." Paper presented at the joint session of the American Economic Association and the Association for Comparative Economic Studies, Toronto, 30 Dec.

Chapman, Janet G. 1963. *Real wages in Soviet Russia since 1928*. Cambridge: Harvard Univ. Press.

_____. 1970. *Wage variation in Soviet industry: the impact of the 1956–1960 Wage Reform*. Santa Monica: RAND Corporation.

_____. 1971. "Labor mobility and labor allocation in the USSR." Association for Comparative Economics, July.

_____ and H. S. Chou. Forthcoming. *The economies of the Soviet Union and the People's Republic of China: a comparative study*.

Dolgopolova, A., and A. Shakhmagon. 1963. *Oplata truda na predpriiatiiakh pishchevoi i rybnoi promyshlennosti* (*Payment of labor in enterprises of the food and fish industries*). Moscow; VTsSPS Profizdat.

Feshbach, Murray. 1966. "Manpower in the USSR." In *New directions in the Soviet economy*, Joint Economic Committee. Washington: GPO. Part III.

Galenson, Walter. 1963. "Wage Structure and Administration in Soviet Industry." In *Internal wage structure*, ed. J. L. Meij. Amsterdam: North-Holland Publishing Company.

_____ and Alan Fox. 1967. "Earnings and employment in eastern Europe." *Quarterly Journal of Economics* (May): 220–47.

Hamermesh, D. S., and R. D. Portes. 1972. "The labour market under central planning: the case of Hungary." *Oxford Economic Papers* 24, no. 2 (July): 241–58.

Henle, Peter. 1972. "Exploring the distribution of earned income." *Monthly Labor Review*, Dec. 1972.

Kirsch, Leonard J. 1972. *Soviet wages: changes in structure and administration since 1956*. Cambridge: M.I.T. Press.

Kostin, Leonid. 1960. *Wages in the USSR*. Moscow: Foreign Languages Publishing House.

_____. 1973. *Organizatsiia oplaty truda* (*The organization of labor payment*). Moscow: Profizdat.

Kunel'skii, L. 1968. "Sotsial'no-ekonomicheskoe znachenie povysheniia minimal'nykh razmerov zarabotnoi platy (The socio-economic significance of raising the minimum wage)." *Sotsialisticheskii trud*, no. 12, pp. 14–22.

_____. 1972. *Sotsial'no-ekonomicheskie problemy zarabotnoi platy* (*Socio-economic problems of wages*). Moscow: Ekonomika.

Loznevaia, M. 1968. "Matematicheskie metody v planirovanii zarabotnoi platy (Mathematical methods in planning wages)." *Sotsialisticheskii trud*, no. 10, pp. 126–35.

Lydall, Harold. 1968. *The structure of earnings*. Oxford: Oxford Univ. Press.

Maier, V. F., 1963. *Zarabotnaia plata v period perekhoda k kommunizmu (Wages in the period of the transition to communism)*. Moscow: Izd. ekonomicheskoi literatury.

Michal, Jan M. 1971. "Size distribution of incomes under socialism in Czechoslovakia." Research Memorandum no. 57, Institute for Advanced Studies, Vienna, June. Mimeographed.

———. 1972. "Size distribution of earnings and income in Czechoslovakia, Hungary, and Yugoslavia." Paper presented at the joint session of the American Economic Association and the Association for Comparative Economic Studies, Toronto, 30 Dec.

Mozhina, M. 1961. "Izmeneniia v raspredelenii promyshlennykh rabochikh SSSR po razmeram zarabotnoi platy (Changes in the distribution of Soviet industrial workers by size of earnings)." *Biulleten' nauchnoi informatsii: Trud i zarabotnaia plata (Bulletin of Scientific Information: Labor and Wages*, no. 10, pp. 18–25.

Mstislavskii, P. S. 1961. *Narodnoe potreblenie pri sotsializme (Consumption of the people under socialism)*. Moscow: Gosudarstvennoe izdatel'stvo planovo-ekonomicheskoi literatury.

Narkhoz-60: Narkhoz-68. Tsentral'noe statisticheskoe upravlenie (Central Statistical Administration), *Narodnoe khoziaistvo SSSR v 1960 g.* (The national economy of the USSR in 1960). Moscow: Statistika, 1961; *Narodnoe khoziaistvo SSSR v 1968 g.* Moscow: Statistika, 1969.

Narkhoz-22–72. Tsentral'noe statisticheskoe upravlenie, *Narodnoe khoziastvo SSSR 1922–1972*. Moscow: Statistika, 1972.

O.E.C.D. 1965. *Wages and labor mobility*. Paris.

Pak, Iu. 1973. "Novye usloviia oplaty truda i povyshenie ego proizvoditel'nosti (New conditions of payment for labor and increasing its productivity)." *Sotsialisticheskii trud*, no. 9, pp. 14–24.

Pryor, Frederic L. 1973. *Property and industrialization in communist and capitalist nations*. Bloomington: Indiana Univ. Press.

Rabkina, N. E., and N. M. Rimashevskaia. 1966. "Metod perspektivnykh raschetov differentsii zarabotnoi platy (Methods of forecasting the differentials in wages)." *Sotsialisticheskii trud*, no. 7, pp. 124–33.

——— and ———. 1972. *Osnovy differentsiiatsii zarabotnoi platy i dokhodov naseleniia (Principles of the differentiation of wages and income of the population)*. Moscow: Ekonomika.

Raitsin, V. I. 1968. *Planning the standard of living according to consumption norms*. White Plains, N.Y.: International Arts and Sciences Press.

Reder, Melvin W. 1969. "A partial survey of the theory of income size distribution." In *Six papers on the size distribution of wealth and income*, ed. Lee Soltow. National Bureau of Economic Research. Dist., Columbia University Press. New York.

Rimashevskaia, N. M. 1965. *Ekonomicheskii analiz dokhodov rabochikh i sluzhashchikh (The economic analysis of the incomes of wage earners and salaried employees)*. Moscow: Ekonomika.

Sarkisian, G. S. 1972. *Uroven', tempy, i proportsii rosta real'nykh dokhodov pri sotsializme (The level, rate, and proportions of the growth in real income under socialism)*. Moscow: Ekonomika.

Schroeder, Gertrude E. 1972. "An appraisal of Soviet wage and income statistics." In *Soviet Economic Statistics*. ed. V. G. Treml and J. P. Hardt. Durham, N.C.: Duke Univ. Press.

_____. 1973. "Recent developments in Soviet planning and incentives." In *Soviet economic prospects for the seventies,* Joint Economic Committee. Washington: U.S. GPO.

Shutov, I. N., 1972. *Lichnoe potreblenie pri sotsializme (Personal consumption under socialism).* Moscow: Mysl'.

Smirnov, A. 1967. "The Party's chief concern." *Komsomol'skaia pravda,* 30 Sept. Translated in *Current Digest of the Soviet Press* 19, no. 39:6–7.

State Five-Year Plan for the Development of the USSR National Economy for the Period 1971–1975. 1972. Translated from the Russian. Joint Publications Research Service, Arlington, Va., Report 596 70.

Statistički Godišnjak Jugoslavije, 1967. Belgrade.

Trud-68. Tsentral'noe statisticheskoe upravlenie. *Trud v SSSR (Labor in the USSR).* Moscow: Statistika, 1968.

TsUNKhU (Tsentral'noe upravlenie narodno-khoziaistvennogo ucheta). 1936. *Trud v SSSR (Labor in the USSR).* Moscow: Soiuzorguchet.

U.S. Civil Service Commission. 1971. *Pay structure of the federal civil service.* SM33-71, 30 June.

U.S. Department of Commerce. 1973. *Current population reports,* Series P-60, no. 90, Dec.

Wiles, Peter. 1974. "Stalin and British top salaries." Draft of article for *Lancaster,* July.

_____ and Stefan Markowski. 1971. "Income distribution under communism and capitalism: some facts about Poland, the UK, the USA and the USSR." *Soviet Studies,* Jan., pp. 344–69; April, pp. 487–511.

Yanowitch, Murray. 1955. "Changes in the Soviet money wage level since 1940." *American Slavic and East European Review* 14, no. 2 (April).

_____. 1960. "Trends in Soviet occupational wage differentials." Ph.D. dissertation, Columbia Univ.

11

Soviet Wages: Comments and Extensions

Janusz G. Zielinski

University of Glasgow

There is very little for me to quarrel with in the content of the interesting and competent[1] chapter by Professor Chapman. Since, however, I am duty-bound to be critical, let me indicate a certain disappointment that the study concentrates so little on wages as *prices*. In fact, it could just as well be presented at a conference on labor economics as at the conference specifically devoted to "Consistency and efficiency of the price mechanism in Soviet-type economies."

In the context of our Symposium one could actually look at wages directly as a price of a specific factor of production and examine it from three basic viewpoints:

(i) How effectively does it fulfill its basic functions? As for every price, these consist of allocative, measurement, distribution, and equilibrating functions. (The last function is not mentioned in other contributions on prices, but experience of centrally planned economies indicates that it cannot be taken for granted under all institutional arrangements.)

Alternatively, as I personally would prefer to look at the functions of prices in centrally planned economies, the first problem would be to examine what the role of wages is in plan *construction,* distinguishing two subproblems: (1) consistency and optimality requirements, and (2) determining the role of wages in plan *implementation,* distinguishing here the role of wages in implementing the *production* plan, where wages are elements of costs of production, and in implementing the *consumption* plan, where wages are the main source of income of the population.

(ii) What are the *specific* features and problems of this particular price

1. EDITOR'S NOTE. Dr. Zielinski's comments were a response to Professor Chapman's original presentation which was revised extensively for Chapter 10 to take account of some of Dr. Zielinski's remarks, among others. Dr. Zielinski's prior commitments have precluded a revision of his own piece. But since his comments deal with some matters not covered by Professor Chapman's chapter and are of interest on their own account, they are being included here in their entirety. Quotations from and explicit references to pages in Professor Chapman's original draft have undergone minor editorial modification.

in each of its basic functions, e.g., what are the dimensions of the allocative function of wages? These must include not only interindustry allocation but also interskill and interoccupational allocative effects. They must also include the impact of wages on the effectiveness of the use of labor, interskill substitution, and labor/capital substitution. Under this heading of specific features of wages as prices we also have the question of the impact of wages on *total* labor supply, where we have—at least outside agriculture—the well-known paradox that lower wages are associated with a larger supply of labor.

(iii) The third group of problems—when one looks at the wages primarily as a price—consists of identifying those problems where malfunctioning of wages in their particular function is important *operationally*. In the sphere of wages—as in other prices—the atrophy of certain functions is always accompanied by the take-over of the atrophied function by some other institutional arrangement. In the sphere of interindustry pricing we have direct allocations, product-mix targets, import norms, administrative orders, etc. The same is true about wages where wage-fund allocations, output indicators, employment quotas, average wage targets, university field quotas, or the like, are extensively used. What one should examine here is the *effectiveness* of these alternative or "supporting" arrangements, which are employed in place of or in support of "atrophied" functions of wages.

My basic position is that in regard to wages we generally encounter in centrally planned economies the same malfunctions that apply to other types of prices: that is, wages are particularly defective in inducing effective use of labor at the micro level; they promote X-efficiency. Wages, like other prices, have lost in centrally planned economies their equilibrating properties within the socialist sector. There is no wage level or structure which would equilibrate supply and demand for labor, under the present economic working arrangements, just as there are no equilibrating interindustry prices for other inputs purchased within the framework of so-called "transaction demand" or—as Professor Gregory Grossman calls it—"operating outlays."

Some of these problems are mentioned by Professor Chapman, but frequently left unexplored in favor of more traditional labor-economics-type wage problems, and some are completely untouched, in spite of their importance both theoretical and practical. Discussion of the latter would lead me to the ungentlemanly practice of criticizing the author of the study—at least by implication—for things which she did not include, rather than following the standard practice of limiting criticism to what the author chose to include in her presentation. For this reason I shall try to concentrate on those problems which are included in Professor Chapman's chapter. I hope, however, that I shall be forgiven if I depart from time to time from this tradition-imposed limitation when the logic of the problems discussed will take me beyond the problems explicitly included in Professor Chapman's presentation.

There are five groups of problems raised in Professor Chapman's chapter on which I want to comment briefly. These are: (1) wage differentials as an allocative mechanism; (2) wage levels and Soviet economic development; (3) wages and efficient use of labor; (4) wages and capital-labor substitution; and, finally, (5) wages and income distribution.

1. *Are wage differentials an important allocative mechanism?*

This important issue is left undeveloped in the chapter, and moreover the author's own position is not clear. On the first page we read that "the differential wage system . . . has an important allocative function." Later we read that the author herself, and others as well, "have found little correlation between changes in relative wages and [changes] in employment in either market or socialist economies."

I don't think that we can be satisfied with that. First of all we should examine the available *empirical evidence*. I think that regarding market economies there is little doubt that wage differentials are *not* an important allocative mechanism. To the authorities mentioned by Professor Chapman I can add the experience of the British Incomes and Prices Board, as reported by its last chairman, Mr. Aubrey Jones, in his latest book *The New Inflation*. He flatly denies the allocative significance of wage differentials. I have not seen any empirical data for Soviet-type economies — except those quoted by Professor Chapman — but there seem to be numerous reasons to suppose that wage differentials should play an even lesser role in centrally planned economies than in market economies. These are mainly three factors: (1) restrictions of labor mobility due to housing shortage, administrative obstacles to labor mobility (existence of so-called closed cities), and similar causes; (2) no direct allocation (rationing) of the wage fund, which is the *main* allocative device in centrally planned economies; and (3) the relative inflexibility of the wage differentials.

From the planners' viewpoint, however, the crucial question is do they *need* wage differentials for achieving the desired allocation of labor force among industries and skills and professions, or do they have *other* sufficiently effective mechanisms? I think the answer is affirmative. Planners have alternative allocative mechanisms, since centrally planned economies effectively control both structure of demand for labor (better than volume of demand for labor) and structure of supply (via total control of education and training), which is again better than volume (demographic factors). Wage differentials, however, play a supplementary role, and the extent of this role should be examined in all its dimensions, not only for interindustry allocation. Professor Chapman argues, in spite of empirical evidence to the contrary, that wage differentials are significant in the allocation of labor. I am less tolerant and think it is long overdue that we adapt our theories to facts, since facts will not adapt themselves to our theories.

2. *Wage level and Soviet economic development*

Since Professor Chapman considers the role of the wage system in Soviet economic development only in the context of the allocative function of wages, which importance is doubtful, she cannot really make a strong case. If, however, she should include in her analysis the *level* of real wages, then several important aspects of Soviet wage policy and economic development would become immediately apparent.

(i) Low real wages were instrumental in increasing total available labor supply, particularly of women. We know that women's participation in the active labor force is very high in the Soviet Union and East Europe. The extent of this phenomenon rarely strikes us, but it should. To see how striking it is we should make two comparisons: (a) compare participation of women in the labor force in centrally planned economies with market economies with the same GNP per capita; and (b) compare it with pre-communist periods, when, outside agriculture, this share was very low indeed. Without a policy of very low real wages, so low that a family needs for subsistence two or more wage earners, such massive and *rapid* increase in the share of women in the labor force would hardly be possible without much greater use of compulsory labor than was the case in the Soviet Union. This aspect of Soviet wage policy is very important; it played a crucial role during the Second World War. We shall return to it when discussing the problem of wages and capital-labor substitution.

(ii) Another aspect of the absolute level of real wages is connected with the problem of changes in relative real wages for different social strata and their demographic effects. I don't have Soviet data, but according to a study of Professor M. Kalecki, white-collar workers in Poland were earning in the 1960s only 74 percent of their 1937 salaries, as opposed to 145 percent for workers.[2] This drastic drop in the absolute standard of living, according to unofficial calculations of some Polish demographers, caused the Polish intelligentsia (defined as people whose parents had university education) to have, on the average, only 1.08 children per family in the 1960s. This leads to a relatively quick elimination of whole social strata, which may be quite important economically and culturally.

2. *Z zagadnień gospodarczo-społecznych Polski Ludowej* (Warsaw, 1964), p. 97.

3. *Wages and the efficient use of labor*

Several times in her chapter Professor Chapman refers to this problem. She notices that before the 1965 reform, "wage differentials . . .
have been little used as signals for managers to economize on labor
costs" and that other elements of economic working arrangements – the
success indicators used, taut planning, and supply problems – actually
induced managers to hire more labor than could be economically justified.
Then she stresses that the Economic Reform of 1965 made "an attempt
to make management aware of and sensitive to labor costs." We do not
learn, however, whether she considers this attempt successful, and if so,
why and how the result was achieved. This is particularly important and
interesting because similar reforms in other East European countries, e.g.,
Poland, *failed* to improve the effectiveness of labor use at enterprise
level, and this is officially admitted in the literature. To quote one of the
foremost Polish authorities, Mr. Br. Fick, Director of the Department of
Wages and Employment of the Polish Planning Commission: "Wage
costs are the only costs of production which enterprises make no effort
to decrease on their own initiative, but on the contrary aim to maximize."[3]
All the relevant systemic changes, introduced in East European countries
at least, are in the sphere of success indicators and incentive systems.
These are not effective at the stage of plan *construction* – any level of
costs if approved by plan is justified; and at the stage of plan *implementation,* the retention of the ratchet principle of financing transaction demand
according to needs and of internal pricing is more than sufficient to nullify
any improvements in success indicators and incentive systems. In the
practice of all centrally planned economies it is recognized that (1) under
existing economic working arrangements – even after current reforms –
enterprises (and industrial associations for that matter) have no effective
incentives to economize on the wage bill, and (2) under such conditions
a special mechanism to regulate the increase in the enterprise wage fund
according to its "real needs" must be set up. This immediately poses the
problem of assessing these needs and changes in them, objectively.

As we all know, centrally planned economies developed two basic
approaches to the solution of this problem. The prevailing view is that
the enterprise wage fund should be set and corrected *automatically* by
using a properly constructed output indicator as a wage-fund regulator.
There is a very substantial literature on how such an output indicator
should be constructed, and the general trend is to abandon so-called
gross output indicators (gross output, marketable output, etc.) and to
substitute for them so-called net output indicators (value added, output
in cost-of-processing prices, output measured in normative labor costs,

---

3. *Bodźce ekonomiczne w przemyśle* (Warsaw, 1965), p. 317.

etc.). The second approach, usually called the *system of wage reserves,* postulates that automatic setting and correcting of the wage fund should be replaced by directives from higher administrative organs, in particular industrial associations, which would determine the wage fund and any changes really necessary for the given plan period on the basis of economic analysis of each case. For this purpose a system of wage reserves should be set at industrial associations, at economic ministries, and at the national level.[4]

This problem of determining the wage fund regulator is not only one of the key issues of wage policy in centrally planned economies (the output indicator used is in fact the most important single incentive in every centrally planned economy) but it also represents a good illustration of what happens when some functions of prices become inoperative. Since wages under the economic working arrangements of Soviet-type economies fail to allocate labor efficiently between enterprises, and since wages also have lost their equilibrating properties (the demand for labor, which is a part of the so-called "transaction demand of the enterprise," is in fact price-inelastic), it has been necessary to develop substitute institutional arrangements. Accordingly (i) total demand for labor is limited by wage fund rationing; (ii) allocation of the wage fund between enterprises is accomplished by the mechanism of the output indicator; and the whole procedure is (iii) supervised by the wage control system of the National Bank.

Here we have a classic situation:

- —wages cease to perform certain functions;
- —the need for these functions does not disappear; hence
- —the economic system responds with a number of institutional substitutes; but
- —none of them proves satisfactory; and, in my opinion,
- —the problem cannot be solved satisfactorily by any substitute arrangement.

I think that there are limits to successful social engineering at each stage of economic development and the problem we are discussing is a good example of one of these limitations.

If what I have said is correct, and I have Professor Z. Fedorowicz on record, who also argues that, for at least intermediate inputs, and these include labor inputs, price elasticity of demand is close to zero for transactions within the socialist sector, then the proposals of Liberman and Kantorovitch, which Professor Chapman mentions, "to make labor more expensive as a means of inducing management to weed out ineffi-

4. For broader discussion of this issue see my *Economic reforms in Polish industry* (Oxford: Oxford Univ. Press, 1973), ch. 7.

cient and/or superfluous employees," cannot work. But is it likely that changes in relative prices of labor and capital can at least produce incentives for substituting labor by capital, as Soviet economist Sarkisian, quoted by Professor Chapman, hopes? This leads me to my fourth group of problems.

4. *Wages and the relative use of labor and capital*

My general position is that under economic working arrangements existing in centrally planned economies, prices are not an effective instrument for influencing the structure of inputs used. There are numerous institutional arrangements which neutralize incentive effects of relative prices. One of the most glaring is the so-called profit adjustment rule, which nullifies the effects of price/wage changes on enterprise bonuses. Theoretically it neutralizes these changes in a given financial year; in practice, it also neutralizes changes in the subsequent years through corrections of the planned level of success indicators. Since, however, most economists in the Soviet Union and East European countries, as well as in the West, still believe that relative wages are instrumental in effecting factor substitution, I wonder if this expectation cannot explain the real rationale behind so-called two-channel prices (discussed by Professors Brown and Licari).[5] The change of relative prices of labor and capital can be effected not only by raising wages, particularly minimum wages, the process which Professor Chapman refers to in her chapter, but also by *taxing the wage fund,* or putting surcharges on the wage fund as is done in the two-channel price system used in Hungary and now being introduced in Poland.

Could it be that in centrally planned economies we have a situation of underdeveloped countries *à rebours* in regard to actual and shadow wages? It is generally believed that in underdeveloped countries the wages actually paid are *higher* than the appropriate shadow wage. In centrally planned economies, actual wages seem to be *lower* than the appropriate shadow wage, which should properly reflect relative scarcities of labor and capital. This actually is, more or less, the essence of the first "theoretical justification" of two-channel prices quoted by Professors Brown and Licari, namely, that "the true opportunity costs of labor to enterprises is higher than the wage bill." I personally think that this is the most satisfactory theoretical explanation of economic justification of two-channel prices, but that *operationally* it cannot be effective within the framework of existing economic working arrangements, since the latter *neutralize* the effects of relative prices on enterprise behavior.

It is interesting to note that Hungary, which has a labor shortage, and

5. In Chapter 8 [Ed.].

Poland, which has a labor surplus, both want to raise the relative price of labor to capital by introducing two-channel pricing. I think the reason is the same – both want to diminish demand for labor by raising enterprise *accounting* costs of labor above actual wage costs, and the solution in both countries is theoretically correct. For calculation of investment effectiveness, however, shadow wages in Poland should be *below* actual wages, to increase effective employment opportunities, whereas in Hungary shadow wages should be *above* actual wages.

This problem is closely related to our discussion of wage levels and economic development. If my interpretation is correct, centrally planned economies have been so successful in their policy of low wages and high investment that they have achieved a situation in which the *shadow wage is above actual wage.* Underdeveloped countries, on the other hand, have failed to restrict consumption effectively, and this is reflected in those countries by a shadow wage which is well below the actual wage.

5. *Wages and income distribution*

Professor Chapman's chapter contains a substantial and interesting section on wages and distribution of Soviet earnings. I would be the last to deny the inherent interest and importance of this subject. It is treated, however, very much outside what one would consider to be wages as price problems. Since I promised not to go too much beyond what is contained in Professor Chapman's study. I shall confine myself to very brief enumeration of some problems of income distribution from the viewpoint of price policy.

The basic problem seems to me to be the correction of real income distribution through prices with different rates of turnover tax on "essential" and "nonessential" goods and services. We all know that turnover tax rates are highly differentiated in all centrally planned economies, and generally they are much higher on "nonessential" goods, where turnover taxes may be in the range of a few hundred percent, than on "essential" goods, some of which are even subsidized.

This raises several problems:

(*i*) Any analysis of relative *nominal* earnings will deviate far from relative *real* earnings, since the share of goods which are highly taxed increases in the higher income brackets. Since the differentiation of sales taxes is much more pronounced in centrally planned economies than in market economies, the question arises whether intersystem comparison of *nonadjusted* nominal income differentials is justified. This is Professor Chapman's procedure. If we instead compared distribution of relative *real incomes* (adjusted for turnover tax differentials in commodity brackets of different income groups) the picture could be substantially different.

(*ii*) The second question is why centrally planned economies use differential turnover taxes for income distribution much more than market economies do. I would suggest that this is due to the policy of low real wages referred to before. Since *minimum* wages have a physiological and/or social floor below which they cannot be depressed, and the total wage fund is severely limited because of the investment requirements of rapid industrialization, *real* wage differentials out of necessity must be relatively small, and differential turnover taxes are used to keep them *smaller* than *nominal* wage differentials.

(*iii*) My third problem is that maybe we should reexamine the rationale behind income redistribution through prices. The standard reasoning is that this enables the centrally planned economy to have its cake and eat it: centrally planned economies have *nominal* wage differentials substantial enough for incentive purposes, and through prices policy they achieve much more nearly equal distribution of real incomes than differentiation of nominal incomes would suggest. Effectiveness of this policy is based on the assumption of the existence of a strong *money illusion.* For market economies, Aubrey Jones, for example, claims that this illusion is no longer as strong as it was or as we thought it was. Jones claims that nowadays workers react to the changes in their real wages, rather than their purely nominal wages. The experience of the British Prices and Incomes Board indicates that workers (or trade unions) take into account not only changes in prices but also changes in income taxes and social security benefits involved in a given wage award. They recalculate their nominal wage increases in the light of all these factors and base their wage claims policy on this. I suspect that a similar phenomenon may be taking place in centrally planned economies. If this is the case, then the need for and the effectiveness of income redistribution through prices would tend to diminish over time in both systems. The introduction of the value-added tax at a standard rate, with few exceptions, is already a witness to this trend in western Europe. Income redistribution will henceforth be effected mainly through direct taxes and differentiated social benefits payments, rather than through the price mechanism.

Subject Index

(The letter "t" following a reference indicates a table.)

Author Index

(The letter "t" following a reference indicates a table and "R", an appearance in a list of references following a chapter.)